Self-Determination Struggles

Self-Determination Struggles

In Pursuit of the Democratic Confederalist Ideal

Thomas Jeffrey Miley

MONTRÉAL • NEW YORK • LONDON

Black Rose Books No.WW430

Library and Archives Canada Cataloguing in Publication

Title: Self-determination struggles : in pursuit of the democratic confederalist ideal / Thomas Jeffrey Miley.
Names: Miley, Thomas Jeffrey, author.
Description: Includes bibliographical references.
Identifiers: Canadiana (print) 20220470219 | Canadiana (ebook) 20220470278 | ISBN 9781551647906 (hardcover) | ISBN 9781551647883 (softcover) | ISBN 9781551647920 (PDF)
Subjects: LCSH: Revolutionaries. | LCSH: Political activists. | LCSH: Radicalism. | LCSH: Self-determination, National. | LCSH: Democracy.
Classification: LCC JC489 .M55 2023 | DDC 303.48/4—dc23

C.P. 35788 Succ. Léo Pariseau
Montréal, QC H2X 0A4
CANADA
www.blackrosebooks.com

Ordering Information

CANADA
USA/INTERNATIONAL

University of Toronto Press
5201 Dufferin Street
Toronto, ON
M3H 5T8
1-800-565-9523
utpbooks@utpress.utoronto.ca

UK/EUROPE

Central Books
50 Freshwater Road
Chadwell Heath, London
RM8 1RX
+44 20 85 25 8800
contactus@centralbooks.com

Contents

PART TWO

SELF-DETERMINATION AND DEMOCRACY

Introduction

Abdullah Öcalan and the Reinvention of Self-Determination

We live in an era of collective existential crisis, in which it is imperative that we think anew the fundamental categories of political life. The material collected in this volume all reflect a preoccupation with self-determination, a concept and principle as indispensable as it is contentious.

The chapters were almost all composed as essays in the aftermath of my 2014 encounter with the Kurdish Freedom Movement, whose leader and inspiration, Abdullah Öcalan, has undertaken an impressive and valiant effort to redefine self-determination, from his lonely prison cell on Imrali Island.

Before actively engaging with the Kurdish struggle, my orientation towards appeals to self-determination had been perhaps excessively critical. I had long been sceptical of the paradigm of national liberation within which the discourse of self-determination seems to be most frequently situated. My conviction was that there is a relatively ubiquitous tendency to essentialize and reify the collective "self" in this discourse, and that therefore the application of a "hermeneutic of suspicion" seems the most appropriate response to any and all appeals to such a principle. More specifically, I maintained that in any context where the discourse of self-determination emerges as salient, this discourse should be subjected to a sociological interrogation, in order to illuminate just how it is embedded in concrete constellations of material and social power relations, and to decipher whether it tends to legitimate and reinforce or, alternatively, subvert existing hierarchies.

I remain convinced that the cultivation of a sociological sensibility, that is, awareness of how the discourse of self-determination is embedded in and tends to affect existing power relations in any given context, is crucial. However, at the same time, I have become increasingly persuaded that it is equally important to pay attention to the creative appropriations and resignifications of the core categories of this discourse as employed in particular times and places. The transformation of the Kurdish Freedom Movement, its effort to transcend the paradigm of national liberation, to resignify self-determination in terms of the struggle for radical, direct democracy against the state, the struggle for multi-cultural and multi-religious accommodation, the struggle for gender emancipation, and the struggle for ecological sustainability, has impressed upon me the potency and potential for simultaneous discursive continuity and paradigm shift.

In a word, what we witness is a convergence between appeals to the doctrine of self-determination and the pursuit of the democratic confederal ideal in the Kurdish context. This is self-determination of a different kind. It is no longer aligned with the aspiration for a sovereign Kurdish nation-state. Instead, it has come to mean the struggle against illegitimate and unjust hierarchy in all its forms – including the domination by the state over political and ethical society, the domination by one ethnicity or sect over others, the domination of man over woman, the domination of humans over nature.

This is a most ambitious agenda, the extent of acceptance of which by the activists and core constituency of the movement, merits rigorous empirical inquiry, to be certain. However, even at the level of programmatic imperative, the reorientation and rearticulation of self-determination achieved by Öcalan and at least partially emulated by his followers in the movement remains quite remarkable.

The Evolution of the Discourse of Self-Determination

If we are to believe much of the scholarship on the subject, the discourse of self-determination originally emerged in the context of the European Enlightenment. More specifically, in a useful overview of the history of the term, Eric Weitz has traced its usage back to the German Enlightenment and German Romantic Era (2015). The concept initially referred almost exclusively to individual liberty, emblematically in the work of Kant; only later would collectivist interpretations become predominant. According to Weitz, the key figures in this crucial transformation were Fichte and, in the Italian context, Mazzini.

The French Revolution allegedly introduced on the world stage "[t]he doctrine of popular sovereignty." According to E.H. Carr, this notion of popular sovereignty "carried with it by implication the doctrine of national self-determination, which seemed the logical and inescapable corollary of democracy". Even so, Carr is quick to add, "the doctrine of self-determination as proclaimed by the French revolution implied primarily the right of peoples to constitute national states in defiance of the dynastic principle, and was a domestic as well as an international question. It certainly did not contemplate a wholesale process of secession and disintegration" (1978, p.412).

It was in 1848, with the so-called Springtime of the Peoples, when self-determination came to be indispensably associated with an emergent principle of nationality. In Carr's estimation, "1848 saw the first shift from the conception of individual self-determination as a corollary of democracy … to the conception of nationality as an objective right of nations to independent statehood". Then, and only then, Carr insists, were "[t]he rights of man envisaged by the French revolution … transferred to nations" (1978, p.413 n.1).

This genealogy, or historical sequence, which would situate the emergence and evolution of the discourse of self-determination, from Kant to Fichte and Mazzini, and from the French Revolution to the Springtime of the Peoples, is admittedly Eurocentric. It would seem to deliberately exclude from its purview the precedents of the US declaration and war for independence, as well as the Creole revolutions of the Americas more generally, as Benedict Anderson (2006) has stressed, not to mention the impact of the Haitian revolution, and specifically, of Dessalines' 1804 proclamation of independence, which constituted a "formal acknowledgment of the self-determination of those diverse and ordinary individuals of whom the black masses were composed" (Shen 2015).

But be that as it may, Weitz also emphasises the importance of socialist thinkers in the evolution of the discourse and category of self-determination. Perhaps most prominently among them was none other than Karl Marx himself. Notably, in his first use of the term, in his 1843 *Critique of Hegel's Philosophy of Right*, "Marx made self-determination a synonym for democracy and an as yet undefined 'people' – in other words, not a nationality or the proletariat – as its source". Two years later, in *The German Ideology*, he and Engels would chastise Max Stirner "for his individualist conception of self-determination, which, they argued, obfuscated the social determinants of emancipation". Only subsequently, in reaction to "the surge of nationalist movements despite their defeat in the Revolution of 1848," would Marx and Engels come to refer increasingly, nearly exclusively, to the concept of self-determination in relation to the collective subject of the nation.

There has been considerable scholarship in recent years seeking to chart the trajectory of Marx's (and Engels') views on the so-called national question. There is something of a consensus in this emergent literature that their views shifted towards a closer affinity with a variety of nationalist movements between the 1840s and the 1860s (Anderson 2010; Brenner 1995; Kasprzak 2012). In their more mature writings, Marx and Engels sought to emphasise clear distinctions "between hegemonic and defensive nationalism," and between "enlightened working-class patriotism and uncritical support for existing national governments. These distinctions, in turn, led them to upgrade the role of national autonomy within their internationalist strategy" (Brenner 1995, p.172).

By all means, their support for both Polish and Irish independence, as well as for the abolition of slavery in the United States, remained consistent through the years. By the 1860s, they had come to express the firm belief that "labor movements in core capitalist countries that failed to support adequately progressive nationalist movements on the part of those affected by their governments, or failed to combat racism toward ethnic minorities within their own societies, ran the danger of retarding or even cutting short their own development" (Anderson 2010, p.3). Nevertheless, their outlook remained uncompromisingly internationalist in orientation, and their support for any given movement for national self-determination was decidedly dependent upon judgments about that movement's impact upon the broader prospects for world revolution. For this very reason, they consistently "opposed Balkan nationalism that might weaken the Ottoman bulwark against Russian expansionism" (Goldner 2011).

Less often noted – for example, almost entirely absent from Weitz's overview – is the discourse articulated by classical anarchist thinkers in favour of self-determination, understood as implying a right to secession. Bakunin, following Proudhon, espoused the radically voluntarist conviction that "each individual, each association, commune, or province, each region and nation, has the absolute right to determine its own fate, to associate with others or not, to ally itself with whomever it will, or break any alliance, without regard to so-called historical claims or the convenience of its neighbors;" and that, moreover, "[t]he right to unite freely and separate with the same freedom is the most important of all political rights, without which confederation will always be disguised centralization" (in Guérin 1970, p.67). Indeed, Guérin goes so far as to argue that Lenin and the Bolsheviks would later "adopt this concept from Bakunin," making it "the foundation of their policy on nationalities and of their anti colonialist strategy," at least until they "belied it to turn to authoritarian centralization and disguised imperialism" (1970, p.67; and Kinna 2020, p.978).

It is worth emphasising that for anarchists like Bakunin, there is no fetishization of the nation. Far from it. The nation is only one of multiple collective and individual subjects purported to possess a right to self-determination, understood as the right to unite and to separate freely.

The coexistence of a more general democratic principle of self-determination with a more specific national principle would likewise persist for quite some time in the discourse of the Marxist tradition. It is, for example, evident in the work of Karl Kautsky, who was long considered not only the eminent orthodox Marxist theoretician in the decades after the death of Marx and Engels, but also the foremost expert on the so-called national question (Munck 2010, p.50; Nettl 1966, p.853). Yet, we can find among his writings multiple references to self-determination in which the collective subject of the principle is not the nation, but rather workers, such as, in the context of the German revolution, when in a report to the Second Congress of the Councils, he would declare, "[t]he worker wants not only well-being, but also self-determination" (in Salvadori 1990, p.244).

Debates would abound in the Second International around the subject of self-determination. Kautsky was the first to formulate the right to national self-determination as a general principle, a position that would be enshrined in a resolution passed at the Fourth International Congress, held in London in 1896, expressed along the following lines: "it supports the right to complete self-determination of all nations and sympathizes with the workers of all countries presently suffering under the yoke of military, national or other despotism. It invites the workers of all these countries to enter the ranks of class-conscious workers of the whole world, in order to fight with them for the overthrow of international capitalism and the attainment of the aims of international Social Democracy" (in Nettl 1966, pp.98-99).

It was at this very Congress, in London, where a 25-year-old Rosa Luxemburg first burst onto the scene of the Second International. The resolution passed in favour of the general principle of national self-determination was in fact a compromise, formulated by Kautsky, after Luxemburg had delivered an impassioned and brilliant objection to a more specific resolution, one that argued explicitly in favour of Polish independence. Luxemburg's opposition to the prospect of Polish independence, which she would later develop into a more comprehensive critique of the principle of national self-determination *tout court*, "not only contradicted the position of the founding fathers of historical materialism; it would bring her into conflict with the leading lights of both German and Russian ocialism, with Kautsky, with Liebknecht the elder, with Plekhanov, with Lenin, on multiple occasions, over the years".

Luxemburg's posture of thoroughgoing internationalism, including her elaboration of a sophisticated justification along scrupulous historical-materialist lines, arriving at the rejection of the principle of national self-determination, would be one "heresy" that would fester in the Second International in the years leading up to the terrible tragedy of the First World War. Another would be the Austro-Marxist proposal for cultural autonomy, delinked from any principle of territoriality. In their important contribution to the debate, Otto Bauer and Karl Renner would explicitly challenge the assumption "that self-determination of nations requires the constitution of separate nation-states" (Nimni 2000, p.xxvii).

It would be these twin heresies – Luxemburg's anti-nationalist rejection of national self-determination, on the one hand, and the Austro-Marxist reinterpretation of national self-determination as implying cultural autonomy but not territorial secession, on the other – that Lenin would set out to refute (Carr 1978, p.418).

In Russia, the ideas of Bauer and Renner had been "eagerly taken up by the All-Jewish Workers' Union in Russia and Poland, commonly called the Bund," who agitated for national autonomy both within the Social-Democratic Party and within the state. Lenin retorted that the proletariat was not interested in such "national autonomy," that, indeed, "[i]t was interested only in two things" – (1) in "political and civil liberty and complete equality of rights," and (2) in "the right of self-determination for any nationality" (meaning the right of secession) (Carr 1978, pp.419-420). In other words, on the subject of national self-determination, Lenin adopted an "all or nothing" posture. For him, the Austro-Marxists were doubly wrong: their position not only failed to do justice to the aspiration for full-fledged national self-determination understood as the right to secession; but at the same time, it reified national differences and thereby tended to foster simmering national(ist) hostilities.

With respect to the other main heresy – which Carr somewhat cursorily summarises as Luxemburg's contention that "national independence was a bourgeois concern and that the proletariat, being essentially international, had no interest in it" – Lenin largely relied upon Kautsky's earlier effort to refute her line of argument, in the course of elaborating his own three-fold response. Fundamentally, Lenin would insist: first, that since "the formation of independent, national states is a tendency of all bourgeois-democratic revolutions," it follows that "the right of secession is a corollary of the doctrine of proletarian support for the bourgeois revolution;" second, that "the denial by a ruling nation of the right of self-determination for other nations flouted the principle of equality among nations;" and third, that to recognise the right of national self-determination, understood as the right to secession, is not the same thing as actually advocating the decision to secede (Carr 1978, p.423; see also Connor 1984, pp.34-38; and Forman 1998, pp.70-82).

Lenin would commission the young Stalin to further elaborate the Bolshevik doctrine on national self-determination, which he did in a famous essay titled *The National Question and Social-Democracy*, published in the spring of 1913 in the party journal. It should be noted, however, that Lenin's and Stalin's line on self-determination would not go unchallenged, even within Bolshevik party ranks. The outbreak of war triggered further discussion about the principle of national self-determination, provoking intense debate among the adherents of the anti-war parties which had come together in the Zimmerwald Conference, a debate pitting Lenin against the Polish social-democrat Karl Radek, whose position on the subject was very close to that of Rosa Luxemburg. Radek, in turn, would influence prominent Bolsheviks like Bukharin, Bosch, and Piatakov, who in November of 2015 would send the Central Committee "a set of documents outlining their position on self-determination and attacking Lenin's". In these documents, they would dismiss the principle as "utopian (it cannot be realized within the limits of capitalism) and harmful as a slogan which disseminates illusions" (Cohen 1975, pp.36-37; see also Daniels 1969, pp.32-33).

The Leninist-cum-Stalinist line on national self-determination would nevertheless survive such attacks, and would come to be formally recognised after the Bolsheviks' seizure of power, and eventually embedded in the constitution of the new revolutionary regime, albeit amended to accept a federal state structure. The principle of national self-determination would thus be rendered hegemonic, even sacralised, converted into a dogma or doxa, among the Communist left. This despite the fact that, in practice, the new regime did not always abide by its sacred principles.

Upon seizing power, Lenin would be unequivocal in his public commitment to "the full right of separation from Russia of all nations and nationalities, oppressed by tsarism, joined by force or held by force within the borders of the state, i.e. annexed" (Suny 1993, p.87). But on the ground, to the contrary, and despite Lenin's public commitment, in the course of the revolution, "the issue was settled finally, in the way that Rosa Luxemburg had predicted, by force of arms". Accordingly, only "where the Western powers had established their military occupation, as in Finland and the Baltic Republics, or where the Red Army was defeated, as in Poland," would self-determination be recognised and ultimately respected. Elsewhere, in fact, "most of the former tsarist colonies" were destined to be eventually "reincorporated into the USSR" (Davis 1976, pp.30-32).

And yet, the principle remained, in principle, its appeal undeniable amongst oppressed national minorities and, perhaps especially, across the colonized world. The Allied powers, seeking to offset the incipient threat of the spread of revolution, and in an "effort to claim the moral high ground in the debate about war aims," turned to appropriate and resignify the discourse of self-determination. In the early months of 1918, with the peace settlement on the horizon, Lloyd George "updated British war aims to include the principle that territorial settlements must be based on 'the right of self-determination or the consent of the governed'". For his part, Woodrow Wilson famously declared that "[n]ational aspirations must be respected; people may now be dominated and governed only by their own consent," and that "[s]elf-determination is not a mere phrase; it is an imperative principle of action" (Getachew 2019, p.39).

Getachew has forcefully argued that this "Wilsonian moment" represented an effort to "recast self-determination in the service of empire" (2019, p.40). Lenin advocated national self-determination not only in the struggles against Czarist Russia, but in struggles of colonized populations for national liberation outside of Europe as well, because he considered "the liberation of oppressed colonial peoples ... an important potential asset for world revolution" (Hobsbawm 1990, p.148). Not so for Wilson, who sought to fend off revolution, and who never intended the doctrine to apply to colonial possessions beyond the "mature" nations of Europe. Even so, Wilson's Secretary of State, Robert Lansing, was most definitely alarmed at his President's embrace of the phrase, remarking that it "is simply loaded with dynamite" (Fisch 2015, p.135).

With the end of the war, the principle of national self-determination "became the touchstone for the creation of new states that arose out of the rubble of the Austro-Hungarian and Ottoman empires" (Epps 1997, p.434). Yet, as Hobsbawm has emphasised, "[i]nevitably, given the actual distribution of peoples, most of the new states built on the ruins of the Old Empires, were quite as multinational as the old 'prisons of nations' they replaced" (1990, p.132). The new small nations proved equally hostile to national minorities in their midst as had the "great nation chauvinists" towards them.

It should be noted, however, that the Covenant of the League of Nations would not include any reference to the phrase self-determination. And indeed, when in 1920, a dispute over the status of the Aaland Islands off the coast of Finland came before the League, its Commission of Jurists "openly repudiated Wilson," explicitly rejecting the islanders' claim, "based on the right of peoples to dispose freely of their own destinies, proclaimed by President Wilson," while insisting instead that "[p]ositive International Law does not recognize the right of national groups, as such, to separate themselves from the State of which they form part by the simple expression of a wish, anymore than it recognizes the right of other States to claim such a separation" (Fisch 2015, p.139; Epps 1997, p.434).

But the impulse and appeal of the ideal of national self-determination was definitely gaining momentum. In the spring of 1919, anticolonial revolts would break out in Egypt, India, China, and Korea, in which claims would be made about the right to self-determination (Getachew 2019, p.39). Even if Wilson and his co-architect of the League of Nations, the South African Jan

Smuts, intended to "excise the revolutionary implications of the Bolshevik right to self-determination and repurpose the principle to preserve racial hierarchy in the new international organization" (Getachew 2019, p.10), they were not able to fully control or contain the expectations that were generated by the enunciation of the principle.

The influence of the Bolsheviks should not be underestimated in this regard. Weitz goes so far as to argue that the "Wilsonian moment" might more appropriately be considered the "Bolshevik moment" (2015, p.485). Vijay Prashad recounts the coverage by an Indian journalist, K.P. Khadilkar, of the revolutionary developments in Russia. Khadilkar "zoomed in on the most important point from this vantage, 'Lenin has issued a decree declaring the rights of nations to self-determination, and freedom has been given to the Baltic states and the Polish people to exercise that right'". Prashad concludes, rather emphatically: "In the colonies, the declaration of the right to self-determination was powerful. It defined the revolution" (2017, p.36).

The Bolshevik-sponsored Congress of the Peoples of the East, which was held in Baku in September of 1920, and which called for anticolonial uprisings, was indicative of the nexus uniting the October revolution with the surge in anticolonial agitation. In reporting on the agrarian question at the Congress, the Comintern's China expert, Anatoly Skachko, would be clear in linking the embrace of anticolonial national self-determination with a broader revolutionary agenda. For he would insist: "The peasants of the East, now marching arm in arm with their democratic bourgeoisie to win independence for their countries from the Western Imperialist powers, must remember that they have their own special tasks to perform. Their liberation will not be achieved merely by winning political independence, and therefore they cannot halt and rest content when that is won.... For the complete and real liberation of the peasantry of the East from all forms of oppression, dependence, and exploitation, it is also necessary to overthrow the rule of their landlords and bourgeoisie and to establish the Soviet power of the workers and peasants…" (Wikipedia 2021a).

There was, of course, a latent tension between support for bourgeois nationalist movements in the colonial world and support for local communists in revolt against a national bourgeoisie, a tension which was quick to surface in the Comintern, most notably in a debate between Lenin and the Indian delegate M.N. (Manabendra Nath) Roy, in which the latter warned against forging too close an alliance with the class enemy (Carr 1981, pp.252-258). This tension would not go away, and was destined to come to the surface on more than one occasion in years to come.

Meanwhile, closer to the metropolitan capitalist core, though the terms of the peace settlement did not include explicit mention of the notion of national self-determination, the inter-war order was certainly imbued with its spirit. The 1923 Treaty of Lausanne, which recognized the existence of an independent Turkish nation-state, at the same time "legitimized the forced deportations of Christians from Anatolia to Greece and Muslims from Greece to Turkey". The so-called "population exchange," as Weitz points out, "exposed the nether side of self-determination". Indeed, in Weitz's judgment, "[b]oth Greece and Turkey as national states were presumed to be ethnically and religiously homogeneous, even though the presumption covered up significant diversity that remained despite the nearly 1.5 million people who had fled or were forced out of their ancestral homes. Both the rights of national citizens and the deportations of those deemed the 'other' derived from the same concept that nations should be self-determining and, therefore, have their own states" (2015, p.487). In the "population exchange," the national principle was certainly trumping the democratic understanding of self-determination.

But the victors were inconsistent in their application of national self-determination as a criterion for redrawing borders in the wake of the war. This left them open to the charge of hypocrisy, and gave the vanquished a moral-cum-legal argument they could brandish in their attempts to delegitimize and ultimately revise the outcome of the peace settlement. In this vein, it is worth noting that the Nazis, in their first party program, dating from February of 1920, would "demand the unification of all Germans in a Greater Germany on the basis of the right of self-determination of peoples" (Fisch 2015, p.166). Both before and after they came to power, they would not cease to argue the case that "Germany's rights as a nation had been violated by the Versailles Treaty and that German minorities in Central and Eastern Europe were being viciously attacked and persecuted". As Weitz has maintained, the Nazis' version of self-determination was of course restricted to the *Volkgemeinschaft*, or the Aryan racial community, and was indeed conceived "with complete disregard for the concerns, the interests, and the very existence of other national or racial communities" (2015, p.489). Or alternatively, as Fisch has framed it, one could say that Hitler "hid himself behind the right of self-determination until he felt strong enough to go on the offensive" (2015, p.166).

Either way, it is certainly significant that "Hitler's occupation of the Rhineland in 1936 and of Austria and Czechoslovakia in 1938 was carried out under the pretext of unifying all Germans in the name of self-determination," and that when he "marched into Poland in 1939," he did so allegedly "to secure Danzig and the Polish Corridor, both predominantly German in population" (Ronen 1979, pp.4-5).

The principle of national self-determination not only survived the Second World War; indeed, it emerged even stronger. The Atlantic Charter of 1941, signed by Great Britain and the United States, would express the commitment of the two nations to "respect the right of all peoples to choose the form of government under which they will live; and they wish to see sovereign rights and self government restored to those who have been forcibly deprived of them" (Weitz 2015, p.489, n.97). Even more explicit would be Article 1.2 of the UN Charter, which would declare, among the purposes of the United Nations, "[t]o develop friendly relations among nations based on respect for the principle of equal rights and self-determination of peoples". In subsequent years, the principle would be further entrenched and recognised in the Declaration on the Granting of Independence to Colonial Peoples (1960), the Covenants on Human Rights (1966), the Declaration on Principles of International Law Concerning Friendly Relations and Cooperation among States (1970), as well as a host of other declarations (Ronen 1979, p.5).

Not coincidentally, as Weitz has observed, "enshrined as a human right," foundational to the "architecture of the postwar world," the term was destined to be "adopted by countless anticolonial activists and was written into the programs of their movements from Kenya to Algeria to Vietnam" (2015, p.489).

However, the legal status of self-determination would not be unambiguous. The UN Charter also recognized, in Article 2.1, "the sovereign equality of all its members," and in Article 2.4, made reference to a principle of "territorial integrity" for all independent states. Colonial powers such as Belgium, Great Britain, and Portugal would all rely on and invoke these in their own defence (Weitz 2015, p.490).

If the legal status of the principle of self-determination remained ambiguous, its moral force was notably less so. This was in no small part because, as Fisch has emphasized, in the postwar period "self-determination became defined, or at least came to be understood essentially as decolonization. Any form of decolonization was regarded as self-determination, and self-determination consisted almost exclusively in decolonization" (2015, p.191).

Indicative in this regard would be the 1955 Bandung Conference, which brought together some twenty-nine Asian and African states, most of which had only recently acquired their independence. The Conference's final communiqué not only "declared its full support of the principle of self-determination of peoples and nations as set forth in the Charter of the United Nations," but in fact would refer to the principle as "a pre-requisite of the full enjoyment of all fundamental Human Rights" ("Final Communiqué" 1955).

But with decolonization, in the creation of new states, neither the "subjective" will of the population nor "objective" ethnic, linguistic, or other identities or shared histories were, as a rule, taken into account. Instead, "[t]he formal criterion stated that colonial territorial entities were to become independent within their colonial borders" – that is, the principle of *uti possidetis* applied (Fisch 2015, p.206). Nor were these new borders generally conceived as malleable or re-negotiable. To the contrary, as the Ethiopian emperor Haile Selassie and the Indian president Radhakrishan would insist in a joint statement from 1965, "self-determination should apply only to colonial territories which have not yet attained their independence and not to parts of sovereign or independent states". (Fisch 2015, p.200).

The disastrous consequences of the 1947 partition between India and Pakistan did much to dissuade the temptation to apply any objective criteria in pursuit of the homogeneity of new nation-states (Fisch 2015, p.209). As Fisch further explains: "In practice, one drew the conclusion that a partition of colonial territorial units without recourse to *uti possidetis*, and thereby to established borders, was no longer a possibility. There was a remarkable consensus on this point, particularly in Africa. Attempts to proceed otherwise, such as in Katanga and Biafra, were rigorously prevented time and again, and not seldom with military force" (2015, p.210).

Indeed, in general, albeit with some notable exceptions, such as Bangladesh, Eritrea, East Timor, and South Sudan, a prohibition on secession in formerly colonized territories has seemed to hold. The combination of "territorial integrity" with *uti possidetis* has for the most part contained and confined the application of the principle of self-determination of peoples, although secessionist conflicts in the formerly colonised world have not been avoided either. Witness Kashmir, Sri Lanka, Baluchistan, the Western Sahara, Cyprus, to name but a few of the most salient ongoing conflicts, as well as, of course, perhaps the most complicated case, that of Israel-Palestine, though even to label that conflict "secessionist" would seem somewhat contentious.

Hobsbawm has argued, in reference to anticolonial nationalism, that "[t]he leaders and ideologues of colonial and semicolonial liberation movements sincerely spoke the language of European nationalism, which they had so often learned in or from the west, even when it did not suit their situation" (1990, p.136). This emphasis on the imitation and diffusion of national(ist) ideals, including the principle of national self-determination, emanating out, as it were, from Europe, has been challenged by postcolonial scholars. Partha Chatterjee (1986), for example, has attempted to rebut the Eurocentric bias built into much of the scholarly literature on nationalism, which treats the emergence and nature of nationalist thought in the colonial world as if it were but mimicry, or mere imitation of a model that was created by European historical subjects, thereby robbing the colonized of agency, reducing their role to the repetition or playing out of scripts that were written elsewhere, by Europeans, for Europeans. An imitation, not surprisingly, that was doomed to fail once it had been transplanted to radically different circumstances.

Following Chatterjee, Getachew has recently emphasized that, rather than diffusion, imitation, or mimicry, in relation to the idea of the nation and the aspiration for national self-determination, what was at work among anticolonial nationalists is more accurately portrayed as translation, reinvention, and creative appropriation. Just as Wilson had creatively appropriated and reinvented self-determination from Lenin and the Bolsheviks, so too, Getachew insists, did anticolonial nationalists reinvent the ideal. Getachew stresses, in particular, how anticolonial nationalists such as Nnamdi Azikiwe, Kwame Nkrumah, and Julius Nyerere effectively redefined self-determination, not only in the obvious sense, to refer to the colonised world, but also related their "nation-building" projects to broader "world-making" efforts to build legal, political, and economic institutions that they hoped would be capable of transforming the "conditions of international hierarchy that facilitate dependence and domination" (2019, p.5).

Nkrumah's slogan, "seek ye first the political kingdom and all things shall be added unto you," however, would prove perhaps less prescient than his subsequent warning about "neocolonialism," his denunciation of how "[t]he 'end of empire' [would be] accompanied by a flourishing of other means of subjugation" (1966, p.52). Implicit in this denunciation was an understanding of self-determination as requiring more than mere formal independence. For, in the neocolonial situation, he would contend, "the state which is subject to it is, in theory, independent and has all the outward trappings of international sovereignty," even though "[i]n reality its economic system and thus its political policy is directed from the outside" (1966, p.ix). Nkrumah therefore argued "that the mere absence of direct political control was an insufficient guarantee of postcolonial freedom" (Getachew 2019, p.23).

This is why, according to Getachew, anticolonial nationalists in the Black Atlantic world, in particular, would seek to interpret non-intervention in more than purely military terms. They would attempt to exercise self-determination by using state power to "limit [foreign] domination through legal instruments". Not only that, they would be adamant in their pursuit of the construction of regional federations, both in Africa and the West Indies, in an effort "to evade the economic dependence inherent in the global economy by organizing regional institutions that were egalitarian and redistributive". Moreover, they would push for a New International Economic Order, an initiative that "directly challenged the economic hierarchies of the international realm". In sum, as Getachew concludes, "[l]aying claim to [an] expansive account of sovereign equality articulated in the right to self-determination, they envisioned an egalitarian welfare world that would be democratic and redistributive" (Getachew 2019, pp.23-24).

The hegemonic understanding of self-determination as formal decolonization in the postwar period thus did not preclude more expansive conceptions of what the true exercise of the principle in fact required. Nor, for that matter, did it mean that aspirations for national self-determination were confined to the colonial world. To the contrary, in the 1960s, the decade that Weitz refers to as "the halcyon days of self-determination" (2015, p.493), in places like Scotland and Québec, the Basque Country, Catalonia, and Northern Ireland, self-determination struggles would surge with new vigour, as the thesis of "internal colonialism" began to emerge. Likewise, some of the more radical elements in the civil rights movement in the United States would resuscitate the language of self-determination to refer to their struggle. While in the Federal Republic of Germany, the desire for national reunification on the grounds of self-determination would also be kept alive.

Meanwhile, in the context of the Cold War, the principle of self-determination would be invoked with frequency by both sides. In the war in Vietnam, for example, "[t]he Soviets and their allies charged the United States with brutally violating the right of self-determination," while in response, "[t]he US countered that it was defending the right of self-determination for the people of South Vietnam" (Weitz 2015, p.493).

For its part, the United Nations would even come to articulate a notion of self-determination that was closely connected to the concept of "development". In this vein, a 1981 study on "The Right to Self-Determination" prepared by the Special Rapporteur of the Sub-Commission on Prevention of Discrimination and Protection of Minorities would include sections not only on "the right of peoples freely to determine their own political status," but also on "the right of peoples freely to pursue their economic development," as well as on "the right of peoples freely to pursue their social development," and on "the right of peoples freely to pursue their cultural development". The report would end by calling for "the elimination of colonialism, neo-colonialism, racism, apartheid and other forms of the violation of the right to self-determination, and the adoption of strong measures to establish truly democratic relations between States and peoples" (Cristescu 1981, p.123). Tellingly, however, the report would also insist that "this right will always ensure respect for the existence, sovereignty and territorial integrity of States" (Cristecu 1981, p.123). Perhaps even more explicitly, the report would emphasise that "the application of the principle to all peoples should not be interpreted as an encouragement to secessionist or irredentist movements, or as justifying activities aimed at changing a country's system of government" (Cristescu 1981, p.39).

In this respect, the 1981 report by the Special Rapporteur was enunciating an understanding of self-determination as distinctly not implying a right to secession in non-colonial contexts, an understanding which had already been codified in the General Assembly's 1970 Declaration on Principles of Law

Concerning Friendly Relations, which had "link[ed] self-determination with the requirement of a government representing the whole people," and at the same time had "reject[ed] the right of secession if the government meets [that] requirement" (Epps 1997, p.438). That Declaration would make clear that it did not intend to "authoriz[e] or encourag[e] any action which would dismember or impair, totally or in part, the territorial integrity or political unity of sovereign and independent states conducting themselves in compliance with the principle of equal rights and self-determination of peoples ... and thus possessed of a government representing the whole people belonging to the territory without distinction as to race, creed or color" (Epps 1997, p.438).

The collapse of the Soviet Union and the end of the Cold War would trigger another wave of creation of new independent states, and another exercise in redrawing state boundaries, within what had been the Soviet sphere. In "1989-1990, the communist regimes of Soviet satellite states collapsed in rapid succession in Poland, Hungary, Czechoslovakia, East Germany, Bulgaria, Romania, and Mongolia. East and West Germany united, Czechoslovakia peacefully split into the Czech Republic and Slovakia, while in the 1990s Yugoslavia began a violent break-up into six states. Macedonia became an independent nation and broke off from Yugoslavia peacefully. Kosovo, which was previously an autonomous unit of Serbia, declared independence in 2008, but has received less international recognition" (Wikipedia 2021c).

As for the Soviet Union itself, it would be dissolved in December of 1991, and broken up into some fifteen sovereign republics, out of what had been formerly union republics within the USSR, achieved for the most part peacefully. "Inside those new republics, four major areas – [Abkhazia, South Ossetia, Transnistria, and Artsakh] – have claimed their own independence, but not received widespread international recognition" (Wikipedia 2021c). And indeed, secessionist conflicts continue to abound across the post-Soviet sphere (Behrends 2021).

Elsewhere, struggles for national self-determination would persist as well. In Québec, for example, the sovereigntist movement gained sufficient momentum to hold a second referendum on independence in 1995. In contrast to the first referendum, which had been decisively defeated back in 1980, in 1995 the sovereigntist cause would lose by only a very narrow margin. Controversy surrounding the precise wording of the referendum, as well as the

razor-thin margin of defeat, would prompt the Canadian government to ini-
tiate a reference on the legality of a unilateral declaration of independence,
after the Québecois premier threatened to hold a third referendum once the
"winning conditions" were there. In 1998, the Supreme Court of Canada
would issue an historic judgment on the matter, in which it would rule out
the legality of unilateral secession, but also argue that, in accordance with the
union's democratic and federal constitution, the central government would
be obliged to negotiate the terms of sovereignty for Québec, should a referendum deliver a clear majority in favour of a clearly worded question about
independence (Leslie 1999). An important precedent was thus set for a third
way of sorts, in which the principle of self-determination conceived as a right
to unilateral secession was rejected, but so too was disputed the predominance of the principle of territorial integrity.

A further crack in the edifice of the primacy of the principle of territorial
integrity over self-determination, understood as the right to secession, would
come in 2010, when the International Court of Justice would issue an advisory
opinion in which it argued that Kosovo's unilateral declaration of independence did not violate any applicable rule of international law. In its advisory
opinion, the ICJ would emphasise not only that, "[d]uring the second half
of the twentieth century, the international law of self-determination developed in such a way as to create a right to independence for the peoples of
non-self-governing territories and peoples subject to alien subjugation, domination and exploitation," but also that "[t]he practice of States in [instances
of declaration of independence outside this context] does not point to the
emergence in international law of a new rule prohibiting the making of a declaration of independence in such cases" (ICJ 2010 p.30). Moreover, it would
insist that "the scope of the principle of territorial integrity is confined to the
sphere of relations between States" (ICJ 2010, p.30).

Tellingly, though, the ICJ dodged making a more clear-cut statement on
the scope and parameters of the principle of self-determination, understood
as the right to secession. In this vein, while the Court would note that it had
heard "radically different views" about whether "the international law of self-
determination confers upon part of the population of an existing State a right
to separate from that State," as well as whether "international law provides
for a right of 'remedial secession' and, if so, in what circumstances," it never-

theless contended "that it is not necessary to resolve these questions in the present case" (ICJ 2010, p.31).

For its part, the United Kingdom has undergone a series of significant transformations in relation to the recognition of its multinational character, including important concessions to the right to self-determination for both Northern Ireland and Scotland. Tony Blair's New Labour government would promise and deliver two referenda on devolution of autonomy for Scotland and Wales, both of which passed in 1997. It would also promote a successful peace process in Northern Ireland, leading to the 1998 Good Friday Agreement. The Agreement would not only institutionalize a complex, consociational power-sharing arrangement for the deeply-divided Catholic and Protestant communities, but would also recognise a so-called "principle of consent," which would assert both "the legitimacy of the aspiration to a United Ireland and the legitimacy of the wish … to remain part of the United Kingdom," and would also emphasise "the right to self-determination for the people of both jurisdictions in Ireland, Northern Ireland and the Republic of Ireland, without external interference, and only with the consensus of a majority of people in both polities" (Wikipedia 2021b). In 2014, David Cameron's Conservative government would accept the Scottish Nationalist Party's aspiration to hold a referendum on independence. The plebiscite would galvanize a high level of enthusiasm and popular participation in Scotland, but would ultimately be defeated by a margin of 55% to 45%.

In Spain, by contrast, the principle of territorial integrity continues to hold sway. After four decades of Franco's fascist dictatorship, which was characterised by an uncompromising unitary Spanish nationalist conception of the state, since the transition to democracy in the late 1970s, there has been a significant degree of devolution of autonomy for the Basque Country, Catalonia, and Galicia, as part of the process of configuration of the quasi-federal *Estado de las Autonomías*. Furthermore, the country's constitution "recognises the right to self-government of the nationalities and regions of which it is composed;" however, in the same paragraph it also declares the "indissolvable unity of the Spanish nation" (Linz 1989; Martínez and Miley 2010).

In the Basque Country, neither the more moderate and Christian-Democratic Basque nationalist party, in power at the regional level, nor the violent insurgency of the more radical, paramilitary organization ETA, has proven capable of forcing any concessions in this regard. ETA would officially abandon its armed struggle in 2011, despite the absence of any peace process similar to the model of Northern Ireland (Whitfield 2014).

While in Catalonia, after decades of loyalty to the constitutional order on the part of the conservative Catalan nationalist party, long hegemonic at the regional level, since 2012, a wave of separatist mobilization took place, in which the demand for the so-called "right to decide," or *dret a decidir*, a neologism advanced in lieu of a full-throated call for self-determination, has come to the fore (Crameri 2016). In relation to this demand, first in 2014, and then again in 2017, the regional government would organize extra-legal referenda on independence, which, however, have been met with escalating waves of state repression, including significant police brutality on the day of the 2017 referendum, as well as the temporary suspension of regional autonomy, and the imprisonment of leading figures from the regional government, who would be convicted on charges of rebellion and sedition and later pardoned (Bernat and Whyte 2020; Miley 2019).

Meanwhile, across the Americas, and in Australia and New Zealand, among other places, recent decades have witnessed an impressive resurgence in the mobilization of indigenous identities, with claims to self-determination that somehow even question the very form of the nation-state (Murphy 2008, p.186). These developments would lead the United Nations in 2007 to elaborate and issue a Declaration on the Rights of Indigenous Peoples, Article 3 of which would affirm that "[i]ndigenous peoples have the right to self-determination," and Article 4 of which would further clarify that "[i]ndigenous peoples, in exercising their right to self-determination, have the right to autonomy or self-government, in matters relating to their internal and local affairs, as well as ways and means for financing their autonomous functions" (United Nations 2007).

It is within this broader context of resurgent indigenous mobilization that the Zapatista movement's rather unique struggle for self-determination, conceived as autonomy from the state rather than as a right to a separate state, would emerge. As Emilio del Valle Escalante has explained, the Zapatista Army of National Liberation (EZLN) first burst onto the scene in January of 1994, in protest against the passage of the North American Free Trade Agreement. The Zapatistas "began as an armed movement declaring war against the Mexican nation-state, but later turned into a social movement that struggles to promote basic human rights and a level of political and cultural autonomy within Mexico". The movement has made clear that it does "not want to become a democratic political party, since this would perpetuate a political system that, by gaining power, distances itself from the needs of the people, especially those at the margins". Instead, the Zapatistas have been scrupulous in their efforts to "maintain independence from political parties and the state," while "promoting instead a mandate of *mandar obedeciendo* (command by obeying), attempting to transform the political system into one that raises the consciousness of civil society to address the needs and demands of the historically marginalized within modern societies". In this vein, the movement has "developed a discourse that addresses the major critical problems that affect not only indigenous peoples, but all those who suffer repression, poverty, discrimination, and political and economic marginalization" (del Valle Escalante 2014).

From 2003, the Zapatistas established a series of autonomous communities, called *caracoles*, in the areas that they effectively control. And in 2012, they would "mobilize thousands of Indigenous Zapatistas, peacefully taking five municipalities in Chiapas ... and [would] announc[e] how, after decades of struggle, they [had] successfully created self-sufficient and autonomous communities with their own political projects and objectives, independent of the Mexican nation-state" (del Valle Escalante 2014). Theirs is a vision of self-determination from below, so to speak. They have reinterpreted the principle to mean a way of "gaining distance or protection from rather than inclusion in state institutions," towards which they "express a profound sense of alienation," since these "carry the stigma of colonial domination" (Murphy 2008, p.186, in del Valle Escalante 2014). Neither inclusion in the state, nor a state of their own: their struggle for self-determination instead is conceived and practiced as a struggle for direct democratic control, apart from the state, even against the state.

In this respect, the development of the Zapatista movement demonstrates a strong affinity and parallel with the transformation of the Kurdish Freedom Movement. Like the Zapatistas, the Kurdish Freedom Movement has evolved from Marxist-Leninist origins towards the espousal of a more libertarian and autonomist ethos and agenda. Nor is it a coincidence that such an evolution would occur in the wake of the collapse of state communism, with the concurrent questioning of the old paradigm of "national liberation". What we witness with these two movements is the emergence, from below, of a new, direct-democratic, and anti-statist conceptualization and praxis of struggle for self-determination.

In the Kurdish Freedom Movement, in particular, much emphasis has been placed on the importance of centering the struggle for gender emancipation as a key pillar of its self-determination project. There is, of course, a longer history to the link between the objectives and aims of "national liberation" and women's empowerment. For example, Vijay Prashad has recalled how, at an Afro-Asian People's Solidarity Conference, held in Cairo in 1957, Aisha Abdul-Rahman would emphasise both "the central role played by women in [national liberation movements], and in the liberation of women by the struggle". According to Abdul-Rahman, "[t]he renaissance of the Eastern woman has always coincided with liberation movements". Indeed, she would go so far as to insist that "[t]he success of these revolutions depends on the liberation of the enslaved half, on rescuing women from paralysis, unemployment and inaction and eliminating the differences between the two halves of the nation – its men and women". And yet, as Prashad nevertheless also admits, these movements remained too often characterised by a certain "machismo and lack of appreciation for the role of women" (Prashad 2008, pp. 53-54). With its ideological and organizational reorientation, the Kurdish Freedom Movement has sought to tackle this problem of lingering "machismo" head-on.

Likewise, both the Kurdish Freedom Movement and the Zapatistas have stressed the importance of ecological sustainability as a constitutive component of their anti-state self-determination projects. To this end, the Kurdish Freedom Movement has embraced, at least in discourse, the paradigm and program of "social ecology" (Hunt 2021), while the Zapatistas, perhaps more consistently, have come to embody the values and practices of participatory, "ecological self-management" (Nail 2010).

In the discourse and, at least partially, in the practices of the Kurdish Freedom Movement and the Zapatistas, then, the principle of self-determination has once again been reinvented, this time to connote the struggle for direct democratic control and autonomy from the state, the struggle for gender emancipation, and the struggle for ecological sustainability, among other aims.

However, this incipient reinvention still coexists with the classical Leninist understanding of and aspiration for self-determination as the right to a separate and sovereign nation-state. Indeed, as we have seen, the principle of self-determination has been transformed on multiple occasions over the course of the last two centuries. It remains a malleable and multi-valent concept, even as it has been increasingly codified in international law. And so, inevitably, part of the struggle for self-determination in the twenty-first century entails the struggle to frame what the principle itself even means.

Overview of the Book

The essays in this volume are intended as a contribution to this endeavour. The first part of the book brings together some six chapters, each treating different aspects of the relationship between self-determination and the nation. The first chapter, titled "The Nation as Hegemonic Project," begins with a discussion of the categories of nationhood and nationalism, before turning to sketch both the analytical distinction and the historical relationship between states and nations. It then briefly traces the rise of and problems with the principle and practice of self-determination in the post-Wilsonian world, and seeks to problematize still-influential Leninist-cum-Stalinist dogmas regarding the self-determination of nations. It concludes with an extended consideration of Benedict Anderson's sophisticated neo-Marxist apology for nationalist politics and ideology. It takes Anderson to task on three related counts: for paying insufficient attention to power relations; for underestimating the affinities between nationalism and racism; and for denying the intimate connection between nationalism and fascism.

The second chapter, titled "Nationalist Ideology and the State," explores the theoretical significance and methodological consequences of treating the nation as an ideological construct. It is intended as a corrective to the persistent essentialism and widespread reifications that continue to plague the literature on nations and nationalism. It begins with a discussion of the nation as ideology. It then turns to relate the national ideal to the process of self-construction, emphasizing the necessary connection between this process and projections of alterity. It concludes by specifying four sets of Ideological State Apparatuses directly implicated in the cultivation of "nationalizing" hegemonic projects: (1) the educational system, (2) the mass media, (3) the bureaucracy, and (4) political parties. It calls upon scholars to focus on these institutions for the purpose of illuminating the dynamics of national construction.

The third chapter, titled "Towards a New Internationalism," begins with a critique of national populism in historical perspective, before turning to reflect upon the significance of the claim that the worker has no country. It then takes up how the relationship was conceived between the Bolshevik revolution and the prospect for world revolution. It proceeds to revisit Rosa Luxemburg's critique of Bolshevism, and to make the case for a dialectical reading of Luxemburg with Frantz Fanon. It concludes with some reflections about the urgent task of imagining communities beyond the confines of the nation-state.

The fourth chapter, titled "Rosa Luxemburg's Living Legacy," begins by situating this most eminent internationalist revolutionary both outside and against the nation. It then takes up her two-sided critique, first of anarchism, on the one hand, and opportunism on the other. It next turns to treat Luxemburg's understanding of revolution as a process. It proceeds to consider at some length the relationship between different aspects of her prescient critique of Bolshevism, and to expound upon her understanding of the link between organizational form and opportunism. It concludes with an in-depth and sympathetic exploration of Luxemburg's critique of self-determination as utopian. Overall, it insists that Luxemburg's contribution to anti-capitalist thought and praxis remains relevant in at least four ways: (1) she elaborates an alternative, equally anti-capitalist and Marxist vision to Leninism, but one less susceptible to the autocratic inclinations of Lenin and the Bolsheviks; (2) she is equally vehement in her critique of revisionism, reformism and "parliamentary cretinism;" (3) she makes the case persuasively that the effective alternatives are "socialism or barbarism;" and (4) she expresses a powerful "revolutionary, internationalist" alternative to the perils and pitfalls of the "national imaginary".

The fifth chapter, titled "1917 on the Brain," is an extended reflection upon the significance of Murray Bookchin's evocative quip that "[t]he Russian Revolution weighs like a nightmare on the brains of the living". It hones in on two important ways in which this legacy weighs upon us like a nightmare. The first has to do with the equation of any anti-capitalist alternative – call it "socialism," call it "communism" – with state tyranny. The second has to do with Leninist-cum-Stalinist dogmas about self-determination, which continue to plague the left, blinding it to Luxemburg's crucial insight about the need to evaluate such abstract principles in terms of their concrete impact on local and global constellations of power relations. Related to this latter confusion, I contend, is the virtual renunciation of the imperative of world revolution. Such an imperative, I insist, can be glimpsed when we consider the limits of national self-determination, as revealed perhaps most clearly by the post-colonial experience, and by the fact that Marxism-Leninism in power has almost invariably been but a "developmentalist," "modernist" ideology, wielded to legitimate the power of those at the helm of tyrannical states, wielded by those who would *seize* power, rather than *dissolve* it.

The sixth chapter, titled "Anticolonial, Postcolonial, and Decolonial Critiques and Creative Appropriations of Self-Determination: From Fanon to Öcalan," seeks to situate the re-articulation of the principle of self-determination by the imprisoned Kurdish leader Abdullah Öcalan, by relating it to a series of critiques and creative appropriations of the principle as formulated by emblematic figures in the anticolonial, postcolonial, and decolonial traditions. It begins by honing in on a rarely recognised feature of Frantz Fanon's 1961 classic, *The Wretched of the Earth*, namely, the distinction he makes between the abstract principle of self-determination and definite demands for thoroughgoing decolonization. It then turns to consider Adom Getachew's defence of the anticolonial articulation and practice of self-determination, highlighting the creative appropriation and virtual re-invention of the ideal of self-determination in the writings and accomplishments of a host of anticolonial thinkers. It next takes up Gary Wilder's recovery of alternative conceptions of self-determination, not linked to state sovereignty, as espoused by Aimé Césaire and Leopold Sédar Senghor. This leads to a discussion of Walter Mignolo's decolonial critique of the paradigm of the nation-state. The essay concludes by recasting Öcalan in an explicitly anti-/post-/de-colonial light, relating these critiques and creative appropriations of self-determination to Öcalan's renunciation of the goal of a nation-state.

The second part of the book brings together six essays which treat different dimensions of the relationship between self-determination and democracy. The seventh chapter, titled "Representative Democracy and the Democratic Confederal Project: Reflections on the Transformation of the Kurdish Movement in Turkey," begins with an overview of the context of state terror, and of the dialectical dynamic of the conflict between the state and the guerrillas. It then turns to address the question of the right to rebel, before proceeding to discuss the existence of multiple Kurdish constituencies. The essay next elaborates a comparison between Turkey and Spain, before examining in some depth the crisis of Kemalist hegemony. It goes on to discuss the contradictions and conflict between the nationalizing Turkish state and the Kurdish project of national revival, and hones in on the plight of the Kurds as a "permanent minority". It proceeds to take up the relationship between violence and national consciousness, and to consider the motifs of martyrdom and collective sacrifice in the discourse and praxis of the Kurdish Freedom Movement. It considers at some length Öcalan's status within the movement as something akin to that of a prophet, before turning to treat the paradox of democratic leadership. It takes up the question of the limits and logic of representative democracy, and discusses the imperative to participate and the need to raise consciousness. This before addressing the relationship between guerrilla discipline and revolutionary discipline, and then sketching the contours of the transformation from democratic centralism to democratic confederalism. The chapter concludes with an extended consideration of challenges for the movement's new paradigm.

The eighth chapter, titled "Reflections on Revolution, the Spiral of Violence, and the Legitimacy of Self-Defense," begins with a discussion of the appeal of the guerrilla in historical perspective. It then turns to consider the significance of Helder Da Camara's influential model of the spiral of violence. It attempts to situate and complicate the model, by incorporating insights from the works of Paolo Freire, Frantz Fanon, and Walter Benjamin. The chapter treats in some depth the relationship between oppression and necrophilia, and discusses the apocalyptic undertones in Da Camara's model. The chapter concludes by invoking Abdullah Öcalan's argument about the legitimacy of self-defence.

The ninth chapter, titled "Revolutionary Consciousness beyond Militant Secularism," begins with a reconsideration of the widespread bias against belief in the spirit world on the secular left. It treats Frantz Fanon as emblematic in this regard, doubly biased against the religious, doubly indebted to the tradition of European secularism, to the militant atheism of both Marx and of Freud. It contrasts Fanon's attitude to that of Frederick Douglass, and recounts a key passage in Douglass's autobiographical account of the emergence of his will to struggle, honing in on the mystical and spiritual dimensions incorporated into this account. It also recalls C.L.R. James's depiction of how spiritual rituals were central to the revolutionary insurrection in the Haitian

Revolution, among the slaves who worked the land. This before turning to hone in on the problematic relationship between revolutionary consciousness and "homogenous empty time". It takes the examples of Rosa Luxemburg and Buenaventura Durruti, whose consciousness, in the frenzy of activity that characterized the last days of their lives, somehow seemed to transcend the confines of homogeneous, empty time, to be transported into the realm of the *messianic*, the realm of the eternal "now". And it points to Walter Benjamin's theorization and embodiment of this phenomenon as well.

The tenth chapter, titled "Murray Bookchin and Democratic Theory," attempts an overview and assessment of the too-often overlooked contribution of Bookchin to democratic theory. In his work, Bookchin manages to elaborate and combine in an original and creative way a compelling ecological philosophy with an overarching social history, an account of the emergence of hierarchy, alongside a rather detailed sketch of the contours of a complex political program, libertarian municipalism, intended to combat and ultimately dissolve hierarchy in all its forms. In the process, he provides a coherent, and to a large extent plausible, meta-narrative which grounds a unique synthesis of ecological and anarchist, or perhaps more precisely, libertarian socialist, politics. The chapter begins with a summary account of Bookchin's meta-narrative of the emergence of hierarchy. It then turns to a sympathetic examination, at some length, of Bookchin's re-articulation of the democratic ideal. It proceeds to provide a more critical set of considerations, related to the problems of Eurocentrism and secular sectarianism in Bookchin's thought. It concludes by arguing that, in Rojava, Bookchin's social-ecological, communalist project has, through dialectical synthesis with the creative and dynamic Kurdish movement, managed definitively to transcend its Eurocentric origins and to become part of humanity's legacy of freedom.

The eleventh chapter, titled "Marx, Marxism, and the Problem of Eurocentrism: Reflections Inspired by Esteban Torres' *La gran transformación de la sociología*," sets out to review and evaluate the charge of Eurocentrism frequently levelled against Marx and Marxism. The chapter begins with an assessment of Esteban Torres's recent attempt to at least partially acquit Marx and Marxism of this charge. It relates Torres's discussion of the problem to broader polemics surrounding the topic. It hones in on debates about Marx's evolving views on European colonialism, and its relationship to capitalism. It pays special attention to the postcolonial critiques advanced by Edward

Said and Dipesh Chakrabarty, as well as to more recent decolonial critiques advanced by Walter Mignolo and Ramón Grosfoguel. It also considers Marxist responses to these. It concludes with a revindication of the contributions of heterodox "Third World Marxists" such as Frantz Fanon and Aimé Césaire, arguing that what is at work in such figures thinking *from* and *for* the global south is not a logic of diffusion, imitation, and mimicry, but rather, can be more accurately portrayed as translation, reinvention, and creative appropriation.

Finally, the twelfth chapter, titled "'Double Consciousness' Among Moroccan Migrants in the Metropolitan Region of Barcelona," foregrounds the perspectives of Moroccan migrants in the Barcelona area. It is based on a set of focus group discussions conducted with Moroccan migrants in the municipalities of Badalona and Hospitalet de Llobregat, in the Spring of 2013. The focus group discussions related to the subject of "integration," and brought to light lived experiences with and reactions to systemic discrimination, offset in part by material opportunities. The chapter documents these experiences and reactions, interpreting them through the lens of W.E.B. Dubois' concept of "double consciousness". It emphasises the ambivalence produced by the simultaneous recognition of the existence of concrete material advantages associated with life in Catalan society, contrasted with grievances generated by so many racist, xenophobic, and Islamophobic everyday encounters. It highlights the salience and affective responses triggered among Moroccan migrant women by mention of controversies surrounding the practice of veiling. It concludes with reflections about the appeal of the ideal of the Umma, the community of believers, among postcolonial subjects in the former European metropoles, as a response to the experience of systemic discrimination on racialized and religious grounds, especially in contexts in which "integrationist" narratives about "the land of opportunity" begin to ring hollow.

Together, these essays are intended as a contribution to efforts to rethink the concept of self-determination for the twenty-first century. The essays focus on different aspects of struggles for self-determination. They consistently seek to critique and challenge nationalist and statist conceptions of the principle, while taking inspiration in, and attempting to advance, an alternative, radical and direct-democratic, even anti-statist, as well as internationalist, articulation and understanding of the ideal.

REFERENCES

Anderson, B. (2006). *Imagined Communities*. London: Verso.

Anderson, K. (2010). *Marx at the Margins. On Nationalism, Ethnicity, and Non-Western Societies*. Chicago, IL: The University of Chicago Press.

Behrends, J.C. (2021). "Post-Soviet Separatism in Historical Perspective," in D. Minakov, et.al., eds., *Post-Soviet Secessionism. Nation-Building and State-Failure after Communism*. Stuttgart: ibidem Press, pp.213-242.

Benjamin, W. (1999). "Theses on the Philosophy of History," in *Illuminations*. London: Pimlico, pp.245-255.

Bernat, I., and Whyte, D. (2020). "Postfascism in Spain: The Struggle for Catalonia," *Critical Sociology*, Vol. 46, Nos. 4-5, pp.1-16.

Brenner, E. (1995). *Really Existing Nationalisms: A Post-Communist View from Marx and Engels*. Oxford: Clarendon Press, 1995.

Carr, E.H. (1978). *The Bolshevik Revolution 1817-1923. Volume 1*. New York: Norton.

Carr, E.H. (1981). *The Bolshevik Revolution 1817-1923. Volume 3*. New York: Norton.

Chatterjee, P. (1986). *Nationalist Thought and the Colonial World*. London: Zed Books.

Cohen, S. (1975). *Bukharin and the Bolshevik Revolution*. New York: Vintage.

Connor, W. (1984). *The National Question in Marxist-Leninist Theory and Strategy*. Princeton, NJ: Princeton University Press.

Crameri, K. (2016). "Do Catalans Have 'the Right to Decide'? Secession, Legitimacy, and Democracy in Twenty-First Century Europe," *Global Discourse*, Vol. 6, No. 3, pp.432-439.

Cristescu, A. (1981). *The Right to Self-Determination. Historical and Current Development on the Basis of United Nations Instruments*. New York, NY: United Nations. Accessible at: https://undocs.org/pdf?symbol=en/E/CN.4/Sub.2/404/Rev.1

Daniels, R.V. (1969). *The Conscience of the Revolution. Communist Opposition in Soviet Russia*. New York, NY: Simon and Schuster.

Davis, H.B. (1976). "Introduction: The Right of National Self-Determination in Marxist Theory – Luxemburg versus Lenin," in Horace B. Davis, ed., *The National Question. Selected Writings by Rosa Luxemburg*. New York, NY: Monthly Review Press, pp.9-48.

del Valle Escalante, E. (2014). "Self-Determination: A Perspective from Abya Yala," *E International Relations*, May 20th. Accessible at: https://www.e-ir.info/2014/05/20/self-determination-a-perspective-from-abya-yala/

Epps, V. (1997). "The New Dynamics of Secession," *ILSA Journal of International and Comparative Law*, Vol. 3, pp.433-442.

"Final Communiqué of the Asian-African Conference of Bandung" (1955). Accessible at: https://www.cvce.eu/en/obj/final_communique_of_the_asian_african_confer ence_of_bandung_24_april_1955-en-676237bd-72f7-471f-949a-88b6ae513585.html

Fisch, J. (2015). *The Right of Self-Determination of Peoples. The Domestication of an Illusion.* Cambridge: Cambridge University Press.

Forman, M. (1998). *Nationalism and the International Labour Movement. The Idea of the Nation in Socialist and Anarchist Theory.* University Park, PA: The Pennsylvania State University Press.

Getachew, A. (2019). *Worldmaking after Empire. The Rise and Fall of Self-Determination* Princeton, NJ: Princeton University Press.

Goldner, L. (2011). "Theses for Discussion," Insurgent Notes, Internal Conference, July 31st. Quoted at: https://www.prometheusjournal.org/2021/03/21/destined-to-be-caught-and-bloodily-scratched/

Guérin, D. (1970). *Anarchism: From Theory to Practice.* New York: Monthly Review Press.

Hobsbawm, E. (1990). *Nations and Nationalism since 1780.* Cambridge, MA: Cambridge University Press.

Hunt, S., ed. (2021). *Ecological Solidarity and the Kurdish Freedom Movement.* London: Lexington Books

International Court of Justice. (2010). "Advisory Opinion. Accordance of International Law with the Unilateral Declaration of Independence in Respect of Kosovo". Accessible at: https://www.un.org/ruleoflaw/files/ef_KOS_Advisory-opinion_bilingual.pdf

Kasprzak, M. (2012). "To Reject or Not Reject Nationalism: Debating Marx and Engels' Struggles with Nationalism, 1840s-1880s," *Nationalities Papers,* Vol. 40, No. 4, pp.585-606.

Kinna, R. (2020). "What Is Anarchist Internationalism?" *Nations and Nationalism,* Vol. 27, No. 4, pp.976-991.

Leslie, P. (1999). "Canada: The Supreme Court Sets Rules for the Secession of Quebec," *Publius: The Journal of Federalism,* vol. 29, no. 2, pp.135-151.

Linz, J. (1989). "Spanish Democracy and the Estado de las Autonomías," in R. Goldwin, et. al, eds., *Forging Unity out of Diversity: The Approaches of Eight Nations.* Washington, DC: American Enterprise Institute for Public Policy Research, pp.260-303.

Martínez, E., and Miley, T. (2010). "The Constitution and the Politics of National Identity in Spain," *Nations and Nationalism,* Vol. 16, No. 1, pp.6-30.

Miley, T. (2019). "Catalan Self-Determination and the European Project," in D. Duarte and G. Vale, eds., *Catalonia, Iberia and Europe*. Rome: Biblioteca Scientifica Europea 2, Aracne Editrice, pp.291-312.

Munck, R. (2010). "Marxism and Nationalism in the Era of Globalization," *Capital and Class*, Vol. 34, No. 1, pp.45-53.

Murphy, M. (2008). "Representing Indigenous Self-Determination" *University of Toronto Law Journal*, Vol. 58, No. 2, pp.185-216.

Nail, T. (2010). "A Post-Neoliberal Ecopolitics? Deleuze, Guattari, and Zapatismo," *Philosophy Today*, Vol. 54, No. 2, pp.179-190.

Nettl, J.P. (1966). *Rosa Luxemburg*. Volume 2. Oxford University Press.

Nimni, E.J. (2000). "Introduction for the English-Reading Audience," in O. Bauer, *The Question of Nationalities and Social Democracy*. Minneapolis, MN: University of Minnesota Press, pp.xv-xlvi.

Nkrumah, K. (1966). *Neo-Colonialism. The Last Stage of Imperialism*. New York: International Publishers.

Prashad, V. (2008). *The Darker Nations. A People's History of the Third World*. New York, NY: The New Press.

Prashad, V. (2017). *Red Star over the Third World*. New Delhi: LeftWord Books.

Ronen, D. (1979). *The Quest for Self-Determination*. New Haven, CT: Yale University Press.

Salvadori, M. (1990). *Karl Kautsky and the Socialist Revolution, 1880-1938*. London: Verso.

Shen, K. (2015). "Haitian Independence," *History of Haiti*. Department of Africana Studies, Brown University. Accessible at: https://library.brown.edu/haitihistory/11.html

Suny, R. G. (1993). *The Revenge of the Past. Nationalism, Revolution, and the Collapse of the Soviet Union*. Stanford, CA: Stanford University Press.

United Nations. (2007). *United Nations Declaration of the Rights of Indigenous Peoples*. New York, NY: United Nations. Accessible at: https://www.un.org/development/desa/indigenouspeoples/wp-content/uploads/sites/19/2018/11/UNDRIP_E_web.pdf

Weitz, E. D. (2015). "Self-Determination: How a German Enlightenment Idea Became the Slogan of National Liberation and a Human Right," *American Historical Review*, Vol. 120, No. 2, pp.462-496.

Whitfield, T. (2014). *Endgame for ETA: Elusive Peace in the Basque Country*. Oxford: Oxford University Press.

Wikipedia. (2021a). "Congress of the Peoples of the East". Accessible at: https://en.wikipedia.org/wiki/Congress_of_the_Peoples_of_the_East

Wikipedia. (2021b). "Principle of Consent". Accessible at: https://en.wikipedia.org/wiki/
Principle_of_consent

Wikipedia. (2021c). "Self-Determination". Accessible at: https://en.wikipedia.org/wiki/
Self-determination

PART ONE

Self-Determination and the Nation

CHAPTER 1

The Nation as Hegemonic Project[1]

Abstract: *This chapter argues that the nation is best conceived as a hegemonic project. It starts with a discussion of the dialectical intertwining of the categories of nationhood and nationalism, and continues with a treatment of the analytical distinction and historical relationship between states and nations. It sketches the rise of and problems with the principle and practice of "self-determination" in the post-Wilsonian world, and seeks to problematize still-influential Leninist-cum-Stalinist dogmas regarding the "self-determination" of nations. It concludes with an extended consideration of Benedict Anderson's sophisticated neo-Marxist apology for nationalist politics and ideology. It takes Anderson to task on three related counts: for paying insufficient attention to power relations; for underestimating the affinities between nationalism and racism; and for denying the intimate connection between nationalism and fascism.*

Introduction

This chapter argues that the nation is best conceived as a hegemonic project. It starts with a discussion of the dialectical intertwining of the categories of nationhood and nationalism, and continues with a treatment of the analytical distinction and historical relationship between states and nations. It draws on and synthesizes the important work of Juan Linz and Eric Hobsbawm, paying particular attention to the processes of state-building and nation-building in the European "core" of the emergent world system.

The chapter then turns to discuss the rise of and problems with the doctrine and practice of "self-determination" in the post-Wilsonian world. It seeks to problematize still-influential Leninist-cum-Stalinist dogmas regarding the "self-determination" of nations. It briefly revisits and recovers alternatives to the Leninist position within the classical Marxist tradition. More substantially, it returns to Marx himself. It focuses on Marx's early writings, especially "On the Jewish Question," emphasizing the problematic of "demystification". It compares Marx's critique of religion with the critique of the nation, and it criticizes Marx for falling into the trap of "secular dogmatism".

The chapter concludes with an extended consideration of Benedict Anderson's sophisticated neo-Marxist apology for nationalist politics and ideology. It takes Anderson to task on three related counts. First, it chides Anderson for paying insufficient attention to power relations – specifically, for ignoring the ways in which all appeals to national community and national belonging are embedded within concrete struggles to reproduce or transform existing constellations of power. Second, it chastises Anderson for underestimating the affinities between nationalism and racism in his attempt to decouple the emotions of love and hate, not to mention the discourses of destiny and contamination. Finally, it invokes Benjamin and Buck-Morss, in providing grounds for scepticism against Anderson's attempt to distance nationalism from fascism.

Nationhood and Nationalism

In ontological terms, the "nation" is best conceived as a hegemonic project.[2] It exists only insofar as people believe it does. This does not mean that the nation should be equated with an ethereal "system of ideas," nor relegated to the super-structural realm, much less diagnosed or dismissed as a form of "false consciousness". To do so would entail perpetuating a false binary between materialism and idealism, between base and superstructure.[3] Like any other idea, the "nation" can only exist as a material force in history, "embodied in institutions and apparatuses" – in other words, as an "institutionalised form".[4]

Nationalists aspire for their beliefs to be institutionalized, so that such beliefs can be diffused, adhered to by an ever broader public, and reproduced. The process of diffusion and reproduction of nationalist beliefs by state apparatuses has been described in architectural terms as that of "nation-building".[5] More recently, Brubaker has described state apparatuses engaged in such processes as "nationalizing states". He refers to "nationalization" and to "nationalizing nationalisms of the existing state" and to "nationalizing elites".[6] Four sets of Ideological State Apparatuses are especially implicated in the cultivation of "nationalizing" and "nation-building" hegemonic projects: (1) the educational system, (2) the mass media, (3) the bureaucracy, and (4) political parties.[7]

Nationhood and nationalism are dialectically interrelated. Gellner has famously insisted that "[i]t is nationalism which engenders nations, and not the other way around".[8] It is certainly true that nationalists aspire for their beliefs to be institutionalized, so that such beliefs can be diffused, adhered to by an ever broader public, and reproduced. Nevertheless, Gellner's formulation is not quite correct; for nationhood and nationalism cannot be neatly distinguished in terms of cause and effect (at least not when these terms are used in a unidirectional and undialectical way). Rather than fixating on questions about which determines the other, about which comes first (the "chicken or the egg," so to speak), it makes more sense to understand nationalism and nationhood as two dimensions of the same inter-subjective phenomenon, operating simultaneously at different levels of consciousness – corresponding with the "programmatic" and the "banal".[9]

Nationalism operates primarily at the conscious level, manifesting itself as "ideology" – at its core, a political program that "holds that the political and the national unit should be congruent".[10] *Nationhood*, by contrast, operates principally at the semi- and even sub-conscious levels, as a "pervasive system of social classification," an organising 'principle of vision and division' of the social world".[11]

The literature on "nation-building" provides the tools for sketching the blueprint of institutional arenas targeted by "nationalizing elites," as well as of the institutional contexts within and against which these elites operate. However, it does not provide much in the way of tools for accounting for how or why particular "nationalizing elites" come to capture state power, much less how or why particular nationalizing projects eventually succeed or fail. In other words, it is insufficient for understanding how and why the blueprints of particular nationalizing projects come to be "built," converted into inter-subjective common sense, i.e. social reality, whilst others are defeated entirely, or at least relegated to the margins. To answer such broader questions about the political dynamics propelling processes of "nation-building," recourse to the concept and theory of hegemony is required.[12]

The relation between nationhood and nationalism can be usefully compared to Marx's important distinction between *class-in-itself* and *class-for-itself*. In making this distinction, Marx implies an "objective existence to class structure independent of actors' awareness".[13] Strictly speaking, such an implication is mistaken. Like all groups capable of exercising collective agency, classes are *intersubjective*, not *objective*, realities – at least in the first instance. Moreover, they operate at three, not two, dialectically interrelated levels (or "analytical moments"): (1) as cultural rules; (2) as emergent material relations; and (3) as situated human behaviour and self-understanding.

Yet Marx's dichotomy between *class-in-itself* and *class-for-itself* remains nevertheless instructive. For class relations "may exist objectively without actors' being aware of them" (even if it is also true that they can only exist "if actors are doing something of which they are aware").[14] In this respect, the ontology of nationhood is fundamentally different from that of class – except to the extent that nationhood is effectively fused with the state.[15]

Nation and State

"Nation" and "state" are two categories all too often conflated in common parlance and even in scholarly debate. Yet, as Juan Linz has incisively argued, "state-building and nation-building are two overlapping but conceptually and historically different processes".[16] Conceptually, following Rokkan, the term "state refers to the sphere of highest governmental authority and administration". The emergence of the so-called "modern state is synonymous with the gradual concentration of administrative functions in the hands of the central government". In the Medieval kingdoms of Europe, by contrast, "the ruler possessed the highest authority but controlled only his own domains".[17] The process of state-building thus refers to the encroaching concentration of power, more concretely the shift towards a monopoly of administration and coercive force in the hands of the sovereign, in a word, the trend towards absolutism.[18] Historically, this state-building process can be traced back – at least in the European core of the emergent world capitalist system – to the "crisis of feudalism, the Renaissance, and the Reformation," and more specifically, to "rivalries between emerging monarchies in Western and later Northern Europe".[19]

By contrast, the term "nation" has proven notoriously hard to define. The dominant definitional trope today is that a nation is a particular type of "imagined" political community. Indeed, according to Benedict Anderson's highly influential account, the "nation" is a community imagined as both sovereign and limited.[20] However, this definition remains too abstract. In the concrete world, as Hobsbawm perspicaciously lamented, "no satisfactory criterion can be discovered for deciding which of the many human collectivities should be labelled in this way". To begin with, there is no objective "way of telling the observer how to distinguish a nation from other entities *a priori*, as we can tell him or her how to recognize a bird or to distinguish a mouse from a lizard" (or for that matter an NGO from a state).[21] Consequently, all "objective" definitions of the nation not only "have failed" but are bound to fail. Worse yet, the "subjective" alternative of defining the nation in terms of the existence of national consciousness is perhaps more problematic still – open to the objections of tautology and extreme voluntarism.[22]

Max Weber considered the term nation to belong to the sphere not of "facts" but of "values". According to Weber, the nation "means above all else that it is proper to expect from certain groups a specific sentiment of solidarity in the face of other groups".[23] Otherwise put, the term nation is never simply descriptive; instead, it entails, at least implicitly, an imperative of sacrifice, solidarity and ultimate political loyalty. Yet, in the sphere of "facts," similar to Hobsbawm, "Weber also notes, there is no agreement on how these groups should be delimited or about what concerted action should result from such solidarity".[24]

Whereas the term "state" is both a category of praxis and a category of analysis, the term "nation" is best considered a category of praxis alone. The state "involves a series of offices ... highly differentiated in modern bureaucracies, armies, courts of justices, legislatures, etc". The nation does not – "[t]here are no clear rules about membership in a nation and there are no defined rights and duties that can be legitimately enforced".[25] This is the persuasive core of Brubaker's call to reframe the study of nationalism so that it overcomes the insidious propensity to rely upon and reify the category of the nation.

As an historical process, state-building preceded the emergence of specifically "national" consciousness by several centuries. For hundreds of years,
"state-building went on without being based on national sentiment, identity,
or consciousness". Only in the nineteenth century, would the idea of the nation begin to "fire the imagination of the intellectuals and the people".[26]

From early on, "architectonic images" were invoked to describe the state-
building process. Indeed, the state was long associated "with the ideas of creation and craft". To this day, the category "state" continues to connote "artefact,"
not "nature," or "organic birth," the way the category of "nation" does.

If "states" and "nations" are thus imagined quite differently, this is closely
related to the relative newness of the "nation". When states first began to
emerge from the fifteenth century, they "did not require intense identification
of their subjects with territorial boundaries, history, culture, or language". In
fact, "state identification and loyalty were often expected to be *transferable*
merely by virtue of dynastic marriages. That is, loyalty belonged to the dy-
nasty, not to the nation".[27]

The Enlightenment and especially the French Revolution brought with
them a profound and radical alteration of the terms of political legitimation
across much of the continent, in turn both reflecting and propelling forward
underlying transformations in the contours of social-property relations.[28]
The era of the "nation-state" commenced, and with it, sovereignty came to
rest – at least in the realm of dominant social imaginaries – no longer in "di-
vinely-ordained, hierarchical dynasties," but instead, in the horizontally-
conceived, secular and general will of the *third estate*, i.e. "the nation".[29] In
Hobsbawm's formulation, the nation "is a social entity only insofar as it relates
to a certain kind of modern territorial state, the 'nation-state', and it is pointless
to discuss nation and nationality except insofar as both relate to it".[30]

Over the course of the nineteenth century and especially in the early twentieth century, the categories of "nation" and "state" would be progressively
fused in the core of the capitalist world system, as the rulers of many states
chose to pursue deliberate "nation-building" policies. The state made the nation, and it did so because it needed to.[31] Accompanying and in order to spur
on the radical social transformations wrought by industrialization, the state
expanded its reach substantially, descending down from commanding heights
into the "everyday life" of its subjects, "through omnipresent agents, from
postmen and policemen to teachers and (in many countries) railway employ-

ees". Creeping democratization, and the incipient demise of "traditional religion as an effective guarantee of social obedience," rendered it imperative for state authorities to rely upon a new "way of welding together the state's subjects against subversion and dissidence". Enter the nation: "the new civic religion of states," a "cement which bonded ... citizens to their state". The more democracy advanced, "the more masses were drawn into politics by elections," and in turn, "the more scope there was for" appeals to the nation "to be heard".[32]

With technological advances, the administration of the state and the economy, both public and private, came to require mass literacy, and this in turn triggered the trend of linguistic assimilation into a national *lingua franca*. Education and conscription were what turned "peasants into Frenchmen," to invoke Eugen Weber's felicitous turn of phrase.[33] But such deliberate pursuit of "nation-building" policies rarely proved so successful outside of France; for state nationalism "was a double-edged strategy," and though it proved capable of mobilizing some inhabitants, it simultaneously "alienated others – those who did not belong, or wish to belong, to the nation identified with the state".[34]

The link Hobsbawm makes between "nationalization" and "democratization" is most insightful. Elsewhere he has famously equated "the age of democratization" with the "era of public political hypocrisy".[35] For Hobsbawm, "nationalism" is a classic case of such hypocrisy. An ideology capable of manipulating the masses – more often than not – for the benefit of the few. The First World War, at least as much as the Second, reveals it as a most dangerous ideology, a most potent concoction and useful tool for manipulating the masses, a belief system that renders them willing to slaughter one another, all for the sake of the country.

Education for the purposes of creating a literate and nationalized pool of labour, recruitment into war machines capable of mobilizing masses for suicidal sacrifice in total war – these are the motives and mechanisms that underpinned and propelled forward the "nationalization" of the masses throughout much of Europe.[36] "Nationalization" and state-propagated nationalisms were thus the products of deliberate decisions made by European rulers commanding rival ships of state across the tormentous seas in an era marked by creeping democratization, capitalist and Imperialist expansion, and looming Inter-Imperialist War.[37]

The Rise of the Principle of "National Self-Determination"

The so-called "Great War" was a crucial turning point. President Wilson famously insisted at the peace settlement in 1918 that "[n]ational aspirations must be respected; people may now be dominated and governed only by their own consent," and that "[s]elf-determination is not a mere phrase; it is an imperative principle of action". Woodrow Wilson, the man who posed as the great liberator of the nations, himself a staunch nationalist of an unequivocally imperialist, even messianic, bent; an eloquent propagandist of the vision of the United States as a chosen people, a new Jerusalem, a city on the hill: "We are chosen and prominently chosen to show the way to the nations of the world".[38]

In the post-Wilsonian world, the doctrine of self-determination is commonly conceived as holding that "the political and the national unit should be congruent".[39] However, when it first burst onto the historical stage at the time of the French Revolution, the ideal of self-determination "implied primarily the right of peoples to constitute national states in defiance of the dynastic principle, and was a domestic as well as an international question. It certainly did not contemplate a wholesale process of secession and disintegration."[40] The so-called "springtime of the peoples" of 1848, inflected as it was with the ideological currents of romanticism, marked a decisive turning point in the history of the doctrine, a transformation from a claim about sovereignty residing in "the people, not the monarch" into a claim about the right of particular nationalities, increasingly imagined along Herderian *volk-ish* lines, to their own independent states.[41]

Indeed, German thinkers like Fichte and Herder developed an idea of the "nation" which was originally used "to appeal across the boundaries of existing states to achieve the unification of people of the same language and culture".[42] This was the moment of birth of nationalism as a political movement in Europe. At the time of the 1848 revolution, nationalist agitation was "strongly linked with liberal and democratic movements" against the monarchical states, and nationalist ideology was epitomized by radical democrats "like Garibaldi and Mazzini who hoped to combine liberal democratic and republican goals with nationalism". But slowly "nationalism came to take precedence over liberal democratic ideas," and radical democrats like Garibaldi and Mazzini gave way to conservative nation-builders such as Bismarck and Cavour.[43]

It would not be until the end of the First World War, however, that the *nationalist* version of the principle of national self-determination would reach its apogee in legitimating the reconfiguration of state boundaries across the European continent, in accordance with the Wilsonian principle.[44] It is worth remembering, however, that the attempt to apply this principle – that is, the attempt "to make state frontiers coincide with the frontiers of nationality and language" – in inter-war Europe proved utterly impractical. Indeed, it proved ultimately disastrous, as Hobsbawm rightly insists:

> Inevitably, given the actual distribution of peoples, most of the new states built on the ruins of the Old Empires, were quite as multinational as the old 'prisons of nations' they replaced. Czechoslovakia, Poland, Romania and Yugoslavia are cases in point. German, Slovene, and Croat minorities in Italy took the place of Italian minorities in the Habsburg Empire. The main change was that states were now on average rather smaller and the 'oppressed peoples' within them were now called 'oppressed minorities'. The logical implication of trying to create a continent neatly divided into coherent territorial states each inhabited by a separate ethnically and linguistically homogeneous population, was the mass expulsion or extermination of minorities. Such was and is the murderous *reducto ad absurdum* of nationalism in its territorial version, although this was not fully demonstrated until the 1940s.[45]

Nor can the disastrous outcome of the attempt to apply the principle of self-determination in inter-war Europe be dismissed as a mere contingency or freak mistake. Rather, it should be recognized as illustrative of the highly divisive and polarizing populist potential of rendering salient rival ethno-nationalist territorial claims in complexly intertwined demo-scapes of linguistic and cultural diversity. The aspirations of rival contending ethno-national groups simply cannot be fulfilled simultaneously. The victories of the utopian dreams of some necessarily require the defeats of the dreams of others. [46]

Despite this fundamental problem inherent in the Wilsonian principle of national self-determination, the doctrine nevertheless remains at the core of current nationalist mobilization throughout much of the world.[47] However, the appeal of the doctrine cannot be attributed to the pernicious legacy of President Wilson alone. Indeed, Wilson's beliefs about self-determination would surely not be nearly so influential to this day if it were not for their paradoxical convergence with the ideas of Vladimir Lenin as well as – in no small part through the influence of the Bolshevik party line – their subsequent salience in the struggles against oppression throughout the colonial world.[48]

Wilson himself never intended the doctrine to apply to colonial posses-sions beyond the "mature" nations of Europe. It was Lenin who first made that connection – advocating the doctrine of national self-determination in the struggles against Czarist Russia as well as in struggles of colonized pop-ulations for "national liberation" outside of Europe. The particular tactical judgment behind his advocacy for such a universal principle: the considera-tion "that the liberation of oppressed colonial peoples was an important po-tential asset for world revolution".[49]

It should not be forgotten that "Lenin's early enthusiasm for the potential revolutionary role of nationalism in colonial and non-colonial areas," re-flected in "his fervent advocacy of the slogan of national self-determination after 1914," was highly controversial in Marxist circles at the time.[50] To begin with, it brought him into direct confrontation with Austro-Marxists such as Karl Renner and Otto Bauer, who remained committed to balancing the struggle against "national oppression" with a clear-cut rejection of territorial appeals for the disintegration of the Austro-Hungarian multinational state along national lines.[51] It also brought him into sharp conflict with Rosa Lux-emburg, who in the course of debates over the fate of Poland had attacked the bourgeois principle of self-determination for its "abstract" and "utopian" character, dismissing it in no uncertain terms:

> The formula, "the right of nations to self-determination" … gives no practical guidelines for the day to day politics of the proletariat, nor any practical solution of nationality problems. For example, this formula does not indicate to the Russian proletariat in what way it should de-mand a solution of the Polish national problem, the Finnish question, the Caucasian question, the Jewish, etc. … The duty to resist all forms of national oppression does not include any explanation of what con-ditions and political forms the class-conscious proletariat in Russia at the present time should recommend as a solution for the nationality problems of Poland, Latvia, the Jews, etc., or what program it should

present to match the various programs of the bourgeois, nationalist, and pseudo-socialist parties in the present class struggle. In a word, the formula, "the right of nations to self-determination," is essentially not a political and programmatic guideline in the nationality question, but only a means of avoiding that question.[52]

Indeed, Lenin's position on national self-determination was originally sharply contested even amongst fellow Bolsheviks who, "like most radical Marxists, rejected appeals to nationalism as inappropriate and un-Marxist". In this vein, in 1915, Bukharin, Piatokov, and Bosh sent documents to the Central Committee attacking Lenin's slogan of "self-determination" as "first of all *utopian* … and *harmful* as a slogan which *disseminates illusions*".[53]

Lenin's initially contentious position on self-determination would be elaborated, at his behest, by the young Stalin and eventually rendered hegemonic among the Communist left, due to its institutionalization in the Soviet Union at the level of Bolshevik party program and Constitutional principles, if clearly not always in state practice.[54]

Returning to Marx and Engels on the National Question

Marxism-Leninism has thus been complicit in the reification of the nation-form and of nationalism as a dominant ideology. However, the desacralization of Lenin allows in principle for a return to origins of sorts within the Marxist tradition, opening up space for questioning and re-evaluating old Leninist dogmas. Among these, the dogma about national self-determination.[55] At first blush, this task may seem difficult, since it has often been alleged that the founding fathers of historical materialism had surprisingly little to say about nationalism at the level of theory, and that they underestimated the strength of its appeal at the level of practice.[56] In this vein, Pelczynsky complains that "[t]hey had no explanation, for instance, of *why* Polish patriotism in the nineteenth century was so intense and manifested itself in frequent uprisings against foreign powers, although they noted it and praised it often in their writings," before posing the question: "How could Marx, who was such an acute observer of contemporary history as well as a social theorist of genius, have been so theoretically unconcerned about one of the dominant political phenomena of nineteenth-century Europe, and apparently blind to its significance for world history?"[57]

There is some truth in this accusation. Marx and Engels did, after all, famously and falsely diagnose in their *Communist Manifesto* – a document drafted in response to the so-called "springtime of the peoples" of 1848 – that "national differences and antagonisms are daily more and more vanishing, owing to the development of the bourgeoisie, to freedom of commerce, to the world market, to uniformity in the mode of production and in the conditions of life corresponding thereto".[58] Indeed, they even went so far as to insinuate that the dialectical development of the laws of capitalism was leading to an imminent transcendence of "national culture" and "national consciousness" and the emergence of a world culture alongside an international revolutionary class consciousness. In terms of the imminent transcendence of national culture and its replacement with world culture, they described/predicted:

> "In place of old local and national seclusion and self-sufficiency, we have intercourse in every direction, universal inter-dependence of nations, and as in material, so also in intellectual production. The intellectual creations of individual nations become common property. National one-sidedness and narrow-mindedness become more and more impossible, and from the numerous national and local literatures there arises a world literature".[59]

It must be recalled, however, that the Communist Manifesto was a pamphlet drafted in a hurry, as a programmatic, even propagandistic, call to action in response to rapidly developing revolutionary tumult. It was thus intended as a direct public intervention in an on-going political struggle, in which Marx and Engels were explicitly concerned to steer events – in accordance with a roadmap they drew, a roadmap for worldwide revolutionary rupture, expected to erupt in and spread out from the capitalist core. Given the nature of the revolutionary tumult to which they were responding, they were of course well aware of the mobilizational power and popular appeal of the category of the "nation," of its links to struggles for the establishment of bourgeois freedoms in bourgeois republics. Indeed, their document makes explicit appeal across national boundaries to all workers of the world. In their call for all workers to unite, justified by their claim that "workers have nothing to lose but their chains," Marx and Engels are deliberately attempting to counter the emergent hegemony of the category of "nation". They do so by articulating an alternative discourse, one that advocates and foresees a more fundamental revolutionary rupture, a transformation of social-property relations, to be protagonized by the toilers of humanity themselves, destined to unite across national boundaries to struggle against their common lot of misery and exploitation.[60]

It is not fair to consider Marx and Engels naïve on the national question.[61] For starters, especially in the longer term, as Eric Hobsbawm reminded us not so long ago, the expansion of capitalist social-property relations across the globe has indeed created something approximating the "world culture" prophesied in the Manifesto by the founding prophets of the faith in communism.[62] However, the emergence of this "world culture" has only on rare occasions entailed a transcendence of "national" modes of identification, perhaps even especially among the working class. But Marx and Engels then believed the onset of global revolution to be imminent; and they believed as well that along with the imminent realization of human emancipation would come the transcendence of the national "webs of mystification," as well as the religious ones, in which the consciousness of the workers remained for the time being, unfortunately all too often enmeshed.

Because Marx and Engels were confident that such national and religious webs of mystification were destined to soon be washed away by the rising tide of human emancipation and the wave of global communist revolution, they spent little time inquiring into the institutional mechanisms of entrenchment and reification of sometimes conflicting, always ethno-fetishized and particularistic, national modes of consciousness. But alas, the global revolutionary rupture that Marx and Engels thought was imminent never arrived. Instead, the revolutionary tumult of mid-century Europe would soon give way to a quarter century of political stability underpinned by unprecedented capitalist expansion, and then increasing competition among rival capitalist powers, culminating in an Imperial scramble for Africa and ultimately the outbreak of the First World War.[63]

Moreover, when communist revolution finally broke out, nearly seventy years after Marx and Engels had declared its arrival imminent, it erupted not in the capitalist core of Europe but instead in the Eurasian periphery, when the Bolsheviks seized power in defeated Czarist Russia. The coming to power of revolutionary forces in Russia was immediately hailed by many Marxists in the West as a harbinger and trigger of imminent world revolution, and indeed was theorized as such by the Bolshevik leaders Lenin and Trotsky as well.[64] But alas, again, the imminent world revolution never came. The revolution failed to spread from the periphery to the capitalist core, and with this failure, the strategy of "socialism in one country" was over-determined, as perhaps was even the tragic denouement of Stalinist tyranny that ended up extinguishing the emancipatory flame lit in October of 1917.[65]

Though the founding fathers of historical materialism did not spend much time inquiring into the mechanisms of entrenchment and reification of national modes of consciousness, it is a mistake to claim that they were "theoretically unconcerned" with the phenomenon of nationalism. owever, to understand their theoretical posture towards the phenomenon requires coming to grips with their critique of "political emancipation" as such. In this regard, it must be recalled that Marx developed his unique approach to social analysis originally as an internal critique of liberalism: indeed, Marxism grew out of, was born of, such an exercise of ruthless but immanent critique. In two important early writings from the mid-1840's, on the eve of his decisive break with the categories of liberal philosophy and classical political economy, Marx would elaborate a set of weighty theoretical considerations sufficient (1) to conclude that the legal and political theories of liberalism were inadequate for understanding social reality, and (2) to dismiss the conflation between "political emancipation" and "human emancipation" upon which any project of "national liberation" ultimately depends.

The Continuing Relevance of Marx on the Jewish Question

In a word, by the mid-1840s, Marx had come to believe that socialism would necessarily entail "the full emancipation of the individual from the web of mystification which turned community life into a world of estrangement presided over by an alienated bureaucracy".[66] Furthermore, among this "web of mystifications" that needed to be destroyed, Marx had surmised, were situated "not only those bonds rising out of class division and exploitation, but also religious and national ties".[67]

In "On the Jewish Question," Marx confronted head-on a question that is intimately related to debates about the "nation" and "national liberation": that of the extension of the franchise in Germany to a minority, a religious-cum-ethnic minority. The essay takes the form of a critique of Bruno Bauer's analysis of the problem, in which Bauer had urged that the franchise be extended to the Jews. Bauer had advanced a classic liberal argument: the problem defined as some group being denied its rights; the solution, an extension of equality.In fact, Bauer had gone one step further than this classic liberal argument – he maintained that the Jewish question posed the larger problem of the relations between religion and the state, both exposing the hypocrisy of the "so-called Christian state" while demanding "that the Jew should renounce Judaism, and in general that man should renounce religion, in order to be emancipated as a citizen".[68] However, Bauer continued to think the problem could be solved from within the existing political institutions. By contrast, Marx expands the problem further, posing a third question, above and beyond the questions, 'Who should emancipate?' and 'Who should be emancipated?'. Marx asks: What kind of emancipation is involved?

It is at this point where the distinction between "political emancipation" and "human emancipation" comes to the foreground. Marx insists: "To be *politically* emancipated from religion is not to be finally and completely emancipated from religion, because political emancipation is not the final and absolute form of *human* emancipation".[69] He adds that "one should have no illusions about the scope of political emancipation," and proceeds to elaborate a sophisticated denunciation of the alienated, bifurcated double-consciousness and indeed double-existence that almost inevitably permeates the subjectivities and configures the concretely unfree life-circumstances of *politically emancipated* but actually subjugated citizens. Indeed, Marx describes the contradiction between formal freedom and actual subjugation in nothing short of biblical terms:

"Where the political state has attained its true development, man – not only in thought, in consciousness, but in reality, in life – leads a twofold life, a heavenly and an earthly life: life in the political community, in which he considers himself a communal being, and life in civil society, in which he acts as a private individual, regards other men as a means, degrades himself into a means, and becomes the plaything of alien powers."[70]

The subject of Marx's criticism, Bruno Bauer, as a liberal, cannot understand the difference between political emancipation and human emancipation. He cannot see why Jews must be emancipated from the kind of society that brings about such an injustice in the first place. Furthermore, Marx points out, not only the Jewish minority but also the Christian majority need to be emancipated. Indeed, Marx insists, human emancipation cannot be attained for *anyone* within a civil society founded upon radical material inequalities. *Everybody* is alienated in "civil society," and the extension of the suffrage cannot solve such problems.[71]

Marx here diagnoses a fundamental contradiction at the very core of liberal social relations: the distinction between the public and the private, along with the contradictory set of values enshrined for each distinctly-imagined sphere. As if in passing, he adds that, far from being part of the solution, the bourgeois state is actually part of the problem.

In Marx's critique of the limits of "political emancipation" there is embedded a critique of the category of *nation* as a mystified, illusory basis for political community. The unity of the *nation* is always fictive, masking and transfiguring the profane power of the few into sacred form, even trans-substantiating it into the general will. Or more evocatively still, the *nation* as sacred vestment in which the profane naked power exercised by the agents of the *bourgeois state* is cloaked.

At the same time, and perhaps more centrally, the critique of the limits of "political emancipation" entails a critique of the limits of representative democracy. A critique only occasionally recalled by post-Marxists these days, though further elaborated and forcefully articulated by Perry Anderson, who has argued in no uncertain terms:

"Parliament, elected every four or five years as the sovereign expression of popular will, reflects the fictive unity of the nation back to the masses as if it were their own self-government. The economic divisions within the 'citizenry' are masked by the juridical parity between exploiters and exploited, and with them the complete *separation* and *non-participa-tion* of the masses in the work of parliament".[72]

Faith in the nation, faith in the bourgeois state, faith in juridical equality, faith in representative democracy, all exposed as mystifications and as irrational delusions. Marx's critique of the category of the nation is thus subsumed under the rubric of a more comprehensive critique of mystification. Belief in "political emancipation," like belief in other ethereal myths and abstractions, equally vulnerable to Marx's general critique of religious consciousness. In Marx's own formulation:

> "The members of the political state are religious owing to the dualism between individual life and species-life, between the life of civil society and political life. They are religious because men treat the political life of the state, an area beyond their real individuality, as if it were their true life. They are religious insofar as religion here is the spirit of civil society, expressing the separation and remoteness of man from man".[73]

If the project of "political emancipation" necessarily entails the consum-mation of alienation and the perpetuation of webs of mystified consciousness, the project of human emancipation to which Marx was committed requires precisely the opposite: a thoroughgoing process of demystification. A reverse inversion of the social world. The myths and fables long told to justify and manufacture consent to the looting, the wars, and the lies, mystifications which insidiously invade the consciousness of victimizers and victimized alike – these myths and fables need to come crashing down, Marx insists.

How to precipitate the crash? By subjecting all dominant worldviews and interpretations to "ruthless criticism" – in Marx's words "ruthless both in the sense of not being afraid of the results it arrives at and in the sense of being just as little afraid of conflict with the powers that be". Ironically enough, given the subsequent conversion of Marxism-Leninism into one of the great political religions of the twentieth century, Marx himself stressed that such a ruthlessly critical posture demanded opposition to "raising any dogmatic banner" whatsoever. According to Marx, the task of critical theory was largely deconstructive in spirit. Its main purpose is not the propagation of a new dogma; to the contrary, Marx prescribes, "we must try to help the dogmatists to clarify their propositions for themselves".[74]

Marx's Critique of Religion and the
Problem of Secular Dogmatism

Even so, the rehabilitation of an anti-dogmatic Marxist perspective requires more than a mere return to the "sacred texts" of Marx. After all, Marx himself was not altogether free of the sin of dogmatism. Indeed, in his critique of religious consciousness there is a clear hint of atheist dogmatism, evident in his diction and analogy of ruthless criticism with "demystification".

Marx's critique of religion was part of his broader critique of ideology. He critiqued religion as a form of ideology. His account of religious consciousness explicitly built upon Feuerbach's "critique of religion as projection".[75] In the introduction to his *Contribution to the Critique of Hegel's Philosophy of Right*, Marx argues that religious consciousness is best understood as a coping mechanism for bearing tyrannical social relations, exploitation and oppression. According to Marx, in fact such conditions "produce religion, which is an inverted consciousness of the world, because they are an inverted world".[76] Indeed, he insists, with considerable rhetorical flourish:

"Religion is the general theory of this world, its encyclopaedic compendium, its logic in popular form, its spiritual *point d'honneur*, its enthusiasm, its moral sanction, its solemn complement, and its universal basis of consolation and justification. It is the fantastic realization of the human essence since the human essence has not acquired any true reality".[77]

Marx is willing to admit that religious suffering is "the expression of real suffering and a protest against real suffering". Indeed, he goes so far as to label religion *"the sigh of the oppressed creature, the heart of a heartless world, and the soul of soulless conditions,"* before quickly turning to denounce it nevertheless as "the opium of the people".[78] But this denunciation of religion as opiate does not, strictly speaking, follow. At least insofar as the consumption of opiates is understood to produce pacifying effects, lulling users into acquiescence, undermining the will to struggle, the analogy between religion and opiates seems an overgeneralization, at best. After all, the *"jihadis"* of the Islamic State can be plausibly criticised for many things, but quiescence is not one of them. Religious consciousness as such evidently does not determine a penchant for quiescence in the face of injustice. Much depends on the content and interpretation of the religious convictions in question.

In Christianity, the millenarian tradition including the Puritan revolutionaries or, more recently, liberation theology are sufficient to demonstrate the relative autonomy of the theological and metaphysical from the ethical and political. As Alysdair MacIntyre reminds us, all robust cultural traditions are malleable and characterised by conflict and competition among multiple, competing, even radically opposed, interpretations of their core metaphysical messages and implications for conduct in this world.[79] In other words, religious traditions, like all traditions, are always susceptible to multiple interpretations with very different ethical and political implications, some revolutionary, others status quo, others reactionary. Revolutionary consciousness and praxis need not take the form of a struggle against religion; for these can also take shape in a struggle for the heart and soul of a religion. That is, they can be born out of immanent critique.

Nor does Marx's denunciation of religion as an "opiate" follow from a second meaning of the reference – probably the one Marx had in mind – namely, insofar as the consumption of opiates is understood to produce merely "illusory" rather than "real" happiness. For starters, this juxtaposition between "illusory" and "real" is an oversimplification, at best, perhaps especially when it comes to the consumption of opiates or other narcotics. The claims of those who profess the capacity of certain mind-altering substances to open the doors to alternative perceptions and perspectives, much less the practices of shamanic rituals, should not be dismissed tout court – lest ruthless criticism of everything existing be rendered and reduced to a petty posture of postprotestant prudishness. But perhaps more importantly, with respect to religious consciousness proper, Marx's certainty that it can be dismissed as merely "illusory" seems epistemologically unfounded, even reflective of a certain secular dogmatism, a certain atheist fundamentalism – which, like all dogmatisms, actually stands in sharp tension with Marx's simultaneous commitment to ruthless criticism.

As Benedict Anderson has cogently argued, the secular dogmatism espoused by Marx reflects a weakness shared by all "evolutionary/progressive styles of thought". In a word, such secular dogmatism grossly underestimates a "great merit of traditional religious world-views," which Anderson rightly insists "naturally must be distinguished from their role in the legitimation of specific systems of domination and exploitation". The merit in question – "their concern with man-in-the cosmos, man as species-being, and the contingency of life".[80] According to Anderson:

> "The extraordinary survival over thousands of years of Buddhism, Christianity or Islam in dozens of different social formations attests to their imaginative response to the overwhelming burden of human suffering – disease, mutilation, grief, and death. Why was I born blind? Why is my best friend paralysed? Why is my daughter retarded? The religions attempt to explain. The great weakness of all evolutionary/progressive styles of thought, not excluding Marxism, is that such questions are answered with impatient silence".[81]

Nevertheless, Marx's criticism of religious consciousness is still powerful and largely accurate as a critique of the dominant interpretations of Christianity in the Europe of his day, and indeed dominant throughout most of Christian history. Interpretations propagated by hierarchical official Churches closely allied with the wealthy and the powerful. Interpretations that preach obedience and servility, acceptance of one's lot in this life, indifference and quiescence in the face of injustice. In this regard, Marx's "secular dogmatism," like that of so many European radicals of his time and up through the present, can be understood and even empathized with as a posture induced in response to the sanctimonious hypocrisy of the established Christian churches. Motivated by the same kind of righteous indignation that led Jesus to denounce the Pharisees and to throw the moneylenders out of the temple. Though closer in praxis to the conclusion reached by the Spanish anarchists – that the temple itself needed to be burned to the ground.

Marx advocates that working people should give up their religious "illusions" not simply out of commitment to the harsh, sobering proposition that there is no God; nor, certainly, does he want to induce despair. Rather, he wants to stir working people to thought and to revolutionary action. In his words, "to call on them to give up their illusions about their condition is to call on them to give up a condition that requires illusions". For this reason, he insists, the criticism of religion "is in embryo, the criticism of that vale of tears of which religion is the halo".[82] Marx likens engaging in religious criticism to plucking imaginary flowers from our chain, the purpose of which is not so "that man shall continue to bear that chain without fantasy or consolation, but so that he shall throw off the chain and pluck the living flower".[83]

Marx's commitment to actively disillusioning working people from their religious faith was linked to his confidence that such religious disillusionment would lead them to "regain their senses" and "think, act, and fashion [their] reality".[84] But revolutionary struggle and praxis are not born of disillusion. They require faith. Faith is a viable and desirable alternative to the existing social order: faith that resistance is not futile, faith that resistance will not make things even worse. Marx was a prophet who preached that the last shall be first and the first shall be last, that inequity and injustice would be redressed and overcome.[85] Indeed, the core of his message was quite similar to that of so many prophets in the Abrahamic tradition, especially those with apocalyptic visions; the main difference – Marx promised redemption and salvation in this earthly realm, human emancipation in this material world.

Yet faith in a socialist future does not emerge spontaneously out of religious disillusionment, certainly not in our post-Stalinist, Orwellian world. Marx can be forgiven for failing to foresee the hypnotic powers of the false idols of consumer society. He was wrong to believe that when humans come to revolve around themselves, they automatically "come to their senses," or that "mystifications" and "idolatry" are diminished in the least.

In sum, not only can religious consciousness not be reduced to mere projection, coping mechanism, or illusion; nor are *religious* delusions the only form that mystified and "inverted consciousness" can take. Marx's critique of religion is thus simultaneously too broad and too narrow – too broad for its reduction of all religious consciousness to alienated delusion; too narrow, for its failure to recognize that secular worldviews are susceptible to dogmatism, projected fantasies, and even idol worship as well.

Religious Community versus National Community?

But what of the relation between *religious* and *national* consciousness? Marx treated the categories of nation and religion as two symptomatic inversions of a social world, both effective smokescreens concealing the brutal reality of material inequities in a world ultimately determined and divided by class. In a word, for Marx, nation and religion were two dominant myths perpetuated to manufacture consent to an unjust order, thus in urgent need of deconstruction. Is Marx's account of national consciousness and, by extension, of mere political freedom, equally susceptible to the charges of reductionism and dogmatism as his critique of religion?

The young Marx tended to treat the categories of religion and nation as two ideologies – two webs of mystification – equally destined to the dustbin of history, certain to be washed away by the rising tide of imminent world revolution. But that revolution never arrived, with inevitable consequences for his prediction about the fate of the two categories. Ironically, despite the continuing tyranny and alienation of capitalism throughout Marx's life across the Western European societies with which he was most familiar, the "dusk of religious modes of thought" that he predicted nevertheless took place. Not so for the category of the nation.

To the contrary, as Benedict Anderson points out, the "dusk of religious modes of thoughts" coincided with the veritable "dawn of the age of nationalism" in Western Europe. In fact, the relation between these two tendencies in Western Europe has frequently been posited, with Anderson, as one of functional equivalence. The "[d]isintegration of paradise" and "the absurdity of salvation" brought on by the secular assault on the realm of the transcendental and the supernatural, issuing in the need for "a secular transformation of fatality into continuity, contingency into meaning," capable of turning "chance into destiny".[86] Thus the simultaneous surge in support for the secular creed and the national creed, so the story goes.[87]

Of course, the triumph of the secular creed should not be overestimated. It certainly remains fiercely contested throughout most of the globe, including even in the world's richest country. What's more, there is, of course, a crucial difference between the categories of religion and nation, since membership in the former are largely "universal by definition, and therefore designed to fudge ethnic, linguistic, political and other differences". Even so, as Hobsbawm has argued, because "universal truths are often in competition … peoples on the borders of one can sometimes choose another as an ethnic badge".[88] Thus the convergence, and sometimes outright conflation, in the dynamics of sectarian and nationalist strife.

The Nation as Artefact

Hegemonic nationalist myths about the "organic" or "natural" ontology of nations notwithstanding, most leading scholars of nationalism nevertheless insist that the nation is "artefact," like the state, a work of art, even the result of "conscious efforts by leaders".[89] On this point, Hobsbawm concurs with Linz, emphasising the "element of artefact, invention, and social engineering which enters into the making of nations".[90] And Gellner concurs with both – in denouncing as myth the idea of "nations as a natural, God-given way of classifying men," and in claiming to have uncovered instead the sobering "*reality*" that nationalism "sometimes takes pre-existing cultures and turns them into nations, sometimes invents them, and often obliterates pre-existing cultures".[91] Or, even more polemically, when Gellner insists that "[n]ationalism is not the awakening of nations to self-consciousness: it invents nations where they do not exist".[92]

Anderson has famously objected to this latter formulation of "nation as invention," on the grounds that it connotes "fabrication" and "falsity," rather than "imagining" and "creation," and thus implies a juxtaposition between "false" and "true" communities. He is certainly right that it does connote and imply such things; but this is hardly grounds for dismissing the cogency of the metaphor. Anderson insists that communities are not to be distinguished by their "truth" or "falsity," since "all communities larger than primordial villages of face-to-face contact (and perhaps even these) are imagined".[93] However, just because nearly all communities are "imagined" does not mean that all *claims* to community are equally "true" or compelling. Claims of community can be distinguished not only by the "style" in which they are imagined; they can also be adjudicated among in terms of the particular interests and particular agendas advanced in the name of some general will.

This is the crux of Rosa Luxemburg's intransigent case against the principle of "national self-determination". For Luxemburg, such a principle seems to presume "uniform social-political whole" that in any class-divided society can never be presumed, indeed there are bound to "exist within each nation classes with antagonistic interests and 'rights'".[94] The point can be made more generally, in a way less constricted by the narrow class bias built into classical historical materialism. In contexts riven by ethno-racialised, gendered, and class divides, any appeal to national community and national belonging is bound to be embedded within broader struggles to reproduce or transform existing constellations of power relations.

Anderson objects to the treatment of nationalism as if it were a mere "ideology," akin to "liberalism" or "fascism". He likens it instead to a broad cultural system such as "kinship" or "religion".[95] But the attempt to distinguish religion and kinship from *mere* "ideology" suggests a peculiarly narrow concept of the latter, and one that certainly cuts against the grain of the well-trodden terrain of not only Marx's but Freud's or Nietzsche's famous critiques of religious consciousness as a paradigmatic case of "*false* consciousness," not to mention feminist critiques of patriarchy and of discursive tropes that reify the gendered division of labour through appeals to categories like "family values".

Even if one rejects the idea that *all* manifestations of religious consciousness can be reduced to or dismissed as opiate, fantasy, or outlet for *ressentiment*, certainly some, perhaps even most, modes of religious consciousness are vulnerable on at least one of these counts.[96] What's more, not only is *all* religious consciousness certainly *ideological* when the term is used in the broad sense as entailing a comprehensive world view; so too are nearly all manifestations of religious consciousness *ideological* in the narrower sense of being ubiquitously marshalled in concrete political struggles to reproduce or transform existing constellations of power relations.

The Nation, the Family, and Love

The other category to which Anderson compares the nation in his attempt to render it beyond susceptibility to ideology critique is that of "kinship". The attempt to liken nationalism to "kinship" is especially problematic because it reifies and reproduces perhaps the quintessential nationalist trope or presumption – what David Theo Goldberg has referred to as its "abstract presumption of familialism". This presumption of the "familiar," that "I am like them," and therefore that we *must* be "familially connected," of course, ultimately implies – "if often silently" – a negation of those branded as nationally or racially other, those "differentiated and disconnected".[97]

The "familial" analogy is central to the imagining of national community, which helps to explain the oft-observed emotive force of appeals to the nation, as well as the close affinities between nationalism and patriarchy.[98] Anderson chides critics of "Nationalism with a capital N" for focusing too much on all the murders committed in the name of the nation, and focusing too little on the effectiveness of appeals to the nation at inducing a willingness to sacrifice and even to die for the sake of one's country. He also insists that critics of nationalism too often conflate nationalism with racism, too often try to depict it as motivated exclusively by hate, and too infrequently emphasise the links between nationalism and the emotion of love.[99]

Anderson would pose the question: how can the nation, if it is a community based on the emotion of love, be dismissed as an "ideology," as but a manifestation of false consciousness? Freud remains on this count most instructive, as Sarah Ahmed has reminded. "Love makes the subject vulnerable, exposed to, and dependent on another," and is "linked profoundly to the anxiety of boundary formation," whereby what is not me and what is me to some extent even merge.[100] Love is perhaps the ultimate form of desire; as such, it is ubiquitously infused with projections of ideals. "Desire creates an ideal object".[101] And thus the potential for love to bleed into an acute form of false-consciousness, self-destructiveness, even self-loathing. As Ahmed insists: "[e]ven though love is a demand for reciprocity, it is also an emotion that lives with the failure of that demand often through an intensification of its affect (so, if you do not love me back, I may love you more as the pain of the non-loving is the sign of what it means not to have this love)".[102] Likewise, witness the frequent invocation of love in justifications for staying the course and enduring abusive familial relationships. Like an abused spouse who continues to love their partner, to stand by that partner despite repeated infidelities and transgressions, one can "love the nation out of hope and with nostalgia for how it could have been," one can "keep loving rather than recognizing that the love that one has given has not and will not be returned".[103]

What's more, the connection between the "national idea" and "national ideals" is such that perceived failure to live up to or "embody" such "ideals" serves to justify exclusion and marginalization. Indeed, the untrustworthy "others" are cast out, as foils, even scapegoated for national failings.[104] In the face of the failure of the nation to return the love, i.e. to deliver on the emancipatory promises so frequently associated with it, "defensive narratives" can quickly surface. All too easily, the "failure of return is 'explained' by the presence of others," the ungrateful, the unpatriotic, those who do not belong.

Thus the ubiquity of lurking projected shadows, of racialized "others," of those symbolically and materially marginalized and excluded, of the "wretched," of those who serve to fix the boundaries of the body politic, of those imagined to intrude like a virus.[105] Those from other countries; those without a country. No imagined self without imagined others. The discourses of destiny and contamination, it turns out, cannot be so easily decoupled.

Ultimately, love and grief are inextricably intertwined. A human who one loves is a human whose death will be grieved, whose death is worth grieving. And so, in the ideology of national belonging, as Ahmed – following Butler – points out, co-nationals' lives are elevated and imagined as "grievable;" and ritualized expressions of national grief in the wake of the death of "co-nationals" has the effect of reproducing and inducing the recognition, "that could have been me".[106]

Love of nation, like love of family, never takes place in a vacuum. Instead, as the emotional expression of identification and desire, it is always shot through with power relations. More specifically, shot through with intimately intertwined systems of class, ethno-racialised, and gender domination. As such, appeals for loyalty to the nation, demands for sacrifice in its name, can only be adequately understood, much less evaluated, in context – that is, by illuminating how such appeals are "incorporated," and how they affect the balance of concrete forces engaged in concrete and overlapping political struggles to reproduce and/or transform existing constellations of material and social power relations.

The Nation and Ideology Critique

Anderson is perhaps correct to insist – contra Luxemburg – that *national* consciousness is not necessarily an impediment to emancipatory political goals, nor an alternative to class consciousness, nor necessarily reducible to "false consciousness".[107] But he is wrong to suggest that nationalist movements cannot be adequately understood through an interpretive lens emphasizing the specifically "ideological" dimension of the phenomenon, in the narrow sense; that is, through an analytic of *ideology critique*.[108]

Anderson is right to insist as well that the categories and preconditions of "national consciousness" are deeply rooted in the structure of contemporary society, including technologies of social communication and basic features of capitalist as well as state-socialist social-property relations. No doubt, one of the great virtues of Anderson's book is the breadth and complexity of the causal account he provides.

Indeed, Anderson compellingly links the emergence of "national consciousness" to broader conditions of epistemic possibility – including crucially the rise of the scientific worldview in Europe, the process of secularisation, and the consubstantial emergent dominant conception of time as "homogenous and empty," all mediated through the machinations of print capitalism.[109]

The notion of "homogenous, empty time" comes from Walter Benjamin, upon whom Anderson's causal account relies significantly. In this respect, it is more than a little ironic that he attempts to divorce "nationalism" from "fascism," by elevating the former to the status of "cultural system," while demoting the latter to the level of mere *ideology*, alongside the likes of liberalism. For Benjamin offered a prescient and piercing early diagnosis of "mass society," and even "the society of the spectacle"- a condition (a) underpinned and propelled forward by transformations in art and in the "mass media" in the age of mechanical reproduction; and (b) intimately intertwined with the rise of fascism.

According to Benjamin, Fascism is best understood as "an attempt to organize the newly created proletarian masses without affecting the property structure," promising them salvation not by giving the masses "their right," their due, but instead merely giving them "a chance to express themselves, resulting in the "introduction of aesthetics into political life". Benjamin hones in especially on the significance of the Futurists' glamorization and glorification of the alleged beauty of war, adducing it as evidence of the extent of human "self-alienation" experienced in "mass society". In his words: "Mankind's ... self-alienation has reached such a degree that it can experience its own destruction as an aesthetic pleasure of the first order".[110]

Benjamin, like Freud, held the modern experience to be centered principally on "shock". As Buck-Morss has explained: "In industrial production no less than modern warfare, in street crowds and erotic encounters, in amusement parks and gambling casinos, shock is the very essence of modern experience". Under such conditions, "response to stimuli *without* thinking has become necessary for survival". Consciousness comes to serve largely as a "shield" and a "buffer," protecting the organism by preventing the retention of external stimuli from being "impressed as memory," even "isolating present consciousness from past memory". The depth of memory thus flattened, "experience is impoverished".[111] This "crisis in cognitive experience" is in turn linked to the cultivation of narcissism, a narcissism which "functions as an anaesthetizing tactic against the shock of modern experience," which is "appealed to daily by the image-phantasmagoria of mass culture," and which renders fertile "the ground from which fascism" can spring forth.[112]

But Anderson's attempt to divorce "nationalism" from "fascism" is ultimately unconvincing, regardless of one's views about Benjamin.[113] The experience of the first half of the twentieth century in Europe cannot be brushed aside so easily, as if a fluke. Hobsbawm's comparative evidence is compelling. In the fifty years or so leading up to the outbreak of Continental-cum-World War in 1914, all versions of nationalism that "came to the fore" had *one* thing in common: "a rejection of the new proletarian socialist movements, not only because they were proletarian, but also because they were, consciously and militantly *internationalist*, or at the very least non-nationalist". Indeed, in this crucial prelude to the unprecedented level of human destruction of the so-called Great War, mass nationalism competed directly for appeal amidst a host of rival *ideologies* – "notably, class-based socialism" – which, tragically, it vanquished.[114]

Conclusion

This chapter has defended the proposition that the nation is best conceived as a hegemonic project. The nation as a category is analytically distinct from the state; even so, it is a category with a very definite history, in which it has been inextricably intertwined with the legitimation of "modern" and of "modernizing" states, perhaps particularly but certainly not only in Europe.[115]

The chapter traces the rise and problems associated with the doctrine of "self-determination". It builds on Hobsbawm's account of the impractical and ultimately disastrous consequences of the attempt to render state frontiers convergent with the frontiers of ethnicity and language in Interwar Europe, before turning to advocate a recuperation of more critical alternatives to the ossified Leninist-cum-Stalinist dogmas about self-determination within the classical Marxist tradition.

The repertoire of critical reflections on the limits and alternatives to national "self-determination" from the classical Marxist tradition can of course be amplified much further. Most importantly, a host of other relevant and critical voices can be recovered, especially voices reflecting the experiences of struggles against colonialism and the challenges faced in the post-colonial world. Voices such as that of Frantz Fanon, who warned early on against the "pitfalls of national consciousness;" or that of Julius Nyerere, who insisted upon distinguishing between "the task of the nationalist," which he considered "simply to rouse the people to a confidence in their power to protest," on the one side, and "the real freedom which socialism represents," on the other, "a very different thing".[116]

Such a task would certainly take us beyond the limits of this chapter. Indeed, it would require us to transcend the epistemological confines of much of the theoretical and comparative scholarship on nationalism in the English language, which remains all-too-complacently anchored in a Eurocentric outlook and focus. The historical configuration of relations between states and nations no doubt vary in significant ways in and across post-colonial contexts.[117]

In practice, self-determination has rarely resembled anything approximating human emancipation. Instead, the slogans of national belonging and appeals to the general will of the national community have served to advance particular interests – indeed, to cover over and conceal inequities, injustices, and exclusions within and between the boundaries of the imagined body politic. Thus the urgency of the task of deconstructing the category of the nation, of rendering it susceptible to "ruthless criticism," i.e. to the method and practice of *ideology critique*. This requires locating the source and delineating the resonance of any and all appeals to the nation within concrete struggles to reproduce or transform existing constellations of power relations. Comprehending the ideological efficacy of recourse to national community and national ideals does not require downplaying or denying the affinities among nationalism, racism, and fascism. To the contrary, such comprehension requires recognition and critical analysis of the intimate connections between the group emotions of love and hate, the discourses of destiny and contamination, and the political logics of belonging and exclusion.

NOTES

1   A somewhat abbreviated version of this chapter was first published in the *Journal of Political Ideologies*, Vol. 23, Issue 2, 2018: 183-204. Accessible at: https://doi.org/10.1080/13569317.2018.1449576 Portions of the chapter were also published as "Marxism, the Nation, and the Problem of Secular Dogmatism" by *Peace in Kurdistan* (London, 2019).

2   The term "hegemonic project" is taken from Bob Jessop, *State Power* (Cambridge, UK: Polity Press, 2008), which he defines, following Gramsci, as a project "to secure the political, intellectual, and moral leadership of the dominant class(es)," p.12. For the genealogy of the term hegemony, see P. Anderson, "The Antinomies of Antonio Gramsci," *New Left Review*, 100 (Nov. 1976 – Jan. 1977), pp.5-78; and E. Laclau and C. Mouffe, *Hegemony and Socialist Strategy* (London: Verso, 1985), ch.1.

3   G. Therborn, *The Ideology of Power and the Power of Ideology* (London: Verso, 1980).

4   R. Brubaker, *Nationalism Reframed* (Cambridge: Cambridge University Press, 1996); and Laclau and Mouffe, *op. cit.*, p.67.

5   M. Hroch, "From National Movement to Fully Formed Nation: the Nation-Building Process in Europe," in G. Balakrishnan, ed. *Mapping the Nation* (London: Verso, 1993), pp.78-97; S. Rokkan, *Nation-Building and Citizenship* (New York: Anchor Books, 1969); J. Linz, "State building and nation building," *European Review* 1:4 (1993), pp.355-369; S. Rokkan, "Nation-Building: A Review of Models and Approaches," *Current Sociology*, Vol. 19, No. 3 (1971): pp.7-38; and S. Rokkan, "Dimensions of State Formation and Nation-Building: A Possible Paradigm for Research on Variations within Europe," in Charles Tilly, ed. The Formation of National States in Western Europe (Princeton, NJ: Princeton University Press, 1975), pp. 562-600.

6   Brubaker, *op. cit.*

7   See L. Althusser, *On Ideology* (London: Verso, 2008 [1971]).

8   E. Gellner, *Nations and Nationalism* (Ithaca, NY: Cornell University Press, 1983), p.55.

9   For classic analyses that focus on the "programmatic" level, see E. Kedourie, *Nationalism*. 4th edn (Oxford: Blackwell, 1993); and H. Kohn, *Nationalism: Its Meaning and History* (Princeton, NJ: Van Nostrand, 1955). For an analysis focusing on the level of the "banal," see M. Billig, *Banal Nationalism* (London: Sage Publications, 1995).

10 Gellner (1983), *op. cit.*, p.1.

11 P. Bourdieu, "Social Space and Symbolic Power," *Sociological Theory*, 7(1) (1989), pp.14-25.

12 On Gramsci's treatment of the "national question," see E. Nimni, *Marxism and the National Question: Theoretical Origins of a Political Crisis* (London: Pluto Press, 1991), ch. 4. For relevant applications of Gramsci's theory of hegemony to the analysis of nationalist dynamics, see I. Lustick, *Unsettled States, Disputed Lands* (Ithaca: Cornell University Press, 1993); M. Beissinger, *Nationalist Mobilization and the Collapse of the Soviet State* (Cambridge: Cambridge University Press, 1996); T. Miley, "Blocked Articulation and Nationalist Hegemony in Catalonia," *Regional & Federal Studies* 23(1) (2013), pp. 7-26; and T. Miley, "Democratic Representation and the National Dimension in Catalan and Basque Politics," *International Journal of Culture, Politics, and Society* 27 (2014), pp. 291-322.

13 D. Porpora, "Cultural Rules and Material Relations," *Sociological Theory*, 11(2) (1993), pp.212-229. Quote from p.217.

14 Ibid., p.222.

15 c.f. H. Bhabha, "DissemiNation: time, narrative, and the margins of the modern nation," in H. Bhabha, ed. *Nation and Narration* (London: Routledge, 1990), p.294.

16 Linz, *op. cit.*, p.355. See also H. Seton-Watson, *Nations and States: An Enquiry into the Origins of Nations and the Politics of Nationalism* (Boulder, CO: Westview Press, 1977).

17 R. Bendix, *Kings or People. Power and the Mandate to Rule* (Berkeley: University of California Press, 1978), p.605, fn.1.

18 See also P. Anderson, *Lineages of the Absolutist State* (London: New Left Books, 1974); T. Ertmann, *Birth of the Leviathan* (Cambridge: Cambridge University Press, 1997); G. Poggi, *The Development of the Modern State* (Stanford, CA: Stanford University Press, 1978); and M. Weber, "Politics as a Vocation," in H.G. Gerth and C. Wright Mills, eds., *From Max Weber: Essays in Sociology* (New York: Oxford University Press, 1958), pp.129-156.

19 Linz, *op. cit.*, p.356.

20 B. Anderson, *Imagined Communities* (London: Verso, 1983/2006).

21 E. Hobsbawm, *Nations and Nationalism since 1780* (Cambridge, MA: Cambridge University Press, 1990), p.5.

22 Ibid., p.8. On the "essentially contested" nature of alternative definitions of the nation, see also C. Calhoun, "Nationalism and Ethnicity," *Annual Review of Sociology* 19 (1993), pp.211-239, especially pp.215-216.

23 M. Weber, "The Nation," in *Economy and Society*, Vol. 2 (Berkeley, CA: The University of California Press, 1978), pp.921-926.

24 J. Linz and A. Stepan, *Problems of Democratic Transition and Consolidation* (Baltimore, MD: The Johns Hopkins University Press, 1996), p.21.

25 Linz, *op. cit.*, p.359.

26 Ibid., p.356. See also W. Connor, "When Is a Nation?," *Ethnic & Racial Studies* 13(1) (1990), pp. 92-103; D.D. Laitin, *Nations, States, and Violence* (Oxford: Oxford University Press, 2007); M. Hechter, *Containing Nationalism* (Oxford: Oxford University Press, 2001); and E. Hobsbawm (1990), *op. cit.* Cf. A.D. Smith, *Nationalism and Modernism* (London: Routledge, 1988), for the classic "anti-modernist" counter-argument, which would locate the origins of the nation much deeper in history. More recently, however, Smith has significantly amended his original position to accommodate the "modernist" thesis. See his *Ethno-symbolism and Nationalism: A Cultural Approach* (London: Routledge, 2009), and J. Hutchison and M. Guibernau, eds., *History and National Destiny: Ethno-Symbolism and its Critics* (London: Blackwell, 2004).

27 Linz and Stepan, *op. cit.*, pp.20-21. However, on "proto-national" sentiments associated with loyalty to a common monarch, see L. Greenfeld, *Nationalism: Five Roads to Modernity* (Cambridge, MA: Harvard University Press, 1992).

28 D. Conversi makes a persuasive case that nationalism should be considered one of the chief long-term political consequences of the French Revolution, and emphasises in particular the role of the Napoleonic wars in its spread. See "Modernism and Nationalism," *Journal of Political Ideologies* 17(1) (2012), pp.13-34.

29 B. Anderson, *op. cit.*, p.7.

30 E. Hobsbawm (1990), *op. cit.*, pp.9-10.

31 J. Breuilly, *Nationalism and the State* (Chicago, IL: The University of Chicago Press, 1994); and C. Tilly, "States and Nationalism in Europe 1492-1992," *Theory and Society* 23(1) (1994), pp.131-146.

32 E. Hobsbawm, *The Age of Empire* (New York: Pantheon Books, 1987), pp.148-149.

33 E. Weber, *Peasants into Frenchmen* (Palo Alto, CA: Stanford University Press, 1976).

34 E. Hobsbawm (1987), *op. cit.*, p.150.

35 Ibid., p.88. For a more sanguine version of the link between nationalism and democracy, see T. Nairn, "The Modern Janus," in *The Break-Up of Britain* (London: New Left Books, 1977), pp.317-350; and T. Nairn, *Faces of Nationalism: Janus Revisited* (London: Verso, 1998).

36 For the role of the educational system in the construction of the French nation,

see E. Weber, *op. cit.* Gellner (1983), *op. cit.*, goes so far as to claim that "the monopoly over legitimate education is now more important than the monopoly of legitimate violence" in the maintenance of social order (p.34). For an account of patterns of post-communist collapse that focuses on the legacies of pre-communist nationalization in the educational system, see K. Darden and A. Grzymala-Busse, "The Great Divide: Literacy, Nationalism, and the Post-Communist Collapse," *World Politics* 59 (Oct. 2006), pp.83-115.

37 E. Weber, *op. cit.*, also emphasises the role of conscription in the making of the French nation. On the relation between mobilization for war and 'nationalization' more generally, see D. Conversi, "Homogenisation, Nationalism, and War. Should We Still Read Ernest Gellner?," *Nations and Nationalisms*, 13(3) (2007), pp.371-394; and D. Conversi, "'We Are All Equals!' Militarism, Homogenisation, and 'Egalitarianism' in Nationalist State-Building (1789-1945)," *Ethnic and Racial Studies* 31(7) (2008), pp. 1286-1314.

38 In P. Anderson, "Imperium," *The New Left Review*, 83, Sept.-Oct. 2013, pp.5-111. Quoted on p.10.

39 Gellner (1983), *op. cit.*, p.1. For the seminal treatment of the history of the principle of self-determination, see A. Cobban, *The Nation State and National Self-Determination* (New York: Thomas Y. Crowell Co., 1969).

40 E.H. Carr, *The Bolshevik Revolution 1817-1923. Volume 1* (New York: Norton, 1950), p. 412.

41 Breuilly, *op. cit.*, ch.5; and O. Pflanze, "Nationalism in Europe, 1848-1871," *The Review of Politics* 28(2) (Apr., 1966), pp.129-143.

42 Linz, *op. cit.*, p.357. On the liberalism originally associated with romantic nationalism in Germany, see B. Vick, "The Origins of the German Volk: Cultural Purity and National Identity in Nineteenth Century Germany," *German Studies Review* 26(2) (2003), pp. 241-256.

43 Linz, *op. cit.*, p.357. On nationalism in nineteenth-century Italy, see L. Riall, *The Italian Risorgimento: State, Society, and National Unification* (London: Routledge, 2004). On Bismarckian "nation-building," see O. Pfanze, *Bismarck and the Development of Germany* (3 vols., Princeton, NJ: Princeton University Press, 1990); and G. Eley, "Society and Politics in Bismarckian Germany," *German History* 15(1) (1997), pp.101-132.

44 On the application of the principle of self-determination in the peace treaties at the end of the First World War, see Cobban, *op. cit.*, ch.3.

45 E. Hobsbawm (1990), *op. cit.*, pp.132-133. For a similar judgment about the lessons

of the interwar European experience, see J. Coackley, "National Minorities and
the Government of Divided Societies: A Comparative Analysis of Some European
Evidence," *European Journal of Political Research* 18 (1990), pp.437-456.

46 Gellner (1983), *op. cit.*, p.2.

47 For discussions of the moral legitimacy and sociological dynamics of contemporary appeals for national self-determination, see A. Buchanan, "Theories of
Secession," *Philosophy and Public Affairs*, 26(1) (1997), pp.31-61; V.O. Bartkus, *The
Dynamic of Secession* (Cambridge: Cambridge University Press, 1999); L.C. Buch-
heit, *Secession* (New Haven, CT: Yale University Press, 1978); J. Linz, "Cautionary
and Unorthodox Thoughts about Democracy," in D. Chalmers and S. Mainwaring,
eds. *Problems Confronting Contemporary Democracies* (Notre Dame, IN: Notre
Dame University Press, 2012), pp.227-252; R. Bauböck, "Paradoxes of Self Determi-
nation and the Right to Self Government", in C. Eisgruber and A. Sajo, eds.,
Global Justice and the Bulwarks of Localism: Human Rights in Context (Leiden:
Martinus Nijhoff Publishers, 2005), pp. 101 128; and D. Ronen, *The Quest for Self-
Determination* (New Haven, CT: Yale University Press, 1979).

48 For Lenin's most significant writing on the right to national self-determination,
see H.B. Davis, *Nationalism and Socialism* (New York: Monthly Review Press,
1967), ch.8.

49 Hobsbawm (1990), *op. cit.*, p.148.

50 S. Cohen, *Bukharin and the Bolshevik Revolution* (New York: Vintage, 1975), p.36.

51 Carr, *op. cit.*, p.422; O. Bauer, *The Question of Nationalities and Social Democracy*
(Minneapolis, MN: University of Minnesota Press, 2000 [1924]). For summary
views of the Austro-Marxist position in historical context, see also S. Avineri,
"Marxism and Nationalism," *Journal of Contemporary History* 26(3/4) (1991),
pp.636-657; J. Coakley, "Approaches to the Resolution of Ethnic Conflict: The
Strategy of Non-Territorial Autonomy," *International Political Science Review* 15(3)
(1994), pp.297-314; M. Löwy, "Marxists and the National Question," *New Left
Review* 96 (1976), pp.81-100; R. Munck, "Marxism and Nationalism in the Era of
Globalization," *Capital & Class* 34(1) (2010), pp.45-53; E. Nimni, *op. cit.*, ch.5-7;
and J. L. Talmon, *The Myth of the Nation and the Vision of Revolution* (Berkeley,
CA: University of California Press, 1981), part 3.

52 R. Luxemburg, "The National Question and Autonomy," in Horace B. Davis, ed.,
The National Question. Selected Writings by Rosa Luxemburg (London: Monthly
Review Press, 1976 [1909]), pp.109-110. For scholarly treatments of Luxemburg on
the "national question," see H.B. Davis, "Introduction. The Right of Self-Determi-

nation in Marxist Theory – Lenin versus Luxemburg," in Davis, *op. cit.*, pp.9-48; N. Ito, "Is the National Question an Aporia for Humanity? How to Read Rosa Luxemburg's 'The National Question and Autonomy,'" *Research in Political Economy* 26 (2010), pp.3-68; Löwy, *ibid.*, pp.85-89; J.P. Nettl, *Rosa Luxemburg*, 2 Volumes (London: Oxford University Press, 1966), especially Appendix II, pp.842-862; A. Nye, *Philosophia: The Thought of Rosa Luxemburg, Simone Weil, and Hannah Arendt* (New York: Routledge, 1994), pp.18-23; Talmon, *ibid.*, part 2; A.K. Shelton, "Rosa Luxemburg and the National Question," *East European Quarterly* XXI(3) (Sept. 1987), pp.297-303; and D. Whitehall, "A Rival History of Self-Determination," *European Journal of International Law* 27(3) (2016), pp.719-743.

53 Quoted in Cohen, *op. cit.*, pp.36-37. See also R.V. Daniels, *The Conscience of the Revolution* (New York: Simon and Schuster, 1969), pp.32-33.

54 On Lenin's collaboration with Stalin in the formulation of Bolshevik policy on nationalities, see I. Deutscher, *Stalin: A Political Biography* (London: Penguin Books, 1990), ch.4-6. For a succinct discussion of the Bolshevik doctrine of self-determination before and during the revolution, see Carr, *op. cit.*, note B, pp.410-428. For subsequent Soviet practice, see G. Smith, ed., *The Nationalities Question in the Soviet Union* (London: Longman, 1991); R. G. Suny, *the Revenge of the Past: Nationalism, Revolution, and the Collapse of the Soviet Union* (Stanford, CA: Stanford University Press, 1993), ch. 4; and I. Bremmer, "Reassessing Soviet Nationalities Theory," in I. Bremmer and R. Taras, eds., *Nations and Politics in the Soviet Successor States* (Cambridge: Cambridge University Press, 1993), pp.3-28. On the treatment of the "national question" in other Marxist-Leninist states, see W. Connor, *The National Question in Marxist-Leninist Theory and Strategy* (Princeton, NJ: Princeton University Press, 1984).

55 Multiple promising efforts have been made along such lines. For a recent powerful defence of Luxemburg's stance on self-determination, see D. Whitehall, *op. cit.* From a perspective closer to anarchism, see M. Bookchin, "Nationalism and the 'National Question,'" *Society and Nature* 2(2) (1994), pp.8-36. For two recent engagements with African anti-colonial thinkers that seek to recover imaginings of decolonization and "self-determination" alternative to the form of the "independent" nation-state, see F. Cooper, *Africa in the World: Capitalism, Empire, Nation-State* (Cambridge, MA: Harvard University Press, 2014); and G. Wilder, *Freedom Time: Negritude, Decolonization, and the Future of the World* (Durham, NC: Duke University Press, 2015). Perhaps the most creative attempt to redefine "self-determination" as radical democracy against the nation-state has come from the im-

prisoned leader of the Kurdish Freedom Movement, Abdullah Ocalan. See his *Democratic Confederalism* (London: Transmedia Publishing Ltd., 2011); and *Manifesto for a Democratic Civilization* (Cologne: New Compass Press, 2015).

56 For such allegations, see S. Avineri (1991), *op. cit.*; R. Debray, "Marxism and the National Question,"*New Left Review*, 105 (1977), pp.20-42; Löwy, *op. cit.*; Nairn (1977), *op. cit.*; and R. Munck, *Marxism and Nationalism: The Difficult Dialogue* (London: Zed Books, 1986).

57 Quoted in R. Szporluk, *Communism and Nationalism* (Oxford: Oxford University Press, 1988), pp.57-58.

58 K. Marx and F. Engels, "Manifesto of the Communist Party," in R. Tucker, ed., *The Marx-Engels Reader. Second Edition* (New York: Norton, 1978 [1848]), pp.469-500. Quote from p.488.

59 Ibid., pp.476-477.

60 J.L. Talmon, *op. cit.*, p.27.

61 See K. Anderson, *Marx at the Margins. On Nationalism, Ethnicity, and Non-Western Societies* (Chicago, IL: University of Chicago Press, 2016); and E. Brenner, *Really Existing Nationalisms: A Post-Communist View from Marx and Engels* (Oxford: Clarendon Press, 1995). However, for a cogent critique of the chauvinistic German prejudices clouding both Marx's and especially Engel's approach to matters associated with nationhood, nationalism, race, and ethnicity, see C. Robinson, *Black Marxism* (Chapel Hill, NC: The University of North Carolina Press, 2000), pp.52-61.

62 E. Hobsbawm, "Introduction," in K. Marx and F. Engels, *The Communist Manifesto* (London: Verso, 2012 [1848]).

63 See Hobsbawm (1987), *op. cit.*

64 For reactions to the Bolshevik revolution among Marxists in the West, see M. van der Linden, *Western Marxism and the Soviet Union* (Leiden: Brill, 2007), ch.2. For the views of Lenin and Trotsky on the prospects for world revolution, see E. Van Ree, "Socialism in One Country: A Reassessment," *Studies in East European Thought* 50(2) (1998), pp.77-117; and I. Deutscher, *The Prophet Armed. Trotsky 1879-1921* (London: Verso, 2003).

65 See Deutscher (1990), *op. cit.*; and Daniels, *op. cit.*, pp.398-412.

66 Kolakowski, quoted in Szporluk, *op. cit.*, p.59.

67 Ibid., p.60.

68 K. Marx, "On the Jewish Question," in R. Tucker, ed., *The Marx-Engels Reader. Second Edition* (New York: Norton, 1978 [1843]), pp.26-52. Quotes from pp.36, 29.

69   Ibid., p.32.

70   Ibid., p.34.

71   See D. McLellan, *Karl Marx: A Biography* (London: MacMillan, 1995), pp.72-77;
     and S. Avineri, "Marx and Jewish Emancipation," *Journal of the History of Ideas*
     25(3) (1964), pp.445-450.

72   P. Anderson, "The Antinomies of Antonio Gramsci," *The New Left Review*, 100
     (Nov.-Dec. 1976), pp.5-78. Quote from p.28.

73   Marx (1843/1978), *op. cit.*, p.39.

74   K. Marx, "Letter to Ruge" (1843). https://www.marxists.org/archive/marx/works/
     1843/letters/43_09.htm.

75   See J. Marsh, *Process, Praxis, and Transcendence* (Albany, NY: State University of
     New York Press, 1999), pp.177-185.

76   K. Marx, "Contribution to the Critique of Hegel's *Philosophy of Right*. Introduc-
     tion," in Tucker, ed., *op. cit.*, pp.53-65. Quote from p.53.

77   Ibid., pp.53-54.

78   Ibid., p.54. See A.M. McKinnon, "Opium as Dialectics of Religion: Metaphor,
     Expression, and Protest," *Critical Sociology* 13(1/2) (2005), pp.15-38.

79   A. MacIntyre, *After Virtue. Second Edition* (Notre Dame, Indiana: University of
     Notre Dame Press, 1984).

82   P. Anderson, *op. cit.*, p.10.

81   Ibid., p.10.

82   Marx (1844/1978), *op. cit.*, p.54.

83   Ibid., p.54.

84   Ibid., p.54.

85   For similar judgments about Marx as a secular prophet, albeit from different
     value-orientations, see H. Arendt, "Tradition and the Modern Age," in *Between
     Past and Future* (New York: Penguin Books, 1993); R. Niebuhr, "Introduction," in
     Marx & Engels on Religion (New York: Schocken Books, 1964); M. Nomad, *Apostles
     of Revolution* (New York, NY: Collier Books, 1961); and Talmon, *op. cit.*, part one.

86   Anderson, *op. cit.*, p.12.

87   See also C.J.H. Hayes, *Nationalism: A Religion* (New York: MacMillan, 1960); J.
     Llobera, *God of Modernity* (Herdon, VA: Berg Publishers, 1994); L. Greenfeld, "Is
     Nationalism the Modern Religion?," *Critical Review* 10(2) (1996), pp.169-191; and
     Breuilly, *op. cit.*, ch.1.

88   Hobsbawm (1990), *op. cit.*, p.69.

89   Linz, *op.cit.*, p.360.

90 Hobsbawm (1990), *op. cit.*, p.10.

91 Gellner (1983), *op. cit.*, pp.48-49.

92 E. Gellner, *Thought and Change* (Chicago: University of Chicago Press, 1978 [1964]), p.169.

93 B. Anderson, *op. cit.*, p.6.

94 Quoted in Nettl, *op. cit.*, p.849.

95 P. Anderson, *op. cit.*, p.5.

96 See J. Marsh, *op. cit.*, pp.158-190.

97 D.T. Goldberg, *The Threat of Race. Reflections on Racial Neoliberalism* (Oxford: Wiley-Blackwell, 2009), pp.5-6.

98 On the affinities between familial and national ideologies, see also E. Balibar, "The Nation Form: History and Ideology," in E. Balibar and I. Wallerstein, *Race, Nation, Class. Ambiguous Identities* (London: Verso, 1991), pp. 86-106. On the relation between nationalism and gender oppression, see N. Yuval-Davis, *Gender & Nation* (London: SAGE, 1997); A. McClintock, "'No Longer in a Future Heaven' Nationalism, Gender, and Race," in *Imperial Leather: Race, Gender, and Sexuality in the Colonial Contest* (New York, NY: Routledge, 1995), pp.352-389: R. Radhakrishnan, "Nationalism, Gender, and the Narrative of Identity," in A. Parker, M. Russo, et. al., eds., *Nationalisms & Sexualities* (New York, NY: Routledge, 1992), pp.77-95; and S. Walby, "Woman and Nation," *International Journal of Comparative Sociology* XXXIII(1-2) (1992), pp.81-100. On the relation between nationalism and hegemonic norms of masculinity, see P. Holden, *Autobiography and Decolonization. Modernity, Masculinity, and the Nation-State* (Madison, WI: The University of Wisconsin Press, 2008); and G.L. Mosse, "Nationalism and Sexuality in Nineteenth-Century Europe," *Culture and Society* XX(5) (Jul-Aug 1983), pp.75-84.

99 P. Anderson, *op. cit.*, pp.5, 141.

100 S. Ahmed, *The Cultural Politics of Emotion* (New York: Routledge, 2014 [2004]), p.125

101 Ibid., p.127.

102 Ibid., p.130.

103 Ibid., p.131.

104 See E. Balibar, "Racism and Nationalism," in E. Balibar and I. Wallerstein, *op. cit.*, pp.37-68; G. Eley and R. Suny, "Introduction: From the Moment of Social History to the Work of Cultural Representation," in G. Eley and R. Suney, eds., *Becoming National: A Reader* (Oxford: Oxford University Press, 1996) pp.3-37, p.28; S. Hall, "Introduction: Who Needs Identity?," in S. Hall and P. Du Gay, eds., *Questions of*

Cultural Identity (London: SAGE, 1996); and K. Tölölyan, "The Nation-State and its Others: In Lieu of a Preface," *Diaspora: A Journal of Transnational Studies*, 1(1) (1991), pp.3-7.

105 E. Balibar, *op. cit.*, pp.42-43; P. Gilroy, "Nationalism, History and Ethnic Abso-lutism," *History Workshop Journal* 30 (Autumn 1990), pp.114-120; and D. Mertz, "The Racial Other in Nationalist Subjectivations: A Lacanian Analysis," *Rethinking Marxism* 8(2) (1995), pp.77-88.

106 Ahmed, *op. cit.*, p.130; J. Butler, *Precarious Lives. The Powers of Mourning and Violence* (London: Verso, 2006).

107 For a sophisticated defence of the irreducibility of national identity to "false-consciousness," see R. Smith, *Stories of Peoplehood: The Politics and Morals of Polit-ical Membership* (Cambridge: Cambridge University Press, 2003).

108 For a forceful argument that "nationalism" is best conceived as a component of the broader dominant ideology of "modernism," see D. Conversi (2012), *op. cit.* Along compatible lines, M. Freeden has made a strong case that "nationalism" is most accurately considered an "embellisher" and "sustainer" of such host ideologies as "liberalism," "socialism," or "fascism." See "Is Nationalism a Distinct Ideology?," *Political Studies*, XLVI (1998), pp.748-765. However, *pace* Anderson, neither Con-versi's nor Freeden's arguments would seem to imply that nationalism should be considered "beyond" or "above" ideology critique.

109 P. Anderson, *op. cit.*, pp.24, 37.

110 W. Benjamin, "The Work of Art in the Age of Mechanical Reproduction," in *Illuminations* (London: Pimlico, 1999 [1920]), pp.234-235.

111 S. Buck-Morss, "Aesthetics and Anaesthetics: Walter Benjamin's Artwork Essay Reconsidered," *October*, Vol. 62, Autumn 1992, pp.3-41. Quote from p.16.

112 Ibid., pp.37, 41.

113 On the impossibility of divorcing nationalism from fascism, see also Conversi (2012), *op. cit.*

114 Hobsbawm (1990), *op. cit.*, pp.122-123.

115 See Conversi (2012), *op. cit.*

116 F. Fanon, *The Wretched of the Earth* (London: Penguin Books, 2001 [1961]); H. Davis, *op. cit.*

117 For exemplary examinations of some such configurations, see R. Aminzade, *Race, Nation, and Citizenship in Postcolonial Africa: The Case of Tanzania* (Cambridge: Cambridge University Press, 2014); N.P. Applebaum, A.S. MacPherson, et. al., eds., *Race and Nation in Latin America* (Chapel Hill, NC: University of North Carolina

Press, 2003); L.W. Barrington, ed., *After Independence: Making and Protecting the Nation in Postcolonial and Postcommunist States* (Ann Arbor, MI: The University of Michigan Press, 2006); J.F. Bayart, *The State in Africa. The Politics of the Belly* (London: Longman, 1993); P. Chatterjee, *The Nation and its Fragments: Colonial and Post-Colonial Histories* (Princeton, NJ: Princeton University Press, 1993); P. Duara, "Historicizing National Identity, or Who Imagines What and When," in G. Eley and R. Suny, *op. cit.*, pp. 151-177; F. Halliday, *Nation and Religion in the Middle East* (London: Saqi Books, 2000); M. Mamdani, *Citizen and Subject. Contemporary Africa and the Legacy of Late Colonialism* (Princeton, NJ: Princeton University Press, 1996); and A. Stepan, J. Linz, and Y. Yadav, *Crafting State Nations. India and Other Multinational Democracies* (Baltimore, MD; The Johns Hopkins University Press, 2011).

CHAPTER 2

Nationalist Ideology and the State[1]

Co-authored with Dr. Enric Martínez-Herrera

Abstract: *This chapter argues that the nation is best conceived as an ideological construct. It explores the theoretical significance and methodological consequences of treating the nation as such. It is intended as a corrective to the persistent essentialism and widespread reifications that continue to plague the literature on nations and nationalism. It begins with a discussion of the nation as ideology. It then turns to relate the national ideal to the process of self-construction, emphasizing the necessary connection between this process and projections of alterity. It concludes by specifying four sets of Ideological state apparatuses directly implicated in the cultivation of "nationalizing" hegemonic projects: (1) the educational system, (2) the mass media, (3) the bureaucracy, and (4) political parties. It calls upon scholars to focus on these institutions for the purpose of illuminating the dynamics of national construction.*

Introduction

This chapter advances the proposition that the nation is an ideological construct embedded in concrete constellations of power relations, produced and reproduced by state apparatuses. It explores the theoretical significance and methodological consequences of treating the nation in such a way. It is intended as a corrective to the persistent essentialism and widespread reifications that continue to plague the literature on nations and nationalism, despite the proliferation of explicit professions of allegiance to a constructivist paradigm among contemporary scholars.

The chapter begins with a discussion of the nation as *ideology*. Following Gramsci, it conceives of ideology as a material force in history, capable in principle of serving as either *political cement* or *political dynamite*. In practice, however, the national ideal – more specifically, the idea of the national community as a primary basis of political allegiance – ranks among and works in conjunction with other dominant political myths of the contemporary world, operating to ensure the reproduction of social-property relations. In a word, it functions most often as a legitimating myth.

The chapter continues with a treatment of the nation as an ideological *construct*. It relates the national ideal to the process of self-construction more generally. It stresses the intimate – indeed necessary – connection between the process of self-construction and the construction and projection of alterity, the marginalization and exclusion, even demonization, of specific *others*. It also emphasizes the centrality of and obsession with "normalization" versus "deviance" in this project.

The chapter concludes by specifying the *state apparatuses* involved in the production and reproduction of the nationalized self. More specifically, it hones in on four sets of ideological state apparatuses directly implicated in the cultivation of "nationalizing" and "nation-building" hegemonic projects: (1) the educational system, (2) the mass media, (3) the bureaucracy, and (4) political parties. It makes the case that both (a) struggles within and (b) the workings of these institutions should be at the very centre of critical analyses by scholars interested in understanding and elucidating the dynamics of national construction.

Nationalist Ideology as a Material Force

The "nation" is a category of vision and division of the social world, an "imagined community" (Anderson 1983/2006) produced, enshrined, perpetuated, and sometimes contested within the horizons of concrete institutional orders and apparatuses. "Nationalism" is the political doctrine associated with struggles to achieve or defend the "sovereignty," "independence," or "self-determination" of a given "nation". As such, the "nation" and "nationalism" operate at different levels of subjectivity – the former pertaining to the level of (often implicit) perceptual schema; the latter, to the level of explicit political program. Nevertheless, both categories are fundamentally "ideological constructs," at least insofar as "ideology" is conceptualized broadly, following Althusser and Gramsci, as encompassing the "imaginary relations of individuals and classes to their conditions of existence" (Balibar 1995/2007, p.31).

Like all ideological phenomena, the "nation" and "nationalism" are "material" in a double sense. First, these imaginings and aspirations are "material" insofar as they exist not merely in the ethereal realm of ideas, but instead, are always already "embodied in institutions and apparatuses". Second, they are material insofar as they constitute "material forces" in history. In Gramsci's words, "'popular beliefs' and similar ideas are themselves material forces" (1971, p.165). Belief in the nation, more specifically, allegiance to the national community, serves as a particularly powerful *political cement*, capable of producing the effect of "social cohesion," indeed of "welding" together and fortifying existing constellations of power relations; though at other times, it can serve as powerful *political dynamite* as well, and in many contexts has proven capable of destroying and overthrowing existing constellations of power relations, or at least radically transforming them.

The nation is imagined as a "collective subject". Like all subjects, it is a construct. Reification and essentialism are therefore to be avoided by critical social scientists. An important task is to elucidate the social forces and processes at work in subject construction. This in accordance with the goal of Althusser to "demonstrate the materiality and historical efficacity of ideologies," as well as the ambitious outline sketched by him in his later work of "a general theory of ideology as the 'interpellation of individuals as subjects' and as a system of both public and private institutions ensuring the reproduction of social relations" (Balibar 1995/2007, p.31).

The Nation and Other Legitimating Myths

The national community as the basis of political allegiance constitutes one of the dominant political myths operative in ensuring the reproduction of social relations in the contemporary world. Alongside and intertwined with other *hegemonic* myths of "modernity" and "post-modernity" – myths that act to "submerge consciousness," "to domesticate" (Freire 1970/1972, pp.27-

28) even to "manufacture consent". Consent – like the will, or the subject from whom it is alleged to emanate – is never spontaneous, but is always "organized through specific institutions and always (and necessarily) backed up by the potential application of force" (Buroway 2003, pp.214-15; Gardner 2015).

Legitimating myths abound in unequal and unjust contemporary societies. Such myths are presented to the public "by well-organized propaganda and slogans". They help keep people passive via "subjugation," and therefore facilitate the preservation and reproduction of the status quo. They include and are also intimately associated with the "national idea" and with "national ideals," and have proven capable on many crucial occasions of eliciting allegiance, including even the willingness to kill and to die, perhaps especially in defence of "national security" and for the sake of the "national community". Freire has elaborated an illustrative, if non-comprehensive, list of some of the most common domesticating and legitimating tropes or myths in and around his native Brazil. For example:

> "[T]he myth that the oppressive order is a 'free society'; the myth that all men are free to work where they wish, that if they don't like their boss they can leave him and look for another job; the myth that this order respects human rights and is therefore worthy of esteem; the myth that anyone who is industrious can become an entrepreneur - worse yet, the myth that the street vendor is as much an entrepreneur as the owner of a large factory; the myth of the universal right of education; the myth of the equality of all men when the question 'Do you know who you're talking to?' is still current among us; the myth of the heroism of the oppressor classes as defenders of 'Western Christian civilization'; the myth of the charity and generosity of the elites; the myth that the dominant elites, 'recognizing their duties', promote the advancement of the people, so that the people, in a gesture of gratitude, should accept the words of the elites and conform to them; the myth that rebellion is a sin against God; the myth of private property as fundamental to personal human development; the myth of the industriousness of the oppressors and the laziness of the oppressed, as well as the myth of the natural inferiority of the latter and the superiority of the former" (1970/1972, pp.109-110).

Such myths are ubiquitous. This is because they span across and correspond to three underlying "fundamental modes of ideological interpellation".

Subjects are always "subject[ed] and qualif[ied]" – "we" are told, related to, and made to recognize three kinds of ideas, as Göran Therborn has explained. First, ideas about "what exists, and its corollary, what does not exist" – that is, about "who we are, what the world is, what nature, society, men and women are like," and their corollaries, what these things are not. Second, ideas about "*what is good*, right, just, beautiful, attractive, enjoyable" and their opposites. The realm of desire is itself structured, "norm-alized," if not always "normal-ized". Third, ideas about "*what is possible* and impossible, our sense of the mutability of our being-in-the-world," i.e. what can be changed, as well as "the consequences of change" – these ideas, too, are patterned, our "hopes, ambitions, and fears," are always interpellated, that is, they are "given shape," conditioned, even constituted, by systemic social forces in which "we" subjects are always embedded and formed (Therborn 1980, p.18).

Ideology and the Construction of the Subject

The power of ideology is most insidious indeed. It "functions by moulding personality," subjecting "the amorphous libido of new-born human animals to a specific social order," and qualifying "them for the differential roles they will play in society" (1978/2008, p.172). It is thus not merely a matter of doctrinal conscious convictions. As Nietzsche put it, consciousness is but a surface (1888/1992, p.35).

Nietzsche may have introduced the concept of the unconscious; but it was Freud who developed it. As Althusser reminds us, Freud "discovered for us that the real subject, the individual in his unique essence, has not the form of an ego, centred on the 'ego', on 'consciousness' or on 'existence'" (1971/2008, p.70). A momentous discovery, that of the depth of the human psyche, though like most "discoveries," it is most certainly a re-discovery, albeit an original synthesis and re-articulation. Momentous nonetheless, opening up the intellectual space for exploring consciousness as construct, as artefact. The human subject is thus revealed to be "de-centred by a structure which has no 'centre' either – except through misrecognition and projection of an imaginary 'ego', i.e. in ideological formations in which it 'recognizes' itself" (1971/2008, p.171). The imagined "centres of sovereignty" in whose likeness and image the subject is constructed and projected, these central Subjects (with a capital S) – be they "God, Father, Reason, Class, or something more diffuse" – serve to pattern the "super-ego of subjects" (with a lower-case s), providing them with "ego goals". Conscious convictions, best interpreted as but the surface manifestation of a deeper and complex set of semi- and sub-conscious forces of interpellation at work, a double process of "subjection and qualification" (Therborn 1980, p.18).

Althusser also reminds us that desire is "the basic category of the uncon-scious," that it is perhaps even "the sole meaning of the discourse of the human subject's unconscious," a "meaning that emerges in and through the 'play' of the signifying chain" (1971/2008, p.164). Conscious affiliations always correspond with so many unconscious desires. Desire for proximity, for near-ness, or for their opposites, underlying and reinforcing "forms of social and political allegiance," not to mention forms of social and political exclusion (Ahmed 2006, p.145).

The "self," the "subject," as imaginary misrecognition, and as construct, as artefact. And with the self comes its corollary, the Other. Indeed, the projec-tion and construction of the "self" always entails the projection and construc-tion of an Other, indeed, multiple Others. Every ego has an alter-ego, multiple alters, every ideology an alter-ideology, multiple alter-ideologies. Alter-ide-ologies which refer to "the ideological dimension of the form in which one relates to the Other: to perceptions of the Other and of one's relationship to him/her," to "them," to those who are not "me/us," to those who are "like me/us," to those who are "unlike me/us," to those who are "beneath me/us," to those who are "above me/us" (Therborn 1980, p.28). Belonging and exclu-sion, it turns out, are but flips sides of the same projected and constructed subject, two sides of the "same coin". The question of 'the subject' thus emerges as "crucial for politics".

As Butler has famously insisted, "exclusionary practices" are invariably in-volved in the production of "juridical subjects," though these practices are often effectively concealed, and "do not 'show' once the juridical structure of politics has been established". In other words, the "subject" is always con-structed in accordance "with certain legitimating and exclusionary aims". Po-litical analysis therefore must pay close attention to these exclusionary operations at work in the construction of the subject. If it fails to do so, if in-stead it takes "juridical structures" as "foundation" or starting point, it runs the risk of reifying, concealing, and naturalizing political processes of sub-ject-formation and exclusion (1990/1999, p.5).

The self is constructed and *constricted*, always operating with relatively fixed and "durable" – though "transposable" – dispositions. Operating with a "habitus," as Bourdieu has rightly emphasized, that is, with "structured structures predisposed to function as structuring structures," in accordance with "principles which generate and organize practices and representations". Principles which are "objectively adapted" to produce particular outcomes and patterns of behaviour, but which do not require or presuppose "a conscious aiming at ends or an express mastery of the operations necessary in order to attain them" (1990).

Habitus disposes and orients the subject, and it operates beneath the surface of consciousness. Something similar can be said for the Foucaultian categories of "epistemes" or "discursive formations," which are "systems of thought and knowledge governed by rules beyond those of grammar and logic" and that work to delimit "conceptual possibilities," in effect, to constrain and *constrict* "the boundaries of thought in a given domain and period". Epistemes and discursive formations are sometimes depicted as operating "beneath the consciousness of individual subjects," though – given Foucault's famous rejection of psychoanalysis, it would seem more accurate to say that they serve to fix its horizons (Stanford 2003/2013).

Ideology, broadly conceived, includes not only (1) conscious convictions, but also (2) subconscious, even subliminal, symbolic associations and projections; (3) habitus, durable dispositions and orientations; and (4) epistemes or discursive formations. Consciousness revealed not only as a surface, but as a *bounded* surface, de-limited by definite frontiers.

The notion of durable dispositions returns our attention again to the "material existence of ideology," that it always "exists in an apparatus, and its practice, or practices" (Althusser 1971/2008, pp.39-40). These "apparatuses" crucially include the body itself. Ideology is thus material in the literal sense that it is embodied, incorporated, incarnated, made flesh as well.

Bio-Power and Normalization as "Modern" Techniques of Social Control

Another Foucaultian category – that of *bio-power* – deserves mention in this regard. In *The History of Sexuality*, Foucault vividly depicted the emergence of *bio-power* in eighteenth-century Europe as an innovative "technique of power," one "utilized by very diverse institutions," spanning across "the family and the army, schools and the police, individual medicine and the administration of collective bodies," and working to sustain the forces and relations of "economic development," acting simultaneously "as factors of segregation and social hierarchization," facilitating and guaranteeing "relations of domination and effects of hegemony". *Bio-power* as a quintessentially "modern" technique of social control, achieved through the "investment of the body, its valorization, and the distributive management of its forces" (1978/1990, p.141).

Along with *bio-power* – indeed, as a consequence of it – came "the growing importance assumed by the action of the norm". The pursuit of control over life, an ambitious new task, required "continuous regulatory and corrective mechanisms," which in turn effected a profound transformation in European institutions of justice. The law came to operate "more and more as a norm," and the judicial system was progressively "incorporated into a continuum of apparatuses (medical, administrative, and so on) whose functions are for the most part regulatory". The result: the *normalizing society*, as corollary and historical outcome of the new "technology of power centred on life" (Foucault 1978/1990, p.144). Disciplinary control and normalization as "distinctive features of modern power," the "concern with what people have not done," with "failure to reach required standards," the obsession with correcting "deviant behaviour," so pervasive in the contemporary world (Stanford 2003/2013).

The impulse to "normalize" and the obsession with "deviance" thus go together. "Normalization" is always an unfinished project. Indeed, the sign of "normalising society" is not "that everyone becomes the same, but that more and more people deviate in some way or other from evolving standards of normality, opening themselves through these multiple deviations to disciplinary strategies of neutralization" (Connolly 1991/2002, p.150).

As Sayer and Paige have noted, "Foucault's exploration of the disciplinary mechanisms of modernity" contains striking parallels with Max Weber's "notion of the disciplined self of ascetic Protestantism". In his classic, *The Protestant Ethic*, "Weber famously argued the ideal self for capitalist social relations is the disciplined, ascetic, industrious, frugal and rational personal ideal of Puritanism and its sectarian offshoots". More recently, Gorski has argued that the same can be said for "the ideal citizen of the modern nation-state and for the employees of its bureaucratic apparatus" as well. Both accounts, like Foucault, emphasize the uniquely "modern" emphasis on attaining "strictly regulated, reserved, self-control" (in Paige 2000, p.4).

The subject is constructed, constricted, and normalized; it is itself a process and product, a "consequence of certain rule-governed discourses that govern the intelligible invocation of identity". But "signification" is never a *founding act*. Rather, it is produced through "*a regulated process of repetition*," one that "both conceals itself and enforces its rules through the production of substantializing effects". The subject is therefore *constituted*, but never definitively *determined* (Butler 1990/1999, p.185).

To insist upon the social construction of the subject thus does not entail any ultimate ontological denial of agency. It does, however, require a renunciation of the possibility that agency could ever be exercised outside of power relations. As Foucault puts the point: "Where there is power, there is resistance, and yet, or rather consequently, this resistance is never in a position of exteriority in relation to power" (1978/1990, p.95). Therborn, too, has likewise insisted that the "formation of humans by every ideology ... according to whatever criteria" always involves the double process of "subjection and qualification". More precisely, a *dialectical* double process, through which subjects, "[a]lthough qualified by ideological interpellations," also "become qualified to 'qualify' these in turn" (1980, p.17).

Even so, the effects of interpellation within systems of domination should not be underestimated, either. The transformation from *amorphous libido* into *human child* is one which requires survival, one which requires "having escaped all childhood deaths, many of which are human deaths, deaths punishing the failure of humanization". All adults have passed this test. We are all "the *never forgetful* witnesses, and very often the victims, of this victory," we all bear in our "most clamorous parts, the wounds, weaknesses and stiffnesses that result from this struggle for human life or death". Even if some of us, perhaps "the majority, have emerged more or less unscathed – or at least give this out to be the case". Still, other "veterans bear the marks throughout their lives". Some will eventually succumb, dying from the old battles, though "at some remove," after the festering "old wounds" burst out again in a fit of "psychotic explosion," in "madness, the ultimate compulsion of a 'negative therapeutic reaction". As for the "normal" majority, their demise is not so spectacular; instead, it usually takes "the guise of an 'organic' decay". As Althusser disturbingly concludes: "Humanity only inscribes its official deaths on its war memorials ..." (1971/2008, p.157). The "fallen heroes" at least get remembered, if only tendentiously, that is, officially and superficially. By contrast, we who survive and are ground down by the everyday struggle, whether we burn out or slowly decay and fade away, we are destined to be forgotten.

The Machinery of Self-Construction

Having thus sketched the scope and effects of interpellation, let us now turn to examine more closely what Foucault referred to as "the machinery of production," in which "manifold relations of force ... take shape and come into play," together working to produce the subject (1978/1990, p.94). Althusser used the term "state apparatuses (SAs)" to specify such "machinery," and distinguished between repressive and ideological SAs.

Althusser's distinction runs the risk of reifying a misleading binary between institutions of coercion and institutions of consent, as if hegemony pertained to a "pole of consent in contrast to another of coercion". However, the Gramscian notion of hegemony, more accurately conceived, always reflects a "*synthesis* of consent and coercion" (Carnoy 1984, p.73).

However, the balance of consent and coercion varies systematically across institutional arenas. Those arenas that function most explicitly and prominently in terms of physical coercion and the threat of violence – institutions such as the army, the police, and the prisons – these constitute the repressive state apparatus. Which is not to say that they function by physical violence alone. To the contrary, as Weber rightly insisted, the effectiveness of the repressive apparatus itself always relies to a significant degree on issues of obedience and morale among the rank and file.

Other institutions of the state proper rely on a more balanced mix of coercion and consent. These include "the government, the administration, the courts," all of which are referred to by Althusser as both repressive and ideological state apparatuses.

Yet other apparatuses rely less immediately still upon physical coercion, and are engaged more directly with the "manufacturing of consent". These institutional arenas are what Althusser had in mind by "ideological state apparatuses," among which he included the following suggestive list: (1) the religious ISA (the system of the different churches); (2) the educational apparatus (the system of the different public and private schools); (3) the family ISA; (4) the legal ISA; (5) the political ISA (the political system, including the different parties); (6) the trade union ISA; (7) the communications ISA (press, radio and television, etc.); and (8) the cultural ISA (literature, the arts, sports, etc.) (1971/2008, pp.17-18).

For Althusser, like Gramsci, "hegemony is everywhere," though it manifests itself "in different forms" across different institutions and institutional arenas. The state proper is enveloped within a broader "apparatus of hegemony," one that encompasses nominally "private" institutions in so-called "civil society" (Carnoy 1984, p.73).

Althusser goes farther than Gramsci in elaborating an expanded concept of the state, though in making the case he relies quite heavily on appeals to Gramsci's authority. Indeed, he portrays Gramsci as having insisted that "the distinction between the public and the private is a distinction internal to bourgeois law;" that it is thus only "valid in the (subordinate) domains in which bourgeois law exercises its 'authority';" and that therefore, the state itself is most accurately considered not "public," but instead, as the "precondition for the distinction between private and public" (1971/2008, pp.17-18).

Althusser thus invokes Gramsci's authority in order, effectively, to "obliterat[e] the peculiar apartness of the state from the rest of society". In so doing, he is certainly treading on heretical terrain within the Marxist tradition. After all, the apartness of the state had "always been regarded as a distinctive feature of the state in the theory of historical materialism," as Therborn would insist. Indeed, according to Therborn, it "is precisely because of the cleavage of society into a *separate* state body and other social institutions that the state is bound up with the division of society into classes" (1978, p.172).

With the paradigm of historical materialism having entered into a degenerative phase, if not yet terminal decline, the heresy involved in Althusser's interpretation of Gramsci has been largely forgotten, or at least its significance seems no longer so obvious. Even if the specificity of state institutions, narrowly conceived – their *apartness* from the rest of society – is crucial for the reproduction of class divisions in the rest of society, the thrust of Althusser's expansionary conceptualization of the Ideological state apparatuses remains forceful, persuasive, even clear: nominally "private" institutions can certainly perform important, delegated functions in the ideological construction of the subject.

The State as Educator

Moreover, Althusser's interpretation of Gramsci is not bereft of textual support either, especially given Gramsci's own shifting and ambiguous conceptualization of the state, and of the state's role in the production and reproduction of hegemony. On the whole, Gramsci did hold an expansive conception of the State. He viewed "the State as an extension of the hegemonic apparatus – as part of the system developed by the bourgeoisie to perpetuate and expand their control of society in the context of class struggle" (Carnoy 1984, p.74). In this crucial respect, Gramsci's analysis converges with that of Foucault. He announced not merely an expansive state, but an ever-expanding one, a state progressively creeping in to control every aspect of life. More directly and explicitly than Foucault, Gramsci attributes this transformation to the rise of the class project of the bourgeoisie, a "revolutionary" class who he believed had "revolutionized" the State. According to Gramsci:

> "The revolution which the bourgeois class has brought into the conception of law, and hence into the function of the State, consists especially in the will to conform (hence ethicity of the law and of the State). The previous ruling classes were essentially conservative in the sense that they did not tend to construct an organic passage from the other classes into their own, i.e., to enlarge their class sphere 'technically' and ideologically: their conception was that of a closed caste. The bourgeois class poses itself as an organism in continuous movement, capable of absorbing the entire society, assimilating to its own cultural and economic level. The entire function of the State has been transformed; the State has become an 'educator', etc". (1971, p.261).

Struggle for control and revolutionary expansion of the state apparatus thus characterized the ascent of the bourgeoisie in Europe. As an ascendant class, its emergent hegemony was increasingly manifested in the form of the state. Indeed, it had to be. "The State, as an instrument of bourgeois domination" had to be "an intimate participant in the struggle for consciousness". The bourgeois project could never depend on "the development of the forces of production" alone, but instead required "hegemony in the arena of consciousness" as well. As a result, the state came to be progressively instrumentalized and "involved in this extension;" its role expanded well beyond that of "the coercive *enforcement* of bourgeois power" (Carnoy 1984, p.76). In a word, it turned into an educator. As Gramsci would again insist:

> "In reality, the State must be conceived of as an 'educator', in as much as it tends precisely to create a new type or level of civilization. Because one is acting essentially on economic forces, reorganizing and developing the apparatus of economic production, creating a new structure, the conclusion must not be drawn that superstructural factors should be left to themselves, to develop spontaneously, to a haphazard and sporadic germination. The State, in this field, too, is an instrument of 'rationalisation', of acceleration and of Taylorisation. It operates according to a plan, urges, incites, solicits, and 'punishes'; for once the conditions are created in which a certain way of life is 'possible', then 'criminal action or omission' must have a punitive sanction, with moral implications, and not merely be judged generically as 'dangerous'. The Law is the repressive and negative aspect of the entire positive, civilising activity undertaken by the State. The 'prize-giving' activities of individuals and groups, etc., must also be incorporated in the conception of the Law; praiseworthy and meritorious activity is rewarded, just as criminal actions are punished (and punished in original ways, bringing 'public opinion' as a form of sanction" (1971, p.247).

"Public opinion," not merely manufactured; but manufactured *and deployed* as a new form of sanction. The institutional arenas of the ISAs thus come into focus as critical sites for concrete political struggles, commanding heights to be controlled or captured, for the purpose of manufacturing and reproducing the horizons of consciousness, not to mention the rhythms and reflexes of embodied subconscious desires, and with these, the terms of consent. The ISAs as critical sites of struggle for the institutionalization and materialization, of different ideologies, are always organically linked with different social forces in conflict, in struggle – especially different social classes.

The Doctrine of Historical Materialism and the Dominant Ideology Thesis

The "bottom line" of the historical materialist thesis regarding ideology, classically conceived, largely hinges on this last point. In Marx's felicitous turn of phrase from the *German Ideology*, "the ideas of the ruling class are in every epoch the ruling ideas" (1845/1978, p.172). Or, as Therborn would reformulate the idea, perhaps more precisely: in class societies "the patterning of a given set of ideologies" is always "overdetermined by class relations of strength and by the class struggle". This goes for all ideologies, not just explicitly ideologies about class. For example, "if we want to explain the different relative positions of Catholicism and nationalism in contemporary France and Italy," historical materialism thesis directs us to "look at how these ideologies have been linked with different classes, and at the outcome of struggles between these classes" (1980, p.39).

Laclau and Mouffe are right to notice subtle but important differences between the "classic problematic" of historical materialism and more recent reformulations such as those advanced by Althusser or Therborn, reformulations heavily indebted to Gramsci. In this regard, Laclau and Mouffe insist upon "two fundamental displacements" brought about by Gramsci. The first, which we have already emphasized, is Gramsci's "conception of the materiality of ideology" – that is, that ideology is always "an organic and relational whole, embodied in institutions and apparatuses," and that, furthermore, it serves to "weld together" and "unify" disparate fragments of society into "cohesive" social forces, indeed, into "historic blocs" themselves organized "around a number of base articulatory principles". The second, related displacement: for Gramsci, "organic ideologies" never represent "a purely classist and closed view of the world;" instead, they are always formed "through the articulation of elements which, considered in themselves," cannot be reduced to "class belonging" (1985, p.67).

However, Laclau and Mouffe mislead insofar as they suggest that the irreducibility of "elements of articulation" to "class belonging" should lead to neo-Gramscians to stress agency and contingency, rather than over-determination by intersecting but irreducible systems of domination. In this latter vein, critical race and feminist theorists have persuasively chastised the classical exponents of the doctrine of historical materialism for their tendency to vulgar economistic reductionism, not to mention their excessively narrow and commodified conception of toil. "Historic blocs" and "counter blocs," it turns out, are never only embedded within class relations and are never only organically linked to specific social classes, classically conceived. Instead, they are always simultaneously embedded within multiple, intersecting constellations of power relations. More specifically, they are always organically linked to subjects and subjectivities interpellated not only by formal class relations, but by ethno-racialized and gendered categories of consciousness and of praxis as well.

In sum, contending "blocs" are always located and recognizable only within intersecting, irreducibly interdependent systems of domination, they are destined to inhabit social landscapes structured by intersecting constellations of power relations, constellations currently categorized and divided by three main, globally-coordinated, regionally-patterned, interdependent systems of domination: class, ethno-racialized and gendered hierarchies.

The State and the Concrete Coordination of "Fictive Universalities"

If ideology "represents the imaginary relationship of individuals," a preliminary task for social science is to decipher and elucidate the *"structure of misrecognition"* operative in a given context (Althusser 1971/2008, pp.37, 171); to pursue a hermeneutic of de-masking the "fictive universality" of hegemonic ideologies (Balibar 1995/2007, p.47); even to purposively disenchant "the imaginary participant in an imaginary sovereignty," to awaken her to the cold, disturbing, even brutal reality that she has been "robbed of [her] real life," only "filled with an unreal universality" (in Paige 2000, p.4). For at the level of consciousness, at least, ideology primarily manifests itself as "the dream of an impossible universality" (Balibar 1995/2007, p.48).

The state provides a crucial terrain for struggles to produce, reproduce, and propagate precisely such impossible dreams, such fictive universalities. Indeed, according to Balibar, the state "is a manufacturer of abstractions precisely by virtue of the unitary fiction (or *consensus*) which it has to impose on society". In the process, the state tends to dawn the mask of the "nation," though underneath this mask it always remains "a fictive community," even if its "power of abstraction," its power to "universalize particularity," serves to compensate somewhat "for the real lack of community in relations between individuals" (1995/2007, p.48).

This peculiar power of the state, its ability to represent and produce "fictive universalities," renders the state a most useful instrument and therefore site of struggles to perpetuate and/or transform the horizons of contestation, the terms of ideological hegemony, in a given context. Privileged minorities manage to mask their specific advantages, to represent their particular wills as "the general will," to portray their particular interests as the "national interest," and thereby to mystify the masses, to exercise a magical, quasi-hypnotic power. This is the power of ideological hegemony. It expresses itself – indeed, is embodied – most manifestly in the state machinery, which in turn can be subdivided into so many institutional instruments and arenas, capable of being effectively employed to mesmerize, to mis-recognize, and to otherwise hide structures of advantage, indeed of domination, covered over and concealed in the heavy romantic mist of "fictive unity".

Thus we return to the state's propensity to be instrumentalized in pursuit of always incomplete projects of "ideological hegemony," projects protagonized by contending groups in society. In pursuit of "ideological hegemony," through which "the development and expansion of the particular group" come to be "conceived of, and presented, as being the motor force of a universal expansion, of a development of all the 'national' energies;" perchance a performance, through which "the dominant group is coordinated concretely with the general interests of the subordinate groups" (Gramsci 1971, pp.161, 182).

The concrete coordination of collective illusions, the manufacturing of collective fantasies, among the central educational tasks carried out by the state. The propagation of the "semblance" that "the rule of a certain class is only the rule of certain ideas," and with it the "sublimation of particular interests in the general interest," carried out by loyal ideologues, in collaboration with, organically linked to, particular state apparatuses. Ideologues whose most remarkable quality with all too disturbing frequency comes down to their ability to "*mystify themselves*, 'in their questions', i.e. in their mode of thinking" (Balibar 1995/2007, p.50).

The state as conductor in the orchestration and production of what Gramsci called "common sense," of "the sense held in common," of the proto-typical conformist underpinnings working to "ground," to produce, and to reproduce "passive quiescence" at the very least, and more optimally, "active consent". "Common sense" is frequently "constructed out of long-standing practices of cultural socialization," and thus can be effectively mobilized to "mask other realities," to conceal specific patterns of advantage, to legitimate specific patterns of disadvantage (Harvey 2005, p.39).

Political elites have thus long used the state machinery to diffuse among the population the set of beliefs and values they deem to be useful to secure the legitimacy of, or at least consent to, the political system. This is certainly the case of elites who rely on nationalist ideology as a major basis of their power. Let us conclude by focusing on four sets of ideological state appara-tuses centrally associated with the representative-democratic state and di-rectly implicated in the cultivation of "nationalizing" and "nation-building" hegemonic projects: (1) the educational system, (2) the mass media, (3) the bureaucracy, and (4) political parties.

The Educational System

The most potent of the ideological state apparatuses in this "educational" process, the educational system itself, is rivalled only by the family. The "ed-ucational ideological apparatus," identified by Althusser as having been "in-stalled in the *dominant* position in mature capitalist social formations as a result of a violent political and ideological class struggle against the old dom-inant ideological State apparatus" – namely, the established churches. Perhaps more accurately, according to Althusser, "the School-Family couple has re-placed the Church-Family couple" (1971/2008, pp.26, 28).

The schools, which take "children from every class at infant-school age, and then for years, the years in which the child is most 'vulnerable', squeezed between the family state apparatus and the educational state apparatus, it drums into them, whether it uses new or old methods, a certain amount of 'know-how' wrapped up in the ruling ideology ... or simply the ruling ideology in its pure state". The specific leverage and utility of the schools should not be underestimated. After all, no "other ideological State apparatus has the obligatory (and not least, free) audience of the totality of the children in the capitalist social formation, eight hours a day for five or six days out of seven" (1971/2008, pp.29-30).

The educational system thus comes into focus as a "key institution of civil society within which consent is cultivated," within which subjectivity is interpellated. In fact, well before Althusser, Gramsci had already described the school as "the State institution *par excellence* that prepares children and youth for their appropriate economic and political niches within the prevailing order", functioning as one of the "primary sites for achieving mass consent for social rule" (Aronowitz, 2002, p. 113). In the school the pupil "breathes in the dominant order of normality" (Gramsci, 1971, p. 31) (Gardner 2015, p.2).

Like Gramsci before Althusser, so too with Foucault after Althusser. For Foucault the school is depicted as crucial, too. According to Foucault, the role of the schools "developed within the framework of the 'new micro-physics' of power," involving "the disciplining of bodies for the control, development, health and fecundity of the population (Foucault, 1978, 1979)". As with the soldier and the madmen, the pupil is "disciplined", is "subjected, used, transformed and improved" (Foucault, 1971, 1979, pp. 138,136; Gardner 2015, p.4). The school's "disciplinary" techniques include the "timetable (to 'establish rhythms, impose particular occupations, regulate the cycles of repetition') and the examination (which 'combines the techniques of an observing hierarchy and those of a normalizing judgement')". Such techniques have been effectively "employed in order to mould, reshape and improve the pupil" (Foucault, 1979, p. 149,184). Indeed, Foucault insists, in the schools "the more or less simple transfer of knowledge from one person to another cannot be disentangled from those authoritative processes which seek to instil discipline into the moral fibres of its inmates and thus differentiate between them, their nature, potentialities, levels and values" (Deacon 2006, pp. 181–182). In sum, Foucault persuasively portrays the school as a "disciplinary institution," as "a technology of control over a population" (Gardner 2015, p.4).

More specifically, the educational system emerges as a "key site for enculturation into collective senses of the self". Indeed, according to Barrett (2007) and Gardner (2015), there is a burgeoning academic literature that has documented at least "three ways in which schools enculturate pupils toward particular identities"' – first, through providing "direct, explicit" information and narratives about "ethnic, national" and other collective groups; second, "through an implicit ethnocentric bias within the curriculum (both what is taught and how it is taught)"; and third, "through normative-performative constructions of daily life". Through such processes, schools serve to "enculturate pupils in official knowledges, schemes of normativity, and methods regulating the self" (Foucault, 1988, 2003). Such enculturation crucially includes enculturation into national, ethno-racialized, "linguistic, and religious collective senses of self," all of which are "absorbed and cultivated through the education system, both overtly and covertly" (Gardner 2015, p.6).

More precisely still, the educational system performs several important functions related to nationalization and to nation-building. The most obvious is its role in the compulsory socialization of youth into particular nationalist "imaginaries". This includes: (1) fostering different degrees of fluency in a given standardized language or languages; (2) fostering different degrees of knowledge about particular political communities (as well as overarching interpretations of their historical trajectories), be these communities local, regional, state-wide, or supra-national; and (3) fostering different degrees of attachment to such communities.

The schools transmit with insistence knowledge of flags and other symbols, hymns, and heads of state. They also transmit selective knowledge about and interpretations of historical episodes, leaders, individual and collective "heroes" and "foes," a corpus of literature, poetry, music, and art, as well as information about distinctive geographical characteristics of the alleged "fatherland". Usually underlying such selection is a conception of certain collectives as "nations," a positive valorisation of chosen "core values" of those "nations," and an assignment of the criteria for individual membership in them.

However, the educational system's ability to socialize students into these beliefs, values, and identities is, to a substantial degree, dependent upon the congruence between such cognitive and normative systems with those to which students are exposed in their families (Percheron 1982).

Another, less obvious function of the educational system concerns its role in facilitating or hindering social mobility. This includes not only class and status mobility in absolute terms, but also in relative terms. Various mechanisms are involved here. One of them is the socialization and selection (or co-optation) of individuals who could potentially resist a given hegemonic project. This process takes place through the provision of a system of rewards and penalties granted in accordance with social conformity and the extent to which an individual consistently shows she can be trusted to merit a position of leadership. Negative selection produces and is produced by feelings of social distance, low self-esteem, alienation, and school failure. Opposite feelings are produced by and produce positive selection.

Yet another role performed by the educational system is to reinforce favourable predispositions among those segments of the population bound to gain the most from the perpetuation and/or full realization of hegemonic aspirations. Students who come from dominant groups benefit from a school system which provides them with relative advantage in terms of contents covered in the curriculum, privileged status, feelings of comfort, and a sense of entitlement associated with collective ownership of a given territory and its institutions, broadly understood. Such advantages reinforce self-confidence, a sense of group belonging, and success, which in turn set in motion a process of self-selection for better employment opportunities and leadership positions in society.

The Mass Media

All ideological state apparatuses, Althusser insisted, "contribute to the same result: the reproduction of the relations of production". The communications apparatus works towards this end "by cramming every 'citizen' with daily doses of nationalism, chauvinism … by means of the press, the radio and television" (1971/2008, p.28). Likewise, Freire has argued, hegemonic myths and biases, the internalization of which are essential to the subjugation of the oppressed," are consistently "presented to them by well-organized propaganda and slogans, via the mass 'communications' media" (1970/1972, pp.27-28, 190-110).

The mass media is another important instrument through which hegemonic projects – including "nationalizing" ones – are realized. Admittedly, the impact of the mass media is relatively weak in comparison with other agents of socialization closer to individuals, such as the family, schools, and religious communities. Even so, the mass media contributes greatly to socialization into "national imaginaries" both through its role in diffusing standardized languages and through its role in diffusing political information, historical narratives, and geographical frames of reference (Rokkan 1971, Gellner 1983, Anderson 1983/2006, Hobsbawm 1990, Billig 1995).

In representative-democratic contexts, the state does not exercise monolithic control over the mass media. Instead, the state-owned "public" media compete alongside alternative, "private" sources. Nevertheless, the state regulates and sometimes subsidizes these "private" competitors, and for decades, in many countries it monopolized television channels. Nor should the impact of competition among multiple sources of mass media be overstated. For frequently, similar networks of powerful corporate interests exercise considerable influence over the content of information as well as the dominant interpretive lenses provided across the mainstream media, both state-owned and especially private. Moreover, competing media outlets all rely to a substantial degree upon the same governmental sources for providing news (Herman and Chomsky 1988).

The media play an important role in "setting the agenda" of public attention and debate. In selecting news items, editorial boards contribute substantially to forging perceptions about politics. Consumers of the news are provided not only with information about particular issues, but are also given cues about the relative importance of different news items (McCombs and Shaw 1972; Lang and Lang 1981). In fact, the media help determine not only the salience of issues but also help frame the way that people think about them (Iyengar and Kinder 1988; Ghanem 1997).

In comparison with other agents of socialization the mass media have the advantage of being present throughout the entire process of socialization, both pre-adult and adult, and of being somewhat ubiquitous. Indeed, studies of contemporary democratic contexts have shown that the first contact of most children with politics tends to occur through the television. After entering the educational system, children encounter on the television images that illustrate and reinforce the political ideas about the "nation" and about the contours of "national history" to which they have been exposed in school. Moreover, panel studies have shown that adults are also highly sensitive to learning from the contents of television news. In addition, research on the effects of the mass media has also found that those who consume the most news show a higher degree of differentiation from their parents' political views (Chaffee and Yang 1990).

The media successfully compete with traditional ideological organizations such as parties, trade unions, and churches in the selection, diffusion, and interpretation of political information. In so doing, they have substantially diluted the segmentation and compartmentalization of different social groups common in the age of mass parties, and thereby have facilitated the emergence and consolidation of a "nationalized" public sphere (Dalton and Wattenberg 2000).

Nevertheless, survey research on media consumption has also demonstrated that people tend to consume those media that are closest to their own cultural codes, be these codes ideological, class, linguistic, or lifestyle. Semiconsciously, individuals tend to seek consistency among their beliefs and values and avoid cognitive dissonance by filtering out, ignoring, or treating with scepticism sources of information and/or interpretive lenses that challenge or contradict their already-established convictions (Greenstein 1965; Eckstein 1988). In the same vein, albeit somewhat more controversially, some researchers contend that issues are affectively-charged, such that individuals hold feelings on most issues, even if they can't recall either the facts related to these issues or even the factors which led to the development of their feelings about them. Thus, as individuals encounter new information, they update their opinions, seeking out information that is consonant with their running tally and processing contrary information differently than affirming information (Lodge and Taber 2000; cf. Zaller 1992).

With respect to the diffusion of "national imaginaries," we can derive, for one, that the influence of media content will be stronger among primary groups which are privileged by nationalizing projects as compared to those which are marginalized by such projects. As a case in point, in societies that have not been nationally "homogenized," the media can be expected to reinforce support for a nationalist agenda among the group of reference to whom the territory allegedly "belongs". Second, we can also derive that children and adolescents will be more sensitive to nationalist narratives propagated in the media than adults.

The Bureaucracy

Alongside the educational system and the mass media, governmental bureaucracies are another important factor in the realization of hegemonic projects, including those of "nationalization" and "nation-building". Eric Hobsbawm (1990) and Eugen Weber (1976) have highlighted the extremely important role that conscripted armies of nineteenth- and twentieth-century Europe played in forging national imaginations and strong feelings of attachment and solidarity. Citizen armies produced such effects through two main mechanisms: (1) indoctrination of officers and conscripts; and (2) shared experiences of mutual aid and solidarity as well as suffering and pride in wartime. Today, conscripted armies are less common in advanced capitalist representative democracies. However, governmental bureaucracies are in some significant respects comparable, since they are state organizations that serve "national interest" and that forge a sense of *esprit de corps*. In fact, they are comparable in another respect as well. In the decades following the Second World War, in most advanced capitalist countries the size of the state grew substantially, due to the universalization of the provision of public education, public health and a wide array of other welfare policies (Esping-Andersen 1990). As a consequence, the proportion of social resources administered by – and the number of jobs depending on – the public sector increased dramatically.

Admittedly, the intensity of indoctrination characteristic of conscripted armies is difficult to find in today's public administration. Nevertheless, in the process of recruitment and training, public servants are usually compelled to learn a corpus of specialized rules. Moreover, promotion in the administrative ranks depends heavily upon successful internalization of a sense of "common good," "public service," and *esprit de corps*. Though the experience of bureaucrats is hardly comparable to that of soldiers who risk their lives in war, public servants definitely share experiences on the job, and assimilate standardized patterns of behaviour, codes and symbols associated with the social body for which they work and with which they come to identify (Weber 2013).

The shared experiences of bureaucrats also include their interaction with and intervention in the broader social environment of a given territory and population, in the pursuit of implementing what they perceive as public values. In addition, such shared experiences sometimes extend as well to competition with other organizations such as private administrations, rival governmental agencies, and "supra-national" organizations. The correspondence between administrative organizations and a given political community makes them prone to perceive themselves (and be perceived) as defenders of the community. In the context of such competition, it frequently occurs that public servants confound their particular, corporate interest with that of the public good. This is because the prospects for retaining their jobs and getting promoted are highly dependent upon the continuing existence and growth of the organization (cf. Linz 1993). A final relevant psychological factor is that, as implementers of the law, public servants tend to reduce their cognitive dissonance by adapting their belief systems to those of the legislative institutions.

All these tendencies render government bureaucrats privileged bearers of the concept of the state, and in "nationalizing states" this simultaneously makes them privileged bearers and disseminators of the "national ideal". They are particularly prone to disseminate their values among their networks of relatives and friends, thus comprising an even wider share of the population.

In multilingual contexts, the use of a given standardized language as an official language of state provides an additional basis for affinity between holders of bureaucratic office and nationalist ideology. In such contexts, passing an examination to demonstrate fluency in the standardized language employed by the administration is a key prerequisite for access to employment in bureaucratic posts. The advantages that fluent speakers of an official language experience in terms of their bureaucratic employment prospects provides them with a vested interest in the protection and promotion of the chosen vernacular (Gellner 1983, Hobsbawm 1990).

More generally, public sector agencies and staff, including bureaucrats as well as policemen and teachers, are both bearers and disseminators of the "national ideal". In their interactions with the citizenry, they help forge the "national imaginations" of the populations they serve. Primary and secondary school teachers play an especially important role in this respect. Moreover, even unintentionally, public administrations generate and transmit notions of political community as citizens interact with them on a daily basis. In other words, over the course of their lives, citizens experience the presence of the "national ideal" incarnated in the administrative structures with which they deal when, for instance, they comply with laws and regulations, pay taxes or fines, receive welfare and educational services, and take advantage of public infrastructure.

Political Parties

Finally, there is the ideological state apparatus of the political party. Parties are hierarchically-structured organizations that play a crucial role in the transmission of political ideologies, beliefs, and values both to party members and to targeted constituencies more generally. After the extension of the franchise to a majority of adult males and the subsequent advent of mass parties in Western Europe, such parties contributed substantially to the training of prospective political staff as well as to the supply of political information, interpretations, and identities to their wide mass of followers. This was the case of both social democratic and Christian democratic organizations. They achieved this not only directly through meetings with party members but also indirectly through the party press, youth branches, affiliated trade unions, and social centres, in which they shared the worldviews of the party (Duverger 1951/1963; Von Beyme 1985; Panebianco 1988; Przeworski and Sprague 1986; Dalton and Wattenberg 2002).

Although the compartmentalization of social groups associated with the era of mass parties was largely overcome with the arrival of the radio and television, parties still play a role in socializing wide swathes of the general public. For one, they continue to use their own organizational resources. Moreover, they also broadcast their messages through the mass media, and thereby manage to contribute to the process of agenda setting.

With respect to the diffusion of "national imaginaries," the embrace of political parties of a particular "nationalist agenda" or of a particular conceptualization of the "national interest," not to mention of particular "nationalizing" frames of reference – these all serve to "socialize" and/or "educate" party constituencies into a distinctly "national" point of view.

Because parties are organizations that are structured hierarchically, party leadership is susceptible to being captured by particular (usually relatively affluent) segments of the population with particular sensibilities, beliefs, and opinions – which do not necessarily reflect those of the rank and file of party members, much less the party's electoral constituency. A "principal-agent" problem is thus posed, by which the agents of representation could conceivably opt to pursue their own agendas, rather than represent the beliefs, preferences, or interests of their constituencies. Indeed, such a "principal-agent" problem has sometimes been considered a fundamental flaw of the representative-democratic ideal (notwithstanding its multiple interpretations as an ideal), perhaps most notoriously by Michels (1915/2001).

It follows that the leadership of the main parties in a given political system can be virtually monopolized by specific segments of the population in which adherence to a specific hegemonic agendas is strongest – including specific "nationalizing" or nation-building projects. The main parties can be captured by an "overwhelming minority" of sorts, organically linked with particular core constituencies. Conversely, the articulation of opposition to a hegemonic agenda can be effectively blocked within the hierarchical power structures of party organizations.

The capture of parties can in turn be reinforced by the co-opting and partial assimilation of exceptional 'representatives' hailing from different social backgrounds into the attitudes and preferences of those who dominate the political establishment. This pattern of adaptation can be interpreted in both psychological and sociological terms – as reflecting in part the distinctive psychic propensities for adaptation to dominant norms of upwardly-mobile "social climbers," and in part the distinctive social contexts in which such "climbers" are immersed. Consequently, such a pattern need not be a product of explicit ideological barriers to entry erected by party leadership. But the result is nevertheless much the same – insofar as the articulation of opposition to the nationalist agenda is effectively blocked by the dynamics of ascension within party hierarchies.

These dynamics of ascension are conditioned by institutional design, such as electoral laws. For instance, where competitive party politics takes place in a proportional system with closed party lists, individual representatives are not chosen directly by voters, but are instead appointed a place on a list by an electoral committee. Such a procedure entails a substantial concentration of power in the hands of the party bureaucracy.

Nevertheless, despite the susceptibility of the dynamics of ascension within parties to be conditioned by institutional design, the possibility of capture of leadership and representative positions by relatively privileged segments of the population remains strong. Indeed, it was precisely this concern that motivated Miliband's critique of the limits of democracy in the context of Great Britain's "representative" institutions. Miliband documented the extent to which the party hierarchies, parliamentary representatives, and state bureaucracy were manned by people who came from extremely privileged class and educational backgrounds; and he proceeded to argue that the organic links connecting the political and state representatives with the socio-economic elite effectively explained why the tensions between capitalism and democracy were nearly unanimously negotiated in terms highly favourable to the former, regardless of the party in power. Indeed, the relatively privileged class backgrounds, as well as educational and occupational trajectories, of political representatives have been documented across a wide spectrum of representative-democratic contexts (Putnam 1976; Miller et. al. 1999; Domhoff 2013).

The argument can be extended beyond the conflict between capitalism and socialism. This especially because other axes of political contention can overlap with and reinforce class cleavages. Where class cleavage overlaps with other social divisions, the relatively privileged segments of the population are prone to be significantly overrepresented amongst the political establishment and bureaucracy.

This argument is relevant for "nationalizing" and nation-building projects as well. Positions of power in hierarchically-organized party structures and highly-coveted representative posts can be captured by sympathizers of particular peoplehood projects. Such sympathizers can then use their strategic location to structure the terms of political contestation in such a way as to effectively exclude opposition to these peoplehood projects; and in so doing, they can effectively contribute to the construction of the "nation" (i.e. the institutionalization of nationalist hegemony) by "setting the agenda" and passing and implementing policies even in the absence of much in the way of popular support.

Conclusion

Despite the emergent nominal consensus in the academic literature in favour of the notion that nations are social constructs, few scholars have followed the call to treat the nation as a "category of practice" alone rather than to continue relying upon it as a category of analysis as well (Brubaker and Cooper

2000). Reification remains relatively ubiquitous in scholarly accounts of nations and nationalism. This chapter is intended as a corrective to such lingering essentialist tendencies.

A serious take on the claim that nations are ideological constructs requires both an understanding of the nature of ideology and concentration on processes of self-construction. This chapter provides theoretical clarification on both of these fronts. It also sketches an agenda for future research, by specifying the machinery of national construction and explaining its operation. More precisely, it focuses on four sets of Ideological state apparatuses directly implicated in the cultivation of "nationalizing" and "nation-building" hegemonic projects: (1) the educational system, (2) the mass media, (3) the bureaucracy, and (4) political parties. It calls upon scholars of nations and nationalism to focus on struggles to capture these state apparatuses as well as the workings of them, for the purpose of illuminating the dynamics of national construction.

NOTE

1   A portion of this essay was first published by *Peace in Kurdistan*, accessible at: https://www.peaceinkurdistancampaign.com/wp-content/uploads/2021/03/ Edition-2.Nationalism-and-the-State-March-2021.pdf

REFERENCES

Ahmed, Sarah, 2006. *Queer Phenomenology*. Durham, NC: Duke University Press.

Anderson, Benedict, 1983/2006. *Imagined Communities*. London: Verso.

Aronowitz, Stanley, 2002. "Gramsci's Theory of Education: Schooling and Beyond," In C. Borg, J. Buttigieg, & P. Mayo, eds., *Gramsci and Education*. Oxford: Rowman & Littlefield.

Balibar, Etienne, 1995/2007. *The Philosophy of Marx*. London: Verso.

Barrett, M. 2007, "Children's Knowledge, Beliefs and Feelings about Nations and National Groups: Essays," in *Developmental Psychology*. New York: Psychology Press.

Billig, Michael, 1995. *Banal Nationalism*. London: Sage Publications.

Bourdieu, Pierre, 1990. *The Logic of Practice*. Cambridge: Polity Press.

Brubaker, Rogers and Frederick Cooper, 2000. "Beyond Identity," *Theory and Society* 29: pp.1-47.

Buroway, Michael, 2003. "For a Sociological Marxism: The Complementary Convergence of Antonio Gramsci and Karl Polanyi," *Politics and Society*, 31(2): pp.193–261.

Butler, Judith, 1990/1999, *Gender Trouble. Feminism and the Subversion of Identity*. New York: Routledge.

Carnoy, Martin, 1984. *The State and Political Theory*. Princeton, NJ: Princeton University Press.

Chaffee, S.H. and S. Yang, 1990. "Communication and Political Socialization," in O. Ichilov, ed., *Political Socialization, Citizenship Education, and Democracy*. New York: Teachers College, Columbia University, pp.137-157.

Connolly, William, 1991/2002. *Identity/Difference*. Minneapolis, MN: University of Minnesota Press.

Dalton, R.S. and M.P. Wattenberg, eds., 2000. *Parties Without Partisans: Political Change in Advanced Industrial Democracies*. Oxford: Oxford University Press. pp.208-237.

Deacon, R., 2006. "Michel Foucault on Education: A Preliminary Theoretical Overview," *South African Journal of Education*, 26(2): pp.177–187.

Domhoff, G. William, 2013. *Who Rules America? The Triumph of the Corporate Rich*. Columbus, OH: McGraw-Hill Education.

Duverger, Maurice, 1951/1963. *Political Parties: Their Organization and Activity in the Modern State*. Hoboken, NJ: Wiley.

Eckstein, Harry, 1988. "A Culturalist Theory of Political Change," *The American Political Science Review.*, 82(3): pp.789-804.

Esping-Andersen, Gosta, 1990. *The Three Worlds of Welfare Capitalism*. Princeton, NJ: Princeton University Press.

Foucault, Michel, 1971. *Madness and Civilization*. London: Routledge.

Foucault, Michel, 1978/1990. *The History of Sexuality. Volume One*. New York: Vintage Books.

Foucault, Michel, 1979. *Discipline and Punish*. Harmondsworth: Penguin.

Foucault, Michel, 1988. "Technologies of the Self, in L.H. Martin, H. Gutman, and P.H. Hutton, eds., *Technologies of the Self: A Seminar with Michel Foucault*. Amherst: The University of Massachusetts Press.

Freire, Paolo, 1970/1972. *Pedagogy of the Oppressed*. Middlesex, England: Penguin Books.

Gellner, Ernest, 1983. *Nations and Nationalism*. Ithaca, NY: Cornell University Press.

Gardner, Peter R., 2015. "Bifurcated Education and Youth Identities in Northern Ireland". Chapter 3 of *Ethnolinguistic Mobilisation and Consociational Democracy: Ulster-Scots Education in Northern Ireland*. Ph.D. Dissertation, Department of Sociology, University of Cambridge.

Ghanem, Salma, 1997. Filling in the Tapestry: The Second Level of Agenda Setting. In M. McCombs, D. Shaw, and D. Weaver, eds., *Communication and Democracy: Exploring the Intellectual Frontiers in Agenda-Setting Theory*. Mahwah, NJ: Lawrence Erlbaum Associates. 3-14

Gramsci, Antonio, 1971. *Selections from the Prison Notebooks*. New York: International Publishers.

Greenstein, Fred I., 1965. *Children and Politics*. New Haven, CT: Yale University Press.

Harvey, David. 2005. *A Brief History of Neoliberalism*. Oxford: Oxford University Press.

Herman, Edward S. and Noam Chomsky, 1988. *Manufacturing Consent*. New York: Pantheon Books.

Hobsbawm, Eric, 1990. *Nations and Nationalism since 1780*. Cambridge, MA: Cambridge University Press.

Iyengar, Shanto and Donald R. Kinder, 1988. *News That Matters: Television and American Opinion*. Chicago, IL: University of Chicago Press.

Laclau, Ernesto and Chantal Mouffe, 1985. *Hegemony and Socialist Strategy*. London: Verso.

Lang, G.E. and Lang, K., 1981. "Watergate: An exploration of the agenda-building process," in G.C. Wilhoit and H. DeBock, eds., *Mass Communication Review Yearbook 2*. Newbury Park, CA: Sage. pp. 447-468.

Linz, Juan, 1993. "State building and nation building," *European Review* 1:4: pp.355-369.

Lodge, Milton and Charles S. Taber, 2000. "Three Steps Toward a Theory of Motivated Political Reasoning," in Arthur Lupia, Matthew McCubbins and Samuel Popkin, eds., *Elements of Reason*. Cambridge: Cambridge University Press, pp. 183-213.

Marx, Karl, 1845/1978. "The German Ideology," in Robert C. Tucker, ed. *The Marx-Engels Reader*. New York: Norton.

McCombs, M.E. and Shaw, D., 1972. "The Agenda-Setting Function of Mass Media," *Public Opinion Quarterly*, 36: pp.176-187.

Michels, Roberto, 1915/2001. *Political Parties. A Sociological Study of the Oligarchical Tendencies of Modern Democracy*. Kitchener, Ontario: Batoche Books.

Miller, Warren, R. Pierce, J. Thomassen, R. Herrera, S. Holmberg, P. Esaisson, and B. Wessels, eds., 1999. *Political Representation in Western Democracies*. Oxford: Oxford University Press.

Nietzsche, Friedrich, 1888/1992. *Ecce Homo*. London: Penguin Books.

Paige, Jeffery M., 2000. "Abstract Subjects: 'Class', 'Race', 'Gender', and Modernity," University of Michigan.

Panebianco, Angelo, 1988. *Political Parties: Organization and Power*. Cambridge: Cambridge University Press.

Percheron, Annik, 1982. "Religious Acculturation and Political Socialisation in France," *West European Politics*, 5(2): pp.8-31.

Przeworski, Adam and John Sprague, 1986. *Paper Stones*. Chicago: University of Chicago Press.

Putnam, Robert, 1976. *The Comparative Study of Political Elites*. Ontario: Pearson Education Canada.

Rokkan, Stein, 1971. "Nation-Building: A Review of Models and Approaches," *Current Sociology*, Vol. 19, No. 3: pp.7-38.

Stanford Encyclopedia of Philosophy, 2003/2013. "Michel Foucault," http://plato.stanford.edu/entries/foucault/.

Therborn, Göran, 1978/2008. *What Does the Ruling Class Do When it Rules?* London: Verso.

Therborn, Göran, 1980. *The Ideology of Power and the Power of Ideology*. London: Verso.

Weber, Max, 2013. "Bureaucracy," in G. Roth and C. Wittich, eds., *Economy and Society*. *Volume 2*. Berkeley, CA: The University of California Press, pp. 956-1005.

Von Beyme, Klaus, 1985 *Political Parties in Western Democracies*. Burlington, VT: Ashgate.

Zaller, John, 1992. *The Nature and Origins of Mass Opinion*. Cambridge: Cambridge University Press.

CHAPTER 3

Towards a New Internationalism[1]

The Critique of National Populism in Historical Perspective

The tyranny of capitalist social-property relations, ever more consolidated across the globe, leads humanity to perpetual war and ecological catastrophe. The very future of life on the planet is under threat, the cancerous contradiction between the imperative for growth built into capitalism and the finitude of natural resources ever more manifest. The entrenched obstacles to collective rationality that we must successfully surmount if we are to avoid a brutal and tragic denouement are immense and global in scope. We desperately need a new revolutionary internationalism, capable of coordinating and connecting local struggles against global capitalism and against related, intersecting systems of domination – of ethnicity and race, of gender, over nature. And yet, the spectre of nationalism continues to haunt hegemonic social imaginaries, thus hindering the urgent task of organizing anti-capitalist resistance both above and below the level of the nation-state.

Parts of the left move to embrace anew the tactic and strategy of national populism, when we need instead a thoroughgoing internationalism. We have seen such opportunist capitulation to the appeal of national chauvinism before, with devastating human consequences. There is no plausible reason to believe that riding the nationalist tiger again will lead to a socialist destination this time around. To the contrary, there are good reasons to be even more sceptical. Not only is the global scope and coordination of capitalist production, finance and, consequently, capitalist political dominance more intense and cohesive than ever before in history, a state of affairs sufficient to render promises of a renaissance of the "golden age" of social democracy smacks of utopianism. More disturbingly, so too are these neo-social-democratic agendas tainted by national chauvinist compromises, especially on matters of "foreign policy," that is, in relation to policies of neo-imperial intimidation, sanctions, violent aggression and natural resource plunder. Worse than compromise: complicity.

When the Worker Had No Country

In the middle of the nineteenth century, Marx and Engels could famously declare that "the worker has no country". The origins of working class internationalism lie in the absence of political representation and of material integration into the nation-state. The working class was at first beneath and beyond the nation. Its nationalization took place rather late in the day, in the last decades of the nineteenth century, and especially in the first decades of the twentieth. Compulsory education for the purposes of creating a literate and nationalized pool of labour; recruitment into war machines capable of mobilizing masses for suicidal sacrifice in total war – these were the motives and mechanisms that underpinned and propelled forward the "nationalization" of the masses throughout much of the capitalist core. "Nationalization" and state-propagated nationalisms were the products of deliberate decisions made by rulers commanding rival ships of state across the stormy seas in an era marked by creeping democratization, capitalist and imperialist expansion, and looming inter-imperialist war.

As Hobsbawm has eloquently insisted, during this era, all versions of nationalism that "came to the fore" had *one* thing in common: "a rejection of the new proletarian socialist movements, not only because they were proletarian, but also because they were, consciously and militantly *internationalist*, or at the very least non-nationalist". Indeed, in the crucial prelude to the unprecedented level of human destruction of the so-called Great War, mass nationalism competed directly for appeal amidst a host of rival *ideologies* – "notably, class-based socialism" – which, tragically, it vanquished.

The Second International succumbed to the opportunism of social democracy, and to the intimately connected contagion of nationalism. Working class solidarity was undermined by the machinations of divide and conquer, crushed in the context of inter-imperial rivalry, and buried in the trenches of the First World War.

In the paradigmatic case of Germany, Rosa Luxemburg famously diagnosed and sought to explain opportunism as a fundamental obstacle to the victory of revolutionary struggle, as a pathological but historical phenomenon, which she persuasively interpreted, through the lens of historical materialism, as related to the infiltration of a creeping petit-bourgeois mentality by the growth of the Social Democratic party and its corresponding bureaucratization. The arc of the party's organizational trajectory was thus: from a small group of professional revolutionaries to an ever-bigger bunch of reformist bureaucrats.

This was a trajectory which mirrored and corresponded with the growth of the state itself in Germany, and indeed, across much of Europe and North America, in the so-called "capitalist core," from the third quarter of the nineteenth century, and that continued with an ever-more militarist bent with the onset of the age of imperial scramble.

Only the most revolutionary, who were by no coincidence among the most profound theorists and thorough-going critics of imperialism, most prominently Lenin and Luxemburg, but also all the individuals and organizations involved in the Zimmerwald movement, held true to internationalist principles; only they proved capable of resisting the hegemonic current towards "national integration" and ultimately capitulation before the warring idols of the nation.

Where was the mass mutiny? Where was the will to resist a meaningless and brutal death? Where was the solidarity among the workers of the world? Where was their will to unite, to break the chains that bound them together, despite and across national boundaries? Even Luxemburg's faith was shaken by the outbreak of war, causing her, from the prison cell in which she would pen her *Junius Pamphlet*, to double down, or up the ante, formulating the alternatives in the famous phrase "socialism or barbarism" – a phrase which she attributed to Engels.

If, and only if, out of the ashes of the catastrophe, the phoenix of the world revolution were to arise, then, and only then, could humanity avoid an endless descent into "barbarism," a telling term in its own right. A world revolution, nothing less, was what anti-capitalist internationalists believed the necessary outcome and denouement of the contradictions, the crisis, the total war. The alternative was simply unthinkable, or at least unspeakable, for them.

The Russian Revolution and the World Revolution

The Russian Revolution, when it came, was hailed among internationalists – Luxemburg, Trotsky, and Lenin alike – as a precursor and trigger for world revolution. Such was the criterion upon which all the most prominent revolutionaries – in the Marxist tradition, at least – agreed was most relevant for judging the ultimate success or failure of the "local" revolution: whether it served to set off the world revolution.

All the great Marxist internationalists concurred: the revolution to overthrow capitalism was bound to be global in scope. Lenin, for certain, had a very hard time conceiving of the prospect of a Russian revolution without "further repercussions," "abandoned to itself". Indeed, as Paul Mattick pointed out long ago, Lenin seemed to assume "that the onslaught of the imperialist nations against the Bolsheviks would break the back of the Russian revolution if the proletariat of Western Europe failed to come to the rescue".

However, when the world revolution in fact failed to materialise, the Bolshevik party in power did not put down its weapons and simply give up. Instead, it proceeded to improvise, to further fasten its grip on the levers of power, its fusion with the state apparatus, and ultimately to forge ahead with the project of "socialism in one country". A hyper-centralized dictatorship of the Bolshevik party in a one-party state; and within the party, a hyper-centralised dictatorship of the Central Committee over the members; and within the Central Committee, a hyper-centralised dictatorship of the Chair. In sum, a dictatorship of the party, over the proletariat, and over the population more generally. This was the governing model of Marxist-Leninist democratic centralism in practice, in the USSR., and, with some variation, in all the states where Marxism-Leninism subsequently came to power, most frequently transforming into state capitalist "*developmentalist*" dictatorships. A tyrannical model, a far cry from human emancipation as envisioned, for example, in Marx's early writings, or for that matter, in his depiction of the dictatorship of the proletariat in his later work on the Paris Commune; or even as envisioned by Lenin in *State and Revolution*, on the eve of the Bolshevik seizure of power.

Luxemburg against Bolshevism

If only Luxemburg had lived! There is a case to be made that her martyrdom, along with that of her comrade Karl Liebknecht, in January of 1919, marks a world-historic turning point, a critical juncture at which the world revolutionary tide began definitively to ebb, and the countervailing forces of fascism began to gain momentum instead. In the wake of her martyrdom, Luxemburg's image was elevated to the status of sacred, hoisted amid the revolutionary pantheon; but too often, her fierce polemics against the opportunistic and tyrannical tendencies inherent in the Bolshevik model have been altogether ignored, when not patronizingly dismissed.

But Red Rosa was certainly right in her early criticism of the Bolshevik organizational form for its authoritarian structure and style, its promotion of "blind subordination, in the smallest details, of all party organs, to the party centre, which alone, thinks and decides for all" – a criticism she first formulated as far back as 1904. Though it is more controversial to say so, Red Rosa was also more right than wrong in her tenacious opposition to nationalism in all its manifestations. She, not the Bolsheviks, proved the more "far-sighted about the dangers lurking in nationalism for revolutionary internationalism". She was indeed correct to emphasise the link between Bolshevik opportunism and its espousal of the dogma of national self-determination, a piercing criticism for which she has been much caricatured and maligned. Not that Luxemburg was opposed to national freedom; she was not. As Talmon pointed out, she was just more honest, more sober, more incisive than the Bolsheviks in her two-pronged assessment that (1) "[s]ocialism could not be reached via national liberation struggles;" and, inversely, that (2) "[n]ational freedom could be obtained only through an international social revolution"; together, these led her to espouse the programmatic conclusion that (3) "[t]he first and categorical imperative was therefore to sink all national differences and to unite in a common anti-imperialist front". Easier said than done; more difficult to practice than to preach.

The First World War and the Bolshevik revolution may not have spread across Europe and triggered the world revolution, as its protagonists had initially hoped and believed it should. But it did certainly contribute to the percolation of anti-colonial consciousness throughout the colonized world – with the conscription of colonial subjects into Imperial armies playing a significant part in the process. As Timothy Mitchell has emphasised, "Lenin's declaration the day after taking power that 'any nation that desires independence' should be allowed 'to determine the form of its state life by free voting'" definitely had a broad appeal among the colonized, and beyond; indeed, it "echoed wider campaigns, emerging across several continents, against the violence and injustice of Empire".

After all, Lenin's own theory of imperialism was largely derivative of the work of J.A. Hobson, the British liberal who provided the seemingly paradoxical connection between Lenin's ideas about self-determination and those of Woodrow Wilson. Hobson had "supported the Afrikaner republics that Britain defeated in the South African war," and had befriended the Afrikaner military and political leader Jan Smuts, "who fought the British but then negotiated the incorporation of the Boer republics into the Union of South Africa," and who later joined his 'old friend' on the British war cabinet "to participate in framing the post-war settlement". Indeed, as Mitchell has provocatively but compellingly argued, it was Smuts who would "in fact guide the formulation of the 'ideal' of self-determination later attributed to Woodrow Wilson". The model for self-determination in practice? None other than "[t]he development of self-government in South Africa, which became a method of empowering whites and further disempowering non-whites". The experience of the Boer republics thus shaped "the wider solution to the claims of subject populations after the First World War," in a way that subtly transformed "the demand for democratization into the very different principle of self-determination, or 'the consent of the governed". The regime of self-determination as an alternative to more thorough-going democratic demands, as an efficient means to fend off the threat and the spectre of an emergent global demos; in sum, decolonization as a re-equilibration and transition to a neo-colonial global system of "decentralized despotism," to invoke Mamdani's most suggestive term.

Luxemburg, like no other, saw right through the pious cant about self-determination. She cogently insisted, against Lenin, in no uncertain terms, that "[s]o long as capitalist States endure, particularly so long as Imperialist world-politics determines and gives form to the inner and outer life of the States, the national right of self-determination has not the least thing in common with their practice either in war or in peace". Nor did she refrain from drawing far-sighted conclusions from this analysis, urgently appealing to her fellow revolutionaries to resist at all costs the siren song of the nation, clairvoyant in her warning that "any socialist policy which fails to take account of this definite historical level and which in the midst of the world vortex lets itself be governed merely by the isolated viewpoints of a single country is doomed in advance" (Mattick, p.23). A more concise description and diagnosis of the inherent limits of the tactics, strategies, and (lack of) principles destined to be pursued by the Third International would indeed be hard to find.

To side with Luxemburg against Lenin on the matter of self-determination of course begs the question of the relationship between revolutionary internationalism and anti-imperialism. One could argue, with Mattick, that anti-capitalist internationalism must certainly be anti-imperialist; but at this point in history, we simply can no longer afford to delude ourselves into thinking that putting an end to imperialism can be achieved by any other means than by destroying the capitalist system in the so-called "advanced capitalist core". In the absence of such destruction, we can rest assured, sooner or later, "'[l]iberation' from one type of imperialism leads to subordination to another".

Reading Luxemburg with Fanon

In his May 2018 article in *Al Jazeera*, Hamid Dabashi called Luxemburg "an unsung hero of postcolonial theory". This perhaps takes the point too far; but Luxemburg's revolutionary internationalism certainly has a lot more in common with later postcolonial thinkers than is too often assumed. Emblematically, with Frantz Fanon, who lived long enough to witness the "pitfalls of national consciousness," to see with his own eyes that "nationalism, that magnificent song that made the people rise against their oppressors, stops short, falters, and dies away on the day that independence is proclaimed". Indeed, he was particularly acute in his observations about the degeneration of party politics in the post-colonial context, in his denouncement of nascent national despotism and creeping corruption. As Dabashi astutely surmised:

"After independence, the party sinks into an extraordinary lethargy. The militants are only called upon when so-called manifestations are afoot, or international conferences, or independence celebrations. The local party leaders are given administrative posts, the party becomes an administration, and the militants disappear into the crowd and take the empty title of citizen ... After a few years, the break-up of the party becomes obvious, and any observer, even the most superficial, can notice that the party, today the skeleton of its former self, only serves to immobilize the people. The party, which during the battle had drawn to itself the whole nation, is falling to pieces. The intellectuals who on the eve of independence rallied to the party, now make it clear by their attitude that they gave their support with no other end in view than to secure their slices of the cake of independence. The party is becoming a means of private advancement".

Even so, Fanon remained perhaps overly optimistic in his formulation of the remedy for this collective ill, in what now appears a rather naïve prescription: "If you really want your country to avoid regression, or at best halts and uncertainties, a rapid step must be taken from national consciousness to political and social consciousness" (p.163). In retrospect, Smuts and Hobson were more realistic, in their judgment that national consciousness was the precise antidote and alternative necessary for fending off and domesticating the prospects of revolutionary internationalist challenges to the tyranny of global capitalism, for translating and transforming threatening claims about global justice into more innocuous matters of international charity.

Less naïve on Fanon's part were his two additional, related points of counsel: the first, about the vital urgency of the task of "political education;" the second, intimately related point, about the need for "decentralization in the extreme". To open peoples' minds, to "awaken them," means nothing else, for Fanon, than "allowing the birth of their intelligence". This task cannot be confused with "making a political speech". It means, on the contrary, "to try, relentlessly and passionately, to teach the masses that everything depends on them; that if we stagnate it is their responsibility, and that if we go forward it is due to them too". To put such revolutionary pedagogy into practice, Fanon continues, "in order really to incarnate the people," extreme decentralization is essential.

A political education into self-determination, understood and practiced, literally, as taking matters into one's own hands. This is Fanon's radically decentralizing spin on self-determination. It constitutes a crucial, dialectical counterpart to Luxemburg's emphasis on thoroughgoing, revolutionary internationalism.

Imagining Community beyond the Confines of the Nation

The nation as a mystified basis of community has not only defeated revolutionary, class-based alternatives at multiple critical junctures over the course of the past century; so too has it been institutionalised and thus reified in the educational system, the mass media, the state bureaucracy, as well as by political parties, including the representatives of social democracy. The forces of social democracy, along with their allies in the trade union movement, were together responsible for many of the democratic limits to commodification imposed upon capitalism, especially in the north and west of Europe, in the decades after the Second World War, when social rights expanded, provided by the welfare state. Yet, such accommodation came at a price – namely, the disorganization and depoliticization of the working class, their progressive conversion into passive spectators of politics at most, more often than not, into mere consumers. This waning, if not death, of class consciousness helped paved the way for the subsequent victory of neoliberalism, the triumph of the cult of the market, not to mention the resurgence of the cult of the nation.

The manifold ways in which national consciousness has been institutionalized, reinforced by the frequent appeals of political elites to supremacist, exclusionary, and patriarchal conceptions of national belonging, for the purposes of dividing and conquering the exploited and oppressed, have effectively hindered the popularity and salience of feelings of transnational empathy, solidarity, loyalty, community, and belonging.

In sum, the cult of the nation constricts and constrains the horizons of our collective consciousness. It thus undermines our capacity for exercising collective rationality in the face of the urgent social and political problems we must confront together, as members of the human race, if we are to stand a chance of successfully transforming global constellations of social-property relations. Such a transformation is urgently needed not just for the sake of justice. The privileges of the plutocrats, the tyrants, and the war-mongers must be checked, they must be held accountable, because their greed, their lust for power, their lethal ineptitude and their colossal irresponsibility are literally threatening the future of life on our planet. But so long as the cult of the nation continues to mystify our consciousness, we will remain disempowered, or worse, we will remain complicit, condemned to aiding and abetting their crimes.

There is a long history of crimes committed in the name of the nation, especially in the name of those nations that can be classified as "Great Powers". In fact, the crimes of the past can in large part account for the "Great Power" status of some nation-states today. In this sense, these crimes do not remain in the past, but live on in the present. And they live on in another sense as well: for the lies and propaganda employed to justify the crimes of the past continue to resonate in the present, even when they are not explicitly repeated and defended, but simply downplayed and whitewashed, or even covered over in an attempt to induce historical amnesia. When not confronted directly and deliberately deconstructed in the name of truth and more than mere reconciliation, in the pursuit of just compensation, the lies and propaganda inherited from the past will continue to weigh on the collective guilty conscience. They will continue to contaminate the collective subconscious and they will thus inevitably seep into, be inflected and reflected in, the contours of contemporary collective consciousness. This is why conflicts and taboos about collective memory are never just about how the past is remembered, but are instead so often central to struggles for hegemony in the present, pitting those committed to the preservation of the status quo against those committed to alternative projects seeking to contest and transform existing constellations of material and social power relations. "The tradition of all dead generations weighs like a nightmare on the brains of the living".

People on the left must denounce in no uncertain terms any and all concessions to resurgent national chauvinism. Once again, workers must come to realize that they have no country. The transnational cohesion and global coordination of the capitalist class has effectively outflanked and progressively undermined the class compromises and limits to commodification that had been negotiated and institutionalised at the level of the nation-state in response to the collective demands of organized labour. As a consequence, the working class finds itself ever more disorganized, un-incorporated, disenfranchised. Now, more than ever, it is scattered across the globe, multi-ethnic in composition, below and beyond the nation. If the class struggle is to be reignited, both locally and globally, it is imperative that it reorganize and re-articulate itself accordingly.

NOTES

1 This chapter was first published by *Roar Magazine*. Issue #8, *Beyond the Border* (October 2018), pp.102-115. Accessible at: https://roarmag.org/magazine/towards-new-internationalism/ A Spanish version is accessible at: https://rojavaazadi madrid.org/hacia-un-nuevo-internacionalismo/ The original draft of the article contains a substantially different ending veering toward liberation theology is published by *Peace in Kurdistan* in its series on self-determination. Accessible at: https://www.peaceinkurdistancampaign.com/wp-content/uploads/2021/04/PIK-Issue-2-Towards-a-New-Internationalism-April-2021.pdf

CHAPTER 4

Rosa Luxemburg's Living Legacy[1]

Prologue

The author had the opportunity to visit Rojava in December of 2014, when the siege on Kobane, Syria was still under way. The heroic resistance of the people there, their will to struggle in self-defence, in defence of their revolution, was of world-historical significance. It rekindled a revolutionary flame, it awoke a long-slumbering revolutionary imagination. Indeed, the Kurdish Freedom Movement, a movement never co-opted, never defeated, kept the flame of world revolution alive. Inspired by the philosophy and example of Abdullah Öcalan, chained to the rock of Imrali for twenty years now, whose contribution to revolutionary thought and praxis, whose critique of hierarchy in all its manifestations, whose persistent efforts to transcend the nationalist paradigm of liberation, whose powerful and persuasive re-articulation, re-definition, of self-determination as democracy against the state, whose democratic-confederal ideals and model, constitute an act of resistance and intellectual achievement of epic proportions, reminiscent of revolutionary heroes of a bygone era.

On one of the walls at a women's academy there hung a portrait of Rosa Luxemburg. The portrait was not out of place. For Red Rosa is one of the great revolutionary martyrs, perhaps the most famous woman revolutionary of all time. And like so many women in the Kurdish Freedom Movement, Red Rosa fought and died for a distinctly libertarian revolutionary ideal, for an ideal of world revolution that could only begin, that had to begin, with a revolution in consciousness.

This chapter is intended as a modest contribution to such a desperately-needed revolution in consciousness, an attempt to "wrest tradition away from conformism" (Benjamin), in commemoration of the hundredth anniversary of Luxemburg's untimely death, an explication of the many ways in which her legacy endures.

Introduction

More than 100 years after Rosa Luxemburg's murder, it is worth emphasizing the ways in which her legacy remains very much alive. In this – an apocalyptic – age, when we are forced to confront an ongoing, Orwellian war on terror, which has done much to provoke a resurgence of the far-right around the globe, when "national" and "transnational" governing institutions have been thoroughly co-opted by a plutocratic clique determined to plunder the globe, when the spectre of climate catastrophe begins to unfold, Luxemburg's thought and her praxis, her principled articulation and embodiment of a distinctly anti-dogmatic, libertarian and thoroughgoing, internationalist version of Marxism, provides an invaluable intellectual resource, a source of inspiration, and she herself, a desperately-needed role model for those of us still committed to the struggle against capitalism and Imperialism.

Red Rosa, the revolutionary martyr, the woman who first made famous the phrase "Socialism or Barbarism," whose earthly fate - shot in the head, dumped in the Landwehr Canal – was certainly an early indicator of which of the two alternatives was destined to come out on top in the twentieth century, and indeed, may even have helped tip the balance against Socialism, in favour of Barbarism. And yet, her ideals and her example, are more relevant now than ever, for us in the twenty-first century, in an age in which the complicity and defeat of social democracy have been rendered increasingly transparent, after the crimes of state communism even blurred the very distinction between "socialism" and "barbarism" in the eyes of so many.

Barbarism is, of course, a loaded term – one whose very use reflects and perpetuates a still deeply ingrained modernist prejudice, the binary pitting "civilization" against "savagery," a binary which long served, and continues to serve, to legitimate and justify imperial conquest, pillage and plunder. But Luxemburg was certainly no apologist for imperialism. To the contrary, her acute analysis of the contradictions of capitalism was centrally concerned with the theory (and critique) of Imperialism. And indeed, her formulation is even subversive, insofar as she implies that socialism is civilization's last chance, that failure to overcome capitalism will mean nothing short of civilizational collapse.

So too did her formulation prove prophetic, insofar as she glimpsed, albeit for but a moment, from behind prison bars, beyond the bounds of her epistemic certainty, of her faith, in the inevitability of the victory of socialism. The outbreak of the First World War had shaken her conviction to the core.

Strictly speaking, the possibility of civilizational collapse, of "common ruin," did not lie beyond the parameters of the Marxist imaginary. In point of fact, towards the very beginning of the *Communist Manifesto*, just after Marx and Engels declare the class struggle to be the hermeneutic key for unlocking the mysteries of all history, or at least the mysteries of all written history, the founding fathers of historical materialism go on to explicitly add that, across this long span of (written) history, the battle between oppressor and oppressed had "each time ended, either in a revolutionary re-constitution of society at large, or in the common ruin of contending classes".[2] Revolutionary re-constitution or common ruin as alternative outcomes, alternative possibilities, for the class struggle had thus been envisioned from the start, recognized in the movement's founding document, revealed in its sacred text. And indeed, Luxemburg attributes the formulation she rendered famous to none other than Engels himself.

And yet, if anything had characterized the Marxist mentality from its inception all the way up through the outbreak of the Great War, it was its steely confidence, the unflinching conviction, that the future belonged to socialism, that victory was inevitable, that the demise of capitalism was foreordained. Not just in one country, but on a global scale.

The Great War changed things forever. It was a calamity of unprecedented proportions, no doubt, though not one whose outbreak Luxemburg had failed to anticipate. She sniffed out the SPD's – and Kautsky's – ever-increasing opportunism a lot sooner than others, and so could see right through her party's appeals to "peace utopias," could denounce her party's creeping inclination to capitulate to the machinations and manoeuvres of the right, to militarism, to nationalism, and, ultimately, to war. Indeed, as early as 1911, she had insisted that the only way to avoid the outcome of war was through the outbreak of revolution, and that therefore the party's main priority and mes-sage should be "ruthlessly to scatter all illusions with regards to attempts made at peace on the part of the bourgeoisie".[3]

Even so, the onset of the war proved quite the shock to her system. Accord-ing to her comrade and first biographer, Paul Frölich:

> "The capitulation of German Social Democracy, its desertion to the im-perialist camp, the resultant collapse of the International, indeed the seeming collapse of her whole world, shattered her spirit. For a moment – probably the only time in her life – she was seized by despair. But only for a moment! She immediately pulled herself together, and by a sheer act of will, overcame her sudden sense of weakness".[4]

The workers of the world were destined to unite. Why, then, had they so stubbornly insisted on clinging to their chains instead, even to the point of opting for meaningless and brutal death in the trenches? Why had they been so easily seduced by all the lies and propaganda, by all the appeals to national glory? Why could they not understand that the worker has no country?

Outside and Against the Nation

Contrary to what has too often been suggested, Luxemburg was no naïve op-timist about the spontaneous inclination or propensity of the working class to overcome the blinders of the nation. Not in the least. Rather, her implacable hostility towards nationalism in all its manifestations was motivated by a deep-seated recognition of its powerful allure and therefore its destructive potential. She was well aware, more aware than all the others, and rightly afraid, of its ideological efficacy when it came to dividing and conquering workers. She rightly realized the nation to be the main alternative, the most fundamental danger, the biggest obstacle to the elevation of class conscious-ness, to the cultivation of class loyalties, both within and beyond the confines of state boundaries.

Luxemburg was a triple outsider. A woman, a Jew, a Pole; but at the same time, on intimate terms with the leaders of German social democracy, her charisma and intellectual acumen was recognized by friend and foe alike from very early on. Her solidly middle-class background and doctoral degree no doubt facilitated her ability to connect with the German party leaders, despite their differences. So, perhaps more precisely, she was a triple outsider-insider, an immigrant at home among an inner circle of professional activists, bourgeois socialist agitators, leaders of an oppositional party that conjured and claimed to represent the working class.

This outsider-insider status no doubt helped render Luxemburg uniquely immune to the twin temptations of either espousing big-nation chauvinism or embracing the dogma of self-determination. Her positionality granted her an epistemic privilege, as social theorists would say today. She could see through the nationalist blinders and illusions of both camps. Outside the nation, she proved capable of seeing beyond it. Indeed, as Whitehall argued: "Her marginal status arguably shaped her empathy for community in its international orientation of borderless solidarity, propelled by and for the global proletariat". Moreover, recovering her perspective allows us to glimpse "the richness of the contests for self-determination before the ideal settled according to liberal priorities after the war".[5]

Luxemburg's initial splash in the Second International came at a congress held in London in 1896 when, at the tender age of 25, she eloquently and vehemently objected to a resolution in favour of Polish independence, arguing against "providing an effective cover for social patriotism's total lack of any scientific basis," against "raising it to the level of dogma". Her opposition to the prospect of Polish independence not only contradicted the position of the founding fathers of historical materialism; it would bring her into conflict with the leading lights of both German and Russian socialism, with Kautsky, with Liebknecht the elder, with Plekhanov, and with Lenin, on multiple occasions over the years. But it was an issue on which she would never waver; nor would her passion ever wane. She would return to it again and again, to articulate and reconfirm her consistent and principled point of view.

As for her discrepancy with Marx and Engels on the subject, she brushed off all accusations of heresy or sacrilege with a counter-attack against dogmatic modes of thought. As she would succinctly put the point in her 1915 *Anti-Critique*: "It has always been the privilege of the 'epigones' to take fertile hypotheses, turn them into rigid dogma, and be smugly satisfied, where a pioneering mind is filled with creative doubt".[6] Or, in a somewhat more direct and elaborate formulation, from a decade earlier, in a foreword she wrote for an anthology on "The Polish Question and the Socialist Movement," where she patiently explained the difference between historical materialism as fluid method of analysis and point of departure versus historical materialism as rigid dogma and foregone conclusion:

> "[T]he vital core, the quintessence, of the entire Marxist doctrine is the dialectical materialist method of social inquiry, a method for which no phenomena, or principles, are fixed and unchanging, for which there is no dogma, for which Mephistopheles' comment, 'reason turns to madness, kindness to torment', stands as a motto over the affairs of human Society; and for which every historical 'truth' is subject to a perpetual and remorseless criticism by actual historical developments".[7]

She was no dogmatist; but she was no revisionist either. She was first and foremost a *revolutionary* Marxist, committed to the overthrow of capitalism on a global scale. Her revolutionary Marxism was firmly rooted in a liberationist but "orthodox" interpretation of the core of the historical materialist faith – an interpretation grounded in a conscientious commitment to the "ruthless criticism of everything existing", along with a visceral rejection of opportunism.

Indeed, it is the visceral rejection of opportunism that united her critique of nationalism with her critique of revisionism, and of its associated pathology, "parliamentary cretinism". As Nettl has explained, for Luxemburg the program of national self-determination was but the first of her "many indices of opportunism which tied socialism to the chariot of the class enemy".[8]

Between Anarchism and Opportunism

From her debut on the German scene, Luxemburg cut her teeth and made her mark as a thorough-going critic of opportunism in both the theory and praxis of the SPD. As Mattick has contended, of all the attacks on revisionism, hers were the most powerful.[9] In her famous polemic against Bernstein, she diagnosed his "opportunist theory" as "nothing else than an unconscious attempt to assure predominance to the petty bourgeois elements" that had infiltrated the party, attracted by its inexorable electoral advances, like bears to honey.[10] In this respect, her analysis anticipated and converged with Michels' perceptive observations about the "iron law of oligarchy". But unlike Michels, she never turned against parliamentary politics *tout court*.

Luxemburg was eloquent and persuasive in her warnings against those who espoused "the method of legislative reform *in place of and in contradistinction to* the conquest of political power and social revolution". She insisted that such a manoeuvre did not mean merely opting for "a more tranquil, calmer and slower road to the *same* goal, but a *different* goal". The "realization of socialism" was reduced to the more limited task of reforming capitalism. From courageously "taking a stand for a new society," the party is transformed into simply "taking a stand for a surface modification of the old society". Rather than seeking to eradicate the crisis-prone capitalist system underpinning and driving the perpetuation of oppressive social relations, the party comes to accommodate itself comfortably within the system, to lower the bar of its demands, to seek only to assuage the worst of the system's abuses.[11]

In this sense, Luxemburg was the consummate "orthodox" Marxist, a revolutionary who remained true to Marx's aspiration for human emancipation, conceived as fundamentally incompatible with life under capitalism, regardless of the level of one's wages. As Marx had insisted in his youth, when he was still more inclined to employ philosophical and moral modes of argumentation, better payment for the wage-slave would not and could not mean the same thing as the conquest of "human status and dignity" by the worker.[12] (Though, tellingly, Marx wrote *for* the worker, not *by* the worker).

For that matter, she also remained true to Marx's (and Engels') early and unflinching belief that the struggle for representative democracy constitutes a first step in the struggle for socialism. She argued, like Therborn would much later, that representative democratic institutions are themselves best understood as the product and reflection of the contradictions of capitalism, and that, inevitably, within the arena of "bourgeois parliamentarianism, class antagonism and class domination are not done away with, but are, on the contrary, displayed in the open".[13]

Access to, and operation within, the parliamentary arena proves "necessary and indispensable to the working class" nonetheless. Necessary "because it creates the political forms, (autonomous administration, electoral rights, etc.)

which will serve the proletariat as fulcrums in its task of transforming bourgeois society". Indispensable because "only through the exercise of its democratic rights, in the struggle for democracy, can the proletariat become aware
of its class interests and its historic task". Whereas Bernstein and the revisionists conceived of parliamentary politics as an alternative route to socialism,
an alternative to revolution, Luxemburg insisted instead that such an arena
is valuable insofar as it paves the way for the revolutionary "conquest of
power".[14] It does so both (1) by providing necessary political forms and (2)
by facilitating the indispensable spread and promotion of revolutionary class
consciousness.

Here her argument proved overly optimistic, at least as a prediction of
the trajectory that awaited Social Democracy, in which the trend of opportunism among the leadership and the weight of national consciousness
among the workers proved capable of fending off the spectre of revolutionary class consciousness among sufficiently broad swathes of the German
working class. And yet, as a set of guidelines for the proper aims, goals, and
necessary limits of participation in the parliamentary arena, it remains nevertheless most instructive.

Revolution as Process

Make no mistake: Luxemburg was by no means sanguine about the enormous
effort that would be required, and the enormous difficulty of achieving victory, regardless of her confidence that the winds of history were blowing in a
definite direction. And not the one that Benjamin glimpsed a few decades
later, after the outbreak of the Second World War. Indeed, in her polemic
against Bernstein and the revisionists, she went to great lengths to charge
them of precisely the sin of underestimating just how perilous and complicated "a transformation as formidable as the passage from capitalist society
to socialist society" was bound to be, at least to the extent that they could be
judged sincere, that they really believed the sand-castle of arguments they
had so studiously constructed.

As Luxemburg points out, the revisionists suggest that socialism could be
introduced through the passage of parliamentary legislation, "in one happy
act," so long as the party remains patient, so long as it doesn't play its hand

too early. But this smooth and peaceful, legal route to socialist transformation envisioned by the revisionists is in fact "impossible to imagine". To the contrary, she cogently contends, "socialist transformation supposes a long and stubborn struggle, in the course of which, it is quite probable, the proletariat will be repulsed more than once, so that the first time, from the viewpoint of the final outcome of the struggle, it will necessarily come to power 'too early'".[15]

Luxemburg diagnosed and sought to explain opportunism as a fundamental obstacle to the victory of revolutionary struggle, as a pathological but historical phenomenon, through the lens of historical materialism, as related to the infiltration of a creeping petit-bourgeois mentality by the growth of the party and its corresponding bureaucratization. The arc of the party's organizational trajectory was thus: from a small group of professional revolutionaries to an ever-bigger bunch of reformist bureaucrats.

This was a trajectory which mirrored and corresponded with the growth of the state itself in Germany, and indeed, across much of Europe and North America, in the so-called "capitalist core," from the third quarter of the nineteenth century, and that continued with an ever-more militarist bent with the onset of the age of Imperial scramble. This was a subject about which Luxemburg would have much to say, most elaborately in her 1913 book *The Accumulation of Capital*.

Despite the clear trend towards creeping opportunism imposed by increasing bureaucratization, Luxemburg pinned her hopes on the potential for ever-more elements of the working class to wake up, to come to realise a revolutionary destiny. She hoped this counter-trend could flourish as the contradictions of capitalism in the age of imperialism inevitably sharpened, and crisis inevitably ensued.

She was well aware that "the forward march of the proletariat, on a world historic scale, to its final victory" would not be "so simple a thing". But forward it was bound to march. Its revolutionary *will* was bound to be forged in struggle. Indeed, it could only be formed "*in opposition* to the ruling classes," in "a constant struggle against the existing order". A constant struggle capable of conjuring a collective *will*, "from outside the present society," from the future perhaps, or at least, from "beyond the existing society". The movement for social democracy, its role conceived as helping the "broad popular masses" recognize "an aim reaching beyond the existing social order," as coordinating, linking, uniting their "daily struggle with the great world transformation". In this process, the movement "must logically grope" between "two rocks: abandoning the mass character of the party or abandoning its final aim, falling into bourgeois reformism or sectarianism, anarchism or opportunism".[16]

The juxtaposition Luxemburg draws between anarchism and opportunism, her portrayal of them as two opposite and "extreme deviations," two temptations to be avoided or surmounted, is noteworthy.[17] It helps her situate her position, in Aristotelian fashion, as a golden mean of sorts. Whereas the anarchists objected to any and all participation in the realm of parliamentary politics, on the one side, and the opportunists would reduce all politics to the parliamentary arena, on the other, Luxemburg advances a vision of tactics and strategy for the movement for social democracy that embraces parliamentary activity as a necessary but insufficient step in the process of forging revolutionary consciousness. Electoral politics as an opportunity to evangelise, to spread the Good News of socialism among "the masses," as a platform for consciousness-raising, for engaging in revolutionary pedagogy. But never for playing the role of *loyal* opposition, much less for harbouring or nurturing illusions about an eventual transition to socialism via legislative reform.

As Mattick has succinctly summarised Luxemburg's position in the longstanding, too-often oversimplified, too-often binary debate about revolution versus reform:

"[R]evolutionary Marxism, too, fights to improve the workers' situation within capitalist society. But in contrast to revisionism, it is interested far more in how the fight is conducted than in the immediate objectives. To Marxism the matter of the moment in the trade-union and political struggle is the development of the subjective factors of the working class revolution, the promotion of revolutionary class consciousness. The blunt statement of reform over revolution is a false statement of the question; these oppositions must be given their proper place in the whole of the social process. We must avoid losing sight of the final goals, the proletarian revolution, through the struggle for everyday demands".[18]

Easier said than done. But it is worth emphasizing that for Luxemburg, capitalism was doomed to collapse from its internal contradictions. In the turbulence surrounding this collapse, there would be opportunities to make revolutionary leaps and bounds. In the run-up to the collapse, the urgent mission was to promote the spread of revolutionary consciousness among the working masses, so that when the fatal moment arrived, they would be prepared to seize power for themselves. The movement, its leaders, should focus their energy and resources on consciousness-raising for the self-empowerment of the working class. Consciousness-raising in the process of fierce oppositional struggle.

The idea of political conflict as a process pervades Luxemburg's thought, as James Scott has rightly stressed.[19] Luxemburg spoke of revolution itself as necessarily a long and fraught struggle, a process bound to suffer serious set-backs, violent opposition, even defeat, only to emerge stronger anew. The process of struggle itself, she expected, would provide the most valuable lessons and would contribute to raising and spreading revolutionary consciousness. A learning process, and one which would be thoroughly dialectical, capable of erasing the very boundaries separating leaders from those who were led.

What Is to Be Done?

Towards the end of her polemic against Bernstein and the revisionists, Luxemburg quotes Marx at length, from his essay on the 18th *Brumaire*, to sketch the learning process that a proletarian revolution entails. First and foremost, ruthless criticism. Indeed, proletarian revolutions must "criticise themselves constantly;" they must "constantly interrupt themselves in their own course;" they must, again and again, "come back to what seems to have been accomplished, in order to start anew;" they must assess and "scorn with cruel thoroughness the half-measures, weaknesses, and meanness of their first attempts". Not only that, just when they seem "to throw down their adversary," they are bound to find they have only "enabled him to draw fresh strength from the earth and again to rise up against them in more gigantic stature". Even worse, they are bound "to constantly recoil in fear about the undefined monster magnitude of their own objects – until finally that situation is created which renders all retreat impossible and conditions themselves cry out: *'Hic Rhodus, hic salta!'* ('Here is the rose. And here we must dance!')".[20] Such is the torturous, perilous, winding path of proletarian revolution, as envisioned by Marx, and as Luxemburg reminds us.

Luxemburg's deep-seated faith in the dialectical learning process of class conflict, class struggle, anticipates and converges quite closely with the conception and prescriptions of liberationist pedagogy so forcefully articulated by Paolo Freire many decades later.[21] Moreover, her profoundly democratic convictions led her into early and frequent clashes with authoritarian tendencies within the movement for social democracy including, perhaps most prominently, with Lenin and the Bolsheviks.

One of the great advantages of Luxemburg's liminal positionality was her intimate familiarity with the movements in both Germany and Russia. She had grown up in Russian Poland, and had helped found the Social Democratic Party of Poland and Lithuania (SDKPiL). The SDKPiL had been present at the 1903 Congress that led to the division in the Russian party between Bolsheviks and Mensheviks, though the SDKPiL had left the Congress before the debate that provoked the split. The SDKPiL was at the Congress to discuss unification with the Russian party, but tellingly, negotiations broke down over the issue of self-determination, the first of many conflicts between Luxemburg and Lenin on the matter.

It was in two texts written in the wake of the fateful split between Bolsheviks and Mensheviks at that Congress – the first *One Step Forwards, Two Steps Back*, followed by *What Is to Be Done?* – where Lenin elaborated his theory and justification for "democratic centralism". And in 1904, Luxemburg would reply with a blistering and prophetic critique of Lenin's arguments, which cuts to the core, and locates quite precisely the spectre of tyranny lurking within the postulates and practices of the "democratic centralist" model.

Luxemburg has no problem with "centralism" *per se*. She is not, like latter-day Bookchinites or the anarchists in her time, prone to fetishize the local as the primary or privileged scale for political action. Her understanding of the dynamics and contradictions of capitalism in the age of Imperialism disabused her of any such naïve and/or antiquated notions. Indeed, for Luxemburg – and on this crucial point she was in agreement with Lenin – in the age of Imperialism, capitalism is global in scope; and so the revolution must be global in scope as well, or bound inevitably to fail, bound to be crushed by imperialist reaction.

In accordance with her historical materialist perspective, always attuned to the expansionary imperative and dynamics of global capitalism, Luxemburg emphasises that the scope of economic centralization under capitalism explains the "strong tendency toward centralization ... inherent in the social democratic movement".[22] She does not object in principle to such centralizing tendencies insofar as they allow for effective coordination of the class struggle, both at the "national" level and beyond, in the politics of the Second International. Nevertheless, she does object, quite vehemently, to what she considers Lenin's "ultra-centralist" ideas about organizational structure.

Luxemburg accuses Lenin of pushing the agenda of centralization in the party to an extreme; she argues that his impulse to hyper-centralize is both symptomatic of the immaturity of the social democratic movement in the Russian "backwaters" of global capitalism, and at the same time guilty of unconsciously mirroring a cult of hierarchy inherited from the Czarist autocracy against which the Bolsheviks were struggling. A case of what Nietzsche diagnosed as trans-valuation, in which the original values of hegemonic social relations still shine through in the very terms of their prefigured negation. Luxemburg pushes her point further by attacking the overly-mechanistic and overly-militaristic pedagogical premises and presuppositions built into the Leninist model.

The Bolsheviks as Control Freaks

To use a contemporary turn of phrase, Luxemburg considered Lenin a "control freak". She scoffed at what she considered his little-General complex, and rejected his reasons for institutionalising a quasi-military chain of command, insisting instead: "[e]xcept for the general principles of the struggle, there do not exist for social democracy detailed sets of tactics which a Central Committee can teach the party membership in the same way as troops are instructed in their training camps". According to Luxemburg, such a rigid and hierarchical chain of command contradicts fundamentally the urgent necessity of fostering reflexive and critical consciousness via truly revolutionary pedagogy, and propagates in its place the perpetuation of servility among party members, of propensities for "mechanical subordination and blind obedience ... to the leading party centre".[23]

At the same time, by erecting an "airtight partition" and "rigorous separation" between party members and the broader mass of the working class, Lenin cuts the party off from fluid, more organic, less formalized and hierarchical social relations with the working class, and in effect, therefore treats the community as if it were but a headless body, somehow incapable of thinking, guiding, or deciding for itself. Bolshevism as a "Blanquist" deviation in disguise, Luxemburg thus surmised.[24]

Centralized coordination cannot be forced in such a fashion without it becoming conspiratorial and dictatorial. Truly *democratic* coordination would require two conditions "not yet fully formed in Russia," from Luxemburg's perspective. The first of these, indispensable, being "[t]he existence of a large contingent of workers educated in the political struggle"; the second, equally indispensable, "[t]he possibility for the workers to develop their own political activity through direct influence on public life, in a party press, and public congresses, etc".[25] These conditions simply cannot be conjured into being by organisational fiat, as Lenin would appear to believe. Such a short-cut is in fact a short-circuit, one that threatens to undermine a process of organic development of ever-expanding concentric circles of democratic social relations facilitating the emergence of democratic coordination, of democratic organizational forms.

Luxemburg goes on to emphasise again that Lenin's "conception of socialist organization" is "quite mechanistic". She hones in on his conflation of two fundamentally contradictory forms of discipline, charging Lenin with an attempt to impose and "implant" within party ranks "the entire mechanism of the centralised bourgeois state" – the discipline of the factory, of the military, of the existing state bureaucracy. A kind of discipline that is top-down, vertical in form, characterised by "the absence of thought and will in a body with a thousand automatically moving hands and legs". She contrasts this to the type of discipline required for the realisation of social democracy, one that is bottom-up and horizontal in form, reflecting "the spontaneous coordination of the conscious, political acts of a body of men". The "regulated docility of an oppressed class," on the one side, "the self-discipline and organization of a class struggling for its emancipation on the other".[26] There is nothing in common between these two forms of discipline, they could hardly be further from one another in ethos and praxis.

Self-discipline is the negation of discipline imposed from above. An ethic of revolutionary discipline, linked to the practice of revolutionary pedagogy, through role models who strive for an ever-closer unity of revolutionary theory with personal ethics and praxis, as an alternative to Lenin's "rigid school-master approach". As Luxemburg so eloquently insists: "The self-discipline of the social democracy is not merely the replacement of the authority of the bourgeois rulers with the authority of a socialist central committee". To the contrary, the discipline of the revolutionary workers forged in struggle would have to be a new form of discipline altogether, a "freely-assumed self-discipline," the alternative to and negation of the interpellated subjectivity of servility so famously analysed decades later by Foucault.[27]

An alternative and negation, indeed: a form of discipline that emerges "not as a result of the discipline imposed upon it by the capitalist state," as Lenin would assume, but rather, through a process of struggling against, of purging, that hegemonic form of vertical, unthinking discipline". Revolutionary struggle as a pedagogical and even collective-therapeutic process for the working class, in which its "old habits of obedience and servility" are "extirpat[ed], to the last root".[28]

What this means in organizational terms, in relation to her dispute with the Bolshevik model, she would further expand upon a few years later, in the wake of the 1905 Russian revolution, in her brilliant and provocative analysis of the mass strike. In that essay, she deftly applies the historical materialist method to confront dogmatic socialist opposition to this form and tactic, so associated with anarchism, effectively re-appraising its positive revolutionary potential in certain concrete contexts, such as that of Russia. Her profound analysis of the revolutionary dynamics on display in Russia in 1905 leads her back again to broader programmatic conclusions, against the Bolsheviks' obsession with ultra-centralist control. Luxemburg contends that the experience of the mass strike in the 1905 revolution, the outbreak of which had caught Lenin and his party comrades completely off-guard, has demonstrated that "during the revolution it is extremely difficult for any directing organ of the proletarian movement to foresee and calculate which occasions and factors can lead to explosions and which cannot".

This is precisely what Luxemburg had in mind when she referred to Lenin's "mechanical, bureaucratic conception" of leadership, an objection to which she returns. Such a "rigid" conception, she insists, "cannot conceive of the struggle save as the product of organisation at a certain stage of its strength". By contrast, she concludes, "the living, dialectical explanation makes the organisation arise as a product of the struggle".[29] Bureaucratic, top-down rigidity versus living and dialectical flow.

But to return to her 1904 essay focusing on "Organisational Questions of Social Democracy," her conception of collective revolutionary will forged in struggle not only demonstrated sensitivity to later Foucaultian motifs about discipline and servility, but, in some ways like Butler's work, managed to combine such motifs with explicit appeals to psycho-analytic categories, like the unconscious, and the ego, too. In discussing the relation between struggle and consciousness, Luxemburg insists: "The unconscious comes before the conscious. The logic of the historic process comes before the subjective logic of the human beings who participate in the historic process".[30]

Luxemburg's stress on the unconscious is linked to her understanding of freedom as a manifestation of humanity's "creative spirit". She chastised Lenin's "ultra-centralism" as imbued with and embodying "the sterile spirit of the overseer," predisposed to stifle rather than nurture the "creative spirit" – with the consequence of "narrowing" rather than "developing" the movement, of "binding" rather than "unifying" it.[31]

Organization and Opportunism

This brings her again to the theme of opportunism, so central to her earlier essay on *Reform or Revolution*. Lenin, like Luxemburg, was eager to denounce any and all manifestations of opportunism; but the Bolshevik leader acted as if the phenomenon could be avoided, magically fended off, merely by designing and abiding by the right organisational design. To this extent, Luxemburg insists, Lenin is guilty of underestimating the opportunists – who know "only one principle: the absence of principle".[32] Indeed, Luxemburg goes further still, to sketch an endogenous, "developmental" trajectory, in accordance with which the organisational preferences of opportunist elements change over time, across distinct phases.

At a first moment, "when the revolutionary elements among the workers still lack cohesion and the movement is groping its way," like in Russia, "opportunist intellectuals" will tend to prefer "despotic centralism".[33] The implicit accusation thus being that the Bolsheviks themselves were not merely misguided, but in fact infected with opportunism to the core.

Later on, in a different phase, "under a parliamentary regime and in connection with a strong labour party, the opportunist tendencies express themselves in an inclination towards 'decentralization'". For a "young labor movement," Luxemburg concludes, the surest way to "enslave" it to "an intellectual elite hungry for power" is to impose a "bureaucratic straightjacket," likely to "immobilize the movement," even convert it "into an automaton manipulated by a Central Committee".[34]

In sum, the basic premise underlying Lenin's justification for "unqualified centralism – the idea that the road of opportunism can be barred by means of clauses in a party constitution," Luxemburg concludes, is "fundamentally false".[35] What's worse, though "the attempt to exorcise opportunism by means of a scrap of paper," by organizational fiat, simply cannot eradicate opportunism, it may definitely hinder the advance of the socialist movement".[36]

The fundamental tension, the "dialectical contradiction through which the socialist movement" must manoeuvre, is between the logic and imperatives imposed upon the working class by the need to survive in this existing society, on the one hand, and "its historic goal, located outside existing society," on the other. The immediate task, "the day-to-day struggle," versus the equally urgent but nevertheless longer-term imperative of "social revolution". And thus, the twin dangers "constantly threatening" the movement, caught between the Scylla of "losing its mass character," and the Charybdis of "abandoning its goal," the spectre of "sinking back to the condition of a sect," or simply "becoming a movement of bourgeois social reform".[37] This "dialectical contradiction" and dilemma helps explain the tremendous difficulties of uniting revolutionary theory with the realities of and problems associated with daily struggle and praxis.

We mentioned above that, in her account, Luxemburg makes use of the concept of the unconscious, or subconscious, though as Fromm has pointed out, she uses the concept more "in the sense of blindly acting historical forces," and less in the sense of "subconscious psychic forces," as Freud did.[38] At the end of her essay on "Organisational Question of Social Democracy," she again invokes a psycho-analytic category, that of the "ego". She sums up her assessment of the situation with a damning indictment and portrait of the psychological motives of the Bolshevik leaders, a blistering depiction of how they internalise and reflect the brutal context against which they are trying to struggle:

"Knocked to the ground, almost reduced to dust, by Russian absolutism, the 'ego' takes revenge by turning to revolutionary activity. In the shape of a committee of conspirators, in the name of a non-existent Will of the People, it seats itself on a kind of throne and proclaims it is all-powerful. But the 'object' proves to be stronger. The knout is triumphant, for Czarist might seems to be the 'legitimate' expression of history".[39]

As much as Lenin may try to act the part of the "nimble acrobat," he nevertheless "fails to perceive that the only 'subject' which merits today the role of director is the collective 'ego' of the working class". In a word, he stands guilty of substituting his own ego for the collective ego, and thus usurps the voice of the working class. But the working class, Luxemburg insists, "demands the right to make its own mistakes," demands the right to learn for itself "in the dialectic of history". Such a learning process is indispensable and simply cannot be curtailed or head off at the pass by party leaders. Indeed, as Luxemburg forcefully concludes, "the errors committed by a truly revolutionary movement are infinitely more fruitful than the infallibility of the cleverest Central Committee".[40]

"Self-Determination" as Utopia

Luxemburg followed the revolutionary events of 1905 in Russia very closely, seeking to learn from the dynamics and flow of pent-up social forces suddenly unleashed across the Tsarist Empire. Her positive reassessment of the value of the tactic of the mass strike, long dismissed by the leading lights of social democracy, to which we briefly referred above, was one of the lessons she tried to transmit to the movement, to get the "collective ego" to recognize, to see for itself, to learn. Another such lesson had to do with the issue of "self-determination". Her opposition to the principle had already brought her to loggerheads with the Bolsheviks, ever since the party's inception, and in a series of articles she would pen between 1908 and 1909 on "The National Question," she would again return to the point of dispute, to elaborate her position more thoroughly, to continue her polemic against Lenin, her convictions reinforced by the course of events in Russia.[41]

A first line of argument Luxemburg would pursue against the espousal by the social democratic movement of an abstract "right of nations to self-determination" is that such an abstract policy in fact resolves nothing concretely. Indeed, "[i]t gives no practical guidelines," certainly not for the daily struggle of the working class; nor, for that matter, does it provide any "practical solution to nationality problems". Indeed, in terms of practical guidelines, Luxemburg insists, recognition of such a principle adds nothing to the general duty to resist oppression in all its forms. Such a duty, she continues, should not be conceived as "arising from any special right of nations," just as "the striving for political and social equality of sexes" does not come "from any special rights of women," either. General opposition to oppression in all its forms, a firm stance against "every form of social inequality and social domination," is the principled position required of the movement for social democracy; it is, after all, "the basic position of socialism". What can proclamations about "an unlimited authorization to all interested 'nations' to settle their national problems in any way they like" add to this general affirmation and point of principle against oppression? The answer, Luxemburg concludes, is nothing at all. In her words:

> "The duty to resist all forms of national oppression does not include any explanation of what conditions and political forms the class-conscious proletariat in Russia at the present time should recommend as a solution for the nationality problems of Poland, Latvia, the Jews, etc., or what program it should present to match the various programs of the bourgeois, nationalist, and pseudo-socialist parties in the present class struggle. In a word, the formula, "the right of nations to self-determination," is essentially not a political and problematic guideline in the nationality question, but only a means of *avoiding that question*".

In sum, for Luxemburg, the "fine-sounding formula of the right of nations to self-determination," at the end of the day, amounts to little more than a "vague cliché". Either it expresses a truism, "an empty, noncommittal phrase," or it expresses a blatant falsehood, an alleged "unconditional duty of socialists to support" any and all national aspirations, regardless of the concrete circumstances in which such aspirations arise. But the historical materialist method must always resist, by definition, calls to ignore concrete circumstances, how particular movements are embedded in concrete constellations of material and social power relations. Such matters require "historical and political discrimination," and therefore need to be judged on a case-by-case basis, and even any one case can change over time. In sum, rendering judgment on all such movements, abstractly, will definitely not suffice.

To add force to her argument against the abstract, and in favour of the concrete, Luxemburg next turns to compare the alleged "right of nations to self-determination" to another abstract rights claim, the so-called "right to work". In this case, Luxemburg praises the movement for social democracy for having rightly recognised that such rhetoric is but an "empty sound," that until "the capitalist regime is abolished ... the chronic unemployment of a certain part of the industrial proletariat" will be perpetuated, since it "is a necessary condition of production". As such, she remarks with approval, the movement is correct not to "demand a declaration of that imaginary 'right' on the basis of the existing system," but instead "strives for the abolition of the system itself by the class struggle, regarding labour organizations, unemployment insurance, etc., only as temporary means of help", the rise of opportunist, revisionist tendencies and practices notwithstanding.

The next weapon in Luxemburg's verbal arsenal against the "right of nations to self-determination" is the claim that such a right "is a complete utopia," in a rather precise historical materialist sense: namely, that it cuts clearly against "the trend of historical development of contemporary societies". What does she mean by such a claim? For starters, she emphasises the inescapability of ethnic and national heterogeneity, the intertwining and intermixing of nationalities in "all the ancient states without exception," as a consequence of a "long history of political and ethnic upheavals".

But even more importantly, Luxemburg goes on to insist, as well, that the brutal reality of imperialism, including "[t]he development of *world powers*, a characteristic feature" of the age, "from the very outset condemns all small nations to political impotence". At least outside the metropole, or what has sometimes been referred to in more recent literature as the advanced capitalist core, "the independent existence of smaller and petty nations, is an illusion, and will become even more so".

Capitalist imperialism further compounds the illusory nature of "self-determination" through the mechanism of "international trade," which "brings with it the inevitable, though at times slow ruin of all the more primitive so-cieties, destroys their historically existing means of 'self-determination,'" thereby rendering "them dependent on the crushing wheel of capitalist de-velopment and world politics". From these definite tendencies Luxemburg infers that "colonialism will inevitably accompany the future progress of cap-italism, and that only the innocuous bourgeois apostles of 'peace' can believe in the possibility of today's states avoiding that path", a prescient glimpse of the gathering clouds and approaching storm of the First World War. Though, at the same time, it is apparent from such claims that Luxemburg failed to anticipate the percolation of anti-colonialist consciousness in the decades after the so-called "Great War" (an oxymoron if ever there was one).

Even the most far-sighted of dialecticians proved incapable of seeing be-yond the storm from paradise in this regard. Luxemburg's conclusion that "the form that best serves the interests of exploitation in the contemporary world is not the 'national' state, but a state bent on conquest," was certainly accurate in the decades running up to the outbreak of world war. But if there is one thing that distinguishes the global capitalist system – that Luxemburg, like Lenin, underestimated, no doubt, despite their vehement denunciations of opportunism – it is the system's ability and agility in co-opting and trans-forming counter-currents and movements of opposition. The Wilsonian em-brace of the doctrine of self-determination, the convergence of the rising American capitalist project with the Bolshevik creed, the turbulent but suc-cessful transition from the era of imperialism to the era of neo-colonialism, was something that Luxemburg could not, or at least did not, foresee.

Luxemburg continues her attack on "the formula of the right of nations to self-determination" with one last line of argument. According to her, at the end of the day, such a formula is not only inadequate for being overly ab-stract and utopian, for "failing to take into account the wide range of histor-ical conditions" and for failing to "reckon with the general current of the development of global conditions". At perhaps an even more fundamental level, she insists, the formula is inappropriate because "it ignores completely" the very core of the historical materialist method: namely, "the theory of so-cial classes". Luxemburg contends:

"When we speak of the 'right of nations to self-determination', we are using the concept of the 'nation' as a homogeneous social and political

entity. But actually, such a concept of the 'nation' is one of those categories of bourgeois ideology which Marxist theory submitted to a radical re-vision, showing how that misty veil, like the concepts of the
'freedom of citizens', 'equality before the law', etc., conceals in every case
a definite historical content".

To put the point bluntly, belief in the "nation," conceived as "a homogeneous socio-political entity" is itself an illusion, a trap, a ploy. "Under the
identity of forms and slogans," fundamentally contrasting, "diametrically opposed" political programs and worldviews are concealed, covered over, reified
into an essentialist whole. In a world torn asunder by the spread of capitalist
social property relations, "there can be no talk of a collective and uniform
[national] will". Ruthless criticism requires deep suspicion towards all such
fictitious universalities which most often serve merely to divide and conquer
the exploited masses, and thereby to mask the particular interests of the ruling
class. Luxemburg thus continues:

> "The 'nation' should have the 'right' to self-determination. But who is
> that 'nation' and who has the authority and the 'right' to speak for the
> 'nation' and express its will? How can we find out what the 'nation' ac-
> tually wants? Does there exist even one political party which would not
> claim that it alone, among all others, truly expresses the will of the 'na-
> tion', whereas all other parties give only perverted and false expressions
> of the national will? All the bourgeois, liberal parties consider them-
> selves the incarnation of the will of the people and claim the exclusive
> monopoly to represent the 'nation'. But conservative and reactionary
> parties refer no less to the will and interests of the nation, and within
> certain limits, have no less of a right to do so. The Great French Revo-
> lution was indubitably an expression of the will of the French nation,
> but Napoleon, who juggled away the work of the Revolution in
> his *coup* of the 18th Brumaire, based his entire state reform on the prin-
> ciple of '*la volonté generale*' [the general will]".

So much for the conflation between the nation and the "general will". But
what about the relation between the nation and the will of the majority, at
least? On this point, Luxemburg appears more willing to concede: "[t]he na-

tion wants what the majority of the people want". However, she immediately proceeds to admonish: "woe to the Social Democratic Party which would ever take that principle as its own yardstick: that would condemn to death Social Democracy itself as the revolutionary party". Its task must never be simply to pander to the will of the present majority. To the contrary, "the historical mission of Social Democracy is based above all on revolutionizing and forming the will of the 'nation'," understood as the working-class majority. Even to the point of getting the workers to reject any and all appeals to "national integration," of persuading them to resist, to transcend, never to succumb or capitulate, nor to "humbly prostrate" themselves, before the warring idols of the nation. Though prostrate themselves they would.

Conclusion

"Are we not touched with the same breath of air which was among that which came before? Is there not an echo of those who have been silenced in the voices to which we lend our ears today?"
– Benjamin, Thesis II.

Rosa Luxemburg was murdered over a century ago. But her voice still echoes in our ears; indeed, it gets louder each day. As the current crisis of capitalist civilization pursues its genocidal-cum-ecocidal course, its contradictions ever more exacerbated, with the social-democratic compromise ever more outflanked and defeated, and with the Marxist-Leninist state-communist alternative forever discredited, Luxemburg's articulation and principled commitment to a distinctly libertarian and thoroughly internationalist brand of anti-capitalist resistance re-emerges as a source of insight and inspiration for those of us engaged in the struggle for humanity, for life on the planet, against tyranny in all its forms.

Her liminal position, as a triple outsider among the milieu of the leaders of German Social Democracy – as a woman, a Jew, a Pole – afforded her epistemic privilege when it came to the so-called "national question". She could see more clearly than perhaps any of her contemporaries the pitfalls of national consciousness in the European context of inter-imperialist rivalry and looming world war.

Her internationalist critique of the dogma of national "self-determination" put her at odds with Lenin and the Bolsheviks; in fact, it was the matter of multiple polemics between them, which would persist from her arrival on the international revolutionary scene up to her untimely death. In the course of these often fierce polemics, Luxemburg forcefully depicted adherence to nationalist ideology as the first among many "indices of opportunism," a Trojan horse for and harbinger of capitulation to the aspirations and agenda of the (petit) bourgeoisie.

Indeed, her critique of nationalism was part of a broader, multi-faceted critique of opportunism, which pitted her against both Bolsheviks and reformists alike. At the same time, her understanding of revolution as a process led her to embody and espouse a form of revolutionary pedagogy that pit her against anarchists, too, especially in relation to her distinctive articulation of the purpose of participation in parliamentary politics.

In sum, Luxemburg's contribution to anti-capitalist thought and praxis remains relevant in at least four ways: (1) she elaborates an alternative, equally anti-capitalist and Marxist vision to Leninism, but one less susceptible to the autocratic inclinations of Lenin and the Bolsheviks; (2) she is equally vehement in her critique of revisionism, reformism and "parliamentary cretinism;" (3) she makes the case persuasively that the effective alternatives are "socialism or barbarism;" and (4) she expresses a powerful "revolutionary, internationalist" alternative to the perils and pitfalls of the "national imaginary". For all of these reasons, her thought and example remain extremely relevant for the urgent task of rethinking the critique of capitalism, especially in light of the failures of state socialism and the defeat of social democracy, in an era in which an alternative to capitalism seems necessary for the very survival of life on the planet.

Epilogue

Let us return to the portrait of Red Rosa hanging on that wall in the woman's academy in northern Syria, to emphasise both a Luxemburgian lesson *for* and a Luxemburgian lesson *from* the revolutionaries in Rojava. The Luxemburgian lesson *for* the Rojava revolution has to do with her critique of the dogma of self-determination, and in relation to her thoroughgoing internationalism. In a world of nation-states, to rescind the goal of achieving a nation-state of one's own is not enough to make the dilemmas of socialism in one country disappear. Direct democracy, local assemblies, and even the organization of militias for self-defence should not, cannot, be confused with the substantive achievement of liberation, of self-determination, not when you cannot control what crosses the borders, up against a brutal embargo, or what comes out of the ground, when the soil bleeds oil, or what falls from the sky, when iron maiden heavy metal death threatens to rain down on a territory. And so, the revolution finds itself surrounded, forced to choose between collaborating with the United States or being pummelled by Turkey, or perhaps both. For the revolution to survive, it must spread.

The Luxemburgian lesson *from* Rojava has to do with the question of revolutionary faith. People in the so-called "West" no longer have faith that the future belongs to them. The murderous century that separates us from Red Rosa renders it seemingly impossible for us to believe, like she still could, with her characteristically charismatic zeal, that "[i]t is we who are marching for the conquest of the world as he did formerly who proclaimed that it is easier for a camel to pass through the eye of a needle than for a rich man to enter the kingdom of heaven".[42] The brutality and ruthless determination of the counter-revolutionary forces, combined with the crimes of state communism, appear to have definitively crushed our capacity for such kind of certainty, such full-throttled conviction, that we are inevitably marching towards the abolition of capitalism. The abolition of life on the planet seems more likely to us.

Our episteme would seem thoroughly disenchanted; if only we could face the future with the same steely confidence of Luxemburg, who, while still in prison, never ceased to anticipate a moment of messianic rupture: "I have the feeling that all this moral filth through which we are wading, this huge madhouse in which we live, may all of a sudden, between one day and the next, be transformed into its very opposite, as if by the stroke of a magician's wand; may become something stupendously great and heroic, must inevitably be transformed".[43] Where is our faith in the magician's wand now? Dumped in the Landwehr Canal?

Or perhaps, just perhaps, can we find that faith again, restored by the heroes fighting for survival, fighting for revolution, rekindling the flame of world revolution, in Kobane? Red Rosa and her revolutionary descendants in the Kurdish Freedom Movement embody, exemplify, in their courageous will to struggle, a crucial message for humanity at the brink: the message that, come what may, resistance is life.

NOTES

1 This chapter was first published by the *Komun Academy for Democratic Modernity* (January 15, 2019). Accessible at: https://komun-academy.com/2019/01/15/rosa-luxemburgs-living-legacy/

2 In R. Tucker, *The Marx-Engels Reader* (New York: W.W. Norton and Company, 1978), p.474

3 "Peace Utopias" (1911), in M. Waters, ed., *Rosa Luxemburg Speaks* (New York: Pathfinder Press, 1970), p.254.

4 P. Frölich, *Rosa Luxemburg: Her Life and Work* (New York: Monthly Review Press, 1972), p.205.

5 D. Whitehall, "A Rival History of Self-Determination," *European Journal of International Law*, Vol. 27, No. 3, p.726.

6 Cited in E. Ettinger, *Rosa Luxemburg: A Life* (George G. Harrap & Co. Ltd., 1987), p.184.

7 "Foreword to the Anthology: The Polish Question and the Socialist Movement" (1905), https://www.marxists.org/archive/luxemburg/1905/misc/polish-question.htm.

8 J.P. Nettl, "Appendix: The National Question," in *Rosa Luxemburg*, Vol. II (Oxford: Oxford University Press, 1966), p.845.

9 P. Mattick, "Luxemburg versus Lenin," in *Anti-Bolshevik Marxism* (Monmouth, Wales: Merlin Press Ltd., 1978), p.21.

10 Ibid., p.37.

11 "Reform or Revolution" (1898-1899), in M. Waters, ed., *Rosa Luxemburg Speaks*, *op. cit.*, pp.77-78

12 "Economic and Philosophical Manuscripts," in R. Tucker, *The Marx-Engels Reader*, *op. cit.*, p.80.

13 "Reform or Revolution" (1898-1899), in M. Waters, ed., *Rosa Luxemburg Speaks*, *op. cit.*, p.80. See also G. Therborn, "The Rule of Capital and the Rise of Democracy," *The New Left Review* #103 (May-June, 1977).

14 Ibid., pp.80-81.

15 Ibid., p.82.

16 Ibid., pp.88-89.

17 Ibid., p.89.

18 P. Mattick, "Luxemburg versus Lenin," *op. cit.*, p.22.

19 See J. Scott, "The Revolutionary Party: A Plan and a Diagnosis," in *Seeing Like a State* (New Haven: Yale University Press, 1998), pp. 147-179.

20 "Reform or Revolution" (1898-1899), in M. Waters, ed., *Rosa Luxemburg Speaks*, *op. cit.*, p.89.

21 See P. Freire, *The Pedagogy of the Oppressed* (New York: Continuum, 2010).

22 "Organisational Question of Social Democracy" (1904), in M. Waters, *Rosa Luxemburg Speaks, op. cit.*, p. 116.

23 Ibid., p.118.

24 Ibid., p.117.

25 Ibid., p.119.

26 Ibid., p.119.

27 See M Foucault, *Discipline and Punish* (New York: Vintage Books, 1995).

28 "Organisational Question of Social Democracy" (1904), in M. Waters, *Rosa Luxemburg Speaks, op. cit.*, pp.119-120.

29 Cited in Mattick, "Luxemburg versus Lenin," *op. cit.*, p.44.

30 "Organisational Question of Social Democracy" (1904), in M. Waters, *Rosa Luxemburg Speaks, op. cit.*, p.121.

31 Ibid., p.122.

32 Ibid., p.126.

33 Ibid., p.126.

34 Ibid., pp.126-127.

35 Ibid., p.127.

36 Ibid., p.128.

37 Ibid., pp.128-129.

38 See E. Fromm, "Marxism, Psychoanalysis and Reality" (1966). https://www.marxists.org/archive/fromm/works/1966/psychoanalysis.htm

39 "Organisational Question of Social Democracy" (1904), in M. Waters, *Rosa Luxemburg Speaks, op. cit.*, p.130.

40 Ibid., p.130.

41 See "The National Question" (1908-1909), https://www.marxists.org/archive/luxemburg/1909/national-question/index.htm

42 "On Socialism and the Churches," in M. Waters, *Rosa Luxemburg Speaks, op. cit.*, p.151.

43 "Letter from Prison to Sonia Liebknecht," in M. Waters, *Rosa Luxemburg Speaks, op. cit.*, p.337.

CHAPTER 5

1917 on the Brain[1]

"The Russian Revolution of 1917 weighs on the brains of the living like a nightmare" (Bookchin 1999, p.132). Especially given the urgency of the task of raising anti-capitalist and internationalist consciousness at this critical historical moment, a task as urgent as it is difficult to even imagine, but a task nonetheless required: (1) for effectively and collectively confronting the collective-existential problem of climate change; (2) for stopping the Orwellian War on Terror and dismantling the collectively-suicidal war-machine; and (3) for putting an end to the tyranny of the oligarchs, the kleptocrats, in cahoots with the war-mongers, the tyranny of an irresponsible few who jeopardize the very future of humanity (and of many other species), all for the sake of their single-minded obsession with material gain, their ruthless commitment to defend and further entrench their unjust privileges, their ill-begotten gains, their unsustainable "way of life".

And yet, again and again, the urgent task of raising anti-capitalist and internationalist consciousness comes up against the spectre of the Russian Revolution (Chomsky 1986, 2013). Without a doubt, its tragic, tyrannical *denouement* serves to constrict and constrain the rebirth of revolutionary imagination. The idea that there is a viable and desirable alternative to capitalism has been seemingly discredited, rendered naïve and utopian. The link between anti-capitalist revolution and human emancipation, seemingly severed. The tyranny of capitalist social-property relations, or tyranny *tout court*, the only imaginable options.

Socialism as required for environmental stability? What about the disastrous environmental record of state "communism"? Socialism or barbarism? What about socialism as barbarism? The tyranny of Stalin; his thuggery; the brutality of the purges. Like a nightmare, indeed. Though give the devil his due: it was Stalin's totalitarian, industrial war-machine which effectively defeated Hitler, despite the lies you probably learned in school.

The rise of fascism was itself a consequence of the defeat of the revolution. And make no mistake, for Lenin and for Trotsky, as for Rosa Luxemburg, the revolution had to be international, *global* in scope, for it to succeed. The hypothesis was that Russia was the weakest link of the Imperialist and capitalist chain, that revolution in Russia would detonate a world revolution, more specifically, that it would spread from the Eurasian semi-periphery to the Imperialist and capitalist "core" of the world system, and then across the globe. But instead, the dream of global revolution gave way to the nightmare of "socialism in one country".

For a brief moment, though, in the autumn of 1918 through the winter of early 1919, that revolution *was* on the agenda in Germany. The fatal failure of the Spartacus uprising, and the brutal murders of Rosa Luxemburg and Karl Liebknecht, killed by the *Freikorps*, betrayed by the Social Democrats, was perhaps *the* fatal turning point, after which the world-revolutionary tide began to ebb, and the forces of fascist reaction began to gain momentum. Marx's prognosis from 1844 thus remains more valid than ever: "There can be no doubt about the task confronting us at the present: *the ruthless criticism of everything existing*, ruthless in that it will shrink neither from its own discoveries, nor from conflict with the powers that be" (Marx 1843). Nothing less than a ruthless criticism of the defeated Russian revolutionary dream, a dream which died long before 1989, is required.

Such ruthless criticism must include recognition and comprehension of the revolutionary trajectory along two inter-dependent paths. The first was the path from Lenin to Stalin and his tyranny, most notably, the crushing of the peasantry, and the purges of the Bolshevik revolutionaries. Call it the question of democracy and dictatorship. The second was the path from international revolution to "socialism in one country". Call it the question of internationalism versus nationalism, in turn intimately related to the utopian principle and program of national self-determination.

The tyrannical potential of the Bolshevik project was evident from the very start. Luxemburg's 1904 critique of the Bolshevik party form, its cult of hierarchy, in her answer to Lenin's *What Is to Be Done?*, proved prophetic (Luxemburg 1970, pp.112-130; Scott 1998, pp.168-174). As did her early critique, written from jail in Germany in the summer of 1918, in which she denounced the Bolshevik's suppression of the Constituent Assembly, their repression of the opposition, their restrictions of democratic freedoms: "Freedom only for supporters of the government, only for the members of one party – however numerous they may be – is no freedom at all. Freedom is always and exclusively freedom for the one who thinks differently" (Luxemburg 1970, p.389).

Then there was the question of "workers' control" versus "state capitalism". Soon after coming to power, Lenin pragmatically and opportunistically retreated from the radical vision espoused in *State and Revolution*, in which he had called for "the destruction of all bureaucratically organized political authority and the establishment of control by the masses over the existing capitalist economy" (Daniels 1969, p.52). March 1918 would constitute a critical turning point in this regard, when Lenin made it clear that "the workers would have to accept discipline and the Taylor system of scientific management;" and insisted that "industrial anarchy had value only to effect the transition between the old 'slave' discipline and the new 'conscious' discipline" (Daniels 1969, p.52); but discipline, and being disciplined, nonetheless.

Yet it was the Kronstadt revolt of March 1921 that sealed the fate of the revolution. The Kronstadters, who called for "a third revolution," who "revolted against the Soviet leaders in the name of the October revolution itself," who defiantly insisted: "The time has come to overthrow the *commissarocracy*" (Daniels 1969, pp.143-144). The brutal suppression of the Kronstadt revolt brought in its wake the suppression of the Workers' Opposition, one of whose most prominent leaders, Aleksandra Kollontai, had already warned: "The task of the party in its present crisis is to face its mistakes fearlessly and lend its ear to the healthy class call of the broad working masses. Through the creative powers of the working class in the form of industrial unions we shall go towards the reconstruction and development of the creative forces of the country; toward purification of the party itself from the elements foreign to it; toward correction of the activity of the party by means of going back to democracy, freedom of opinion, and criticism inside the party" (Daniels 1969, p.128; Scott 1998, pp.175-179) – echoes of Luxemburg's prophecy.

The Kronstadters were crushed, insulted and defamed as counter-revolutionaries, even denounced as foreign agents; soon thereafter, the Workers' Opposition was suppressed and persecuted as a counter-revolutionary current as well. One of the great ironies of the Kronstadt revolt was Trotsky's protagonism in its violent repression, a sad fact all-too-conveniently forgotten by his defenders and disciples. Another sad fact was the silence of the doomed opposition. The trajectory from revolutionary hopes to Bolshevik tyranny was traced in and through this silence.

This trajectory coincided with, and was highly influenced by, even likely overdetermined by the path from international revolution to "socialism in one country". The October Revolution did not trigger revolution in the West, as expected; rather, it triggered an imperialist counter-assault and civil war. The retreat at Brest-Litovsk in March of 1918 along with the concession of huge portions of the Russian Empire to the German and Ottoman Empires were seen by Lenin as temporary, bound to be reversed by imminent world revolution. But in the meantime, the western allies armed and supported the opponents of the Bolsheviks. Churchill famously declared that Bolshevism must be "strangled in its cradle". Centralization, prompted by war conditions, strengthened and fuelled the regime's dictatorial tendencies and its treatment of dissident voices as counter-revolutionary threats.

The question of internationalism and the imperative of world revolution was in turn intimately related to the doctrine of self-determination. Luxemburg had long polemicized with Lenin about the concrete impact of the abstract utopia of national self-determination that the Bolsheviks had upheld as a point of principle. Luxemburg criticized this policy as a "variety of opportunism," calculated to "bind the many foreign nationalities present in the Russian empire to the cause of the revolution" (Mattick 1935).

The calculation was, however, mistaken. As Paul Mattick long ago pointed out: "Contrary to what the Bolsheviks had expected, one after another, the 'liberated nations' took advantage of the freshly granted freedom to take a position of deadly enmity to the Revolution, combining against it with German imperialism, under whose protection they carried the banner of counter-revolution to Russia itself". And as Luxemburg had predicted: "With the phrase about the self-determination of nations, the Bolsheviks furnished water for the mills of the counter-revolution and thus furnished an ideology not only for the strangling of the Russian Revolution itself, but for the planned counter-revolutionary liquidation of the entire World War" (Mattick 1935).

Most historians have been more generous in their judgments about the effect of the Bolshevik policy of self-determination on the course of the revolution. But even admirers of Lenin's political line from Isaac Deutscher to E.

H. Carr have nevertheless admitted that the choice was never really one "between dependence and independence, but between dependence on Moscow or dependence on the bourgeois governments of the capitalist world" (Carr 1978, p.268; Deutscher 2003, pp.312-313). Moreover and as a matter of fact, above and beyond the slogan and the propaganda, "on the ground, communists decided themselves who was the carrier of the nation's will, and after the initial recognition of independence for Poland, Finland, the Baltics, and (for a time) Georgia, few other gestures were made towards 'separatists'" (Suny 1993, p.90). Indeed, as Horace Davis has surmised and summarised: "Eventually most of the former tsarist colonies were reincorporated into the USSR. But where the Western powers had established their military occupation, as in Finland and the Baltic Republics, or where the Red Army was defeated, as in Poland, it was the self-determination of the bourgeoisie that won out". In effect, "the issue was settled finally, in the way that Rosa Luxemburg had predicted, by force of arms" (Davis 1976, pp.30-32).

As Mattick has emphasized, "Luxemburg died too early to see that the Bolshevik policy, even though it ceased to further the world-revolutionary movement, was yet capable of assuring the rule of the Bolsheviks". In this respect, Luxemburg's revolutionary companion and fellow martyr, Karl Liebknecht, was perhaps the more precise prophet of the two, when he, too, wrote from jail: "If the German revolution fails to take place, there remains for the Russian revolution the alternatives: to go down fighting or to present a mere wretched appearance of life" (Mattick 1935).

To sum up, there are two fateful legacies of the Russian revolution that weigh upon us like a nightmare. The first is the equation of any anti-capitalist alternative – call it "socialism," call it "communism" – with state tyranny. The second has to do with Leninist-cum-Stalinist dogmas about self-determination, which continue to plague the left, blinding it to Luxemburg's crucial insight about the need to evaluate such abstract principles in terms of their concrete impact on local and global constellations of power relations. Related to this confusion, the virtual renunciation of the imperative of world revolution, though it is certainly more imperative today than ever, despite the difficulty we have to even imagine it. On the other hand, this is an imperative that should come across all the more clearly, given the limits of national self-determination and of "socialism in one country". This is revealed by the postcolonial experience, by the fact that Marxism-Leninism in power has almost

invariably been but a "developmentalist," "modernist" ideology, wielded by
those who would *seize* power, rather than *dissolve* it in order to legitimate the
power of those at the helm of tyrannical states (Balibar 2007, pp.85-88;
Bookchin 1999, p.134).

This chapter concludes with the verdict of yet another imprisoned revolutionary, Abdullah Öcalan, leader of the Kurdish Freedom Movement: "The
inadequate analysis of the question of the state by socialist ideology obscures
the problem of the nation-state's place in the hegemonic system of capitalist
modernity. And in the 'right of nations to self-determination', the vision of a
state for every nation was fundamental in aggravating the issue even further"
(Öcalan 2017, p.105). Such flawed analysis ended up: (1) propagating the cult
of the state, the religious conviction that a state is needed for a nation to be
free; and even (2) conflating the proliferation of "independent" state apparatuses with the smashing of the state apparatus, which is the fundamental revolutionary task, and which is not at all the same thing as "seizing" state power.

NOTE

1   This chapter was first published as a postscript for *1917: Revolution and its After-*
    math. Goldman, Berkman, Bookchin, Mett (Montreal: Black Rose Books, 2018),
    pp.404-411.

REFERENCES

Balibar, Étienne. 2007. *The Philosophy of Marx* (London: Verso).

Bookchin, Murray. 1999. "Marxism," in Janet Biehl, ed., *The Murray Bookchin Reader*
    (Montréal, Québec: Black Rose Books), pp.122-142.

Carr, Edward Hallett. 1978. *The Bolshevik Revolution 1917-1923*. Volume One (New York,
    NY: W.W. Norton & Company).

Chomsky, Noam. 1986. "The Soviet Union versus Socialism," *Our Generation* (Spring/
    Summer). https://chomsky.info/1986____/

Chomsky, Noam. 2013. "Noam Chomsky on Revolutionary Violence, Communism,
    and the American Left. Noam Chomsky Interviewed by Christopher Helali".
    https://chomsky.info/20130312/

Daniels, Robert Vincent. 1969. *The Conscience of the Revolution. Communist Opposition in Soviet Russia* (New York, NY: Simon and Schuster).

Davis, Horace B. 1976. "Introduction: The Right of National Self-Determination in Marxist Theory – Luxemburg versus Lenin," in Horace B. Davis, ed., *The National Question. Selected Writings by Rosa Luxemburg* (New York, NY: Monthly Review Press), pp.9-48.

Deutscher, Isaac. 2003. *The Prophet Armed. Trotsky 1879-1921* (London: Verso).

Luxemburg, Rosa. 1970. "Organizational Questions of Social Democracy," and "The Russian Revolution," in Mary-Alice Waters, ed., *Rosa Luxemburg Speaks* (New York, NY: Pathfinder Press, 1970), pp.112-130; pp.365-395.

Marx, Karl. 1843. "Letter from Mark to Arnold Ruge," (September). https://www.marxists.org/archive/marx/works/1843/letters/43_09-alt.htm

Mattick, Paul. 1935. "Luxemburg versus Lenin". https://www.marxists.org/archive/mattick-paul/1935/luxemburg-lenin.htm

Öcalan, Abdullah. 2017. "Democratic Nation," in *The Political Thought of Abdullah Öcalan. Kurdistan, Women's Revolution and Democratic Confederalism* (London: Pluto Press).

Scott, James C. 1998. *Seeing like a State* (New Haven, CT: Yale University Press).

Suny, Ronald Grigor. 1993. *The Revenge of the Past. Nationalism, Revolution, and the Collapse of the Soviet Revolution* ((Stanford, CA: Stanford University Press).

CHAPTER 6

Anticolonial, Postcolonial and Decolonial Critiques and Creative *Appropriations of the Principle of Self-Determination: From Fanon to Öcalan*

Abstract: *This chapter seeks to situate the re-articulation of the principle of self-determination by the imprisoned Kurdish leader Abdullah Öcalan, by relating it to a series of critiques and creative appropriations of the principle as formulated by emblematic figures in the anticolonial, postcolonial, and decolonial traditions. It begins by honing in on a rarely recognised feature of Frantz Fanon's 1961 classic,* The Wretched of the Earth, *namely, the distinction he makes between the abstract principle of self-determination and definite demands for thoroughgoing decolonization. It then turns to consider Adom Getachew's defence of the anticolonial articulation and practice of self-determination, highlighting the creative appropriation and virtual re-invention of the ideal of self-determination in the writings and accomplishments of a host of anticolonial thinkers. It next takes up Gary Wilder's recovery of alternative conceptions of self-determination, not linked to state sovereignty, as espoused by Aimé Césaire and Leopold Sédar Senghor. This leads to a discussion of Walter Mignolo's more recent decolonial critique of the paradigm of the nation-state. The essay concludes by recasting Öcalan in an explicitly anti-/post-/de-colonial light, relating these critiques and creative appropriations of self-determination to Öcalan's renunciation of the goal of a nation-state.*

Introduction

The purpose of this chapter is to situate the historic re-articulation of the principle of self-determination achieved by the imprisoned leader of the Kurdish freedom movement, Abdullah Öcalan, and pursued by those inspired by him, most notably in the revolutionary developments in Rojava, in the northeast of Syria (Allsopp and Van Wilgenburg 2019; Knapp et. al. 2016; Schmidinger 2018). This will be attempted by relating this re-articulation to a series of critiques and creative appropriations of the principle as formulated by emblematic figures in the anticolonial, postcolonial, and decolonial traditions.

We begin by honing in on a rarely recognised feature of Frantz Fanon's 1961 classic, *The Wretched of the Earth*, namely, the distinction he makes between the abstract principle of self-determination and definite demands for thoroughgoing decolonization. Fanon's critical orientation towards the category of self-determination was motivated by his sociological sensibility, that is, by his penchant for locating the enunciation of the discourse of self-determination within concrete constellations of material and social power relations, both at the domestic and the international levels. According to Fanon, it is both nationalist elites and American diplomats who wax most eloquent about the principle of self-determination. Awareness of this fact leads Fanon to espouse a sceptical attitude towards the category, which he suggests is best conceived as a reactionary discourse espoused by the partisans of order, intended to fend off the spectre of a more radical, revolutionary transformation of power relations, only achievable through violent struggle.

We then turn to consider Adom Getachew's defence of the anticolonial articulation and practice of self-determination, which she explores in her recent book, *Worldmaking after Empire: The Rise and Fall of Self-Determination* (2019). Getachew emphasises the creative appropriation and virtual re-invention of the ideal of self-determination in the writings and accomplishments of a host of emblematic anti-colonial figures. She stresses the imperative to pay careful attention to the contexts in which and purposes for which the ideal has been mobilized. She further highlights the international, "worldmaking" dimension to the aspiration for self-determination as envisioned by a wide variety of anti-colonial protagonists, ranging from Nnamdi Azikiwe, W.E.B. Du Bois, Michael Manley, and Kwame Nkrumah, to Julius Nyerere,

George Padmore, and Eric Williams. Yet, she also admits the limits and constraints to their achievements, limits foreseen by Fanon.

We next take up Gary Wilder's recovery of alternative conceptions of self-determination, not linked to state sovereignty, as espoused by the important anti-colonial figures Aimé Césaire and Leopold Sédar Senghor (Wilder 2015). Wilder brings into focus the fact that both Césaire and Senghor refused to equate decolonization with nation-state independence. He stresses instead how they both advocated the transformation of the French Empire into a multi-national, democratic federation. Wilder's work helps open up space for rethinking as contingent rather than inevitable the pathway traversed by the colonial world from empire to nation-state. He effectively captures the untimely quality of Césaire and Senghor's dissent from what came to constitute the hegemonic program and parameters of anti-colonial nationalism in their own era. Paradoxically, perhaps, Césaire and Senghor's untimely message re-emerges as quite pertinent today, in an era in which the contradictions and confines of nation-state sovereignty have become overwhelmingly evident.

This leads us to a discussion of Walter Mignolo's decolonial critique of the paradigm of the nation-state (Mignolo 2011; Mignolo and Walsh 2018). Mignolo draws a contrast between decolonization and decoloniality. The former, he contends, was linked to the aspiration for the achievement of an independent nation-state. However, for Mignolo, this aspiration led ultimately up a blind alley, because the nation-state remains embroiled in what he calls, following Alonso Quijano, "the colonial matrix of power" (Quijano 2000). By contrast, the project of decoloniality, Mignolo insists, encourages an opening to imagining "forms of governance beyond the nation-state". In this vein he points to the experience, the embodied knowledge and praxis, of the Zapatistas in Chiapas as emblematic of the virtues of such a decolonial approach.

This brings us, finally, to Abdullah Öcalan, and to his renunciation of the goal of a nation-state, not just as a matter of pragmatism, but out of principle (Akkaya and Jongerden 2012; Guneser and Finley 2019; Jongerden 2016; Öcalan 2017). Öcalan manages an impressive re-articulation of self-determination, away from the goal of an independent nation-state, instead positioning himself in favour of a form of radical, direct democracy against the state. This is an historic move, because it has led to a corresponding transformation of the Kurdish freedom movement, indeed, towards its transcendence of the paradigm of national liberation, and its espousal of the principles and program, the ethos, of democratic confederalism instead (Dinc 2020; Fadaee and Brancolini 2019; Jongerden 2019; Ustundag 2016).

The version of grassroots democracy sketched by Öcalan and under construction in Rojava includes, crucially, autonomous assemblies and self-defence militias for all salient ethnic groups (Colsanti et. al. 2018; Gunes 2020; Knapp et. al. 2016). This is a strategy for multi-cultural accommodation, an effort to overcome the spectre of the tyranny of the majority, that is in some ways reminiscent of the Austro-Marxist attempt to delink the recognition of cultural rights from the principle of territoriality (Coakley 1994; Nimni 1999).

At the same time, the self-determining, grassroots democracy envisioned by Öcalan and incarnated in Rojava seeks to centre and institutionalize gender emancipation, through autonomous women's assemblies and a women's militia for self-defence, as well as a co-chair system that guarantees the presence of women in leadership positions, and quotas for women in all delegated posts (Burç 2020; Dirik 2018; Rasit and Kolokotronis 2020; Shahvisi 2021). This is also part of the democratic confederal program as expressed by Öcalan and embodied in the institutions being built in Rojava, which seek to enshrine principles of ecological sustainability as a third fundamental pillar in its approach (Ayboga 2021; Hildyard 2018; Hunt 2019).

In sum, Öcalan and the Kurdish freedom movement have effectively accomplished a redefinition of self-determination, now conceived in relation to a version of grassroots democracy that seeks to ensure multicultural accommodation, to prioritize gender emancipation, and to guarantee ecological sustainability. All this occurs in a region that finds itself at the very epicentre of neo-imperialist conflict, where ethnic and sectarian groups are so often pitted against one another, where ultra-reactionary forces seek to subjugate women, and where the soil bleeds oil.

This is a most impressive achievement, which in some ways amounts to a full-circle moment for the principle of self-determination, born out of the imperative of the sovereignty of people/s. Perhaps too often this achievement has been chalked up to the influence of Murray Bookchin upon Öcalan's thought (e.g. Cemgil and Hoffman 2016; Gerber and Brincat 2021; Harned 2019). Bookchin has been influential, no doubt (Biehl 2012; Hammy 2021). But there are other affinities, albeit not direct influences over Öcalan, but affinities nonetheless, convergences with a critical orientation towards the understanding of self-determination in terms of nation-state sovereignty, articulated along expressly anti-colonial, postcolonial, and decolonial lines.

Fanon's Critique of Self-Determination

Let us begin with Fanon. In *The Wretched of the Earth*, Fanon mentions the term self-determination only twice, both times in a critical vein. The first such occasion comes in the chapter "Concerning Violence," in his discussion of nationalist political parties, which he critiques for "proclaim[ing] abstract principles" while "refrain[ing] from issuing definite demands". He portrays these parties as pursuing exclusively "action of the electoral type". Among such actions, he includes composing "a string of philosophical political dissertations on the themes of the rights of peoples to self-determination, the rights of man to freedom from hunger and human dignity, and the unceasing affirmation of the principle 'one man, one vote'". But when it comes to the matter of violence, he contends, "[t]he national political parties never lay stress upon the necessity of a trial of armed strength, for the good reason that their objective is not the radical overthrowing of the system" (1963, p.59). Fanon thus seems to dismiss talk of self-determination as but a ploy on the part of nationalist elites who are not really interested in a process of thorough-going decolonization – a process which would require nothing less than the putting into practice of the sentence, "[t]he last shall be first and the first last" (1963, p.37). Their "pacifist" and "legalist" reflexes, their harping on about the self-determination of peoples, Fanon insists, are instead reflective of the fact that these nationalist elites are actually "partisans of order," albeit "the new order". They are but "blunt[ly] posing" the main demand which they put to the colonialist bourgeoisie, namely, "[g]ive us more power" (1963, p.59).

The second occasion on which Fanon mentions the term self-determination comes again in the chapter "Concerning Violence," this time in the context of his discussion of American geo-strategic designs. Fanon remarks that "the Americans take their role of patron of international capitalism very seriously," and as such, acting in this role, "[e]arly on, they advise the European countries to decolonize in a friendly fashion". This same role leads them, subsequently, not "to hesitate to proclaim first the respect for, then the support of, the principle of 'Africa for the Africans'," and, ultimately, to be unafraid to "state officially that they are the defenders of the rights of all peoples to self-determination". Their purpose, Fanon contends, is to avoid the outbreak of violence. Because with the outbreak of such violence, with the outbreak of real nationalist wars, comes "the opportunity for socialist propaganda to infiltrate among the masses and to contaminate them" (1963, p.79). The principle of self-determination is thus again seized upon by Fanon, identified as part of a discursive repertoire aimed at defusing the threat of thoroughgoing decolonization, now somehow explicitly aligned with the cause of socialism.

Be it in the slogans of nationalist elites, or in the mouths of American diplomats, such talk of the principle of self-determination, Fanon warns, should be met with scepticism. It is, for Fanon, an abstract principle which he compares to definite demands, a legalist and pacifist ideal which he compares to the kind of core commitment to a revolutionary transformation of concrete constellations of material and social power relations only achievable through violent struggle. In a word, Fanon suggests, the principle of self-determination promises an orderly alternative to the spectre of bloody, thoroughgoing decolonization for local elites, and for the patrons of international capitalism.

Fanon's critique of the principle of self-determination was, in turn, linked to his denunciation of what he termed "the pitfalls of national consciousness" in general, and his specification of the "historic mission" of the "national middle class" in particular, a mission which, he insisted, "has nothing to do with transforming the nation," and everything to do with serving as an "intermediary" for international capital. According to Fanon, this mission "consists, prosaically, of being a transmission line between the nation and a capitalism, rampant though camouflaged, which today puts on the mask of neo-colonialism". As such, like Nkrumah, Fanon is quick to diagnose the onset of the era of neo-colonialism, even under the rubric of self-determination. And he seems set to emphatically dismiss the idea that the national middle class can play a progressive role in the pursuit of a strategy of independent, national development under its leadership. To the contrary, he contends, that in the African colonies, at least, "the dynamic, pioneer aspect, the characteristics of the inventor and the discoverer of new worlds which are found in all national bourgeoisies, are lamentably absent," that, instead, "the spirit of indulgence is dominant at [its] core" (1963, pp.152-153).

This critique by Fanon is, interestingly enough, broadly in line with the tenor of Timothy Mitchell's argument in his 2011 book, *Carbon Democracy*, in which Mitchell sketches the genealogy and function of the ideal of self-determination as articulated after the First World War in relation to the so-called Middle East. In the book, Mitchell shows how, in the process of elaboration and consolidation of the mandate system, the demand for democratization of transnational relations was effectively transformed into "the very different principle of self-determination, or 'the consent of the governed'" (2011, p.78). Such a contrast between the "democratization of transnational relations" and "self-determination" resonates with the similar contrast drawn by Fanon between thoroughgoing "decolonization" and "self-determination". For Mitchell, like Fanon, the translation of demands for the former category into respect for the latter principle are seen as a strategy for salvaging fundamental hierarchies in the constellations of power relations characteristic of the international and domestic orders, respectively.

As George Ciccariello-Maher has emphasized, Fanon warned how "emancipation — and formal equality more broadly speaking — [could] reinforce ontological hierarchy by masking it beneath a false universalism that became white supremacy's best alibi". But "from a dialectical perspective," Ciccariello-Maher continues, "for this alibi to function on both the objective and subjective levels, for it to deactivate struggles and freeze dialectical movement at the level of the merely formal, something essential must have been lacking from the emancipation process itself. That something was struggle" (2017, p.64). Indeed, to this end, "Fanon draws upon the centrality Hegel ascribes to struggle for subjective transformation as leverage to insist that freedom cannot be given, but must instead be fought for" (2017, p.65).

This point made by Ciccariello-Maher about the centrality of struggle for Fanon can help us understand the scepticism that he registers towards appeals for formal recognition of self-determination. Fanon was concerned that such recognition could effectively short-circuit the combative confrontation required for the revolutionary transformation of power relations in both the international and domestic orders that thoroughgoing decolonization by definition must entail.

Fanon thus anticipates a state of affairs that would be perceptively diagnosed by Nkrumah, a half a decade later, that "[t]he 'end of empire' [could be] accompanied by a flourishing of other means of subjugation" (1966, p.52).

Most menacingly, by the spectre of neo-colonialism, which would be succinctly described by Nkrumah as follows: "[t]he essence of neo-colonialism is that the State which is subject to it is, in theory, independent and has all the outward trappings of international sovereignty. In reality its economic system and thus its political policy is directed from the outside" (1966, p.ix).

Getachew's Defence of Anti-Colonial Self-Determination

Fanon's critical orientation towards the category of self-determination serves, too, as a counterpoint and partial corrective to the full-throated defence of the dynamics and achievements of the era of anti-colonial self-determination articulated by Adom Getachew in her important contribution, *Worldmaking after Empire: The Rise and Fall of Self-Determination* (2019). In the book, Getachew "draw[s] on the political thought" of a diverse array of thinkers and activists, including "Nnamdi Azikiwe, W.E.B. Du Bois, Michael Manley, Kwame Nkrumah, Julius Nyerere, George Padmore, and Eric Williams, [in order to] argue that decolonization was a project of reordering the world that sought to create a domination-free and egalitarian international order" (2019, p.2). Getachew takes issue with what she calls "the standard view of decolonization as a moment of *nation-building* in which the anticolonial demand for self-determination culminated in the rejection of alien rule and the formation of nation-states" (2019, p.2). Rather than this *nation-building* dimension, a dimension which she does not deny, Getachew emphasizes instead that these anticolonial nationalist projects were simultaneously projects of *worldmaking*. The protagonists of Getachew's story, she persuasively contends, did not only seek to extend the doctrine of self-determination, to apply a fixed doctrine to their colonized nations; rather, they reinvented the doctrine altogether, so that it could "reach beyond its association with the nation". Indeed, they would "insist that the achievement of this ideal required juridical, political, and economic institutions in the international realm that would secure non-domination" (2019, p.2).

Getachew is careful to situate the worldmaking projects at the core of her narrative within a series of successive subversive and globally ambitious projects. In the process, Getachew provides a very illuminating, synoptic sketch of the trajectory of the doctrine of self-determination, whose eruption on the international scene she traces back, notably, to Vladimir Lenin and the Bolshevik Revolution. Getachew highlights how, after the Bolsheviks came to power in October of 1917 in a Russia that was thoroughly devastated by the so-called Great War, they began to call for, to demand, "'a democratic peace between the nations, without annexations and indemnities and on the basis of the free self-determination of nations'". This call on the part of Lenin's revolutionary government, in turn, would have tremendous ramifications, with "observers among the Allied powers and elsewhere" fearing its impact upon the exploited and dispossessed around the world. In a word, "the Russian Revolution 'seemed to have all the qualities of the opening act of a revolutionary drama shortly to be enacted all over Europe'. According to then-US Secretary of State Robert Lansing, the revolution threatened the domestic stability of states and the prospects for a stable postwar world order" (2019, pp.37-38).

The capitalist powers responded accordingly, with American President Woodrow Wilson, alongside the South African Jan Smuts, coming to embrace the doctrine of self-determination, only to recast it in the context of the emergent institutional order of the League of Nations as a racially differentiated principle in the service of empire. This is what Getachew means by referring to the post-War "Wilsonian moment" as a "counterrevolutionary moment". And she goes on to emphasize the more general methodological point that "the principle of self-determination must be excavated through careful attention to the contexts in which it emerges and the uses for which it is mobilized" (2019, p.40).

Flash forward to the end of the Second World War, and we come to another moment of recasting, of reinvention, in which "anticolonial nationalists [would] appropriate the principle of self-determination [and] reinvent its meaning through a novel critique of imperialism that centered on the problems of slavery and racial hierarchy" (2019, p.74). In terms of the logic of question and answer, as Getachew frames it, anticolonial nationalist "framed empire as enslavement and conceived of the right to self-determination as the response to this problem". In other words, "[i]n this pairing of question and answer, the anticolonial account of self-determination was invented" (2019, p.77).

The institutional and discursive openings for the anticolonial reinvention of self-determination were not, of course, unlimited. Instead, the context was one of both "possibility and constraint," Getachew claims, invoking the eminent historian Frederick Cooper's "felicitous phrase" to this effect (2019, p.79). And in terms of contextual constraints, most significantly, "the more radical demands around economic self-determination … would have to be set aside in the institutionalization of [the] right to self-determination" (2019, p.79).

This right to self-determination was conceived by anticolonial nationalists as but a first step. And Getachew spends a good deal of time in her book sketching the projects, the ultimately failed institutional experiments, of regional federation and international economic redistribution, intended as complements and counterparts necessary for approximating substantive sovereign equality and non-domination in the international order.

Fanon as Counterpoint

Fanon provides a counterpoint to Getachew's narrative. He specifies the particular domestic and international loci from which the discourse of self-determination emanated in and around the anticolonial struggle. In so doing, he helps explain the contextual constraints, contradictions, and ultimate failure of the promise of self-determination to deliver anything close to substantive sovereign equality, much less non-domination in the international order.

There is, nonetheless, a narrative of national liberation, and of human emancipation, to which Fanon remains undoubtedly committed. One could even say, following Marx's famous formulation from his 1844 essay "On the Jewish Question," that the contrast between self-determination and thoroughgoing decolonization that Fanon makes is reminiscent of the distinction between political emancipation and human emancipation (Marx 1844). But we live in an era in which the category of emancipation itself has come into question. David Scott, for example, has elaborated a rather sophisticated argument along the lines that there is, allegedly, a political and epistemic abyss that separates us from the narrative of emancipation which Fanon articulates in *The Wretched of the Earth*; indeed, that the "problem-space" in which Fanon's anticolonial project made sense and operated has been rendered irredeemably obsolete. This is because, in a word, "the epistemological assumptions that [had] held [the anticolonial project] together and guaranteed the salience of its emancipatory hopes—assumptions about history, about culture, politics, resistance, freedom, subjectivity — have been steadily eroded by the labor of anti-metaphysical and anti-teleological strategies of criticism" (1999, p.199).

It is difficult to deny the at least partial persuasiveness of Scott's line of postmodern and postcolonial argument. This is an age of defeat and disenchantment, no doubt. The revolutionary optimism with which Fanon could still face the future, even from his deathbed, does indeed seem to belong to another era, one that sometimes appears irrevocably lost to us. And yet, the aspiration for radical freedom is quite stubborn in its persistence. Anywhere there is tyranny, domination, exploitation, and oppression, sooner or later the will to resist is bound to emerge. The revolutionary impulse and imperative, the dictum that "the last shall be first," can only be suppressed for so long. As the terminal crisis of capitalist modernity continues to unfold around the globe. The brutal consequences of never-ending neo-imperialist wars, of never-equalled levels of plutocratic plunder, of always-worsening climate catastrophe become increasingly obvious. More people may just realize that, in crucial ways, Fanon must remain our contemporary, if we are to stand a chance to survive.

Wilder on Césaire and Senghor and Alternative Anti-colonial Conceptions of Self-Determination

We have seen how Fanon's distinction between self-determination and decolonization can serve as a partial corrective to Getachew's revindication of the achievements of the anticolonial era. Let us now turn to look at a narrative which complements Fanon's distinction. The contrast between the abstract principle of self-determination and the concrete struggle for decolonization as sketched by Fanon tends to converge with the recent attempt by Gary Wilder in his book, *Freedom Time* (2015), to recover alternative understandings of colonial emancipation, not reducible to national liberation and state sovereignty, alternative understandings articulated by the likes of Césaire and Senghor.

Wilder emphasizes the dual nature of decolonization: on one side, it represented "an emancipatory awakening of peoples;" and simultaneously, on the other, "a heteronomous process of imperial restructuring". Yet most actors and agencies on both sides of the imperial divide tended to "share the assumption that self-determination meant state sovereignty".

Césaire and Senghor, by contrast, refused to "reduce decolonization to national independence". This refusal on their part, Wilder argues, "derived from their convictions about the difference between formal liberation and substantive freedom". Moreover, there was both a pragmatic and an ethical dimension to this refusal. According to Wilder: "Pragmatically, they believed that autarchic national solutions could not adequately address the problem of colonial freedom in an epoch of global interdependence. Ethically, they believed that the history of imperial entanglement allowed them to claim the legacies, resources, and rights supposedly reserved for metropolitans" (2015, pp.241-242).

In different ways, Césaire and Senghor both called for the radical reconfiguration of political relations within the French Empire for its transformation into a multi-national, democratic federation. Wilder urges us to imagine what might have been had such a vision been realized. He contends: "Africans *sans papiers* in metropolitan France would not be foreigners demanding hospitality but citizens whose rights of mobility, family reunification, social security, and political participation were legally protected. Africans would not be outsiders appealing for economic aid from a foreign French state nor targets of dehumanizing humanitarianism. Violations of their human rights could be adjudicated in a federal justice system rather than depend on the weak ethical norms of international law or the good will of powerful nations. West African peoples would be integral members of an expanded European Union" (2015, p.244).

Even more forcefully, Wilder sums up his argument by insisting that "the nationalist logic of decolonization has contributed to dispossession; state sovereignty has neither been a recipe for self-determination in postcolonial Africa nor a guarantor of basic rights for Africans in the metropolitan postcolony" (2015, p.246). As such, a radical rethinking of what self-determination would require, indeed, a decoupling of the ideal from the paradigm of nation-state sovereignty, would seem in order. Césaire and Senghor stand out as untimely thinkers, whose dissent from what came to be the hegemonic program and parameters of anti-colonial nationalism in their own era, emerges again today, capable of speaking directly to the dilemmas of our era, in which the promises of nation-state sovereignty have come to ring increasingly hollow.

Wilder's recovery of futures that might have been, as envisioned by Césaire and Senghor, in turn allows us to historicize the equation of self-determination with nation-state sovereignty, and thus to come to terms with the profound significance of Frederick Cooper's reminder that "[a]nticolonial movements were not a stage along an inevitable pathway from empire to nation, but part of a wider pattern of struggle whose culmination in the multiplication of nation-states was conjunctural and contingent" (2005, pp.153-154). Indeed, even that "[n]ationalism was part of the repertoire of political opposition, but not necessarily the most important one" (2005, p.156).

There are thus resources within the anticolonial tradition for critiquing the principle of self-determination and/or for questioning its reducibility to the demand for state sovereignty. Such resources can be fruitfully seized upon today, in our quest to reimagine what self-determination can and must mean in the twenty-first century. For we must come to terms with the limits and failures of decolonization, understood as the achievement of formal state sovereignty, en route to a revival of the critique of the state.

The Decolonial Critique of the Nation-State Paradigm

Decolonial thinkers such as Walter Mignolo, perhaps unexpectedly, turn out to be quite helpful in this regard. With Catherine Walsh, Mignolo has emphasised that, for the decolonial paradigm and project, "the horizon is not the political independence of nation-states (as it was for decolonization)," but rather, it is concerned "with the habits that modernity/coloniality implanted in all of us; with how modernity/coloniality has worked and continues to work to negate, disavow, distort and deny knowledges, subjectivities, world senses, and life visions" (Walsh and Mignolo 2018, p.2).

According to Walsh and Mignolo, the decolonial project came into focus in the 1990s, by which time "decolonization's failure in most nations had become clear; with state in the hands of minority elites, the patterns of colonial power continued both internally (i.e., internal colonialism) and with relation to global structures," and thus "decoloniality was born in the unveiling of coloniality" (Walsh and Mignolo 2018, pp.5-6).

Not coincidentally, it was around the same time that, in Bolivia, "the 500-kilometer March of Indigenous Peoples from the lowland Amazon region to the capital ... made visible a people that the so-called nation-state had historically denied" (Walsh 2018, p.25).

Mignolo describes the result of struggles for independence as entailing merely a shift from "outward coloniality," by which he means "European direct control over the colonies," towards "internal colonialism," by which he means "local elites managing the building of colonial nation-states according to the script of the European idea of modernity" (Mignolo 2018, pp.122-123).

Indeed, Mignolo is emphatic that "[t]he state politics of decolonization failed, and among the consequences are the failed modern/colonial nation-states created after independence, as seen today in several regions of Asia and Africa" (Mignolo 2018, p.128). He goes on to specify that though "[d]ecolonization ... was successful in sending the colonizer home," it was a failure nonetheless, "for it ended up creating nation-states that remained within the management of the colonial matrix of power even if imperial settlers were no longer in the terrain". To this end, he contends: "Knowledge was not called into question, but it was accepted as if decolonization could be achieved without delinking from the knowledge of political theory and political economy, and the corresponding subject-formation that these knowledges entail" (Mignolo 2018, p.222).

The pursuit of the independent nation-state, which characterized "the project of decolonization during the Cold War," Mignolo insists, fell "into the trap of coloniality without colonialism" (Mignolo 2018, p.234). This is because, he argues, "nation-states, the very idea of uniform nationality, was a European imperial imposition" (Mignolo 2018, p.237). Accordingly, the goal of decolonization, to "take hold of the state," proved "insufficient" (Mignolo 2018, p.136).

Elsewhere, he highlights that among the reasons for the failure of decolonization during the Cold War, two stand out: the first being "that local elites wanted something (the nation-state) that was alien to them but that was desirable because of the persuasive rhetoric enticing people to become modern and jump on the bandwagon of universal history". The second was the fact "that the elites founding, and controlling the newly formed nation-state also took the opportunity of the personal advantage that decolonization offered them". As a result, he concludes, "[a]ll the dreams of Amilcar Cabral and Patrice Lumumba were taken away from them and distorted by the elites trapped in the interstate system web regulated by the colonial matrix of power" (Mignolo 2018, p.238).

In a word, the project of decoloniality, in contrast to that of decolonization, is characterised by an opening to imagining "forms of governance beyond the nation-state". According to Mignolo, "decoloniality has changed the terrain from aiming at forming sovereign nation-states (decolonization) out of the ruins of the colonies to aiming at decolonial horizons of liberation (decoloniality) beyond state designs, and corporate and financial desires". Exemplary in this regard, he contends, is the "engaged praxis of living and knowing" allegedly embodied by the Zapatistas (Mignolo 2018, p.125).

Decoloniality, he goes on to insist, cannot be achieved "via state politics and regulation". To the contrary, he argues, "it requires a political structure of governance (not the current nation-state) that rules and obeys at the same time …, that supports people's organizations and creativity, that could be thought of as part of a communal decolonial horizon". Nor are the Zapatistas alone in such an endeavour. Rather, he insists, "[i]n the second decade of the twenty-first century, the number of organizations denying the authority of the colonial matrix of power and the empty promises of the rhetoric of modernity is growing around the planet" (Mignolo 2018, p.126).

Öcalan and the Re-Articulation of Self-Determination

He might have mentioned the Kurds. The project of democratic confederalism espoused by the Kurdish freedom movement, inspired by the writings of the imprisoned leader Abdullah Öcalan, and institutionalised in the revolutionary developments in Rojava in northeastern Syria, is expressly framed as such a form of governance beyond the nation-state. Öcalan has argued that though "[t]he right of self-determination of the peoples includes the right to a state of their own," it turns out that, nevertheless, "the foundation of a state does not increase the freedom of a people;" indeed, that "nation-states have become serious obstacles for any social development" (2017, p.46).

Elsewhere, Öcalan has stressed that "[t]he inadequate analysis of the question of the state by socialist ideology obscures the problem of the nation-state's place in the hegemonic system of capitalist modernity". Moreover, he continues, "in the 'right of nations to self-determination', the vision of a state for every nation was fundamental in aggravating the issue even further" (2017, p.105). Such flawed analysis, he insists, ended up propagating the cult of the state, the religious conviction that a state is needed for a nation to be free.

The paradigm and program Öcalan advances, that of democratic confederalism, he contends, "is the contrasting paradigm of the oppressed people. [It] is a non-state social paradigm. It is not controlled by a state". It is conceived as a form of radical, direct democracy, "based on grassroots participation," in which "decision-making processes lie with the communities," and in which "the basic power of decision rests with the local grassroots institutions" (2017, pp.46-47).

This re-articulation of self-determination, away from the goal of the nation-state, instead in favour of the construction of institutions for grass-roots democratic participation, is presented as a paradigm shift, and as a response to the failure of formal state sovereignty to bring about real freedom, or the substantive emancipation of colonised peoples.

The transformation of the Kurdish freedom movement, born as a movement that espoused the classic goals of national liberation, but coming to embrace the democratic confederal, non-state alternative, indeed, its attempt to transcend the nationalist imaginary, resonates with the decolonial impulse to "deny the authority of the colonial matrix of power". This is so, even if Öcalan does not reject altogether as "empty promises ... the rhetoric of modernity" (Mignolo 2018, p.126), but rather re-vindicates the potential for a "democratic modernity," conceived to be in dialectical tension and opposition to "capitalist modernity" (Öcalan 2017, pp.99-105).

Likewise, Öcalan's anti-statist turn resonates not only with decolonial but also with certain postcolonial sensibilities. For example, Partha Chatterjee insists on the distinction between community and state in his 1993 book, *The Nation and Its Fragments: Colonial and Postcolonial Histories*. Chatterjee contends that "autonomous forms of imagination of the community were, and continue to be, overwhelmed and swamped by the history of the postcolonial state". In this vein, he emphasizes: "[h]ere lies the root of our postcolonial

misery: not in our inability to think out new forms of the modern community but in our surrender to the old forms of the modern state" (1993, p.11).

The influence of Murray Bookchin on Öcalan's thinking has been much
emphasized, indeed, somewhat exaggerated. But Bookchin was an unabashed
and unapologetic Eurocentrist, whereas Öcalan is coming from a very different place (Muhammad 2018; Venturini 2015). Öcalan does undoubtedly take
inspiration in Bookchin, but he appropriates his categories creatively, incorporating them into his own, idiosyncratic and synthetic vision, a vision which
tends to converge with many of the anticolonial, postcolonial, and decolonial
critiques of self-determination that we have already reviewed.

In her thoughtful preface to the English-language translation of the second
volume of Öcalan's five-volume *Manifesto for a Democratic Civilization*,
Radha D'Souza has emphasized how "common words with shared meanings
acquired diverse meanings under specific contexts of anticolonial movements," and from this fact proceeds to stress "the need for caution in the way
ideas about nation, nation-state, and communities are understood in English
and Eastern languages" (2017, p.24). D'Souza thus poses a difficult question
about what might be lost in translation, a question whose significance, upon
reflection, goes beyond just the meaning of specific words, to include the
broader frames of reference, the cultural context within which any specific
articulation takes place. In this vein, D'Souza dismisses the "rough and ready"
interpretation according to which "Öcalan comes close to a synthesis of
Marxism and anarchism," an interpretation which she alleges relies on the
assumption that "liberalism, socialism, Marxism, and anarchism are the only
possible political theories and that Greco-Roman philosophical schools are
the only schools of philosophy that we have as sources for our conceptual
repertoire" (2017, p.17). Öcalan no doubt engages in a dialogue with these political theories and these philosophical schools, but he does so from a standpoint in which he is immersed in so many other sources as well. It is
important that we not forget this crucial point. Indeed, openness to just such
a sensibility is what motivates my desire to situate Öcalan's re-articulation of
self-determination in relation to the traditions of anticolonial, postcolonial,
and decolonial critiques of the concept.

But be that as it may, Öcalan's reformulation would situate the principle
of self-determination at the ethical core of the democratic ideal. The basic
principle that can be induced from his articulation is that people have a right

to determine the contours and content of the social, political, and economic relations in which their lives are embedded (Akkaya and Jongerden 2012; Jongerden 2016). The realization of such a principle not only includes but would in fact take us well beyond the right to representative rule. It would entail the construction and consolidation of participatory democratic mechanisms in places of worship, in schools, at the workplace, for example, as well as, crucially, the constitution of popular assemblies at the level of neighbourhoods and villages (Conway and Singh 2011; Esteva 2007; Milstein 2020). Furthermore, it would require the confederation of such local outlets for participation to guarantee democratic responsiveness and accountability at larger, regional, 'national', and transnational scales (Grubacic 2019; Öcalan 2017, p.45; Öcalan 2020, p. 357).

Of course, self-determination is a term with many meanings. For some, if not most, it has referred principally to a right that belongs to nations, a right to national independence (Fisch 2015; Weitz 2015). This in turn is usually interpreted in explicitly statist terms as a right to an independent nation-state. Öcalan provides grounds for scepticism about this proposition – not out of any indifference to specifically national forms of oppression, but rather, because he emphasizes that the merits of the ideal of independence in our inextricably interdependent world would seem dubious, at best (Iriye 2014; Öcalan 2011, p.62). By all means, he also points out that the proliferation of nominally independent nation-states has rarely led to substantive independence. Nor, he adds, is nominal independence even a reliable formula for actually reducing the occurrence of national oppression, though it can be quite effective at turning the tables, converting tyrannized national minorities into tyrannical national majorities (Miley 2018; Öcalan 2012, p.90; Öcalan 2017, p.99).

Öcalan's formulation helps us to overcome the statist interpretation of self-determination, as well as indeed the tendency to think about self-determination in exclusively, or even primarily, national terms (Gould 2006; Jongerden 2017). This should not be confused with a call for a purely individualistic understanding of the right to self-determination. To the contrary, he definitely thinks it makes sense to claim that national groups have a right to self-determination, conceived as a right for self-governance or political autonomy. But for Öcalan, other kinds of groups can be considered political communities in the relevant sense, with a right to self-determination as well, including women (Öcalan 2017, p.96; Rasit and Kolokotronis 2020).

The right to self-determination, as articulated by Öcalan, is thus somehow akin to a principle of non-domination (Cemgil 2016; Okçuo lu 2018). It is located at the core of the democratic ideal, but also includes specific group rights for political autonomy, especially for groups that have suffered systemic oppression. Moreover, Öcalan is careful to stress, it must not remain a mere abstract principle; rather, it is a right that can only be realized through the dynamics – the victories – of concrete political struggles (Öcalan 2020, pp.350-354).

Conclusion

In this chapter, we have sought to situate the imprisoned Kurdish leader Abdullah Öcalan's historic re-articulation of self-determination in relation to a series of anti-colonial, postcolonial, and decolonial critiques of the category. Such iconic figures as Fanon, Césaire, Senghor, and Mignolo have stood out most prominently in this account. This may seem like an unlikely pairing, since Öcalan is more often treated in dialogue with people like Murray Bookchin, Andre Gunder Frank, Maria Mies, Immanuel Wallerstein, Fernand Braudel, and Michel Foucault, whose work has more directly influenced Öcalan's thought (Bar-On 2015; Biehl 2012; Hammy 2021; Piccardi 2021). However, our intention has been to highlight other affinities, with figures who have not exercised direct influences over Öcalan, but with whose critical orientation towards the understanding of self-determination in terms of formal nation-state sovereignty, there is a clear convergence nonetheless. In a word, ours is an effort to recast Öcalan in an explicitly anti-/post-/de-colonial light.

Öcalan's re-articulation of the principle of self-determination effectively closes the gap between the category and Fanon's alternative of definite demands for thoroughgoing decolonization. Not only does the ethos of democratic confederalism indeed approximate the dictum that "the last shall be first". So too does it incorporate a model of militant struggle, emphasizing the imperative of self-defence. In Öcalan's words, "[a] society that insists on determining its own course, that rejects colonization or any form of imposed dependency, must be capable of self-defence" (2020, p.190).

Like Fanon, too, Öcalan would seem well aware of the "pitfalls of national consciousness" (Fanon 1963). No doubt, the radical democratic alternative to capitalist modernity that he proposes would seem to leave little room for the exercise of hegemony by the Kurdish national middle class (Öcalan 2011, pp.47-49). Likewise, Öcalan appears perfectly cognizant of the divide and rule tactic motivating any and all American gestures towards the recognition of the right to self-determination, conceived in statist terms, for the Kurds (Öcalan 2011, pp.108-110). Local intermediaries and international agents of capitalist modernity are thus both treated with a similar sort of scepticism by Öcalan as they had been by Fanon. Indeed, such scepticism is in part what motivates Öcalan's critique of the nation-state form.

Moreover, Öcalan's creative appropriation and resignification of the principle of self-determination is reminiscent of a similar move made by emblematic anti-colonial figures in the post-war era, as recounted by Getachew. Indeed, towards the very end of her book, Getachew emphasises how "even instances that appeared as moments of closure—first the decline of interwar internationalisms and the consolidation of a system of nation-states, and later the political and economic limits of the postcolonial state—were occasion for reformulating the contours of an anti-imperial future and enacting new strategies to realize this vision. On this view," she continues, "the fall of self-determination marks not only a dead end but also a staging ground for reimaging that future" (2019, p.181). Getachew perceives "intimations of a new language ... afoot" in a variety of movements across the Black Atlantic World, including Black Lives Matter, calls for reparations by Caribbean nations, and South African calls for social and economic decolonization. But movements can be perceived in the so-called Middle East as well – and Öcalan and the Kurdish freedom movement have staked out a position at the vanguard among these trends.

Similarly, Öcalan's formulation of the "democratic nation" (2012, pp.89-93; 2017, pp.97-144) in particular, recalls in important respects the alternative conceptualization of self-determination, not linked to formal state sovereignty, elaborated by the likes of such emblematic, albeit heterodox, anticolonial figures as Aimé Césaire and Leopold Sédar Senghor. Just as Césaire and Senghor advocated the transformation of the French Empire into a multinational, democratic federation, Öcalan has called not for the construction of new borders but, rather, for their transcendence, through the formation of a democratic confederation of the peoples of the Middle East (Öcalan 2011, p.62, p.90). Wilder has highlighted how the untimely thought of Césaire and Senghor, specifically their dissent from the equation of self-determination with nation-state sovereignty, re-emerges today as capable of speaking to the dilemmas of our era, in which the contradictions and confines of the nation-state have become increasingly obvious (Wilder 2015, pp.244-246). It is these same dilemmas, these same contradictions and constrictions of the nation-state, to which Öcalan's articulation of self-determination as radical, grass roots, direct democracy against the state also speaks.

Finally, Öcalan's elaboration of a distinctly non-state paradigm for self-determination resonates quite closely with Walter Mignolo's decolonial critique of the nation-state as reflecting and perpetuating the "colonial matrix of power". Mignolo points to the Zapatista movement's efforts to rule by obeying as indicative of an alternative, decolonial approach to governance beyond the nation-state (Mignolo 2011, pp.213-251; 2018, p.125). Such an ethos converges rather precisely with Öcalan's insistence that "[d]emocratic confederalism leaves no room for hegemony of any sort" (2020, p.220). The Zapatistas and the Kurdish freedom movement, therefore, in praxis, in subjective knowledge and theoretical orientation are movements that tend to prefigure and embody an alternative understanding of what self-determination can and must come to mean in the twenty-first century (Saed 2017; Venturini 2021). In this vein, Öcalan's efforts to articulate a new paradigm for the emancipation of colonized peoples, which has already inspired the revolutionary developments in Rojava, northeastern Syria, are perhaps just beginning to bear fruit. The proof, as they say, will be in the pudding.

REFERENCES

Akkaya, H. and Jongerden, J. (2012). "Reassembling the Political: The PKK and the Project of Radical Democracy," *European Journal of Turkish Studies. Social Sciences on Contemporary Turkey*, Vol. 14.

Allsopp, H. and Van Wilgenburg, W. (2019). *The Kurds of Northern Syria. Governance, Diversity, and Conflicts.* London: I.B. Taurus.

Ayboga, E. (2021). "Ecology Structures of the Kurdish Freedom Movement," in S. Hunt, ed., *Ecological Solidarity and the Kurdish Freedom Movement.* London: Lexington Books, pp.77-96.

Bar-On, T. (2015). "From Marxism and Nationalism to Radical Democracy: Abdullah

Öcalan's Synthesis for the 21st Century," *Ciencias Sociales y Relaciones Internacionales. Nuevas Perspectivas desde América Latina.* CLACSO, pp.225-256.

Biehl, J. (2012). "Bookchin, Öcalan, and the Dialectics of Democracy". Accessible online at: https://mirror.anarhija.net/theanarchistlibrary.org/mirror/j/jb/janet-biehl-bookchin-ocalan-and-the-dialectics-of-democracy.a4.pdf

Burç, R. (2020). "Non-Territorial Autonomy and Gender Equality: The Case of the Autonomous Administration of North and East Syria – Rojava," *Filosofija i drustvo*, Vol. 31, No. 3, pp.319-339.

Cemgil, C. "The Republican Ideal of Freedom as Non-Domination and the Rojava Experiment: 'States as They Are' or a New Socio-Political Imagination?" *Philosophy and Social Criticism*, Vol. 42, Nos. 4-5, pp.419-428.

Cemgil, C. and Hoffman, C. (2016). "The 'Rojava Revolution' in Syrian Kurdistan: A Model of Development for the Middle East?" *IDS Bulletin*, Vol. 47, No. 3, pp.53-76.

Chatterjee, P. (1993). *The Nation and Its Fragments. Colonial and Postcolonial Histories.* Princeton, NJ: Princeton University Press.

Ciccariello-Maher, G. (2017). *Decolonizing Dialectics.* Durham, NC: Duke University Press.

Coakley, J. (1994). "Approaches to the Resolution of Ethnic Conflict: The Strategy of Non-Territorial Autonomy," *International Political Science Review*, Vol. 15, No. 3, pp.297-314.

Colasanti, N., et. al. (2018). "Grassroots Democracy and Local Government in Northern Syria: The Case of Democratic Confederalism," *Local Government Studies*, Vol. 44, No. 6, pp.807-825.

Conway, J. and J. Singh. (2011). "Radical Democracy in Global Perspective: Notes from the Pluriverse," *Third World Quarterly*, Vol. 32, No. 4, pp.689-706.

Cooper, F. (2005). *Colonialism in Question. Theory, Knowledge, History.* Berkeley, CA: University of California Press.

Dinc, P. (2020). "The Kurdish Movement and the Democratic Federation of Northern Syria: An Alternative to the (Nation-)State Model?" *Journal of Balkan and Near Eastern Studies*, Vol. 22, No. 1, pp.47-67.

Dirik, D. (2018). "Overcoming the Nation-State: Women's Autonomy and Radical Democracy in Kurdistan," in J. Mulholland, et. al., eds., *Gendering Nationalism.* London: Palgrave Macmillan, Cham, pp.145-163.

D'Souza, R. (2017). "Preface," in Abdullah Öcalan, *Manifesto for a Democratic Civilization. Volume II. Capitalism. The Age of Unmasked Gods and Naked Kings.* Cologne: International Initiative Edition.

Esteva, G. (2007). "Oaxaca: The Path of Radical Democracy," *Socialism and Democracy*, Vol. 21, No. 2, pp.74-96.

Fadaee, S. and Brancolini, C. (2019). "From National Liberation to Radical Democracy: Exploring the Shift in the Kurdish Liberation Movement in Turkey," *Ethnicities*, Vol. 19, No. 5, pp.858-875.

Fanon, F. (1963). *The Wretched of the Earth*. New York: Grove Press.

Fisch, J. (2015). *The Right of Self-Determination of Peoples: The Domestication of an Illusion*. Cambridge: Cambridge University Press.

Gerber, D. and Brincat, S. (2021). "When Öcalan Met Bookchin: The Kurdish Freedom Movement and the Political Theory of Democratic Confederalism," *Geopolitics*, Vol. 26, No. 4, pp.973-997.

Getachew, A. (2019). *Worldmaking after Empire. The Rise and Fall of Self-Determination* Princeton, NJ: Princeton University Press.

Gould, C. (2006). "Self-Determination beyond Sovereignty: Relating Transnational Democracy to Local Autonomy," *Journal of Social Philosophy*, Vol. 37, No. 1, pp.44-60.

Grubacic, A. (2019). "Sweeping the World Clean of Capitalism: Samir Amin, Abdullah Ocalan and the World of Autonomous Regions," *Globalizations*, Vol. 16, No. 9, pp.1073-1078.

Gunes, C. (2020). "Approaches to Kurdish Autonomy in the Middle East," *Nationalities Papers* Vol. 48, No. 2, pp.323-338.

Guneser, H. with Finley, E. (2019). "The Evolution of the Kurdish Paradigm," in F. Venturini, et. al., eds., *Social Ecology and the Right to the City*. Montreal: Black Rose Books.

Hammy, C. (2021). "Social Ecology in Öcalan's Thinking," in S. Hunt, ed., *Ecological Solidarity and the Kurdish Freedom Movement*. London: Lexington Books, pp.25-40.

Harned, P. (2019). *Democratic Confederalism: A Radical Model for Political Emancipation in Northern Syria*. University of Texas at Austin Electronic Thesis.

Hildyard, N. (2018). "Where's the Revolution in Democratic Confederalism's Ecology?" Presentation to Seminar on Ecological and Gender Dimensions of the Democratic Confederalist Approach in Kurdistan. An Inter-Cultural Dialogue, SOAS, London, 3 February. Accessible at: http://www.thecornerhouse.org.uk/sites/thecornerhouse.org.uk/files/Where%27s%20the%20revolution.pdf

Hunt, S. (2019). "Prospects for Kurdish Ecology Initiatives in Syria and Turkey: Democratic Confederalism and Social Ecology," *Capitalism Nature Socialism*, Vol. 30, No. 3, pp.7-26.

Iriye, A. (2014). "The Making of a Transnational World," in A. Iriye, ed., *Global Interdependence: The World after 1945*. Cambridge, MA: Harvard University Press, pp.681-848.

Jongerden, J. (2016). "Colonialism, Self-Determination, and Independence: The New PKK Paradigm," *Kurdish Issues. Essays in Honor of Robert W. Olson*, pp.106-121.

Jongerden, J. (2017). "The Kurdistan Workers' Party (PKK): Radical Democracy and the Right to Self-Determination beyond the Nation-State," in G. Stansfield, ed., *The Kurdish Question Revisited*. London: Hurst and Company, pp.245-258.

Jongerden, J. (2019). "Learning from Defeat: Development and Contestation of the 'New Paradigm' within Kurdistan Workers' Party (PKK)," *Kurdish Studies*, Vol. 7, No. 1, pp.72-92.

Knapp, M. et. al. (2016). *Revolution in Rojava: Democratic Autonomy and Women's Liberation in Syrian Kurdistan*. London: Pluto Press.

Marx, K. (1844). "On the Jewish Question". Accessible at: https://www.marxists.org/ archive/marx/works/1844/jewish-question/

Mignolo, W. (2011). *Darker Side of Western Modernity. Global Futures, Decolonial Options*. Durham, NC: Duke University Press.

Mignolo, W. (2018). "The Decolonial Option" in W. Mignolo and C. Walsh, *On Decoloniality: Concepts, Analytics, Praxis*. Durham, NC: Duke University Press, pp.105-244.

Miley, T. (2018). "The Nation as Hegemonic Project," *Journal of Political Ideologies*, Vol. 23, No. 2, pp.183-204.

Milstein, C., ed. (2020). *Deciding for Ourselves. The Promise of Direct Democracy*. Chico, CA: AK Press.

Mitchell, T. (2011). *Carbon Democracy. Political Power in the Age of Oil*. London: Verso.

Muhammad, U. (2018). "An Unsuitable Theorist? Murray Bookchin and the PKK," *Turkish Studies*, Vol. 19, No. 5, pp.799-817.

Nimni, E. (1999). "Nationalist Multiculturalism in Late Imperial Austria as a Critique of Contemporary Liberalism: The Case of Bauer and Renner," *Journal of Political Ideologies*, Vol. 4, No. 3, pp.289-314.

Nkrumah, K. (1966). *Neo-Colonialism. The Last Stage of Imperialism*. New York: International Publishers.

Öcalan, A. (2011). *Prison Writings. The PKK and the Kurdish Question in the 21st Century*. London: Transmedia Publishing Ltd.

Öcalan, A. (2012). *Prison Writings III. The Road Map to Negotiations*. Cologne: International Initiative Edition.

Öcalan, A. (2017). *The Political Thought of Abdullah Öcalan. Kurdistan, Woman's Revolution, and Democratic Confederalism*. London: Pluto Press.

Öcalan, A. (2020). *The Sociology of Freedom*. Oakland, CA: PM Press.

Okçuoglu, D. (2018). "Rethinking Democracy and Autonomy through the Case of the Kurdish Movement," in E. Nimni and E. Aktoprak, eds., *Democratic Representation in*

Plurinational States. Comparative Territorial Politics. London: Palgrave Macmillan, Cham, pp.211-227.

Piccardi, E. (2021). "The Challenges of a Kurdish Ecofeminist Perspective: Maria Mies, Abdullah Öcalan, and the Praxis of Jineoloji," *Capitalism Nature Socialism,* DOI: 10.1080/10455752.2021.1905016

Quijano, A. (2000). "Coloniality of Power, Eurocentrism, and Latin America," *Nepantla: Views from the South,* Vol. 1, No. 3, pp.533-580.

Rasit, H. and Kolokotronis, A. (2020). "Decentralist Vanguards: Women's Autonomous Power and Left Convergence in Rojava," *Globalizations,* Vol. 17, No. 5, pp.869-883.

saed. (2017). "From the October Revolution to Revolutionary Rojava: An Ecosocialist Reading," *Capitalism Nature Socialism,* Vol. 28, No. 4, pp.3-20.

Scott, D. (1999). *Refashioning Futures. Criticism after Postcoloniality.* Princeton, NJ: Princeton University Press.

Schmidinger, T. (2018). *Rojava: Revolution, War, and the Future of Syria's Kurds.* London: Pluto Press.

Shahvisi, A. (2021). "Beyond Orientalism: Exploring the Distinctive Feminism of Democratic Confederalism in Rojava," *Geopolitics,* Vol. 26, No. 4, pp.998-1022.

Ustundag, N. (2016). "Self-Defense as a Revolutionary Practice in Rojava, or How to Unmake the State," *Atlantic Quarterly,* Vol. 115, No. 1, pp.197-210.

Venturini, F. (2015). "Social Ecology and the Non-Western World," in Network for an Alternative Quest, ed., *Challenging Capitalist Modernity II. Dissecting Capitalist Modernity – Building Democratic Confederalism.* Cologne: International Edition, pp.118-124.

Venturini, F. (2021). "The Value of Social Ecology in the Struggles to Come," in S. Hunt, ed., *Ecological Solidarity and the Kurdish Freedom Movement.* London: Lexington Books, pp.3-24.

Walsh, C. (2018). "Decoloniality in/as Praxis," in W. Mignolo and C. Walsh, *On Decoloniality: Concepts, Analytics, Praxis.* Durham, NC: Duke University Press, pp.15-104.

Walsh, C. and Mignolo, W. (2018). "Introduction," in W. Mignolo and C. Walsh, *On Decoloniality: Concepts, Analytics, Praxis.* Durham, NC: Duke University Press, pp.1-12.

Weitz, E. (2015). "Self-Determination: How a German Enlightenment Idea Became the Slogan of National Liberation and a Human Right," *The American Historical Review,* Vol. 120, No. 2, pp.462–496.

Wilder, G. (2015). *Freedom Time. Negritude, Decolonization, and the Future of the World.* Durham, NC: Duke University Press.

PART TWO

Self-Determination and Democracy

CHAPTER 7

Representative Democracy and the Democratic Confederal Project

Reflections on the Transformation of the Kurdish Movement in Turkey[1]

Co-authored with Luqman Guldive

The Context of State Terror

There have been successive attempts to represent Kurdish identities, interests and aspirations in the party system of the Republic of Turkey. The legal obstacles and often harsh persecution that these would-be representatives have faced are testimony to the limits to political freedom imposed by the constitutional order, which enshrines and promotes an aggressive, assimilationist, integral Turkish-nationalist conception of the Republic. Such a conception is incompatible with democracy in a context like that of the Republic of Turkey – a context characterized by "deep diversities," associated with multiple communities of language and religious beliefs; a context with a long and bloody history of salient conflicts amongst citizens divided by alternative, competing and resilient conceptions of group belonging and political loyalty.[2]

Nor is it a coincidence that anti-democratic forces in the Republic of Turkey have so consistently and so vehemently insisted upon – even frequently rallied around – the imperative to repress the Kurdish minority. Recourse to tyranny in the name of the Turkish national majority against a mobilized and defiant Kurdish minority has proven a most effective formula for legitimating authoritarian rule, and indeed for countering any and all emergent challenges to existing relations of hierarchy. Nationalist belligerence as the antidote to the toxic threat of solidarity among the marginalized, the exploited, the oppressed.[3]

Human rights atrocities and state terror have been, and continue to be, inflicted upon the Kurdish minority by Turkish security forces, most brutally in the early 1990s, and again with increasing intensity since the breakdown of peace negotiations in July of 2015. All-out war against the Kurdish Freedom Movement, both inside Turkey and across the border in Syria, has been the centrepiece of President Erdogan's alliance with the far-right. Now, more than ever perhaps, the struggle for democracy in Turkey is thus intimately intertwined with the urgent need for a peaceful resolution to the so-called "Kurdish question". The alternative, as we have seen, is spiralling violence, tyranny and chaos.[4]

So too has the historical trajectory of the Kurdish Freedom Movement been profoundly influenced by the context of militarism, authoritarianism and paramilitary violence in which and against which it initially emerged and has never ceased to be in conflict. The Republic of Turkey was on the frontlines of the Cold War, a NATO member, and its security apparatus was armed to the teeth, and consistently permitted, encouraged, to be ruthless in its efforts to eradicate threats to capitalist social-property relations.

Torture and extra-judicial killings of leftist and pro-Kurdish militants propelled a process of polarization and radicalization that took place from the late 1960s, which escalated after successive coups in 1971 and 1980 that were intended to crush the left, and that reduced the legal channels for mobilizing anti-capitalist opposition to a bare minimum. They included a lethal combination of legal and extra-legal repression which together contributed to the emergence of the very kind of violent opposition whose eradication apologists for such measures claimed was the state's purpose and goal. A spiral of violence and repression was thus conjured, one that continues to this day.

The State and the Guerrilla

The Kurdistan Workers' Party (PKK) was born in this maelstrom. From the outset, it was structured in accordance with the Marxist-Leninist principle of democratic centralism, and conceived simultaneously as a vanguard political party and as a paramilitary force, a *guerrilla*, committed to waging a "prolonged peoples' war" for national liberation. Its goal was the attainment of a Kurdish nation-state, indeed, a state-communist utopia which would unite Kurds from Turkey, Iraq, Iran and Syria in a Greater Kurdistan.[5] It was a utopian dream, no doubt, equal to if not even exceeding in ambition the dystopian project against which it was struggling, that of the Kemalist Republic, with its intransigent goal of assimilating, if need be annihilating, all traces of Kurdish identity into a homogenised Turkish national imaginary.

The PKK acts in the name of the Kurdish nation. But as a proscribed *guerrilla*, it cannot be said to *represent* a Kurdish constituency, at least not in the same way that a legally recognized political party can.[6]

In point of fact, even a legally recognized political party cannot be said to represent a nation, at least not in the same way that it can be described as representing a constituency. This is because, as Max Weber noted long ago, the nation belongs to the sphere of values, not to the realm of facts.[7] The common conflation between nation and state, terms treated so often as synonymous categories in discourse and praxis, must not be reproduced in social-science and political theory; for doing so contributes to the perpetuation of reified and essentialist notions of the nation which cover over and conceal the dynamics of power relations.[8]

Strictly speaking, it is citizens of the state who are represented by parliamentary assemblies, be it at the local, "regional," or "national" (i.e. state-wide) levels. Elected representatives *represent* electoral constituencies, the boundaries of which, and electoral rules for, are established by laws, whose compliance is guaranteed by the judiciary, and ultimately backed by the coercive force of the state. Likewise, the division of competences among different elected assemblies, as well as the balance of power between the legislative, executive, and judicial branches of government are determined by constitutional norms, again, overseen by the judiciary, and ultimately backed by the coercive force of the state.

The state is thus the institutional arena within which claims to representation by politicians (elected or otherwise) are grounded, that is, recognized by law and guaranteed by force. Indeed, the state, to cite Max Weber again, has been famously defined as an organization, or complex of organizations, whose "administrative staff (successfully) claims the monopoly of the legitimate use of physical force within a given territory".[9]

Like all social-scientific definitions, Weber's is of course contentious – but the intimate link he draws between *stateness* and violence is most certainly perceptive. It helps explain, for example, why the term "terrorist" is most frequently reserved for non-state actors alone.[10] It also helps explain why state authorities tend to treat often relatively minor dangers posed to the general citizenry by so-called "terrorist" organisations as if they were existential threats. For indeed, by challenging the state's monopoly on violence, such organisations effectively pose a challenge to what is commonly understood to be the very essence of *stateness*.[11]

Though in practice, not all paramilitary organisations are perceived as equally threatening by authorities of the state, as the experience of the Republic of Turkey confirms. In fact, state authorities have most often turned a blind eye, even collaborated with paramilitary *guerrilla* forces committed to terrorising individuals and communities suspected of actively plotting against "territorial integrity" and/or against existing capitalist social-property relations, or simply sympathising with those who do.[12] Good cop, bad cop, even worse cop.

It is worth emphasizing that Weber does not simply refer to the state as claiming a monopoly on violence, but rather, refers to a monopoly on *legitimate* violence.[13] The exercise of *illegitimate* violence, by contrast, we are led to assume, is the domain of the *criminal*, the *gangster*, the *bandit*, the *terrorist*. Though of course, it can be countered that legitimacy, like beauty, is in the eye of the beholder – as reflected in the relevant, relativist maxim, that one person's terrorist is another person's freedom fighter. But it would perhaps be more prudent to leave such objections to the cynics, the believers in, and practitioners of, *realpolitik*. After all, Socrates made Thrasymachus blush.

The term *terrorism* has a relatively straightforward definition, definitely more straightforward than Weber's difficult definition of the state. According to Wikipedia, "*terrorism* is, in the broadest sense, the use of intentionally indiscriminate violence as a means to create terror among masses of people; or fear to achieve a financial, political, religious, or ideological aim". Although the web's most famous free encyclopedia is quick to add, in a bout of on-line epistemic humility that stands in striking contrast to the boldness with which it dares to define the state, that "there is no commonly accepted definition of terrorism".[14]

In the context of the ongoing Orwellian "War on Terror," the impulse to embrace such reflexivity, to acknowledge the normative dimension and contested nature of the term *terrorism*, is understandable.[15] The term is wielded with worrisome effectiveness by scaremongers-cum-warmongers in the political arena and the mass media in an extremely demagogic fashion, serving simultaneously to silence dissent and mobilize support for draconian measures at home and illegal wars of aggression abroad. A dose of relativism might indeed appear a useful antidote against such mass intoxication by neofascist propaganda techniques.

And yet, as Darnell Stephen Summers has cogently stressed, recourse to this type of relativism in debates about the nature of terrorism has one most unfortunate consequence for defenders of civil liberties and critics of tyranny: namely, it lets the biggest culprits of terrorism off the hook.[16] Who are these biggest culprits? Without a doubt, state actors. Indeed, according to the common-sense definition provided by Wikipedia, the United States of America is by far the most lethal terrorist organisation on the planet. Its NATO partner, the Republic of Turkey, also ranks among the worst offenders as do all of the members of the UN Security Council.[17]

The PKK, as a paramilitary *guerrilla* force, has from the time of its inception been considered by the state authorities of the Republic of Turkey to be a terrorist organization. Indeed, Turkish authorities have consistently treated the PKK as public enemy number one; and as a result, those suspected of belonging to the organization, or even sympathizing with it, have been the victims of successive waves of brutal state terror. At the height of the war between the Turkish state and the PKK in the early 1990s, thousands of Kurdish villages were forcefully evacuated, tens of thousands murdered, and a mass exodus provoked. And after the breakdown of peace negotiations in 2015, another brutal wave of state terror was unleashed, this time including urban settings, leaving another bloody trail of thousands killed and hundreds of thousands forcibly displaced.[18]

There is, of course, blood on the hands of the PKK too, though not nearly as much as that on the hands of the Turkish security forces with which it has been at war since 1984.[19] Still, as PKK founder Abdullah Öcalan has come to lament, the organization has on too many occasions been guilty of behaving like a state.[20] This state-like behaviour on the part of the *guerrilla* cannot be treated lightly, or dismissed as a mere aberration; instead, it merits social-scientific analysis and theoretical reflection, as Öcalan himself has attempted, from the confines of his lonely prison cell on Imrali Island.

The Right to Rebel

Why the resemblance between the *guerrilla* and the state? There are many aspects to this question that must be addressed if we are to provide an adequate explanation. Let us begin with the matter of violence. The PKK launched its military offensive against the Turkish state in 1984, four years after the 1980 coup had triggered a bout of severe state repression, two years after the 1982 Constitutional reform had further entrenched military prerogatives, effectively confining and constricting the terrain of civilian politics. In a word, the PKK's offensive was a product of and response to this context of state aggression and denial of basic civil liberties.

One need not be an anarchist to be able to understand and be willing to apologize for, or even advocate, violent resistance in the face of such conditions of state tyranny. To the contrary, the theoretical tools of classical liberalism should in this regard suffice. After all, the canonical English liberal political philosopher John Locke famously justified the so-called "Glorious Revolution" of the late 17th century, in which he took part, along the following lines:

"*Whenever the Legislators endeavour to take away, and destroy the Property of the People*, or to reduce them to Slavery under Arbitrary Power, they put themselves into a state of War with the People, who are thereupon absolved from any farther Obedience, and are left to the common Refuge, which God hath provided for all Men, against Force and Violence. Whensoever therefore the *Legislative* shall transgress this fundamental Rule of Society; and either by Ambition, Fear, Folly or Corruption, *endeavour to grasp* themselves, *or put into the hands of any other an Absolute Power* over the Lives, Liberties, and Estates of the People; By this breach of Trust *they forfeit the Power*, the People had put into their hands, for quite contrary ends, and it devolves to the People, who have a Right to resume their original Liberty".[21]

To put the point simply, for Locke, and for classical liberal political theory, when the state has declared war upon the people, the people are justified in taking up arms against the state.[22] To translate these terms of Enlightenment-era liberal philosophy into the language of post-Enlightenment Weberian social science, this means that, in conditions of authoritarian encroachments upon civil liberties and infringement of basic human rights, state actors risk losing their ability to exercise a monopoly on the use of legitimate violence.[23] But it is one thing to be justified in taking up arms against state tyranny; another to be successful. Which brings us to the matter of survival. The PKK of course never came close to its original goal of establishing a state-communist Greater Kurdistan; and yet, it has achieved a feat that is rather remarkable nevertheless. It has managed to survive, even to thrive against NATO's second largest army, and maintain a plausible claim to represent a broad constituency of Kurdish people, for over forty years now. How has this virtual stalemate with the Turkish state been possible?

There is an old Kurdish saying that the Kurds have no friends but the mountains. Certainly, the region's mountainous terrain has helped the guerrilla to survive, rendering it logistically difficult for the Turkish security forces to eradicate it. Even so, the many decades of survival would have clearly been impossible if the guerrilla did not count on significant levels of popular support among the Kurdish public.[24]

The racism and systemic discrimination that Kurds have long faced at the hands of the Turkish state, intertwined and combined with the poverty and exploitation that characterizes the lives of so many Kurds, in both rural villages and urban shanty-towns, provides an objective basis, a reservoir of material and symbolic grievances which underpin popular attitudes, helping to account for propensities to support insurrection.[25]

Multiple Kurdish Constituencies

The PKK's efforts and success in recruiting a high proportion of proletarian and *lumpen* members among its early cadres, along with its aggressive pursuit of class warfare in the Kurdish countryside from the outset of its military campaign earned it respect and revolutionary credentials. It became clearly distinguished from all other previous and contemporary rival pro-Kurdish organizations which had been composed of, and catered nearly exclusively to, middle-class activists and sensibilities.[26]

But such respect and support has been by no means unanimous among Kurds. The PKK's ongoing military campaign has also earned it much enmity and fear among certain segments of the Kurdish population, especially those who, for diverse motives, have opted for collaboration with the Turkish authorities.[27] Such "collaborationism" has been frequent not only among the wealthy few, the large-holding landowners who for generations have been integrated into the Republic's clientelistic networks. This is also seen among less wealthy Kurds who over the course of the war have been co-opted or coerced into the village guard system, as well as among others who have been pulled into the orbit of reactionary forms of political Islam. And of course, among the supporters and the collaborators there are those who harbour mixed feelings, are ambivalent or apolitical.

The relative success of Erdogan's ruling AKP in general elections in Kurdish-majority provinces, at least until 2015, is well-documented by Cengiz Gunes. The evidence he presents should be more than enough to correct oversimplified and binary accounts that would divide the Kurdish population into an overwhelming patriotic and revolutionary majority, on the one side, and a collaborationist and reactionary minority, on the other. The spectrum of political identities, opinions and behaviours among Kurds is certainly more complicated than that.

Unfortunately, there is a scarcity of survey research on patterns of national identification in the Republic of Turkey.[28] The formal restrictions on freedom of expression, combined with informal taboos, especially on matters related to Kurdish identity, have to date rendered such research more unfeasible for the most part. Survey research would allow us to measure the diffusion of competing or complementary conceptions and sentiments of national belonging across diverse segments of the population; to see how these conceptions and sentiments relate to aspirations for the recognition of cultural rights, and for various degrees of political autonomy and/or independence; to verify how such conceptions, sentiments and aspirations relate to a host of different political attitudes and behaviours; to locate this variety of individual identities, attitudes and behaviours within existing constellations of material and social power relations; and even to observe with some precision how these patterns evolve over time. The copious public opinion research on nationalist movements in Spain, since the time of the transition to democracy in the late 1970s until the present, is exemplary in this regard.[29]

One of the great virtues of the comparative research project spearheaded by Faleh Jabar, which includes text by Cengiz Gunes, is the systematic effort built into the research design to analyze how political representatives in the Kurdish regions of Turkey, Iraq, Syria, and Iran respond to such questions. But in Bakur, conducting this research was exceedingly difficult in the context of intense repression following the breakdown of peace negotiations in July 2015, and especially in the aftermath of the attempted coup in July 2016. The researcher commissioned by Jabar's team to do the work in Turkey, Luqman Guldive, is to be commended for his bravery. Many of the questions Guldive posed to representatives of the different political parties were very sensitive. Remember that many HDP representatives, including co-chairs Selahattin Demirtas and Figen Yuksekdag, had been imprisoned and charged with treason for making public statements articulating demands for political autonomy.[30]

The literature on nationalism in general, and on Turkish and Kurdish nationalisms in particular, is rich in detail when it comes to tracing the biographies and worldviews of nationalist activists and leaders, as well as the histories and programs of nationalist parties; but we know much less about the perspectives and sentiments of the people in whose names these leaders, activists and parties speak, that is, who they claim to represent.[31]

We can infer some things about the level of acceptance of these elite and activist perspectives among the general public from records of electoral performance. Yet, there are limits to our ability to infer from such records. For starters, because political parties present policy bundles or packages for competition in electoral campaigns.[32] Issues associated with national identity and aspirations are only part of the political programs between which voters choose on election day. So, for example, a voter might opt for the AKP in a general election despite disagreeing with the party's stance on the so-called "Kurdish question," because s/he approves of the ruling party's neoliberal development agenda and/or track record, or, more likely, because s/he approves of the AKP's version of political Islam. Indeed, post-election surveys are good tools for helping researchers decipher the meaning of electoral outcomes.

To make matters worse, in the case of the Republic of Turkey, the history of constitutional and legal proscriptions and restrictions on pro-Kurdish parties further complicates our ability to infer from electoral outcomes alone the contours of public opinion on matters related to national identity.

A Comparison between Turkey and Spain

In Spain, the rich history of public opinion survey research on national identities, a tradition that can be traced back to the efforts of Juan Linz, has been usefully supplemented by an albeit smaller corpus of elite survey research, which allows us to compare and contrast the attitudes, identities and aspirations of parliamentarians with those of the constituencies who they represent. This allows for crucial insights into the nature and limits of political representation regarding such matters in the country.[33] No equivalent scholarly corpus exists for Turkey, despite the valiant inroads made by Faleh Jabar and his associates, including the important text by Cengiz Gunes.

Since the outbreak of the war between the PKK and the Turkish state in the 1980s, there has been an impressive proliferation of scholarly research on the so-called Kurdish question. And yet, we still know very little about what it means for ordinary people to call themselves Kurds. In Spain, to give but one important example, we know that for a clear majority of those who identify as Catalans or Basques, registering such identification does not preclude them from identifying as Spaniards as well. If asked the question, "How do you identify yourself?," and given five options, "Turkish, More Turkish than Kurdish, Equally Turkish and Kurdish, More Kurdish than Turkish, or Kurdish," what would the patterns of responses in Bakur be? Or for that matter, what would the patterns of responses be among migrants from the Kurdish region living in the metropolitan regions of Istanbul and Ankara? Of course, no question is neutral, and how a question is framed can certainly condition responses. But survey research can also shed light on how the same people respond to differently framed questions.

As Juan Linz has explained, such survey research was very difficult to carry out before the transition to democracy in Spain. The fact that this type of research is virtually non-existent in Turkey is indicative of the level of authoritarian restrictions on political freedom in the Republic.[34]

The comparison between the restrictions on freedoms in Franco's Spain and those in the Republic of Turkey raises an interesting question: How should the Republic of Turkey be classified in terms of the typology of political regimes?[35] The transition from a single-party state to competitive party politics occurred alongside, and was spurred on by, the Republic's incorporation into NATO at the onset of the Cold War, following the Second World War.[36] However, the space of permissible party competition remained severely constrained by Kemalist criteria embedded in the constitutional order, with entrenched military prerogatives reinforced after the 1980 coup. The tradition of coups – in 1960, 1971, 1980, and 1997 – long rendered emphatically clear the military's determination to make use of its prerogatives when deemed necessary to ensure the perpetuation of Kemalist ideals, rendering them beyond the scope of permissible political competition.[37] This created a "guarded democracy" at best, with a long track record of constitutional and legal restrictions on representation for anti-capitalist, anti-secular, and pro-Kurdish political organisations, as well as a bloody history of endemic political violence, state terror, and human rights atrocities.

A Crisis of Kemalist Hegemony?

Since the ascension of Erdogan and the AKP to power in 2002, Kemalist hegemony has increasingly given way to what Cihad Hammy has evocatively dubbed "a marriage between Turkish nationalism and authoritarian Islam".[38]

Against the backdrop of ongoing accession talks with the European Union, there was much hope that Erdogan might usher in a more democratic era of politics in the country; but such hopes have gave way to fears of neo-fascist involution, especially after the successive, escalating developments of: (1) the demise of prospects for membership in the EU; (2) the breakdown of the alliance between Erdogan and the Gulen movement, and the subsequent struggle for control over the state apparatus; (3) the end of peace negotiations and the re-ignition of all-out war against the Kurdish Freedom Movement; (4) the massive purges and political repression that followed the July 2016 failed coup; and (5) the hyper-presidentialist reform of the constitution. The constant looming threat of coups might have been vanquished; but the result was far from the liberal democratic "end of history" once promised, but rather, the emergence of yet another case of an increasingly frequent form of hybrid regime – which some scholars have termed "participatory competitive authoritarianism," others "electoral authoritarianism," and yet others called "electoral hegemony".[39]

Robert Dahl famously distinguished "polyarchies" (his preferred term for liberal, representative democracies) from other types of regimes based on two dimensions or criteria: (a) the level of "liberalization" or public contestation permitted; and (b) the level of inclusiveness in political participation permitted. Based on these two dimensions, he came up with a useful fourfold typology of political regimes: (1) closed hegemony (low liberalization, low inclusiveness); (2) inclusive hegemony (low liberalization, high inclusiveness); (3) competitive oligarchy (high liberalization, low inclusiveness); and (4) polyarchy (high liberalization, high inclusiveness).[40] According to this four-fold typology, the Republic of Turkey has long qualified as a regime of inclusive hegemony.

Dahl's choice of terms is in some respects confusing. For those familiar with Gramsci, especially, the distinction he draws between "hegemony" and "polyarchy" (or "liberal democracy") will most certainly seem counter-intuitive.[41] Likewise, for those familiar with the long and bloody history of human rights abuses by state authorities, to consider it "inclusive" would appear to be the wrong term.

However, there is one important sense in which it makes sense to refer to the Republic of Turkey as an "inclusive" regime. Unlike the regime of segregation during the Jim Crow era in the United States, or the regime of apartheid in South Africa, or under colonial regimes, the Republic of Turkey does not have any formal restrictions on the franchise; nor does it make any formal distinction between citizens and subjects. The regime is not formally "exclusionary," but rather, "assimilationist".[42] Indeed, the term long officially used to describe its citizens of Kurdish descent was "Mountain Turks".[43]

Although the regime is not exclusionary in principle, it has indeed proven exclusionary in practice. As the Republic of Turkey was described elsewhere:

"A nationalizing state, dominated by an 'integral' brand of nationalism, assimilationist in principle, exclusionary more often than not in practice (Brubaker 1996). A nationalist mentality captured well by the famous words of the then-Prime Minister, Ismet Inönü, whose father was a

'Turkified Kurd', and who was destined to succeed Kemal as president after Kemal's death in 1938. He would insist, in 1925, in the midst of the wave of brutal repression: 'In the face of a Turkish majority other elements have no kind of influence. We must Turkify the inhabitants of our land at any price, and we will annihilate those who oppose the Turks or '*le Turquisme*'. A supremacist and ultimately exclusionary mentality captured even more bluntly by Kemal's Minister of Justice, who would boast in 1930: 'We live in a country called Turkey, the freest in the world. As your deputy, I feel I can express my real convictions without reserve. I believe that the Turk must be the only lord, the only master of his country. Those who are not of pure Turkish stock can only have one right in this country, the right to be servants and slaves' (Özcan 2006, p.70)".[44]

The Nationalizing State versus the Kurdish Project of "National Revival"

Turkish nationalism is an "integral" one. Why, we may ask, has its assimilationist project failed? Undoubtedly, a significant part of the explanation has to do with the dynamics of what Trotsky called "combined, uneven development". The systemic discrimination faced by people of Kurdish descent is not reducible to, but certainly has a lot to do with, their poverty. The grinding poverty associated with Kurdishness has not only reinforced popular prejudices against Kurds; most likely and even more importantly, it long prohibited the majority of Kurds from the opportunity to assimilate, even if they so desired. Indeed, literacy levels in the Kurdish region have consistently been by far the lowest in the country; in 1960, the literacy rate stood at only 15%; and in 1970, it remained only 30%.[45]

Significantly, it was in the 1960s that Kurdish intellectuals took advantage of the trend of liberalization that characterised that decade both to mobilize in favour of public expression in the Kurdish language, and, increasingly, over the course of the decade to articulate the idea that the Kurdish region constituted an "internal colony". By the 1970s, Kurdish university students came on the scene, including the young Abdullah Öcalan. They were committed to spreading the gospel of "internal colonialism" among the Kurdish masses.[46]

In his classic book *The Social Preconditions of National Revival in Europe*, Miroslav Hroch documents the spread of national consciousness among minorities in Europe and usefully distinguishes among three phases of mobilization: Phase A, in which a minority of intellectuals come to valorize and cultivate awareness about the worth of the minority group's language, culture and history; Phase B, in which a new generation of activists increasingly politicize this project and begin evangelising beyond intellectual circles, among broader segments of the minority group; and Phase C, in which a mass movement emerges.[47] The model he provides need not be interpreted in a deterministic or teleological manner, the transition from Phase A to Phase B to Phase C is not inevitable or unavoidable. However, as the movement gains momentum, with each successive transition among Phases, the task for state authorities of assimilating the minority group into the majority nation is rendered increasingly difficult, if not utopian. Indeed, once a movement of "national revival" has passed the threshold of gaining significant traction among members of a minority group, efforts at assimilation to fend off the emergent threat to the dominant nationalist imaginary, to the one propagated by the state, are likely to be counterproductive, to trigger polarisation, even spiral like a boomerang.[48]

The plight of the Kurds in Turkey, however, is different in important respects from that of the "national minorities" in Europe whose movements are so insightfully analysed by Hroch – the Norwegians, the Czechs, the Finns, the Estonians, the Lithuanians, the Slovaks, the Flemish, the Danes (in Schleswig). It was emphasized above that the "assimilationist," integral nation-building policies of the Turkish state distinguished the Kurdish plight from that of colonialism proper. But the crucial similarities between the Kurdish plight and that of colonised peoples should not be ignored either. These similarities are associated with the sense of quasi-racial superiority propagated by the Turkish nationalizing-state, and reflected in widespread, popular prejudices among the Turkish-speaking national majority vis-à-vis the Kurds.

The Plight of the Kurdish "Permanent Minority"

Robert Dahl has emphasized the problem for democratic theory posed by the plight of permanent minorities.[49] Representative democracy tends to presuppose that groups that constitute minorities today can tomorrow become the majority. But for "national" minorities, their fate is that of a permanent minority, perpetually facing the threat of tyranny exercised in the name of the majority, at least once the threshold of national consciousness among a critical mass has been crossed.

Federal or other "consociational" arrangements can help ameliorate the plight of permanent minorities; but to institutionalize such measures democratically would require the consent of the majority. What's more, even after such measures are institutionalized, the arbiters of the new federal division of powers are likely to enforce the views of the hegemonic majority whenever push comes to shove.

This might sound like an argument in favour of secessionism – if it weren't for the fact that "national" groups are not hermetically sealed, and thus cannot be discretely divided. As such, the creation of new national states is capable of creating new national majorities, but much less likely to resolve the problem of permanent minorities.[50]

The problem for the Kurdish minority in Turkey has been further compounded by the constraints and constrictions, both legal and extra-legal, on political representation for perspectives and projects that would challenge hegemonic, integral Turkish-nationalist conceptions.

It is not a coincidence that the "revival" and mobilization of Kurdish national consciousness took place during the 1960s, a decade of relative liberalization. But the limits of the Republic's newfound tolerane were soon reached. The so-called "coup by memorandum" of 1971 unleashed a crackdown on the anti-capitalist left, as well as on any and all expressions of pro-Kurdish sentiments – a crackdown that included proscriptions on political organizations accused of propagating Kurdish "separatism" and prosecution of prominent pro-Kurdish militants. These were among other, even more repressive police-state tactics that included widespread torture, as security forces combed the Kurdish countryside in an effort to hunt down leftists and "separatist agitators".[51]

The suppression of legal channels for expressing and mobilizing anti-capitalist dissent contributed to the proliferation of leftist *guerrilla* groups over the course of the 1970s, which in turn exacerbated the vehemence and the violence of the security forces, as well as that of far-right paramilitary groups with organic links to the "deep state". A spiral of violence had commenced, albeit one in which, it should not be forgotten, the torture and violence perpetuated by forces on the right far outweighed any human rights violations by forces on the left. The repressive violence would be stepped up even further after the 1980 coup.[52]

Violence and National Consciousness

This is the context in which the PKK emerged, something all-too-conveniently and often ignored or forgotten in moralizing, liberal condemnations of the paramilitary organisation's means and ends. It is, as well, a context which renders the analogy between the Kurdish plight in Turkey and the plight of colonized peoples seem more plausible, indeed, that makes it impossible to dismiss such claims as mere rhetorical bluster or hyperbole.

This brings us, again, to the matter of violence. Decolonization, as Fanon famously insisted, "is always a violent phenomenon". More specifically, in his much-celebrated analysis of the dynamics of the Algerian anti-colonial struggle, Fanon brings to bear insights from psychoanalysis to emphasise the constructive aspect of violence and its ability to generate national consciousness. According to Fanon, this constructive, generative capacity of anti-colonial violence operates at both the collective and the individual levels. Collectively, "[t]he armed struggle mobilizes the people," binding them together, "throw[ing] them in one way and in one direction". Immersion in this process of armed struggle, in turn, has ramifications at the level of the individual psyche and consciousness. Not only does it "introduc[e] into each man's consciousness the ideas of a common cause, of a national destiny and of a collective history;" simultaneously, anti-colonial violence acts as "a cleansing force". It "frees the native from his inferiority complex and from his despair and inaction," "makes him fearless," and "restores his self-respect".[53]

Fanon's text has been frequently misconstrued as a one-sided, even reckless, celebration of anti-colonial violence – perhaps because people pay too much attention to the chapter "Concerning Violence" and not enough attention to the chapter on "Colonial Wars and Mental Disorders".[54] Be that as it may, his point about the capacity of anti-colonial violence to generate national consciousness introduces an important element worthy of consideration in any discussion about representation and the "national question".

Hroch's model of "revival" among national minorities in Europe is one that does not presuppose or require any causal role for violence – except to the extent that the context of the state, in which and against which these movements are mobilized, sets the parameters of peaceful politics, implicitly threatening to make use of its "monopoly on legitimate violence" whenever the ruling class perceives a fundamental threat to its interests. But Hroch himself has very little to say about this.

Even so, from the standpoint of representation, it is worth noting that in the European cases Hroch studies, he finds national consciousness to have been invariably born amongst intellectuals, the "national agitators" *par excellence*, and only subsequently spreads beyond this stratum to be taken up by broader segments of society. Hroch's observation is in line with Eric Hobsbawm's more general historical-materialist claim that national consciousness tends to arise most intensely and most consistently among the "lesser examination-passing classes".[55] Likewise, both Hroch's and Hobsbawm's observations square with those of Max Weber, who advanced a similar argument over a century ago. According to Weber:

> "The significance of the 'nation' is usually anchored in the superiority, or at least the irreplaceability, of the culture values that are to be preserved and developed only through the cultivation of the peculiarity of the group. It therefore goes without saying that the intellectuals, as we have in a preliminary fashion called them, are to a specific degree predestined to propagate the 'national idea', just as those who wield power in the polity provoke the idea of the state. "By 'intellectuals' we understand a group of men who by virtue of their peculiarity have special access to certain achievements considered to be 'culture values', and who therefore usurp the leadership of a 'culture community'".[56]

As such, the "national ideal" does not arise spontaneously; nor does it necessarily even resonate among wide swathes of the toiling masses, among peasants or urban workers, at least not initially. In some cases, the original core of intellectuals who serve as bearers of the national ideal manage to evangelize effectively, and their ideal takes root among the masses. But this is far from always.

Most often, the instrument used for the "nationalization of the masses" has been the state itself. This is largely true even for the prototypical European cases of "national unification," Germany and Italy. Indeed, as Guiseppe Mazzini, the first prime minister of Italy, would emblematically declare: "We have made Italy, now we must make Italians".[57] In other cases, however, in opposition to a state, the instrument has been a party, including – as Fanon observed with the FLN – those organised as *guerrillas*, engaged in armed struggle. Such has been the historic role of the PKK in the Kurdish region of Turkey.

The Motifs of Martyrdom and Collective Sacrifice

To insist upon the PKK's role in generating national consciousness among Kurds is not to deny pre-existing awareness, feelings or shared senses of Kurdishness beyond the core of revolutionary militants. Instead, it is to suggest that intervention by *guerrillas* transformed the significance of such sentiments, rendering Kurdish subjectivity politically salient, increasingly defiant, infused with a collective will to struggle. Even if, in the process, it pitted some Kurds against others, elevating a sanctified few to the status of heroes, while expelling others from the emergent imagined community.

The sanctified few are mostly militants killed in combat, revered as "martyrs," their blood sacrifice commemorated in posters, as a sign of respect, and as a means of strengthening resolve among the living. Their images represent and give meaning to the Kurdish struggle; the "martyrs" provide a model for militant ethics, a vision of revolutionary virtue; they thus exercise a powerful influence over the contours and content of political imagination in and around the movement.[58] We shall prevail, we must prevail, the "martyrs" did not shed their blood in vain. Such are the sentiments evoked. This is how courage is concocted, fortitude forged.

Imagined communities are also about imagined possibilities. They are about what people can imagine to be possible; about what they imagine themselves to be capable of enduring and achieving; about what they can imagine themselves being willing to kill for and, more importantly, what they can imagine themselves being willing to die for. When pragmatic acquiescence to an unjust status quo comes to seem unbearable, when death comes to seem preferable, when resistance comes to seem the only option, this is when new political communities are born.

The "martyrs," through their ultimate sacrifice, helped to create new horizons of imagination among the living. In this respect, they can be said to represent the Kurdish nation. This is despite the fact that they are not "representative" – indeed, in a way, precisely *because* they are not. They represent in a *generative* sense. Through their individual examples and deaths, they bring a new consciousness into being. They *prefigure* and *embody* the ideals of a revolutionary nation to come.

Öcalan as Prophet

There are the "martyrs;" and then there is the leader. He is the one whose appeal and authority is recognized and celebrated by virtually everybody in the movement, whose leadership is treated as indisputable, beyond question or contestation. A secular prophet, the nation in the flesh. Abdullah Öcalan.

It is Öcalan for whom the "martyrs" fell; it is his vision and will that inspire the struggle. The concept of charisma most certainly applies. Max Weber proves again useful in our attempt to comprehend. Weber defined charisma as:

> "[A] certain quality of an individual personality, by virtue of which he is set apart from ordinary men and treated as endowed with supernatural, superhuman, or at least specifically exceptional powers or qualities. These are such as are not accessible to the ordinary person, but are regarded as of divine origin or as exemplary, and on the basis of them the individual concerned is treated as a leader [...]"[59]

Öcalan's followers are bound by his charismatic authority. They recognize in him "exceptional personal qualities" and "extraordinary personal accomplishments," which together inspire their "loyalty and obedience," very much in accordance with Weber's characterization of the phenomenon. But still, the phenomenon remains quite difficult to grasp, at least in purely secular terms. As Charles Lindholm has explained:

> "Charisma as a term, of course, did not originate with Weber. It had a long history in Christian theological discourse, and signified the gift of grace, resembling in some senses the Greek idea of the 'divine man' or the Roman concept of *facilitas*, the hero's innate ability to project to

success due to his connection with the divine. For Christians it meant
the intuitive recognition by laypeople that a saint has intimate contact
with God".[60]

There is something analogous at work in the relationship between Öcalan
and his disciples, which is what makes it appropriate to refer to him as a secular prophet.

Among modern secular leaders, this charismatic relationship resembles in
important respects the reverence long accorded to figures such as Mao and
Mandela. Indeed, it was from Mao, albeit inflected through the example of
Che Guevara, that Öcalan had originally devised and sought to implement
the PKK's initial strategy of a "prolonged peoples' war". And like Mao, Öcalan's
tremendous popularity is linked to his recognition as a hero of the cause of
national liberation. Though crucially, unlike Mao, Öcalan's movement was
never victorious, though it has not been defeated either.

After Mao came to power, the Chinese Communist Party would instru-
mentalize and transform this popular reverence, making use of the state apparatus and of authoritarian controls over political communication to
carefully cultivate "the image of Mao as a saviour of the Chinese nation," as
a means of increasing both "internal cohesion and external appeal". Even so,
as Leese has emphasized, this image "always bore the danger of being hijacked
for contradictory purposes," at least unless it "remained under firm party
control".[61] And in fact, in the mid-1960s, during the Cultural Revolution, Mao
would consciously employ the cult "to mobilize the masses against the party
bureaucracy".[62]

Of course, rather than coming to power, Öcalan was forced into exile in
Syria, where he lived for close to two decades, before being forced out of that
country too, eventually apprehended, and subsequently imprisoned on Imrali
island, where he has remained in virtual isolation, for over two decades. In
this respect, his plight and charismatic appeal is more reminiscent of that of
Nelson Mandela, whose decades-long imprisonment on Robben Island
served to reinforce his moral authority, rendering him a living symbol of the
oppression of his people.

In the end, Mandela, like Mao, also came to power. But, in contrast to Mao,
he was elected into office, and successively and successfully incorporated into

the liberal-democratic, capitalistic mainstream. His charismatic appeal managed to survive for the most part untarnished, even beyond his death, though put to the service of decidedly reformist ends. He is among the pantheon of domesticated myths, right next to Gandhi and Martin Luther King.

Öcalan remains a captive, confined to a lonely existence in conditions of extreme isolation inside his prison cell, "chained to the rock of Imrali".[63] But in a way he has been fortunate, for his captivity has allowed him thus far to avoid succumbing to either of the twin temptations of tyranny and co-option.

The Paradox of Democratic Leadership

Charismatic leadership faces the logic of representative democracy with considerable tension. As a type of authority, Weber contrasted it explicitly to "traditional" modes of rule, on the one hand, and to "legal-rational" ones on the other. Weber conceived of charismatic authority as both a "revolutionary and an unstable form of authority". One of the distinguishing features of charismatic leaders is their ability to "promise change" and to radically alter "peoples' attitudes and values", according Ivan Szelenyi, a prominent interpreter of Weber. This is both the source of charisma's strength as well as its instability, since it tends to "deteriorate if the leader cannot produce the promised changes".[64] In the process, charismatic relationships are routinized, channelled and transformed into one of the other two modes of rule.[65]

The radical alterations in peoples' attitudes and values that charismatic leaders are capable of inducing renders them revolutionary. And yet, the difficulty of delivering on their promises renders their charismatic authority unstable – prone to dissipation, routinization, or both.

Öcalan's imprisonment, like that of Mandela, has resulted in a strengthening of his charismatic appeal, an intensification of devotion to him among his followers. But at the same time, his prolonged isolation has also induced useful self-reflection – about the dangers of the twin temptations of tyranny and co-option. In fact, well before his arrest, Öcalan had begun making calls for peace since 1993, at the height of the war and in the midst of devastating human rights atrocities by the Turkish security forces, including mass village evacuations. Such calls were due in no small part to a pragmatic recognition of the impossibility of ever winning a "prolonged people's war" against NATO's second-largest army, especially given the global balance of power in the post-Cold War world. But the end of the Cold War also got Öcalan thinking about the reasons for the defeat of state communism.[66]

So began a long process of re-assessment, re-articulation and transformation, of both the means and the ends of the movement he had inspired. This process would accelerate in the months and years after his arrest. Paradoxically enough, prison turned out to be a place of mental freedom for Öcalan who, despite very limited access to books, produced a most impressive corpus of writings, both in terms of volume and ambition.

In one of his publications, Öcalan has reflected explicitly on this paradoxically emancipatory impact of imprisonment on the parameters of his thought. In his words:

> "Before prison, while I was able to develop in theory and practical action, I did not have much of a chance to develop the perception of truth. For those who have grave problems, the circumstances of a prison are of educational significance. Thus, though prisons are not areas of theoretical and practical struggle but instead are areas where those who are not crushed by such problems may develop a successful perception of truth and necessary mode of struggle for it. Prison allows those who fight for exceptional causes to work hard each day to attain the truth. Prison time that is spent on the acquisition of truth is, I am certain, worthwhile".[67]

From seeker of power to seeker of truth: such are the terms Öcalan chose to depict the transition of his existential orientation while in captivity. His quest for power was kept in check and he had a lot of time on his hands, to read, to think, to write. This was a monastic life of sorts, which would appear to have opened epistemic horizons previously denied him. Though unlike a monk or an ordinary prisoner, millions hang on his every word.

While in prison, Öcalan has used his charismatic authority to affect a paradigm shift in the Kurdish Freedom Movement – from a Marxist-Leninist conception of national liberation, to a radical democratic critique of the state, and of patriarchy as the root of all hierarchy. Indeed, influenced by the work of the libertarian municipalist and social ecologist Murray Bookchin, Öcalan has elaborated a thorough-going critique of the tenets of democratic central-ism, alongside a principled renunciation of the goal of a Kurdish nation-state. He sees a "democratic confederal" alternative, not just for Kurds, but for the broader Middle East.[68]

This is quite an unexpected, radical-democratic turn coming from a charis-matic *guerrilla* leader of a national liberation movement – perhaps even un-precedented. An attempt to channel his charismatic appeal and influence not towards the conquest of state power, but rather to get his followers to embrace a comprehensive critique of all relations involving hierarchy, oppression, and domination. One is tempted to conclude this is an exercise in democratic leadership.

The theory of democracy has a hard time dealing with leadership.[69] Indeed, to many, the very notion of "democratic leadership" will probably sound like a contradiction in terms, if not a cynical catchphrase, like "democratic cen-tralism".

The Leninist conception of "democratic centralism" served to legitimize a monopoly on power by the Communist Party; in turn, a monopoly on power within the Party by the Central Committee; in turn, most often, a monopoly on power within the Central Committee by the party chairman. In short, au-tocracy, or dictatorship, was couched in the language of democracy. All "lead-ership" and no democracy, if not in theory, certainly in the practice of "democratic centralism".

But what about the theory, and the practice, of multi-party, representative democracy? What space is there for democratic leadership in such regimes? This question is very much related to the concept of representation. Main-stream democratic theorists tend to measure the quality of representation and even define democracy, first and foremost, in accordance with the crite-rion of responsiveness. For example, as Robert Dahl would write on the very first page of *Polyarchy*, "a key characteristic of a democracy is the continuing responsiveness of the government to the preferences of citizens, considered as political equals".[70] Likewise, Adam Przeworski insists: "[a] collectivity gov-erns itself democratically when decisions implemented on its behalf reflect the preferences of its members".[71]

The Limits and Logic of "Representative Democracy"[72]

Such is the theory. However, in practice, the empirical literature has demonstrated a high degree of autonomy, or lack of responsiveness, between the policy preferences of democratic constituencies and those of elected representatives. This can be attributed in no small part to the fact that political parties are hierarchical organizations susceptible to capture by privileged minorities and powerful interest groups.[73]

Competitive, multi-party elections are intended to secure a certain degree of responsiveness by giving the electorate the opportunity to hold unresponsive representatives accountable – the chance "to throw the bums out". However, privileged groups can exercise their power to secure disproportionate influence among multiple parties across the party system, and thus get them to collude to disregard constituency preferences.

Most often the means by which establishment parties so collude is by changing the subject, that is, by "mobilizing biases" and "setting the agenda," so as to reduce the terrain or set of issues over which they compete to begin with.[74] Such de facto reduction of the terrain of party competition means, in practice, that representative democracies most often come closer to Dahl's ideal type of "inclusive hegemony" than to his ideal type of "polyarchy".

The constriction of the space of multi-party competition need not take place through explicit lobbying, direct capture, or conscious collusion among political representatives and the state bureaucracy. Most emblematically, in the case of corporate capitalist interests, because of their control over crucial, productive resources, this minority almost always possesses a "blackmail" power sufficient to limit the policy options that can be seriously considered, much less pursued, by any elected government, regardless of the profile or predilections of those who "man the state apparatus".[75] As Przeworski and Wallerstein have explained:

> "[U]nder capitalism all governments must respect and protect the essential claims of those who own the productive wealth of society. Capitalists are endowed with public power, power which no formal institutions can overcome. People may have political rights, they may vote, and governments may pursue popular mandates. But the effective capacity of any government to attain whatever are its goals is circum-

scribed by the public power of capital. The nature of political forces that come into office does not alter these limits, it is claimed, for they are structural—a characteristic of the system, not of the occupants of governmental positions nor of the winners of elections".[76]

This "blackmail" power is what Marxist scholars have dubbed "the structural dependence of the state on capital". It helps ensure the representation of the preferences of the capitalist minority above and beyond the representation of constituency preferences, and indeed, to encourage the pragmatic adaptation of constituency preferences, to get the majority to accept that catering to the particular interests of the capitalist class is at the same time in the interest of all. The implicit threat and "blackmail" being that the capitalist minority will wreak general havoc on any government that jeopardizes its specific class interests in reproducing the basic parameters of capitalist social-property relations.

The criterion of responsiveness that is built into dominant definitions-cum-defences of representative democracy tends to depend upon a conflation of preferences with interests. Such conflation leads mainstream theorists to downplay the significance of the phenomenon of pragmatic acquiescence, and either to ignore or to explicitly deny the spectre of systematically-distorted preferences. Otherwise put, they treat preferences as exogenous determinants of, rather than endogenous moments within, broader political processes.

Recognition of the endogenous nature of preferences, however, problematizes the reliance upon responsiveness as the sole or primary criterion for judging the quality of democratic representation. Political parties do not merely reflect, but in fact help shape citizen preferences, alongside a whole host of what Althusser termed "ideological state apparatuses," including the state bureaucracy, the schools, the mass media, religious institutions, and the family.[77] These institutions all tend to be organised hierarchically, and they all tend to perpetuate deference to hierarchically-sanctioned values and authorities.

An authoritarian style of political leadership is one that actively seeks to reinforce such deference to hierarchy; by contrast, a democratic style of leadership is one that seeks to promote suspicion and critical reflexivity towards hierarchy in all its forms – including that of the relationship between leaders and followers. Truly democratic leadership is self-liquidating in that sense.

This is why democratic leadership stands in so much tension with the logic of representative democracy, which by its very nature, perpetuates the dialectic of leaders and followers, and institutionalizes submissiveness to elected authorities, indeed, delegates sovereignty to them. Or, perhaps better put, in representative forms of government, the citizens surrender their sovereignty to their alleged representatives. As Rousseau provocatively but perceptively argued a quarter of a millennium ago, in *The Social Contract*, sovereignty cannot be represented; it can only be exercised.[78] Though the genealogy of the notion of sovereignty itself should not be covered over or forgotten, descending as it does from the divine right of kings.[79]

The Imperative of Participation, the Need to Raise Consciousness

As Bernard Manin has emphasised, representative government was originally considered an alternative to democracy, which was until only recently conceived as requiring direct and active citizen participation, that is, self-rule in a literal, not metaphorical, sense.[80]

The passive, largely depoliticized, uninformed electorates in regimes that by contemporary standards qualify as democracies are perhaps more accurately described as subjects and at best "constituencies", not citizens. Despite the formal legal protections contemporary "citizens" enjoy, the fact remains, they do not govern themselves. Instead, their participation is limited to the candidate selection process, otherwise and increasingly known as the electoral circus.[81] This is a spectator sport, and not one of which most people are even big fans.

The adjectives "passive," "depoliticised," and "uninformed" are, of course, causally linked. Participation in decision-making processes clarifies, facilitating the acquisition of knowledge about issues and alternatives being decided upon; whereas exclusion from such processes mystifies, perpetuating ignorance and feelings of incompetence among those left out. This is the core insight of the theory of participatory democracy, as well as the related, still burgeoning body of literature on deliberative democracy.[82]

Participation in institutions of genuine self-governance is thus an educational experience. But it requires, in turn, a citizenry with the time, resources, energy, and predisposition to participate. In other words, genuine self-governance requires a broader educational project, one committed to a radical critical pedagogical approach, in the tradition of Paolo Freire, as outlined in his highly influential contribution, *The Pedagogy of the Oppressed*.[83] This is an educational project that aims to help people unlearn and deconstruct the ubiquitous, hegemonic lies and propaganda that serve to legitimize unjust, oppressive, hierarchical social relations.

For the purposes of initiating and guiding such an educational project, political organization and leadership proves indispensable. Leadership uses the model of radical pedagogy, a project of *paideia*, to invoke and indulge for a moment the preferred terminology of the still-too-influential grecophiles.[84] This is a collective educational project, and one which includes more than just a de-constructive aim of inculcating a *hermeneutic of suspicion*.[85] Indeed, an exclusive focus on the art of deconstruction has an elective affinity with the nihilistic and hyper-individualistic pretensions so pervasive in the neoliberal university.

No, a truly radical and critical pedagogy needs positive commitments, too. It must include a reconstructive goal as well. A commitment to "moral education and character building," albeit not of a traditional sort. An "anti-morality," perchance. Or maybe "faith/anti-faith" would be a better choice of terms, an education into an ethic of solidarity and egalitarian values. And it would foster a collective commitment to forging the capacity for sacrifice, indeed, the will to struggle, against the forces of exploitation, domination, and marginalization, indeed, against injustice in all its forms.

The goals of critical pedagogy for radical democracy may seem contradictory and indeed, to a certain extent, they may be. A healthy balance between a *hermeneutic of suspicion* and an *ethic of conviction* is certainly difficult, but not altogether impossible, to achieve.[86] Given the urgent nature of the need for collective struggle to transform the systemically-entrenched but suicidal, genocidal and "eco-cidal" dynamics of global capitalism and neo-imperialism, those of us who can, *should* make an effort. Each contributes according to their abilities, after all.

Contemporary political theory and dominant, narcissistic culture may be obsessed with the "self" in self-determination; however, it has shockingly little to say about the concept of determination, except as the term is used in debates about causality. But determination, of course, has another meaning as well.

The competitive and consumerist ethos promoted by increasingly unfettered capitalism, combined with the thorough discrediting of capitalism's "state-socialist alter-ego," have together contributed to the emergence of what Bookchin provocatively called *homo consumerans*.[87] Or what Stephen Casmier even more ironically dubbed, "The New Reagan Man".[88] It is a model that is highly influential across the globe, but perhaps most influential in the "West," where the hegemony of capitalism is most deeply entrenched.

Guerrilla Discipline as Revolutionary Discipline?

This brings us back to the subject of the *guerrilla*. The *guerrilleros* were once lionized among some in the western New Left, perhaps most famously by Régis Debray, who remarked in *The Revolution in the Revolution?*:

> "[A]ny man, even a comrade, who spends his life in a city is unwittingly a bourgeois In comparison with a *guerrillero*. He cannot know the material effort involved in eating, sleeping, moving from one place to another – briefly, in surviving".[89]

But he forgot to mention the fact that the *guerrillero* is trained into a revolutionary discipline that includes, first and foremost, following orders; only a select few get to issue commands. This select few is virtually always self-selected, and that exercises a hierarchical authority which cannot be easily revoked or held accountable, at least not through electoral mechanisms.

In a word, the revolutionary *guerrillero* is made in the image and likeness of the very figure against whom s/he is trained to fight, the existential enemy, the state soldier. The dialectical resemblance between the ethic of the *guerrillero* and the ethic of the soldier in turn reflects the similarity in authoritarian command structures shared by the revolutionary *guerrilla* and the bourgeois military alike. It is a microcosm and crucial example of what Bookchin had in mind when he referred to state socialism as capitalism's "alter ego".

Debray's champion and role model was, of course, Che Guevara, one of the last martyrs of the revolutionary pantheon of Marxism-Leninism. This man was often held up as a shining example of heroic selflessness, even a prefiguration of the promise of a state-socialist "New Man," who himself put some thought into the subject of the need for radical pedagogy, and to its links with revolutionary praxis. In Guevara's own formulation:

> "The sermons of the past have been transposed to the present in the individual consciousness, and a continual labour is necessary to eradicate them. The process is two-sided: On the one side, society acts through direct and indirect education; on the other, the individual subjects himself to a process of conscious self-education.
>
> "The new society being formed has to compete fiercely with the past. The latter makes itself felt in the consciousness in which the residue of an education systematically oriented towards isolating the individual still weighs heavily ...".[90]

It is worth noting that the primary feature of the education into the "old society" that Guevara chooses to stress is its orientation "towards isolating the individual," not its tendency to perpetuate deference towards hierarchy. The latter is a virtue in a soldier, which again demonstrates the elective affinity between the *guerrilla* and the state.

Öcalan has expressed some rather piercing, self-critical thoughts in this vein from his jail cell, at the same time implicitly directed at the operational commanders of the *guerrilla* organization he created and continues to inspire and even nominally to lead. In Öcalan's words:

> "The PKK had been conceived as a party with a state-like hierarchical structure similar to other parties. Such a structure, however, causes a dialectic contradiction to the principles of democracy, freedom and equality, a contradiction in principle concerning all parties whatsoever their philosophy. Although the PKK stood for freedom-oriented views we had not been able to free ourselves from thinking in hierarchical structures".[91]

The *guerrilla* has not been disarmed or disbanded – a development which Öcalan has never advocated or foreseen, even at the height of the peace process, his calls for the organization to lay down its arms notwithstanding. This is the crux of the issue from the standpoint of the Turkish state or, for that matter, from the standpoint of any state. But what is more problematic, at least from the standpoint of a commitment to radical democracy; nor has the organization's hierarchical structure, its chain of command, been transformed, despite Öcalan's emphasis and efforts to encourage a "paradigm shift".

From Democratic Centralism to Democratic Confederalism

The Kurdish Freedom Movement, however, encompasses more than the PKK. Indeed, as Akkaya and Jongerdon have insisted, from 2005, "the PKK and all affiliated organizations" were restructured along the lines of the democratic confederal model, "under the name of the Union of Kurdistan Communities (*Koma Civaken Kurdistan*, KCK)," and organized alongside the Democratic Society Congress (*Demokratic Toplum Kongresi*, DTK), conceived as "part of the attempt to forge a new political paradigm, defined by the direct and continual exercise of the people's power through village, town, and city councils".[92]

How has this transition from Marxist-Leninist, democratic centralist *guerrilla* party into a more decentralized, more horizontally-networked movement taken place? What have been the main achievements, challenges and obstacles for this re-organization and re-orientation, this "paradigm shift"? And what have been the consequences of this process of transformation for the movement? These are very important questions, about which the literature on the Kurdish movement – in English, at least – remains equivocal, when not entirely silent. The equivocations, the awkward silences, of the literature are symptomatic of the taboos, contradictions, and limits of human rights normative discourse, exacerbated in the age of the war on terror. They also reflect what Dilar Dirik has perceptively termed the "male state gaze" embedded in the methods and *epistemes* of mainstream social sciences.[93]

The devastation and trauma wrought upon the Kurdish people by the Turkish security forces, the systematic state terror, the total evacuation of thousands of villages, the killing of tens of thousands, the displacement and exile of millions, made it abundantly clear to Öcalan by the early 1990s that the Maoist-cum-Guevarista strategy of a "prolonged people's war" by the PKK could not lead to military victory, to "national liberation," or to the creation of an independent socialist Kurdish nation-state. The military might of NATO's second biggest army, exercised within its own sovereign territory, was simply too brutal, too overwhelming a force to overcome. Faced with the realization of the impossibility of victory, even the prospect of total annihilation, Öcalan began to reach out to European politicians from his refuge in the Bekaa Valley and in Damascus in search of a way to end the war without sacrificing the dignity of the Kurdish people, in search of a way towards a peaceful and democratic resolution to the raging conflict.

The end of the Cold War undoubtedly also influenced Öcalan's burgeoning conviction that the party and the movement which he had brought into being was in dire need of reformation, indeed, of fundamental reorientation. The collapse of the Soviet Union meant the disappearance of a state-communist bloc capable of patronizing and protecting a "liberated," single-party socialist Kurdish republic, inevitably wedged between hostile, neighbouring nation-states. It simultaneously signified the definitive death knell for the credibility of the state-communist ideal. In sum, it induced a crisis both at the level of *realpolitik*, and at the level of principles.

There were also developments originating from the grassroots in Bakur, which were amplified, encouraged and promoted by the organized diaspora in Europe operating within the orbit of the movement. These developments have been well-documented by Gunes himself in his incisive 2012 monograph on *The Kurdish National Movement in Turkey*. They included the spread of "public celebrations and mass protests," most emblematically around the annual *Newroz* festival, reconstrued as a myth of Kurdish resistance; as well as in events organised to commemorate the self-immolation of PKK prisoners and other "heroic acts of sacrifice" among PKK "martyrs". Indeed, a whole repertoire of "representation of resistance practices" emerged, congealing around the myth of *Newroz*, and also hoisting up a host of "exemplars," a veritable pantheon of revolutionary martyrs, the public commemoration, even worship, which burst into the streets in a wave of so-called *serhildan* (or "rebellions").[94] From the early 1990s, such "[b]urgeoning civil resistance" against the security forces became an increasing complement to the ongoing guerrilla campaign.[95]

One of the more remarkable aspects of the repertoire of "representation of Kurdish resistance" that emerged from the early 1990s onwards was the prominent place of women. Not only did women "participate in large numbers in numerous *serhildan*", they also "took an active role in the activities of the legal political Kurdish parties". They "came to the forefront of the resistance" and were increasingly "constituted" and commemorated "as 'exemplars'".[96] Alongside and helping to propel such emergent symbolic and organizational prominence of women in the movement over the course of the 1990s, Öcalan would formulate an elaborate theoretical critique of patriarchy. Indeed, he would come to consider women as the "first colony," and even to "redefine national liberation as first and foremost the liberation of women".[97]

Öcalan's emphasis on the primacy of the struggle against patriarchy was quite developed even before his abduction and imprisonment. It has featured prominently in his copious prison writings, perhaps especially in his original synthesis and articulation of the long history of hierarchy, his vision of the dialectic of domination and resistance.

In Öcalan's account of patriarchy, its origins are intimately intertwined with the emergence of the state. And especially since his imprisonment, Öcalan's thinking has taken a radically anti-statist turn. What began as a pragmatic, realistic appraisal of the impossibility of attaining a Kurdish nation-state through a guerrilla war against Turkish security forces (and as a compromise proposal calling for respect for human rights and cultural rights, alongside measures of decentralization or autonomy) developed, under the influence perhaps especially of Murray Bookchin, into a principled rejection of the state. In effect, Öcalan advanced a redefinition of self-determination, now understood as radical, direct democracy, against the state.[98]

Under Bookchin's influence, Öcalan would also take up the theme of the urgent need for social ecology. Even so, as with the emphasis on the struggle against patriarchy, the sensitivity of the movement to ecological issues was not just born like Athena. It did not just spring spontaneously out of Öcalan's head. Instead, it was forged in concrete struggles, most emblematically in the struggle to save the ancient village of Hasnkeyf in the province of Batman, set to be submerged under water by the Turkish state's Ilisu Dam project. This was a struggle in which the European environmentalist movement would forge organic links with the Kurdish movement, thereby prefiguring the overlapping, decentralized networks of resistance envisioned by the democratic confederal ideal.[99]

Öcalan's articulation of democratic confederalism grows out of a deep dis-enchantment with and critique of Marxism-Leninism, which, in quasi-confessional terms, in a series of penetrating self-criticisms of his own previous mentality, he accuses of reproducing the cult of hierarchy, of behaving as organizations like mini-states, acting in accordance with a logic of conquest and domination, rather than resistance and freedom. The emphasis on the struggle against patriarchy, the fostering of awareness of the urgency of social ecology, the thoroughgoing critique of the state, the promotion of popular assemblies and championing of radically decentralized, direct democracy, all of these components of the "paradigm shift" are explicitly contrasted to the democratic-centralist model and mindset.[100]

Likewise, Öcalan's critique of Marxism-Leninism includes a critique of its scientism, of its hostility to the realm of myth, of its bias in favour of secular-fundamentalism. In this latter vein, in recent years, Öcalan has urged the Kurdish movement to organize a Democratic Islam Congress, with the purpose of elaborating a liberationist interpretation of the ethical and political implications of professing and practising authentic Islamic faith.[101] Whether, in practice, the tradition and perception of militant secularism among movement cadres and supporters has been transformed is another matter – certainly worthy of close empirical investigation, given not only the history of conflict with Kurdish *Hezbullah* to which Gunes' text refers, but also in terms of countering the appeal of Erdogan's AKP and its brand of patriarchal, neoliberal Islam, not to mention the ongoing struggle with reactionary jihadists in Rojava. The fact that the first Kurdish rebellions against the Kemalist republic were mobilised along the secular-religious divide, in the name of the community of believers, is not irrelevant in the present. Indeed, the proper relation between religion and politics continues to be a source of dispute and contestation, capable of dividing contemporary Kurds. The movement's attempt to articulate a Democratic Islam is intended to transcend such divisions; how serious and successful this attempt is will no doubt condition the contours and horizons of support for the ambitious democratic confederal project advanced by the Kurdish Freedom Movement.

Finally, and crucially, the principled rejection of the strategy of "national liberation," understood in terms of the pursuit of a Kurdish nation-state, has included a rather elaborate set of arguments against the insidious evils of what Öcalan refers to as "feudal nationalism," most often in reference to the example of Barzani in South Kurdistan. The ideological and programmatic re-orientation of the Kurdish Freedom Movement thus includes not just a renunciation of the goal of a state, but more ambitiously, the aspiration to transcend altogether the confines of the "nationalist imaginary". This transcendence which should not be confused with repudiating pride in Kurdishness, but rather, with escaping the dialectic of "majority" versus "minority". Indeed, as Öcalan has insisted, "in democratic confederalism there is no room for any kind of hegemony striving".[102]

Self-administration and autonomous organization of direct democratic assemblies, not to mention self-defence militias, for all ethnic and religious groups as the alternative to the tyranny of the majority, to the "hegemonic striving" deeply ingrained in the ideology of nationalism. This is a tall order to ask from a movement that has sacrificed so many lives for the dream of a Greater Kurdistan. It is an exercise in democratic leadership, if ever there was, on the part of Öcalan, his attempt to get his followers to dream internationalist dreams of radical democracy, to imagine forms of confederation that cut across and beyond the mental borders imposed by the cult of national community. Easier to pronounce than to achieve. And so, again, a subject worthy of close empirical investigation, of which the survey of political representatives conducted by Guldive for Gunes' manuscript, under very difficult conditions of state repression, provides a very partial but nonetheless important point of departure.

The struggle against patriarchy, the struggle for social ecology, the struggle against the nation-state, the struggle against sectarianism in all its forms, the struggle for radical, direct democracy – these are all significant departures from the original articulation of the struggle for "national liberation" understood as the creation of a state-communist Greater Kurdistan. Ambitious aspirations indeed. It is a thoroughgoing re-orientation of the goals of the movement: mainstream social scientists interested in understanding the movement too often either ignore or downplay this, and advocates for the movement tend to take (or at least portray) this at face value, when close empirical investigation of the terms of consciousness and praxis of the cadres and supporters of the movement is what the commitment to and search for truth ultimately requires.

Challenges for the "New Paradigm"

The organizational transformations undertaken since 2005 have been conceived and justified as means to decentralize and thus democratize – indeed, de-Leninize – the Kurdish Freedom Movement. But it would be a mistake to think that Öcalan's intention has been to unambiguously compromise or moderate the radicalism, indeed, the profound anti-capitalism, of the movement. To the contrary, if anything, the project of democratic confederalism, articulated as radical, direct democracy against the state, provides a more fundamental, more thorough-going critique and threat to the *status quo* assumptions of the international order in the age of globalised plutocracy and the Orwellian war on terror. This is especially so if the appeal of the program were to spread beyond the project's Kurdish constituency, if it were to be embraced *en masse* by Turks, by Arabs, by Persians, and beyond. The articulation and practice of self-determination as direct democracy, as collective action in accordance with the principles of social ecology, would indeed constitute a major threat for all the geo-political alliances and local power blocs vying for influence and control across a bleeding region and globe. By contrast, the emergence of another independent, crony-capitalist or even state-communist-cum-state-capitalist petro-state would ultimately constitute a much less threatening prospect for the global system.

Though, of course, the discourse of democracy – even the discourse of radical, direct democracy – is sufficiently rife with ambiguity, *aporia*, even contradictions, to be simultaneously susceptible to opportunistic as well as insurrectionist interpretations, intentions, and derivations. The paradoxes of power in politics cannot be abolished by organizational fiat, programmatic pronouncement or ideological catchphrases alone. It is one thing to declare radical decentralisation and horizontal-participatory organizational forms, another altogether to actually operate in accordance with such principles.

An egalitarian and participatory ethos capable of promoting both a deep respect for freedom and a will to struggle for collective justice, to the point of ultimate sacrifice, is indeed hard to come by. Even harder, perhaps, to create. The problems associated with *vanguardism* are difficult to avoid, even in the absence of explicit hierarchical organizational forms. Informal tyranny and effective concentration of power can occur without formal hierarchy; in fact, in some ways, and in some circumstances, "structure-less-ness," or for-mally-horizontal structures, may be even more conducive to tyranny and/or easier for a minority faction to control than organizations structured in ac-cordance with more bureaucratized, formalized hierarchies.[103]

The spectre of tyranny cannot be so easily vanquished; it is inherent to the realm of politics. As Rosa Luxemburg rightly stressed in her own incisive, prophetic polemic against Bolshevism in 1904, an organizational form itself ultimately reveals more about circumstances than it does about principles.[104] Particular historical trajectories and dynamics, concrete political contexts, tend to impose specific organizational forms. Moreover, most crucially, so long as only a minority of the population is mobilized and actively participating, re-gardless of formal organizational structure, the reality of *vanguardism* will remain: decisions affecting broad constituencies, and programmatic pro-nouncements made in their names, will in fact be made by small minorities.

A life-and-death example from the glorious, "structure-less" revolution of the anarchosyndicalists in Spain, in the summer of 1936, proves most illus-trative in this regard. As Burnett Bolloten has explained in vivid detail, the anarchosyndicalist CNT-FAI refused to seize power, despite having protago-nized the successful defence of the populace from the fascist assault on Barcelona. Despite finding itself "at the helm," it opted instead to share power with the constitutional, elected authorities, who ultimately rolled back the revolution. Even so, Bolloten proceeds to point out: "Although opposition to dictatorship was the rationale most frequently used by the anarchosyndicalists to explain their decision not to impose their will in Barcelona, they never-theless established in rural areas a multiplicity of parochial dictatorships with the aid of militia groups and revolutionary tribunals".[105] In short, radical de-centralisation, even "structureless-ness," is no guarantee against tyranny.

The anarchosyndicalists in Spain were notable for their outright rejection of participation in electoral politics. Theirs was a vision of direct democracy, organized primarily at the level of the factory and in self-defence militias, radically decentralized but confederated. Rousseau's objection to the idea of delegated sovereignty animated their bitter opposition to the parliamentary form of representation.

The radically-horizontal, seemingly "structure-less" anarchosyndicalists perhaps paradoxically converge with the hierarchically-structured, centralized Marxist-Leninist *guerrilla* form in their mutual commitment to the conjuring of a new people, a new order, through acts of revolutionary insurgency – or, as Debray provocatively puts it, to the transubstantiation of "the political word into flesh".[106]

The "democratic-confederal" reorientation of the Kurdish movement has, by contrast, facilitated a flourishing of pro-Kurdish, electoral party politics. Admittedly, as Gunes has well documented, there is a deeper history to pro-Kurdish party politics in the Turkish electoral arena, with precedents of victories of pro-Kurdish candidates in municipal elections in Batman and Diyarbakir dating back to 1977, though one of these candidates would be murdered, the other imprisoned.[107]

For its part, the 1982 Constitution "strictly banned any mention of the existence of the Kurds and incriminated any political party or organisation voicing Kurdish demands," thereby severely limiting the space of toleration for pro-Kurdish voices within the realms of municipal and parliamentary representation.[108] Even so, from the early 1990s, coinciding with the outbreak of the *serhildan*, the mass street rebellions, the "burgeoning civil resistance" that came to complement the ongoing *guerrilla* campaign, "pro-Kurdish representation … was able to return," as the movement "managed to build an institutional base and endure the state's numerous attempt to suppress it," with a series of political parties emerging, then being suppressed, then emerging anew, to challenge "the established order in Turkey to recognize Kurdish identity and cultural rights, and putting forward proposals for political reconciliation to end the cycle of violence".[109] In the wake of the "paradigm shift," initially against a backdrop of relative liberalization and efforts to converge with European norms, the advances of the movement in electoral politics, at both the municipal and the parliamentary levels, have been considerable, as Gunes has again well demonstrated.

The prospects for peace, especially in the period between 2013 and 2015, contributed to unprecedented levels of electoral support for the pro-Kurdish HDP. In July of 2015, against a backdrop of escalating tensions, intimidation and harassment, the party nevertheless managed to pass the very high 10% threshold to form a parliamentary group in the Grand National Assembly for the first time, and did so again in the snap election in the fall, amidst the wave of state repression that was unleashed after the breakdown of the peace process. All these developments are treated in considerable detail and with admirable sophistication by Gunes in the text.[110]

The literature on conflict resolution in the English language, which is highly influenced by the paradigmatic case of Northern Ireland, tends to employ a four-fold analytical distinction, ubiquitous in "transitology" studies more generally: namely, the distinction between reformists and revolutionaries in the opposition, on the one side, and between moderates and hardliners in the state on the other.[111] Through this lens, the art of conflict resolution is interpreted as mirroring the "game" of representative democracy, as requiring the forging of a consensus amongst reformists and moderates, and the sidelining, or marginalization, of revolutionaries and hardliners.[112]

Partly overlapping with this distinction between reformists and revolutionaries is another distinction, between the "political" and "military" wings in opposition movements. The examples of Sinn Fein and the IRA, or Herri Batasuna and ETA, are especially relevant in this regard.[113] Integral to the process of sidelining revolutionaries are efforts to coax the "political" wing into dissociating from, even to denounce, the armed struggle, in exchange for measures of compromise and accommodation. This means, in effect, the recognition of and adaptation to the state's monopoly of legitimate violence, in exchange for partial political concessions to the movement's demands. Definitive ceasefire, followed by full-fledged disarmament, are thus envisioned in the model as is incorporation into a state that promises to be more responsive. With the forging of trust the principal task, its absence is the most difficult obstacle on the road to peace and "reconciliation".

The Kurdish Freedom Movement's "paradigm shift" can be understood through such a "conflict resolution" frame to a certain extent – with the HDP in the role of Sinn Fein, and even Demirtas in the role of Gerry Adams. But there are limits to this comparative lens, imposed not only by the extent and brutality of state terror on the part of Turkish security forces; but also in terms of the state-centric terms of reference.

The breakdown of the most recent peace negotiation proves illustrative in this regard. What caused the collapse of these negotiations were not so much events inside of Turkey, but rather events in northern Syria.

Kurdish people are divided across four states, their plight being the incarnation of the contradictions of the dismemberment of the Ottoman Empire and the emergence of the nation-state form in the "Middle East" at the end of the First World War. The Kurdish Freedom Movement may have given up on the goal of an independent nation-state encompassing the whole of

Greater Kurdistan; but it has not surrendered its commitment to some form of political unity among all Kurds. Indeed, the project of "democratic confederalism" explicitly institutionalizes forms of "confederal" collaboration within a transnational "Middle Eastern Union".[114] To this degree, the movement has never ceased to object to the institutional legacies left by Sykes Picot or Lausanne, even if Öcalan has been emphatic that his "paradigm shift" envisions transcending state borders, not creating new ones.

The establishment of a stronghold in northern Syria by the Kurdish Freedom Movement against the backdrop of civil war and state collapse, and the emergence and consolidation of a revolutionary space for constructing democratic confederalism in practice has had tremendous ramifications for political dynamics inside of Turkey. The heroic resistance of the Kurdish forces in Kobane was instrumental in setting off alarms within the Turkish state's security apparatus. Moreover, the Turkish state's selective enforcement of its southern border, its complicity with the crossing of international *jihadis*, contrasted with the vigour and lethal force which it proved willing to exercise in order to prohibit Kurds from Bakur from crossing to help defend Kobane, only served to throw fuel on a simmering fire, especially after Erdogan appeared on television to gloat about the imminent fall of the city. The window of opportunity, the prospects for peace, were thus undermined by developments beyond the Turkish borders. A spill-over of the conflict in Syria, which ultimately precipitated and unleashed the ongoing, all-out war on the Kurdish Freedom Movement, was now operating on both sides of the border, and in Iraqi Kurdistan as well.[115]

Amidst the polarizing dynamics of violent state repression and street mobilization across the Kurdish region of Turkey, in the broader context of the siege of Kobane, latent ambivalences and ambiguities in terms of tactics and strategy associated with the democratic confederal model were thrust to the surface. The detonator was the decision by some urban youth associated with the movement to dig trenches, to attempt to block the access of Turkish security forces from passing into certain neighbourhoods. This was a *de facto* declaration of democratic autonomy, intended as a display of collective self-defence, explicitly justified in terms of Öcalanist principles and goals as an effort to construct democratic confederalism. Some months later, after the PKK had called off its ceasefire in the summer, dozens of pro-Kurdish municipal authorities would in turn issue declarations of democratic autonomy.[116]

First the trenches, then the full-fledged declarations of local autonomy. These actions were interpreted by Turkish security forces as nothing short of treasonous assaults on state sovereignty, and so triggered a swift escalation in the intensity and extent of state repression, including the imprisonment of thousands of political representatives and movement activists (HDP co-chairs and MPs, and BDP mayors and city councillors, among them) as well as the siege of close to 60 municipalities – a veritable human rights atrocity.[117]

This brings us back to Lenin. The fact is, the democratic confederal model, at least as articulated by Öcalan and his followers, may reject the Leninist principle of democratic centralism, and may even reject the Leninist conception of "national liberation"; but it does not abandon the Leninist analysis of the situation of "dual power".[118] Nor does it renounce a willingness to engage in armed insurrection. Indeed, its vision is one of armed militias organized for the purposes of peoples' self-defence, a vision of democracy *against* the state. And so, in Turkey and in Syria, and increasingly in Iraq, too, the Kurdish Freedom Movement now finds itself at the crossroads, in a critical juncture for the future of the democratic confederal ideal – one predicted by none other than Murray Bookchin, whose prophetic words conclude:

"Libertarian municipalists do not delude themselves that the state will view with equanimity their attempts to replace professionalised power with popular power. They harbor no illusions that the ruling classes will indifferently allow a Communalist movement to demand rights that infringe on the state's sovereignty over towns and cities. Historically, regions, localities, and above all towns and cities have desperately struggled to reclaim their local sovereignty from the state (albeit not always for high-minded purposes). Communalists' attempts to restore the power of towns and cities and to knit them together into confederations can be expected to invoke increasing resistance from national institutions. That the new popular-assemblyist municipal confederations will embody a dual power against the state that becomes a source of growing political tension is obvious. Either a Communalist movement will be radicalized by this tension and will resolutely face all its consequences or it will surely sink into a morass of compromises that absorb it back into the social order that it once sought to change. How the movement meets this challenge is a clear measure of its seriousness in seeking to change the existing political system and the social consciousness it develops as a source of public education and leadership".[119]

NOTES

1   This chapter was first published as an extended comment in C. Gunes, with fore-
    word and comment by Thomas J. Miley, *The Political Representation of Kurds in
    Turkey: Actors, Issues and Challenges* (London: I.B. Tauris, 2019).

2   See Juan J. Linz and Alfred Stepan, *Problems of Democratic Transition and Consoli-
    dation* (Baltimore: The Johns Hopkins University Press, 1996), chapter 2; and
    J. Linz, A. Stepan, and Y. Yadav, *Crafting State-Nations: India and Other Multi-
    National Democracies* (Baltimore: The Johns Hopkins University Press, 2011),
    chapter 1; and Mark Redhead, *Charles Taylor: Thinking and Living Deep Diversity*
    (Lanham, MD: Rowman & Littlefield, 2002).

3   Indeed, the Republic of Turkey provides a prime example of the more general ten-
    sion between "nationalizing state policies" and democratic consolidation. Linz and
    Stepan have incisively characterised this tension as follows: "[I]n many countries
    that are not yet consolidated democracies, a nation-state policy often has a differ-
    ent logic from a democratic policy. By a nation-state policy we mean one in which
    the leaders pursue what Rogers Brubaker calls 'nationalizing state policies' aimed
    at increasing cultural homogeneity. Consciously or unconsciously, the leaders send
    messages that the state should be 'of and for' the nation. In the constitutions they
    write, therefore, and the politics they practice, the dominant nation's language be-
    comes the only official language and occasionally the only acceptable language for
    state business and for public (and possibly private) schooling, the religion of the
    nation is privileged (even if it is not necessarily made the official religion), and the
    cultural symbols of the dominant nation are also privileged in all state symbols
    (such as the flag, the national anthem, and even eligibility for some types of
    military service), and in all of the state-controlled means of socialization such as
    radio, television and textbooks. By contrast, democratic policies in the state-
    making process are those that emphasize a broad and inclusive citizenship where
    all citizens are accorded equal individual rights … The neglect in the literature on
    democratic transition and consolidation of the question of the legitimacy of the
    state is unfortunate because this variable, while not always of great importance for
    non-democratic politics, is of fundamental theoretical and political importance
    for democracies," *Problems of Democratic Transition and Consolidation, op. cit.*,
    pp.25-26.

4   As we put the point in a report written in February of 2017: "The events of the past
    year-and-a-half demonstrate very clearly that there can be no democracy in

Turkey without a peaceful resolution of the Kurdish question. The political situation in the country has deteriorated dramatically over the past year-and-a-half, since the breakdown of the peace process in mid-June 2015, and especially since the failed coup in mid-July 2016. President Erdogan has taken advantage of the state of emergency to escalate repression against all opposition, not just those groups allegedly implicated in the coup. The repressive measures include many clear violations of European and human rights norms to which Turkey is bound. These measures have targeted with special intensity the Kurdish Freedom Movement, but also extend to critical media and to dissenting voices in the press and academia, and to trade unions, human rights defenders and wider civil society. To make matters worse, the victims of these repressive measures have virtually no effective recourse to the judiciary, whose independence has been severely undermined. Indeed, the judiciary itself has experienced a massive and unlawful purge, as has the public administration and the educational system." "State Terror, Human Rights Violations, and Authoritarianism in Turkey. Report of the Third Imrali Peace Delegation Based on its Visit to Turkey, Feb. 13-19, 2017," in Thomas Jeffrey Miley and Federico Venturini, eds., *Your Freedom and Mine: Abdullah Ocalan and the Kurdish Question in Erdogan's Turkey* (Montreal: Black Rose Books, 2018), p.226.

5 On the roots of the Turkish-Kurdish conflict, see M. Angrist, "Turkey. Roots of the Turkish-Kurdish Conflict and Prospects for Constructive Reform," in U. Amoretti and N. Bermeo, eds., *Federalism and Territorial Cleavages* (Baltimore: The Johns Hopkins University Press, 2004), pp.387-416; V. Eccarius-Kelly, *The Militant Kurds. A Dual Strategy for Freedom* (Santa Barbara, CA: Praeger, 2011); N. Entessar, *Kurdish Ethnonationalism* (London: Lynne Reinner Publishers, 1992); C. Gunes, *The Kurdish National Movement in Turkey. From Protest to Resistance* (London: Routledge, 2012); M. Gunter, *The Kurds and the Future of Turkey* (London: Palgrave, 1997); J. Jongerden and A. Akkaya, "Born from the Left. The Making of the PKK," in J. Jongerdon and M. Casier, eds., *Nationalism and Politics in Turkey. Political Islam and the Kurdish Issue* (London: Routledge, 2011), pp.123-142; D. McDowall, *A Modern History of the Kurds* (London: I.B. Tauris, 1996); T. Miley with C. Hammy and G. Yildiz, "The Turkish-Kurdish Conflict in Historical Context," in T. Miley and F. Venturini, eds., *Your Freedom and Mine: Abdullah Ocalan and the Kurdish Question in Erdogan's Turkey* (Montreal: Black Rose Books, 2018), pp. 3-123; D. Natali, *The Kurds and the State. Evolving National Identity in Iraq, Turkey, and Iran* (Syracuse, NY: Syracuse University Press, 2005); E. O'Ballance, *The Kurdish Strug-*

gle, 1920-1994 (London: Palgrave MacMillan, 1996); A. Özcan, *Turkey's Kurds. A Theoretical Analysis of the PKK and Abdullah Öcalan* (London: Routledge, 2006); D. Romano, *The Kurdish Nationalist Movement. Opportunity, Mobilization, Identity* (Cambridge: Cambridge University Press, 2006); S. Saeed, *Kurdish Politics in Turkey. From the PKK to the KCK* (London: Routledge, 2017); and P. White, *Primitive Rebels or Revolutionary Modernizers? The Kurdish National Movement in Turkey* (London: Zed Books, 2000).

6   This is not to claim that there is no representative relation between a *guerrilla* force and its purported constituency. In fact, as Che Guevara famously insisted: "In the course of polemics those who advocate guerrilla warfare are often accused of forgetting mass struggle, almost as if guerrilla warfare and mass struggle were opposed to each other. We reject this implication. Guerrilla warfare is a people's war, a mass struggle. To try to carry out this type of war without the support of the population is to court inevitable disaster. The guerrillas are the fighting vanguard of the people, stationed in a specified place in a certain area, armed and prepared to carry out a series of warlike actions for the one possible strategic end - the seizure of power. They have the support of the worker and peasant masses of the region and of the whole territory in which they operate. Without these prerequisites no guerrilla warfare is possible." *Guerrilla Warfare: A Method* (Peking: Foreign Language Press, 1964), p.2. Notably, on the fiftieth anniversary of Guevara's death, PKK co-founder Duran Kalkan would refer to Che as "our principal inspiration" (https://anfenglish.com/features/pkk-commanders-our-strongest-inspiration-was-che-guevara-22628). For a recent sophisticated conceptualization and defence of guerrilla violence as an "imaginative technique of mobilization," at least in some instances, especially among those who suffer from an "extreme lack of voice (representation)," see N. Chandhoke, *Democracy and Revolutionary Politics* (London: Bloomsbury Academic, 2015).

7   M. Weber, "Structures of Power: The Nation," in H.H. Gerth and C.W. Mills, eds., *From Max Weber: Essays in Sociology* (Abingdon, Oxon: Routledge, 1991), pp.171-180.

8   As Linz and Stepan have emphasized: "A nation does not have officials, and there are no defined leadership roles, although there are individuals who act as carriers in the Weberian sense of Träger, of the national sentiment in movements or nationalistic organizations. There are no clear rules about membership in a nation and no defined rights that can be legitimately enforced (although nationalists often try to enforce behaviour on the part of those who identify with the nation or

who they claim should identify with it). However, without control of the state, the desired behaviours cannot be legally or even legitimately enforced. A nation and nationalist leaders in its name do not have resources like coercive powers or taxes to demand obedience; only a state can provide those resources to achieve national goals in a binding way. The nation as such, therefore, does not have organizational characteristics comparable with those of the state. It has no autonomy, no agents, no rules, but only the resources derived from psychological identification of the people who constitute it. Whereas a state can exist on the basis of external conformity with its rules, a nation requires some internal identification. Benedict Anderson is quite right. Without 'imagined communities' there are no nations". *Problems of Democratic Transition and Consolidation, op. cit.*, p.22. Likewise, from a distinctly post-colonial perspective, Homi Bhabha converges with Linz and Stepan when he insists: "To write the story of the nation demands that we articulate that archaic ambivalence that informs modernity. We may begin by questioning that progressive metaphor of modern social cohesion – *the many as one* – shared by organic theories of holism of culture and community, and by theorists who treat gender, class, or race as radically 'expressive' social totalities". "DissemiNation: time, narrative, and the margins of the modern nation," in H. Bhabha, ed. *Nation and Narration* (London: Routledge, 1990), p.294. For a persuasive warning against near-ubiquitous recourse to essentialism in discussions of the nation and nationalism, claims about "social constructivism" notwithstanding, see R. Brubaker, *Nationalism Reframed* (Cambridge: Cambridge University Press, 1996).

9   M. Weber, "The Fundamental Concepts of Sociology," in T. Parsons, ed., *The Theory of Social and Economic Organization* (New York: Free Press, 1964), p.156.

10 In fact, as Henry Commager has argued: "Even when definitions of terrorism allow for *state terrorism*, state actions in this area tend to be viewed through the prism of war or national self-defence, not terrorism." Quoted in L. Donahue, "Terrorism and the counter-terrorist discourse," in V. Ramraj, M. Hor and K. Roach, eds., *Global Anti-Terrorism Law and Policy* (Cambridge: Cambridge University Press, 2005), p.20. For debates about the definition of terrorism, see the informative discussion by Alex Schmid, "The Definition of Terrorism," in A. Schmid, ed., *The Routledge Handbook of Terrorism Research* (Oxford: Routledge, 2011), pp.39-157.

11 As Linz and Stepan have contended, in relation to violence and coercion exercised by "non-state" actors associated with nationalist movements: "[A] nation crystallizing out of a nationalist movement, even when it does not control a state, can exercise power, use violence, or exact contributions without having yet gained

statehood. But in a world system of states this means that the movement is taking over some of the functions of another state, subverting its order, so that a state is breaking down in the process. Nationalists can create private armies to enforce their aspirations and to challenge the authority of the state, which in some cases can lose control over a territory. In that case we are talking of the development of a civil war or a national liberation struggle, which might end in the creation of a new state." *Problems of Democratic Transition and Consolidation, op. cit.*, p.22.

12 For the sordid history of the so-called "counter-guerrilla," much of which came to light during the Ergenekon trials, see D. Ganser, *Nato's Secret Armies. Operation Gladio and Terrorism in Western Europe* (London: Routledge, 2004); T. Miley with C. Hammy and G. Yildiz, "The Turkish-Kurdish Conflict in Historical Context," in T. Miley and F. Venturini, *Your Freedom and Mine: Abdullah Öcalan and the Kurdish Question in Erdogan's Turkey, op. cit.*; K. Yildiz and S. Breau, *The Kurdish Conflict: International Humanitarian Law and Post-Conflict Mechanisms* (London: Routledge, 2010). For information about the Ergenekon trials, see E. Zürcher, *Turkey. A Modern History* (London: I.B. Tauris. Fourth Edition, 2017).

13 The term *legitimate* is notoriously multi-faceted. In normative political philosophy, it tends to be used as an equivalent of fair or just. In empirical political sociology, by contrast, the focus is explicitly on perceptions and justificatory discourses, especially modes of legitimation (i.e. the justifications used by elites for the exercise of political authority). The realms of fact and of value are supposed to remain scrupulously separated, scholars working in this *sociological* tradition/discipline tend to believe, though of course, few if any social-scientific devotees of "value-neutrality" manage to persuasively practice what they preach. In such an effort at "value-free" sociology, Max Weber famously distinguished among three ideal types of legitimation – legal-bureaucratic, charismatic, and traditional. If the discourse and ideology of the nation has proven so attractive to rulers in recent decades and centuries, perhaps this is because it combines a potent blend of Weber's three types of legitimation. The role of charismatic leadership in the "founding" of nations is in this respect a phenomenon that is difficult to deny. Charismatic leaders have often been worshipped as founders of nations, after all. The case of Öcalan is thus no exception in this regard. In point of fact, his figure and resonance paradoxically mirrors and simultaneously sublimates/transvalues the cult of Atatürk, which, by the way, remains compulsory to this day in Turkey, even after close to two decades of hegemony of Erdogan's brand of political Islam. Still, one might wonder, just why has state legitimacy proven so vulnerable to

nationalist challenges over the past century, and what might this have to do with the spread of representative democracy, and relatedly, of democratic ideals? Nationalist conflicts pose a particularly thorny problem for state authorities concerned to legitimate their rule in accordance with democratic principles. This is because, as Sir Ivor Jennings famously emphasised, the notion of rule by (representatives of) the people, for the people – a notion which is arguably the very core of the democratic creed – tends to presuppose an answer to the question, "Who are the people?" By extension, attempts to legitimate the exercise of authority by rulers elected to represent the people run into special difficulties in contexts where large segments of the population are not seen as, and/or do not see themselves as, belonging to the people, i.e. to the nation. Moreover, largely because of the fact that democratic politics tend to be confined within the boundaries of "nation-states" (sic), peoplehood and nationhood are all too often conflated in the terms of contemporary political discourse, certainly but not only in Turkey, indeed, all around the globe. On the flip side, with respect to the question of violence in the phrase "monopoly of legitimate violence," we know from the comparative study of nationalism that violent repression of ethno-cultural minorities more often than not seems to strengthen the cohesion of the victimised group, at least in the longer run, certainly in the contemporary period. The case of the Catalans and the Basques in Spain are quite exemplary in this regard. On the dilemmas for democratic theory posed by peoplehood, see I. Jennings, *The Approach to Self-Government* (Cambridge: Cambridge University Press, [1956]2011); and, more recently, Rogers M. Smith, *Stories of Peoplehood* (Cambridge: Cambridge University Press, 2003). On the causal relation between violent Franquist repression and the subsequent strengthening of national identity in Spain, the work of Juan Linz on the subject remains worthy of close attention. See, in particular, his long essay from 1973, "Early State-Building and Late Peripheral Nationalisms against the State: The Case of Spain," in Shmuel N. Eisenstadt and Stein Rokkan (eds.), *Building States and Nations. Analysis by Region, Vol. II* (Beverly Hills: Sage Publications,1973), pp: 32-116, as well as the chapter on Spain in *Problems of Democratic Transition and Consolidation* (*op. cit.*).

14 https://en.wikipedia.org/wiki/Terrorism

15 On the truly "Orwellian" dimension of the ongoing war on terror, see the prescient 2003 volume published by the Campaign Against Criminalising Communities (CAMPACC), *A Permanent State of Terror?* (London). See also the special issue by the Institute for Race Relation's (IRR) journal, *Race and Class* on *The Politics of*

Fear: Civil Society and the Security State (http://www.irr.org.uk/publications/is
sues/the-politics-of-fear-civil-society-and-the-security-state/); as well as the incisive article by the IRR's emeritus Director, A. Sivanandan, "Racism, Liberty and
the War on Terror" (Institute for Race Relations, 2006) (http://www.irr.org.uk/
news/racism-liberty-and-the-war-on-terror/); and the book by the IRR's current
Director, Liz Fekete, *Europe's Fault Lines: Racism and the Far Right* (London: Verso,
2017). For powerful criticism of the war on terror grounded firmly in a US consti-
tutionalist perspective, see Bruce Ackerman, *Before the Next Attack: Preserving Civil
Liberties in the Age of Terrorism* (New Haven, CT: Yale University Press, 2007); and
David Cole and Jack Dempsey, *Terrorism and the Constitution: Sacrificing Civil
Liberties in the Name of National Security. Third Edition* (The New Press, 2006).
For a critique of the war on terror paradigm from a perspective that nevertheless
remains close to the US foreign policy establishment, see R. Malley and J. Finer,
"The Long Shadow of 9/11. How Counter-terrorism Warps US Foreign Policy,"
Foreign Affairs (July/August 2018), pp.58-69. The consequences of the "war on
terror" for political expression and therefore representation are particularly grave.
The banning of representative symbols such as flags or images of political leaders,
and the prosecution of human rights defenders who seek to give legal and political
advice to outlawed organizations/movements searching for ways to negotiate a
democratic peace, are two pertinent examples of the anti-democratic core of the
paradigm, its commitment to coercion over consensus, to weapons over words,
its substitution of politics by war.

16 See D. Summers, "Dancing with the Devil," as well as his sharp rejoinder to
Michael Gunter in "Consolidating Peace, Democracy and Human Rights after
Raqqa: Prospects for the Region and the Kurds. Panel Discussion at the 14th An-
nual EUTCC Conference," in T. Miley and F. Venturini, eds., *Your Freedom and
Mine: Abdullah Öcalan and the Kurdish Question in Erdogan's Turkey, op. cit.,*
pp.385-389, 396.

17 For a synoptic overview of the most blatant examples of US state terror in the past
60 years, see N. Chomsky, "The Long and Shameful History of American Terrorism" (https://politics1660.wordpress.com/2017/01/22/noam-chomsky-the-long-
shameful-history-of-american-terrorism/). See also the helpful reading list on
state terror, available at: http://www.chomskylist.com/category_page.php?cate
gory_id=97

18 For details of the spiralling violence between the Turkish state and the Kurdish
Freedom Movement and the human rights atrocities against the Kurdish popula-

tion since the breakdown of peace negotiations in mid-2015, see T. Miley, "State Terror, Human Rights Violations and Authoritarianism in Turkey," in T. Miley and F. Venturini, *Your Freedom and Mine: Abdullah Öcalan and the Kurdish Question in Erdogan's Turkey, op. cit.*, pp.221-252.

19 According to most estimates, the number of people killed since 1984 exceeds 40,000; the number of people displaced to date close to 4 million; the number of villages evacuated and destroyed, over 3,000. In 2001, a UN Special Rapporteur on extrajudicial, summary or arbitrary executions was provided by Turkish authorities with official figures in which these human rights atrocities are broken down further, since the declaration of the state of emergency in 1987. These figures help provide a sense of proportion in the balance sheet of suffering: "over 23,000 suspected PKK militants killed, more than 4,400 unarmed civilians killed and 5,400 wounded, more than 5,000 police officers and gendarmes killed and 11,000 injured. See K. Yildiz and S. Breau, *The Kurdish Conflict: International Humanitarian Law and Post-Conflict Mechanisms, op. cit.*, pp.16, 277 fn99).

20 See, for example, A. Öcalan, *War and Peace in Kurdistan. Perspectives for a Political Solution to the Kurdish Question* (Cologne: International Initiative, 2009), especially pp.28-30; and A. Öcalan, *Prison Writings. The PKK and the Kurdish Question in the 21st Century* (Cologne: International Initiative, 2011), especially pp.122-123.

21 J. Locke, "The Right to Revolution," in *The Second Treatise on Government*, section 222. http://press-pubs.uchicago.edu/founders/documents/v1ch3s2.html

22 See R. Aschraft, *Revolutionary Politics and Locke's Two Treatises of Government* (Princeton, NJ: Princeton University Press, 1986).

23 See the relevant conclusions in this regard reached by M. Manwaring, Professor of Military Strategy in the Strategic Studies Institute of the US Army War College, in his chapter, "The Environment as a Global Stability-Security Issue," in M. Manwaring, ed., *Environmental Security and Global Stability. Problems and Responses* (Lanham, MD: Lexington Books, 2002). Manwaring contends: "Instability and violence are the general consequences of unreformed political, social, economic, and security institutions and concomitant misguided, insensitive, incompetent, and/or corrupt (i.e. illegitimate) governance. Thus, governance is the root cause and the central strategic problem in the current unstable security arena," p.168. Translation from social-scientific-cum-military-speak into plain language: no justice, no peace.

24 As was already noted earlier (in footnote 5), Che Guevara stressed the importance of popular support for determining the prospects of survival and ultimate success

of the tactic of guerrilla warfare. In a similar vein, Mao Tse Tung famously insisted in his equally influential writings *On Guerrilla Warfare* (1937) that: "The most important natural quality is that of complete loyalty to the idea of the people's emancipation. If this is present, the others will develop; if it is not present, nothing can be done". https://www.marxists.org/reference/archive/mao/works/1937/guerrilla-warfare/cho5.htm

25 For the most comprehensive and persuasive documentation of the objective, material conditions underpinning and fuelling the Kurdish insurgency in Turkey, see V. Yadirgi, *The Political Economy of the Kurds of Turkey: From the Ottoman Empire to the Turkish Republic* (Cambridge: Cambridge University Press, 2017). See also A. Icduygu, et. al., "The Ethnic Question in an Environment of Insecurity: The Kurds in Turkey," *Ethnic and Racial Studies*, Vol. 22, Issue 6, 1999, pp.991-1010.

26 On the distinctive class composition of the cadres of the PKK, see D. McDowall, *A Modern History of the Kurds, op. cit.*, p.418; D. Romano, *The Kurdish Nationalist Movement. Opportunity, Mobilization, Identity, op. cit.*, p.89; M. Van Bruinessen, "Between Guerrilla War and Political Murder: the Workers' Party of Kurdistan," *Middle East Report*, #153, July-Aug. 1988, p.42; and P. White, *Primitive Rebels or Revolutionary Modernizers? The Kurdish National Movement in Turkey, op. cit.*, pp.155-156.

27 On the role of the "village guards" in the spiral of repression and violence in the Kurdish region, see D. McDowall, *A Modern History of the Kurds, op. cit.*, p.422; D. Romano, *The Kurdish Nationalist Movement. Opportunity, Mobilization, Identity, op. cit.*, p. 83; and K. Yildiz and S. Breau, *The Kurdish Conflict: International Humanitarian Law and Post-Conflict Mechanisms, op. cit.*, p.16.

28 An initial inroad into survey research that focuses on the Kurdish question in Turkey and is available in English was made by Z. Saragil, "Curbing Kurdish Ethno-nationalism in Turkey: An Empirical Assessment of Pro-Islamic and Socioeconomic Approaches," *Ethnic and Racial Studies*, Vol. 33, No. 3, 2010, pp.533-553. Unfortunately, Saragil's article relies on rather dubious extrapolations from the World Values Survey, a point made persuasively by F. Ekmeki, "Understanding Kurdish Ethno-nationalism in Turkey: Socio-Economy, Religion, and Politics," *Ethnic and Racial Studies*, Vol. 34, No. 9, 2011, pp.1608-1617. For a rare example of original survey research conducted in Turkey that explores the political implications of Kurdish ethnicity on support for different political parties, see M. Toprak, et. al., "Transformations of Turkish Politics: Socio-Political, Economic and Ethnic Particularities," *bilig*, No. 50, 2009, pp.199-232.

29 The abundance of research about national identity in Spain that uses general population surveys and elite surveys is thanks in no small part to the research agenda
of Juan Linz, who from the mid-1960s produced a series of pioneering studies
with FOESSA and DATA, and who, alongside some of his many students, would
continue to pursue this agenda until the end of his life in 2013. For an excellent example of such research, see J. Linz, "From Primordialism to Nationalism," in Edward A. Tiriyakian and Ronald Rogowski, eds., *New Nationalisms of the Developed
West* (Boston: Allen & Unwin, 1985), pp.203–253.

30 Gunes's manuscript provides detailed information about the legal and extra-legal
obstacles that pro-Kurdish political parties have faced in recent decades. One
point worth mentioning in this regard is that the repression of parliamentary and
local representation of pro-Kurdish voices directly undermined peace negotiations
on multiple occasions. For example, as was explained elsewhere, after the murder
of President Özal in 1993, "[a]longside stepped-up military assault, the Turkish
government moved to ban the Kurdish political party HEP, which had emerged
after a split with Turkey's Social Democratic Party (Gunes 2012, pp.156-164). Moreover, the Constitutional Court even decided to strip "one of the most moderate
Kurds in the Assembly" of his parliamentary immunity. Further removals of parliamentary immunity soon followed. Moreover, such legal measures were comple-
mented by extra-legal ones as well: assassinations of Kurdish politicians, bomb
attacks on their headquarters and branch offices, and arrests of party members
(McDowall 1996, p.439). The window of opportunity for a negotiated, political solution to the ongoing human rights' tragedy in the Kurdish region was thus
slammed shut." See T. Miley with C. Hammy and G. Yildiz, "The Turkish-Kurdish
Conflict in Historical Context," in T. Miley and F. Venturini, eds., *Your Freedom
and Mine: Abdullah Öcalan and the Kurdish Question in Erdogan's Turkey, op. cit.,*
p.50. For details about the wave of state repression against the HDP since spring
2015, and its contribution to the rapid deterioration of the human rights situation
in the Kurdish region (and beyond) in Turkey, see T. Miley, "State Terror, Human
Rights Violations, and Authoritarianism in Turkey," in the same volume, pp.225-
258. Also accessible at: https://peaceinkurdistancampaign.com/2017/03/20/state-
terror-human-rights-violations-and-authoritarianism-in-turkey/.

31 Indeed, as was argued elsewhere: "The social scientific literature on nationalism is
plagued by empirical deficiencies. Despite the endless debates about how a nation
should be defined, the abundance of general theories of nationalism, the extensive
literature on nationalist ideology, movements and leadership, and even on nation-

alist parties and electorates, there remains a dearth of empirical data in the literature. The social groups in whose names nationalist ideologues speak are themselves poorly described. In most of the literature we find inadequate empirical data on the composition of these groups. There is little empirical research devoted to gauging the feeling of national identity. There is even less research relating patterns of different modes of national identification with the diffusion of different political attitudes." See T. Miley, "Against the Thesis of the 'Civic Nation': The Case of Catalonia in Contemporary Spain," *Nationalism and Ethnic Politics*, Vol. 13, 2007, pp.1-37.

32 See I. Budge and D. McDonald, "Choices Parties Define: Policy Alternatives in Representative Elections, 17 Countries 1945–1998," *Party Politics*, 12(4), 2006, pp.451–466; and J. Roemer et. al., *Racism, Xenophobia, and Distribution: Multi-Issue Politics in Advanced Democracies* (Cambridge: Russell Sage Foundation Books, 2007). For an overview of the significance of this literature for the theory of representative democracy and for the theory of nationalism, see T. Miley, "Democratic Representation and the National Dimension in Catalan and Basque Politics," *International Journal of Politics, Culture and Society*, Vol. 27, 2014, pp.291-322.

33 See X. Coller, et. al., eds., *Political Power in Spain: The Multiple Divides between MPs and Citizens* (London: Palgrave Macmillan, 2018); as well as T. Miley, "Democratic Representation and the National Dimension in Catalan and Basque Politics," *op. cit.*

34 For a good overview of the vast literature on representation in the social sciences, of the many related debates which have developed relatively autonomously, see S. Dovi, "Political Representation," in E. Zalta, ed., *The Stanford Encyclopedia of Philosophy* (Stanford, CA: Stanford University Press, 2007). Available at: https://plato.stanford.edu/entries/political-representation/#PitFouVieRep Several strands in the literature stand out as particularly pertinent to our discussion. First, there is a literature that has developed mainly in normative political philosophy, in which Hanna Pitkin's 1967 classic, *The Concept of Representation* (Berkeley, CA: University of California Press, 1967), still remains central, as exemplified by Gunes's references to it in his manuscript. For an overview of the reception of Pitkin's work, see S. Dovi, "Hannah Pitkin: The Concept of Representation," in J. Levy, *The Oxford Handbook of Classics in Contemporary Political Theory* (Oxford: Oxford University Press, 2015). For a sophisticated critique of much this normative literature from a perspective highly indebted to Hayden White's work in the fields of history and literary criticism, see F. Ankersmitt, *Aesthetic Politics: Political Philosophy Beyond*

Fact and Value (Stanford, CA: Stanford University Press, 1997). Among the most interesting developments in the normative literature in recent years has been the so-called "constructivist" turn, which is in turn indebted to Carole Pateman's famous book from 1970 on *Participation and Democratic Theory* (Cambridge: Cambridge University Press). See, for example, the work of Lisa Disch, including her 2011 article, "Toward a Mobilization Conception of Democratic Representation," *American Political Science Review*, 105(1), pp.100–114.; as well as her more recent piece, "The Constructivist Turn in Democratic Representation: A Normative Dead-End?" *Constellations*, Vol. 22, No.4, 2015, pp.487-499. As is evident in Disch's work, the normative literature has evolved in a more empirical direction, and is now convergent with debates in a second strand, that developed mainly within the tradition of empirical democratic theory, with its long-standing emphasis on the impact of institutional design on the type and quality of democratic representation. One of the most influential "sub-strands" in this more empirically-based literature on representation has been developed by feminist scholars, with Anne Phillips' book, *The Politics of Presence* (Oxford: Oxford University Press, 1995) being a canonical point of reference. There is likewise a related "sub-strand" which focuses on the question of representation of ethnic and religious minorities. See the overview provided in Banducci, S.A., et. al., "Minority Representation, Empowerment, and Participation," *The Journal of Politics*, Vol. 66, No. 2, 2004, pp.534-556. This feminist, critical race and multicultural contribution to the literature on representation in turn builds on related longstanding debates within empirical democratic theory, especially the debate about consociationalism, generated by Arend Lijphart's 1969 article, "Consociational Democracy" *World Politics*, Vol. 25, No. 2, 1969, pp.207-225; as well as the more recent debates about multinational federalism, of which Linz, Stepan, and Yadav's 2011 book, *Crafting State-Nations: India and Other Multi-National Democracies, op. cit.*, is exemplary. See also the volume by J. Cohen and A. Arato, *Forms of Pluralism and Democratic Constitutionalism* (New York: Columbia University Press, 2018), which includes an article by A. Stepan and J. Miley that explicitly addresses the relevance of the Öcalan-inspired, "democratic confederal" Rojava revolution, "Federacy and the Kurds: Might This New Political Form Help Mitigate Hobbesian Conflict in Turkey, Iraq, and Syria." For the significance of all these convergent strands of abundant normative and empirical literature for the theory of representative democracy, see the edited volume by A. Przeworski, et. al., *Democracy, Accountability, and Representation* (Cambridge: Cambridge University Press, 1999); as well as J. Linz with T. Miley,

"Cautionary and Unorthodox Thoughts about Democracy Today," in Douglas Chalmers and Scott Mainwaring, eds., *Institutions and Democracy: Essays in Honor of Alfred Stepan* (South Bend, IN: University of Notre Dame Press, 2012), pp. 227-252. Finally, there is yet another influential strand of literature on representation that deserves mention, which, however unfortunately, remains largely ignored by and in turn largely ignores the convergent debates in normative political philosophy and in comparative politics/empirical democratic theory, but dominates the discussion in cultural studies. Its canonical reference remains the work of Stuart Hall. See, for example, S. Hall, ed. *Representation. Cultural Representation and Signifying Practices* (London: SAGE, 1997).

35 The five-fold typology of political regimes provided by Juan Linz in *Totalitarian and Authoritarian Regimes* (Boulder, CO: Lynne Reinner Publishers, 2000) remains at the centre of debates in comparative political sociology on regime types. Nicos Poulantzas's *Fascism and Dictatorship: The Third International and the Problem of Fascism* (London: NLB, 1970) is probably still the most sophisticated contribution to the debate about regime types from within the Marxist tradition, though Göran Therborn also provides very pertinent reflections about regime types conceptualised as diverse "bourgeois formats of representation" in chapter four of *What Does the Ruling Class Do When It Rules?* (London: NLB, 1978). For the controversy surrounding Linz's description of the Franco regime as an authoritarian regime, see T. Miley, "Franquism as Authoritarianism: Juan Linz and his Critics," *Politics, Religion & Ideology*, Vol. 12, No. 1, 2011, pp.27-50. For the relevant, more recent elaboration of the concept of "competitive authoritarianism," see S. Levitsky and L. Way, *Competitive Authoritarianism: Hybrid Regimes after the Cold War* (Cambridge: Cambridge University Press, 2010).

36 See T. Miley with C. Hammy and G. Yildiz, "The Turkish-Kurdish Conflict in Historical Context," *op. cit.*, pp.10-11.

37 See V. Yadirgi, *The Political Economy of the Kurds of Turkey: From the Ottoman Empire to the Turkish Republic, op. cit.*, p.192.

38 See C. Hammy, "Two Visions of Politics in Turkey: Authoritarian and Revolutionary," *Open Democracy*, Aug. 20, 2016. https://www.opendemocracy.net/north-africa-west-asia/cihad-hammy/two-visions-of-politics-in-turkey-authoritarian-and-revolutionary

39 For an overview of the burgeoning literature on "hybrid regimes," see N. Ezrow, "Hybrid Regimes," in F. Moghaddam, ed. *The SAGE Encyclopedia of Political Behavior* (London: SAGE Publications, 2017). For an elaboration of the concept of

"semiauthoritarianism," see C. Göbel, "Semiauthoritarianism," in J. Ishiyame and M. Breuning, eds., *21ˢᵗ Century Political Science: A Reference Handbook* (London: SAGE Publications, 2011), pp.258-267. On the concept of "competitive authoritarianism," see S. Levitsky and J. Loxton, "Populism and Competitive Authoritarianism in the Andes," *Democratization* Vol. 20, 2013, pp.107-136; and J. Loxton, "Competitive Authoritarianism," in F. Moghaddam, ed., *The SAGE Encyclopedia of Political Behavior, op. cit.*. On the related concept of "participatory competitive authoritarianism," see S. Mainwaring, "Review: From Representative Democracy to Participatory Competitive Authoritarianism: Hugo Chávez and Venezuelan Politics," *Perspectives on Politics*, Vol. 10, No. 4, 2012, pp.955-967. For the concept of "electoralist hegemony," see C. Hacker-Cordón, "Electoral Legitimation, Polyarchy, and Democratic Legitimacy," *American Political Science Association*, Foundations Section, Washington, DC: 2001. Hacker-Cordón draws heavily on P. Anderson's important essay, "The Antinomies of Antonio Gramsci," *New Left Review*, No. 100, 1976, pp.5-78.

40 See R. Dahl, *Polyarchy: Participation and Opposition* (New Haven, CT: Yale University Press, 1971).

41 For the elaboration of the Gramscian concept of hegemony, see P. Anderson, "The Antinomies of Antonio Gramsci," *op. cit.*; as well as his more recent, *The H-word: The Peripeteia of Hegemony* (London: Verso Books, 2017). For a penetrating critique of the Gramscian framework from an anarchist perspective, see J. Scott, *Domination and the Arts of Resistance: Hidden Transcripts* (New Haven, CT: Yale University Press, 1990), especially chapters 3 and 4.

42 On the distinction between "exclusionary" and "assimilationist" nationalisms, see T. Miley, "Against the Thesis of the 'Civic Nation': The Case of Catalonia in Contemporary Spain," *op. cit.*

43 See C. Sagnic, "Mountain Turks: State Ideology and the Kurds in Turkey," *Information, Society and Justice*, Vol. 3, No. 2, 2010, pp.127-134.

44 T. Miley with C. Hammy and G. Yildiz, "The Turkish-Kurdish Conflict in Historical Context," *op. cit.*, p.8.

45 See D. Natali, *The Kurds and the State. Evolving National Identity in Iraq, Turkey, and Iran* (Syracuse, NY: Syracuse University Press, 2005), p.97; and K. Ertur, *The Political Integration of the Kurds in Turkey* (Portland State University PhD. Dissertation, 1979), accessible at: https://pdxscholar.library.pdx.edu/cgi/viewcontent.cgi?article=3897&context=open_access_etds.

46 See T. Miley with C. Hammy and G. Yildiz, "The Turkish-Kurdish Conflict in Historical Context," *op. cit.*, pp.24-27.

47 See M. Hroch, *The Social Preconditions of National Revival in Europe* (New York: Columbia University Press, 2000).

48 For another important book in the literature on comparative nationalisms that makes ample use of the idea of "thresholds," incorporated within a broader neo-Gramscian framework, see I. Lustick, *Unsettled States, Disputed Lands: Britain and Ireland, France and Algeria, Israel and the West Bank-Gaza* (Ithaca, NY: Cornell University Press, 1995). Lustick's account, unfortunately, follows Laclau and Mouffe's post-Marxist reading of Gramsci to excise the political economic dimension almost entirely from the historical narratives that he weaves. For Laclau and Mouffe's highly influential post-Marxist take on hegemony, see *Hegemony and Socialist Strategy* (London: Verso, 1986). For cogent critiques of Laclau and Mouffe's framework in implicit defence of a more orthodox historical materialist perspective, see G. Therborn, *From Marxism to Post-Marxism?* (London: Verso, 2008), and P. Anderson, *The H-word: The Peripeteia of Hegemony* (London: Verson, 2017). See also T. Miley, "Self-Determination in the Twenty-First Century: Beyond the Nation, against the State," (forthcoming).

49 See R. Dahl, *A Preface to Democratic Theory* (Chicago, IL: Chicago University Press, 1956), chapter 4, "Equality, Diversity, Intensity," pp.90-123.

50 See J. Linz, "Democracy, Multinationalism, and Federalism," *Working Paper*, No. 103 (Madrid: Centro de Estudios Avanzados en Ciencias Sociales, Instituto Juan March de Estudios e Investigaciones, 1997).

51 See T. Miley with C. Hammy and G. Yildiz, "The Turkish-Kurdish Conflict in Historical Perspective," *op. cit.*, pp.27-29.

52 Ibid., pp.35-36.

53 F. Fanon, *The Wretched of the Earth* (London: Penguin Classics, 2001), p.74.

54 See E.V. Wolfenstein, *Psychoanalytic-Marxism. Groundwork* (Free Association Books, 1993), p.432, n.3.

55 E. Hobsbawm, *Nations and Nationalism since 1780* (Cambridge: Cambridge University Press, 1990), pp.117-118.

56 M. Weber, "Structures of Power: The Nation," in H.H. Gerth and C. Wright Mills, eds., *From Max Weber: Essays in Sociology, op. cit.*, p.176.

57 Quoted in J. Linz, "State Building and Nation Building," *European Review*, Vol. 1, No. 4, 1993, p.361. See also T. Miley, "The Nation as Hegemonic Project," *Journal of Political Ideologies*, Vol. 23, Issue 2, 2018: 183-204.

58 See M. Koefoed, "Martyrdom and Emotional Resistance in the Case of Northern Kurdistan: Hidden and Public Emotional Resistance," *Journal of Political Power*, Vol. 10, Issue 2, 2017, pp.184-199.

59 M. Weber, "The Sociology of Charismatic Authority," in H.H. Gerth and C. Wright Mills, eds., *From Max Weber: Essays in Sociology*, *op. cit.*, pp.245-246.

60 C. Lindblom, *Charisma* (Oxford: Oxford University Press, 1993), p.192.

61 D. Leese, *Mao Cult: Rhetoric and Ritual in China's Cultural Revolution* (Cambridge: Cambridge University Press, 2011), p.20.

62 Ibid., p.87.

63 A. Öcalan, *Manifesto for a Democratic Civilization. Volume One: The Age of Masked Gods and Disguised Kings* (Prosgrunn, Norway: New Compass Press, 2015), p.21.

64 I. Szelenyi, "Lecture 19: Weber on Charismatic Authority", accessible at: https://oyc.yale.edu/sociology/socy-151/lecture-19

65 H.H. Gerth and C. Wright Mills, "Introduction," in H.H. Gerth and C. Wright Mills, eds., *From Max Weber: Essays in Sociology*, *op. cit.*, p.54.

66 T. Miley with C. Hammy and G. Yildiz, "The Turkish-Kurdish Conflict in Historical Context," *op. cit.*, pp.51-64.

67 A. Öcalan, "Seek the Truth," in T. Miley and F. Venturini, eds., *Your Freedom and Mine: Abdullah Öcalan and the Kurdish Question in Erdgoan's Turkey*, *op. cit.*, pp.315-316.

68 An increasing number of Öcalan's writings have been translated into English. See, for example, A. Öcalan, *The Roots of Civilization* (Transmedia Publishing Limited, 2007); *Prison Writings: The PKK and the Kurdish Question in the Twenty-First Century* (Cologne: International Initiative, 2013); *Prison Writings III: The Road Map to Negotiations* (Cologne: International Initiative, 2012); *Manifesto for a Democratic Civilization. Volume One: The Age of Masked Gods and Disguised Kings*, *op. cit.*; *Manifesto for a Democratic Civilization. Volume Two: The Age of Unmasked Gods and Naked Kings* (Prosgrunn, Norway: New Compass Press, 2017); and *The Political Thought of Abdullah Öcalan: Kurdistan, Women's Revolution and Democratic Confederalism* (London: Pluto Press, 2017).

69 See J. Linz with T. Miley, "Cautionary and Unorthodox Thoughts about Democracy Today," *op. cit.*

70 R. Dahl, *Polyarchy: Participation and Opposition, op. cit.*

71 A. Przeworski, *Democracy and the Limits of Self-Government* (Cambridge: Cambridge University Press, 2010), p.18.

72 This section draws substantially on T. Miley, "Democratic Representation and the National Dimension in Catalan and Basque Politics," *op. cit.*

73 R. Miliband, *The State in Capitalist Society* (New York, NY: Basic Books, 1969).

74 P. Bachrach and M.S. Baratz, "Two Faces of Power," *The American Political Science Review*, Vol. 56, No. 4, 1962, pp.947-952.

75 N. Poulantzas, "The Problem of the Capitalist State," *New Left Review*, Vol. 58, 1969, pp.67-78.

76 A. Przeworski and M. Wallerstein, "The Structural Dependence of the State on Capital," *The American Political Science Review*, Vol. 82, No 1, 1988, pp.11-29.

77 L. Althusser, "Ideology and Ideological State Apparatuses," in *On Ideology* (London: Verso, 2007), pp.1-140.

78 .J. Rousseau, *The Social Contract*, Book 2.1. Accessible at: https://www.early moderntexts.com/assets/pdfs/rousseau1762.pdf

79 See J. Bartelson, *A Genealogy of Sovereignty* (Cambridge: Cambridge University Press, 1993).

80 B. Manin, *The Principles of Representative Government* (Cambridge: Cambridge University Press, 1997).

81 For the conceptualization of elections as a "candidate selection process," see G.W. Domhoff, *Who Rules America?* (McGraw Hill Education, Seventh Edition, 2013). For accounts of democracy that emphasise the primacy of participation, see C. Pateman, *Participation and Democratic Theory*, *op. cit.*; and, more recently, L. Disch, "Toward a Mobilization Conception of Democratic Representation," *op. cit.* For the contrast between "polyarchy" and "popular democracy," see W. Robinson, *Promoting Polyarchy* (Cambridge: Cambridge University Press, 1996). For a vision of direct democracy conceived as an alternative to representative democracy that has had a strong influence on Öcalan, see M. Bookchin, "Libertarian Municipalism," in J. Biehl, ed., *The Murray Bookchin Reader* (Montreal: Black Rose Books, 1999), pp.172-196.; and M. Bookchin, *The Next Revolution: Popular Assemblies and the Promise of Direct Democracy* (London: Verso, 2015).

82 On "deliberative democracy," see J. Cohen, "Deliberation and Democratic Legitimacy," in J. Bohman and W. Rehg, eds., *Deliberative Democracy: Essays on Reason and Politics* (Boston, MA: MIT Press, 1997); J. Fishkin and P. Laslett, eds., *Debating Deliberative Democracy* (Wiley, 2008); A. Gutmann and D. Thompson, *Why Deliberative Democracy?* (Princeton, NJ: Princeton University Press, 2002); E. Leib, "Can Direct Democracy Be Made Deliberative?," *Buffalo Law Review* Vol. 54, 2006,

pp.903-925; J. Mansbridge and J. Parkinson, eds., *Deliberative Systems* (Cambridge: Cambridge University Press, 2012); and C. Ross, *The Leaderless Revolution: How Ordinary People Can Take Power and Change Politics in the 21st Century* (London: Simon and Schuster, 2011).

83 P. Freire, *The Pedagogy of the Oppressed* (Continuum, 30th Anniversary Edition, 2000).

84 See M. Bookchin, *Urbanization without Cities* (Montreal: Black Rose Books, 1992), p.299.

85 For the concept of "the hermeneutic of suspicion," see P. Ricoeur, *Freud and Philosophy: An Essay on Interpretation* (New Haven, CT: Yale University Press, 1993).

86 For the concept of an "ethic of conviction," see M. Weber, "Politics as a Vocation," in H.H. Gerth and C. Wright Mills, eds., *From Max Weber: Essays in Sociology*, *op. cit.*, pp.71-128.

87 M. Bookchin, "The Future of the Left," in *The Next Revolution: Popular Assemblies and the Promise of Direct Democracy, op. cit.*, p.128.

88 S. Casmier, "Subliminal Consciousness in the Killing Fields of Spain." Unpublished Paper delivered at the 16th Annual Conference of the Multidisciplinary Society, *The Space Between: Literature and Culture 1914-1945*, School of Advanced Study, University of London, July 17, 2014.

89 R. Debray, *The Revolution in the Revolution? Armed Struggle and Political Struggle in Latin America* (New York: Monthly Review Press, 1967), p.70.

90 C. Guevara, "Notes for the Study of Man and Socialism in Cuba" (Havana, 1965). Accessible at: https://openrevolt.info/2012/01/01/che-man-and-socialism-in-cuba/

91 A. Öcalan, *War and Peace in Kurdistan, op. cit.*, p.28.

92 A. Akkaya and J. Jongerden, "Confederalism and Autonomy in Turkey: The Kurdistan Workers' Party and the Reinvention of Democracy," in C. Gunes and W. Zeydanliogu, eds., *The Kurdish Question in Turkey. New Perspectives on Violence, Representation, and Reconciliation* (London: Routledge, 2014), pp.186-204. Quote from p.193. See also A. Akkaya and J. Jongerden, "Reassembling the Political: The PKK and the Project of Radical Democracy," *European Journal of Turkish Studies*, Vol. 14, 2012, pp.1-17; and S. Saeed, *Kurdish Politics in Turkey. From the PKK to the KCK, op. cit.*, especially pp.90-91.

93 D. Dirik, *The Uprising of the Oldest Colony: Patriarchy, State and Capitalist Modernity in Kurdistan.* PhD. Dissertation, Department of Sociology, University of Cambridge, 2018.

94 C. Gunes, *The Kurdish National Movement in Turkey: From Protest to Resistance,* *op. cit.*, pp.116-118.

95 D. McDowall, *A Modern History of the Kurds, op. cit.*, p.427.

96 C. Gunes, *The Kurdish National Movement in Turkey: From Protest to Resistance,* *op. cit.*, pp.119-120.

97 A. Öcalan, *Liberating Life: Woman's Revolution* (Cologne: International Initiative, 2013), p.6. One of the institutional corollaries to this emphasis on the struggle against patriarchy is the movement's insistence upon establishing co-chairs and gender quotas for its political organizations and representative positions. This is exemplified not only in the statutes and practices of pro-Kurdish political parties in Turkey such as the Peoples' Democratic Party (HDP) and Democratic Regions Party (DBP), but also in the revolutionary arrangements which have been institutionalised in Rojava, northern Syria, since the middle of 2012. As Saleh Muslim Mohammed, the co-president of the Öcalan-inspired, Syrian-Kurdish Democratic Union Party (PYD) has explained: "We established a model of co-presidency – each political entity always has both a female and a male president – and a quota of 40% gender representation in order to enforce gender equality throughout all forms of public life and political representation". Accessible at: https://kurdish issue.wordpress.com/2014/11/11/a-revolution-of-life-interview-with-saleh-muslim/

98 See D.H. Matthews and T. Miley, "Review of Abdullah Öcalan's *Manifesto for a Democratic Civilization*," in T. Miley and F. Venturini, eds., *Your Freedom and Mine: Abdullah Öcalan and the Kurdish Question in Erdogan's Turkey, op. cit.*, pp.337-352.

99 See K. Geary, N. Hildyard and K. Yildiz, "Holding Investors to Account: The Ilisu Dam Campaign," in E. Schmid, ed., *Listen to the Refugee's Story: How UK Foreign Investment Creates Refugees and Asylum Seekers* (London: Ilisu Dam Refugees Project, The Corner House, and Peace in Kurdistan, 2003).

100 As part of this "paradigm shift," Öcalan has elaborated the concept of a "democratic nation," which he insists can be institutionalised in one of two ways – either through compromise, or unilaterally. In his words: "The first is predicated on finding a compromise with nation-states. It finds its concrete expression in a democratic constitutional solution. It respects the historical-societal heritage of peoples and cultures. It regards the freedom of expression and organisation of these heritages as one of the irrevocable and fundamental constitutional rights. Democratic autonomy is the fundamental principle of these rights. The foremost conditions of this arrangement are that the sovereign nation-state renounces all denial and

annihilation policies, and the oppressed nation abandons the idea of forming its own nation-state. It is difficult for a democratic autonomy project to be implemented without both nations renouncing statist tendencies in this regard. EU countries took more than 300 years of nation-state experience before they could accept democratic autonomy as the best solution for solving nation-states' regional, national and minority related problems. The second path for a democratic autonomy solution – one that does not depend on finding a compromise with nation-states – is to implement its own project unilaterally. In the broad sense, it recognises the Kurdish people's right to become a democratic nation through the implementation of democratic autonomy. It goes without saying that in this case conflicts will intensify with those sovereign nation-states who do not accept this unilateral implementation of becoming a democratic nation. If this happens, the Kurds will have no other choice but to adopt a full-scale mobilisation and war position in order to protect their existence and to live freely against the individual or joint attacks of nation-states (Iran, Syria and Turkey). They will not hold back from becoming a democratic nation with all its dimensions and to develop and realize their aspirations through their own efforts until they either reach a compromise or achieve independence amidst the warfare." *Democratic Nation* (Cologne: International Initiative, 2016), pp.31-32.

101 See R. Dag, "Democratic Islam Congress and the Middle East," *Open Democracy*, June 13, 2014. Accessible at: https://www.opendemocracy.net/north-africa-west-asia/rahman-dag/democratic-islam-congress-and-middle-east

102 A. Öcalan, *Democratic Confederalism* (Cologne: International Initiative, 2011), p.30.

103 See J. Freeman, "The Tyranny of Structurelessness," *Berkeley Journal of Sociology*, Vol. 17, 1972, pp.151-165.

104 R. Luxemburg, "Organisational Questions of the Russian Social Democracy" (1904). Accessible at: https://www.marxists.org/archive/luxemburg/1904/questions-rsd/index.htm

105 B. Bolloten, *The Spanish Civil War. Revolution and Counterrevolution* (The University of North Carolina Press, 1979), p.372.

106 R. Debray, *Revolution in the Revolution?*, *op. cit.*, p.112.

107 C. Gunes, *The Kurdish National Movement in Turkey: From Protest to Resistance*, *op. cit.*, p.152.

108 Ibid., p.155.

109 Ibid., p.152.

110 See also T. Miley with C. Hammy and G. Yildiz, "The Turkish-Kurdish Conflict in Historical Context," *op. cit.*, pp.79-117.

111 For the original formulation of this four-fold distinction, see G. O'Donnell, P. Schmitter, and L. Whitehead, eds., *Transitions from Authoritarian Rule: Tentative Conclusions about Uncertain Democracies* (Baltimore: The Johns Hopkins University Press, 1986). See also J. Linz and A. Stepan, *Problems of Democratic Transition and Consolidation, op. cit.*

112 For example, see A.K. Jarstad and T.D. Sisk, *From War to Democracy: Dilemmas of Peacebuilding* (Cambridge: Cambridge University Press, 2008); and J. Tong, *Comparative Peace Processes* (Wiley, 2014).

113 See J. McGarry and B. O'Leary, "Consociational Theory and Peace Agreements in Pluri-National Places: Northern Ireland and Other Cases," in G. Ben-Porat, ed., *The Failure of the Middle East Peace Process? A Comparative Analysis of Peace Implementation in Israel/Palestine, Northern Ireland, and South Africa* (London: Palgrave MacMillan, 2008), pp.70-96; T. White, ed. *Lessons from the Northern Ireland Peace Process* (Madison, WI: The University of Wisconsin Press, 2014); Robert P. Clark, *Negotiating with ETA. Obstacles to Peace in the Basque Country, 1975-1988* (Reno: University of Nevada Press, 1990); and U. Aiartza and J. Zabalo, "The Basque Country: The Long Walk to a Democratic Scenario," *Berghof Transitions Series No.7*, 2010. Accessible at: https://www.berghof-foundation.org/fileadmin/redaktion/Publications/Papers/Transitions_Series/transitions_basque.pdf

114 A. Öcalan, *Democratic Confederalism, op. cit.*, Part V, pp.35-44.

115 See T. Miley with C. Hammy and G. Yildiz, "The Turkish-Kurdish Conflict in Historical Perspective," *op. cit.*, pp.96-100; and G. Yildiz, "How Did Turkey's Peace Process with the PKK Rebels Fail? How Can It Be Resurrected?," MPhil Thesis, Department of Sociology, University of Cambridge, 2017.

116 See T. Miley with C. Hammy and G. Yildiz, "The Turkish-Kurdish Conflict in Historical Perspective," *op. cit.*, pp.100-116.

117 See T. Miley, "State Terror, Human Rights Violations, and Authoritarianism in Turkey: Report of the Third EUTCC Imrali International Peace Delegation," *op. cit.*

118 V.I. Lenin, "The Dual Power," (1917). Accessible at: https://www.marxists.org/archive/lenin/works/1917/apr/09.htm

119 M. Bookchin, "The Communalist Project," in *The Next Revolution: Popular Assemblies and the Promise of Direct Democracy, op. cit.*, pp.18-19.

REFERENCES

Ackerman, B. *Before the Next Attack: Preserving Civil Liberties in the Age of Terrorism* (New Haven, CT: Yale University Press, 2007).

Aiartza, U. and J. Zabalo, "The Basque Country: The Long Walk to a Democratic Scenario," *Berghof Transitions Series No.7*, 2010.

Akkaya, A. and J. Jongerden, "Reassembling the Political: The PKK and the Project of Radical Democracy," *European Journal of Turkish Studies*, Vol. 14, 2012, pp.1-17

Akkaya, A. and J. Jongerden, "Confederalism and Autonomy in Turkey: The Kurdistan Workers' Party and the Reinvention of Democracy," in C. Gunes and W. Zeydanli-oglu, eds., *The Kurdish Question in Turkey. New Perspectives on Violence, Representation, and Reconciliation* (London: Routledge, 2014), pp.186-204.

Althusser, L. "Ideology and Ideological State Apparatuses," in *On Ideology* (London: Verso, 2007), pp.1-140.

Anderson, P. "The Antinomies of Antonio Gramsci," *New Left Review*, No. 100, 1976, pp.5-78.

Anderson, P. *The H-word: The Peripeteia of Hegemony* (London: Verso Books, 2017).

Angrist, M. "Turkey. Roots of the Turkish-Kurdish Conflict and Prospects for Constructive Reform," in U. Amoretti and N. Bermeo, eds., *Federalism and Territorial Cleavages* (Baltimore: The Johns Hopkins University Press, 2004), pp.387-416.

Ankersmit, F. *Aesthetic Politics: Political Philosophy Beyond Fact and Value* (Stanford, CA: Stanford University Press, 1997).

Ashcraft, R. *Revolutionary Politics and Locke's Two Treatises of Government* (Princeton, NJ: Princeton University Press, 1986).

Bachrach, P. and M.S. Baratz, "Two Faces of Power," *The American Political Science Review*, Vol. 56, No. 4, 1962, pp.947-952.

Banducci, S.A., et. al., "Minority Representation, Empowerment, and Participation," *The Journal of Politics*, Vol. 66, No. 2, 2004, pp.534-556.

Bartelson, J. *A Genealogy of Sovereignty* (Cambridge: Cambridge University Press, 1993).

Bhabha, H. "DissemiNation: time, narrative, and the margins of the modern nation," in H. Bhabha, ed. *Nation and Narration* (London: Routledge, 1990).

Bolloten, B., *The Spanish Civil War. Revolution and Counterrevolution* (The University of North Carolina Press, 1979),

Bookchin, M. *Urbanization without Cities* (Montreal: Black Rose Books, 1992), p.299.

Bookchin, M. "Libertarian Municipalism," in J. Biehl, ed., *The Murray Bookchin Reader* (Montreal: Black Rose Books, 1999), pp.172-196.

Bookchin, M. *The Next Revolution: Popular Assemblies and the Promise of Direct Democracy* (London: Verso, 2015).

Brubaker, R. *Nationalism Reframed* (Cambridge: Cambridge University Press, 1996).

Budge, I. and D. McDonald, "Choices Parties Define: Policy Alternatives in Representative Elections, 17 Countries 1945–1998," *Party Politics*, 12(4), 2006, pp.451–466.

Casmier, S. "Subliminal Consciousness in the Killing Fields of Spain". Unpublished Paper delivered at the 16TH Annual Conference of the Multidisciplinary Society, *The Space Between: Literature and Culture 1914-1945*, School of Advanced Study, University of London, July 17, 2014.

Chandhoke, N. *Democracy and Revolutionary Politics* (London: Bloomsbury Academic, 2015).

Clark, R.P. *Negotiating with ETA. Obstacles to Peace in the Basque Country, 1975-1988* (Reno: University of Nevada Press, 1990.

Cohen, J. and A. Arato, eds., *Forms of Pluralism and Democratic Constitutionalism* (New York: Columbia University Press, 2018).

Cohen, J. "Deliberation and Democratic Legitimacy," in J. Bohman and W. Rehg, eds., *Deliberative Democracy: Essays on Reason and Politics* (Boston, MA: MIT Press, 1997).

Cole, D. and J. Dempsey, *Terrorism and the Constitution: Sacrificing Civil Liberties in the Name of National Security. Third Edition* (The New Press, 2006).

Coller, X., et. al., eds., *Political Power in Spain: The Multiple Divides between MPs and Citizens* (London: Palgrave Macmillan, 2018).

Dahl, R. *A Preface to Democratic Theory* (Chicago, IL: Chicago University Press, 1956).

Dahl, R. *Polyarchy: Participation and Opposition* (New Haven, CT: Yale University Press, 1971).

Debray, R. *The Revolution in the Revolution? Armed Struggle and Political Struggle in Latin America* (New York: Monthly Review Press, 1967).

Dirik, D. *The Uprising of the Oldest Colony: Patriarchy, State and Capitalist Modernity in Kurdistan*. PhD. Dissertation, Department of Sociology, University of Cambridge, 2018.

Disch, L. "Toward a Mobilization Conception of Democratic Representation," *American Political Science Review*, Vol. 105, No. 1, 2011, pp.100–114.

Disch, L. "The Constructivist Turn in Democratic Representation: A Normative Dead-End?" *Constellations*, Vol. 22, No.4, 2015, pp.487-499.

Domhoff, G.W. *Who Rules America?* (McGraw Hill Education, Seventh Edition, 2013).

Donahue, L. "Terrorism and the counter-terrorist discourse," in V. Ramraj, M. Hor and K. Roach, eds., *Global Anti-Terrorism Law and Policy* (Cambridge: Cambridge University Press, 2005).

Dovi, S. "Political Representation," in E. Zalta, ed., *The Stanford Encyclopedia of Philosophy* (Stanford, CA: Stanford University Press, 2007).

Dovi, S. "Hannah Pitkin: The Concept of Representation," in J. Levy, *The Oxford Handbook of Classics in Contemporary Political Theory* (Oxford: Oxford University Press, 2015).

Eccarius-Kelly, V. *The Militant Kurds. A Dual Strategy for Freedom* (Santa Barbara, CA: Praeger, 2011).

Ekmeki, F. "Understanding Kurdish Ethno-nationalism in Turkey: Socio-Economy, Religion, and Politics," *Ethnic and Racial Studies*, Vol. 34, No. 9, 2011, pp.1608-1617.

Entessar, N. *Kurdish Ethnonationalism* (London: Lynne Reinner Publishers, 1992).

Ertur, K. *The Political Integration of the Kurds in Turkey* (Portland State University PhD. Dissertation, 1979).

Ezrow, N. "Hybrid Regimes," in F. Moghaddam, ed. *The SAGE Encyclopedia of Political Behavior* (London: SAGE Publications, 2017).

Fanon, F. *The Wretched of the Earth* (London: Penguin Classics, 2001).

Fekete, L. *Europe's Fault Lines: Racism and the Far Right* (London: Verso, 2017).

Fishkin, J. and P. Laslett, eds., *Debating Deliberative Democracy* (Wiley, 2008).

Freire, P. *The Pedagogy of the Oppressed* (Continuum, 30TH Anniversary Edition, 2000).

Freeman, J. "The Tyranny of Structurelessness," *Berkeley Journal of Sociology*, Vol. 17, 1972, pp.151-165.

Ganser, D. *Nato's Secret Armies. Operation Gladio and Terrorism in Western Europe* (London: Routledge, 2004).

Geary, K., N. Hildyard and K. Yildiz, "Holding Investors to Account: The Ilisu Dam Campaign," in E. Schmid, ed., *Listen to the Refugee's Story: How UK Foreign Investment Creates Refugees and Asylum Seekers* (London: Ilisu Dam Refugees Project, The Corner House, and Peace in Kurdistan, 2003).

Gerth, H.H. and C. Wright Mills, "Introduction," in H.H. Gerth and C. Wright Mills, eds., *From Max Weber: Essays in Sociology*, (Abingdon, Oxon: Routledge, 1991), pp.3-74.

Göbel, C. "Semiauthoritarianism," in J. Ishiyama and M. Breuning, eds., *21st Century Political Science: A Reference Handbook* (London: SAGE Publications, 2011), pp.258-267.

Guevara, C. *Guerrilla Warfare: A Method* (Peking: Foreign Language Press, 1964).

Gunes, C. *The Kurdish National Movement in Turkey. From Protest to Resistance* (London: Routledge, 2012).

Gunter, M. *The Kurds and the Future of Turkey* (London: Palgrave, 1997).

Gutmann, A. and D. Thompson, *Why Deliberative Democracy?* (Princeton, NJ: Princeton University Press, 2002).

Hacker-Cordón, C. "Electoral Legitimation, Polyarchy, and Democratic Legitimacy," *American Political Science Association*, Foundations Section, Washington, DC: 2001.

Hall, S., ed., *Representation. Cultural Representation and Signifying Practices* (London: SAGE, 1997).

Hobsbawm, E. *Nations and Nationalism since 1780* (Cambridge: Cambridge University Press, 1990).

Hroch, M. *The Social Preconditions of National Revival in Europe* (New York: Columbia University Press, 2000).

Icduygu, A., et. al, "The Ethnic Question in an Environment of Insecurity: The Kurds in Turkey," *Ethnic and Racial Studies*, Vol. 22, Issue 6, 1999, pp.991-1010.

Jarstad, A.K. and T.D. Sisk, *From War to Democracy: Dilemmas of Peacebuilding* (Cambridge: Cambridge University Press, 2008).

Jennings, I. *The Approach to Self-Government* (Cambridge: Cambridge University Press, [1956] 2011).

Jongerden, J. and A. Akkaya, "Born from the Left. The Making of the PKK," in J. Jongerden and M. Casier, eds., *Nationalism and Politics in Turkey. Political Islam and the Kurdish Issue* (London: Routledge, 2011), pp.123-142.

Koefoed, M. "Martyrdom and Emotional Resistance in the Case of Northern Kurdistan: Hidden and Public Emotional Resistance," *Journal of Political Power*, Vol. 10, Issue 2, 2017, pp.184-199.

Laclau, E. and C. Mouffe, *Hegemony and Socialist Strategy* (London: Verso, 1986).

Leese, D. *Mao Cult: Rhetoric and Ritual in China's Cultural Revolution* (Cambridge: Cambridge University Press, 2011).

Leib, E. "Can Direct Democracy Be Made Deliberative?," *Buffalo Law Review* Vol. 54, 2006, pp.903-925.

Levitsky, S. and J. Loxton, "Populism and Competitive Authoritarianism in the Andes," *Democratization* Vol. 20, 2013, pp.107-136.

Levitsky, S. and L. Way, *Competitive Authoritarianism: Hybrid Regimes after the Cold War* (Cambridge: Cambridge University Press, 2010).

Lijphart, A. "Consociational Democracy" *World Politics*, Vol. 25, No. 2, 1969, pp.207-225.

Lindblom, C. *Charisma* (Oxford: Oxford University Press, 1993).

Linz, J. "Early State-Building and Late Peripheral Nationalisms against the State: The Case of Spain," in Shmuel N. Eisenstadt and Stein Rokkan (eds.), *Building States and Nations. Analysis by Region, Vol. II* (Beverly Hills: Sage Publications,1973), pp: 32-116.

Linz, J. "From Primordialism to Nationalism," in Edward A. Tiriyakian and Ronald Rogowski, eds., *New Nationalisms of the Developed West* (Boston: Allen & Unwin, 1985), pp.203–253.

Linz, J. "State Building and Nation Building," *European Review*, Vol. 1, No. 4, 1993, pp.355-369.

Linz, J. "Democracy, Multinationalism, and Federalism," *Working Paper*, No. 103 (Madrid: Centro de Estudios Avanzados en Ciencias Sociales, Instituto Juan March de Estudios e Investigaciones, 1997).

Linz, J. *Totalitarian and Authoritarian Regimes* (Boulder, CO: Lynne Reinner Publishers, 2000).

Linz, J. with T. Miley, "Cautionary and Unorthodox Thoughts about Democracy Today," in Douglas Chalmers and Scott Mainwaring, eds., *Institutions and Democracy: Essays in Honor of Alfred Stepan* (South Bend, IN: University of Notre Dame Press, 2012), pp. 227-252.

Linz, J. and A. Stepan, *Problems of Democratic Transition and Consolidation* (Baltimore: The Johns Hopkins University Press, 1996).

Linz, J., A. Stepan, and Y. Yadav, *Crafting State-Nations: India and Other Multi-National Democracies* (Baltimore: The Johns Hopkins University Press, 2011).

Loxton, J. "Competitive Authoritarianism," in F. Moghaddam, ed., *The SAGE Encyclopedia of Political Behavior* (London: SAGE Publications, 2017).

Lustick, I. *Unsettled States, Disputed Lands: Britain and Ireland, France and Algeria, Israel and the West Bank-Gaza* (Ithaca, NY: Cornell University Press, 1995).

Malley, R. and J. Finer, "The Long Shadow of 9/11. How Counter-terrorism Warps US Foreign Policy," *Foreign Affairs* (July/August 2018), pp.58-69.

Mainwaring, S. "Review: From Representative Democracy to Participatory Competitive Authoritarianism: Hugo Chávez and Venezuelan Politics," *Perspectives on Politics*, Vol. 10, No. 4, 2012, pp.955-967.

Mansbridge, J. and J. Parkinson, eds., *Deliberative Systems* (Cambridge: Cambridge University Press, 2012).

Manin, B. *The Principles of Representative Government* (Cambridge: Cambridge University Press, 1997).

Manwaring, M. "The Environment as a Global Stability-Security Issue," in M. Manwaring, ed., *Environmental Security and Global Stability. Problems and Responses* (Lanham, MD: Lexington Books, 2002).

Matthews, D.H. and T. Miley, "Review of Abdullah Öcalan's *Manifesto for a Democratic Civilization*," in T. Miley and F. Venturini, eds., *Your Freedom and Mine: Abdullah*

Öcalan and the Kurdish Question in Erdogan's Turkey (Montreal: Black Rose Books, 2018), pp.337-352.

McDowall, D. *A Modern History of the Kurds* (London: I.B. Tauris, 1996).

McGarry, J. and B. O'Leary, "Consociational Theory and Peace Agreements in Pluri-National Places: Northern Ireland and Other Cases," in G. Ben-Porat, ed., *The Failure of the Middle East Peace Process? A Comparative Analysis of Peace Implementation in Israel/Palestine, Northern Ireland, and South Africa* (London: Palgrave MacMillan, 2008), pp.70-96.

Miley, T. "Against the Thesis of the 'Civic Nation': The Case of Catalonia in Contemporary Spain," *Nationalism and Ethnic Politics*, Vol. 13, 2007, pp.1-37.

Miley, T. "Franquism as Authoritarianism: Juan Linz and his Critics," *Politics, Religion & Ideology*, Vol. 12, No. 1, 2011, pp.27-50.

Miley, T. "Democratic Representation and the National Dimension in Catalan and Basque Politics," *International Journal of Politics, Culture and Society*, Vol. 27, 2014, pp.291-322.

Miley, T. "The Nation as Hegemonic Project," *Journal of Political Ideologies*, Vol. 23, Issue 2, 2018: 183-204.

Miley, T. "State Terror, Human Rights Violations, and Authoritarianism in Turkey. Report of the Third Imrali Peace Delegation Based on its Visit to Turkey, Feb. 13-19, 2017," in T. Miley and F. Venturini, eds., *Your Freedom and Mine: Abdullah Ocalan and the Kurdish Question in Erdogan's Turkey* (Montreal: Black Rose Books, 2018), pp.225-258.

Miley, T. with C. Hammy and G. Yildiz, "The Turkish-Kurdish Conflict in Historical Context," in T. Miley and F. Venturini, eds., *Your Freedom and Mine: Abdullah Ocalan and the Kurdish Question in Erdogan's Turkey* (Montreal: Black Rose Books, 2018), pp.3-123.

Miliband, R. *The State in Capitalist Society* (New York, NY: Basic Books, 1969).

Natali, D. *The Kurds and the State. Evolving National Identity in Iraq, Turkey, and Iran* (Syracuse, NY: Syracuse University Press, 2005).

O'Ballance, E. *The Kurdish Struggle, 1920-1994* (London: Palgrave MacMillan, 1996).

Öcalan, A. *The Roots of Civilization* (Transmedia Publishing Limited, 2007).

Öcalan, A. *War and Peace in Kurdistan. Perspectives for a Political Solution to the Kurdish Question* (Cologne: International Initiative, 2009).

Öcalan, A. *Prison Writings. The PKK and the Kurdish Question in the 21st Century* (Cologne: International Initiative, 2011).

Öcalan, A. *Democratic Confederalism* (Cologne: International Initiative, 2011).

Öcalan, A. *Prison Writings III: The Road Map to Negotiations* (Cologne: International Initiative, 2012).

Öcalan, A. *Prison Writings: The PKK and the Kurdish Question in the Twenty-First Century* (Cologne: International Initiative, 2013).

Öcalan, A. *Liberating Life: Woman's Revolution* (Cologne: International Initiative, 2013).

Öcalan, A. *Manifesto for a Democratic Civilization. Volume One: The Age of Masked Gods and Disguised Kings* (Prosgrunn, Norway: New Compass Press, 2015).

Öcalan, A. *Democratic Nation* (Cologne: International Initiative, 2016).

Öcalan, A. *Manifesto for a Democratic Civilization. Volume Two: The Age of Unmasked Gods and Naked Kings* (Prosgrunn, Norway: New Compass Press, 2017).

Öcalan, A. *The Political Thought of Abdullah Öcalan: Kurdistan, Women's Revolution and Democratic Confederalism* (London: Pluto Press, 2017).

Öcalan, A. "Seek the Truth," in T. Miley and F. Venturini, eds., *Your Freedom and Mine: Abdullah Öcalan and the Kurdish Question in Erdgoan's Turkey* (Montreal: Black Rose Books, 2018), pp.315-322.

O'Donnell, G., P. Schmitter, and L. Whitehead, eds., *Transitions from Authoritarian Rule: Tentative Conclusions about Uncertain Democracies* (Baltimore: The Johns Hopkins University Press, 1986).

Özcan, A. *Turkey's Kurds. A Theoretical Analysis of the PKK and Abdullah Öcalan* (London: Routledge, 2006).

Pateman, C. *Participation and Democratic Theory* (Cambridge: Cambridge University Press, 1970).

Phillips, A. *The Politics of Presence* (Oxford: Oxford University Press, 1995).

Pitkin, H. *The Concept of Representation* (Berkeley, CA: University of California Press, 1967).

Poulantzas, N. "The Problem of the Capitalist State," *New Left Review*, Vol. 58, 1969, pp.67-78.

Poulantzas, N. *Fascism and Dictatorship: The Third International and the Problem of Fascism* (London: NLB, 1970).

Przeworski, A. and M. Wallerstein, "The Structural Dependence of the State on Capital," *The American Political Science Review*, Vol. 82, No 1, 1988, pp.11-29.

Przeworski, A., et. al., eds., *Democracy, Accountability, and Representation* (Cambridge: Cambridge University Press, 1999).

Przeworski, A. *Democracy and the Limits of Self-Government* (Cambridge: Cambridge, University Press, 2010).

Redhead, M. *Charles Taylor: Thinking and Living Deep Diversity* (Lanham, MD: Rowman & Littlefield, 2002).

Ricoeur, P. *Freud and Philosophy: An Essay on Interpretation* (New Haven, CT: Yale University Press, 1993).

Robinson, W. *Promoting Polyarchy* (Cambridge: Cambridge University Press, 1996).

Roemer, J., et. al., *Racism, Xenophobia, and Distribution: Multi-Issue Politics in Advanced Democracies* (Cambridge: Russell Sage Foundation Books, 2007).

Romano, D. *The Kurdish Nationalist Movement. Opportunity, Mobilization, Identity* (Cambridge: Cambridge University Press, 2006).

Ross, C. *The Leaderless Revolution: How Ordinary People Can Take Power and Change Politics in the 21st Century* (London: Simon and Schuster, 2011).

Saeed, S. *Kurdish Politics in Turkey. From the PKK to the KCK* (London: Routledge, 2017).

Sagnic, C. "Mountain Turks: State Ideology and the Kurds in Turkey," *Information, Society and Justice*, Vol. 3, No. 2, 2010, pp.127-134.

Saragil, Z. "Curbing Kurdish Ethno-nationalism in Turkey: An Empirical Assessment of Pro-Islamic and Socioeconomic Approaches," *Ethnic and Racial Studies*, Vol. 33, No. 3, 2010, pp.533-553.

Schmid, A. "The Definition of Terrorism," in A. Schmid, ed., *The Routledge Handbook of Terrorism Research* (Oxford: Routledge, 2011).

Schmid, E., ed. *A Permanent State of Terror?* (London: Campaign Against Criminalising Communities, CAMPACC, 2003).

Scott, J. *Domination and the Arts of Resistance: Hidden Transcripts* (New Haven, CT: Yale University Press, 1990).

Sivanandan, A. "Racism, Liberty and the War on Terror" (London: Institute for Race Relations, 2006).

Smith, R. *Stories of Peoplehood* (Cambridge: Cambridge University Press, 2003).

Stepan, A. and J. Miley. "Federacy and the Kurds: Might This New Political Form Help Mitigate Hobbesian Conflict in Turkey, Iraq, and Syria," in J. Cohen and A. Arato, eds., *Forms of Pluralism and Democratic Constitutionalism* (New York: Columbia University Press, 2018).

Summers, D. "Dancing with the Devil," in T. Miley and F. Venturini, eds., *Your Freedom and Mine: Abdullah Öcalan and the Kurdish Question in Erdogan's Turkey* (Montreal: Black Rose Books, 2018), pp.385-389.

Therborn, G. *What Does the Ruling Class Do When It Rules?* (London: NLB, 1978).

Therborn, G. *From Marxism to Post-Marxism?* (London: Verso, 2008).

Tong, J. *Comparative Peace Processes* (Wiley, 2014).

Toprak, M., et. al., "Transformations of Turkish Politics: Socio-Political, Economic and Ethnic Particularities," *bilig*, No. 50, 2009, pp.199-232.

Van Bruinessen, M. "Between Guerrilla War and Political Murder: The Workers' Party of Kurdistan," *Middle East Report*, #153, July-Aug. 1988.

Weber, M. "The Fundamental Concepts of Sociology," in T. Parsons, ed., *The Theory of Social and Economic Organization* (New York: Free Press, 1964).

Weber, M. "Politics as a Vocation," in H.H. Gerth and C. Wright Mills, eds., *From Max Weber: Essays in Sociology* (Abingdon, Oxon: Routledge, 1991), pp.71-128.

Weber, M. "Structures of Power: The Nation," in H.H. Gerth and C. Wright Mills, eds., *From Max Weber: Essays in Sociology* (Abingdon, Oxon: Routledge, 1991), pp.171-180.

Weber, M. "The Sociology of Charismatic Authority," in H.H. Gerth and C. Wright Mills, eds., *From Max Weber: Essays in Sociology* (Abingdon, Oxon: Routledge, 1991), pp.245-248.

White, P. *Primitive Rebels or Revolutionary Modernizers? The Kurdish National Movement in Turkey* (London: Zed Books, 2000).

White, T. ed. *Lessons from the Northern Ireland Peace Process* (Madison, WI: The University of Wisconsin Press, 2014).

Wolfenstein, E.V. *Psychoanalytic-Marxism. Groundwork* (Free Association Books, 1993).

Yadirgi, V. *The Political Economy of the Kurds of Turkey: From the Ottoman Empire to the Turkish Republic* (Cambridge: Cambridge University Press, 2017).

Yildiz, K. and S. Breau, *The Kurdish Conflict: International Humanitarian Law and Post-Conflict Mechanisms* (London: Routledge, 2010).

Zürcher, E. *Turkey. A Modern History* (London: I.B. Tauris. Fourth Edition, 2017).

CHAPTER 8

Reflections on Revolution, the Spiral of Violence, and the Legitimacy of Self-Defence[1]

The *Zeitgeist* Effect and the Appeal of the Guerrilla

In trying to understand the trajectory of the Turkish and the Kurdish left in the 1970s, it is crucial to situate this trajectory within its global historical context. This was the moment of Regis Debray, *cause célèbre*, jailed by the same thugs in Bolivia who had martyred his friend Che Guevara. The moment when he famously argued that he had glimpsed the future in Cuba along with Che, that guerrilla tactics provided the answer to the question, "How to overthrow the power of the capitalist state?", the guerrilla could become "the nucleus of a people's army" and a harbinger of "a future socialist state" (1967, p.24). It would be when he could confidently dismiss not only "those who are addicted to the electoral opium, for whom socialism will come on the day when half plus one of the electorate vote for it" (1967, p.83), but even those committed revolutionaries who remained believers in the "old obsession," those who "believe that revolutionary awareness and organization must and can precede revolutionary action" (1967, p.83). A moment when it was increasingly fashionable to conclude, with Debray, that "[r]evolutionary politics, if they are not to be blocked, must be diverted from politics as such," that "[p]olitical resources must be thrown into an organization which is simultaneously political and military" (1967, p.123).

This was the moment when Frantz Fanon's last book and testament, *The Wretched of the Earth*, was all the rage as well. Fanon had eloquently defended the recourse to armed struggle on psychological grounds, as a "cleansing force" and practice capable of "mobilizing the people," a practice that "binds them together as a whole, since each individual forms a violent link in the great chain, a part of the great organism of violence which has surged upwards in reaction to the settler's violence in the beginning". What's more, Fanon insisted, the practice of violence, "when it arises out of a war of liberation, introduces into each man's consciousness the ideas of a common cause, of a national destiny and of a collective history;" that "it frees the native from his inferiority complex and from his despair and inaction;" that "it makes him fearless and restores his self-respect" (2001, p.74).

A brilliant and provocative book, no doubt, but one which was all too often interpreted, then as now, nearly exclusively in relation to what Fanon had to say in his chapter "concerning violence;" whereas what he had to say in his chapter on "colonial wars and mental disorders," his qualifications and words of caution, remained (and remains) all too often underemphasized, if not entirely ignored (Wolfenstein 1993, p.432, n3).

The potential for generating a negative dialectic, for precipitating a spiral of violence and repression, was perhaps not sufficiently anticipated. Nor was the political and social consequences of triggering such a spiral sufficiently foreseen or taken into account. The tactical and strategic weaknesses of the pursuit of peaceful and reformist forms of resistance were certainly well-rehearsed. But the perils of the path of violent insurgency were probably less well understood. The far-right was way more brutal, it should not be forgotten; but nor can it be denied that both sides were caught in a vicious spiral.

Enter the Spiral of Violence

In thinking through the dynamics of that spiral we can appreciate the contribution of the great liberation theologian Helder Da Camara, the Archbishop of Olinde and Recife, in impoverished and marginalized northeastern Brazil, whose reflections from that fateful moment, whose interpretation of the appeal of the guerrilla, and whose illumination of the logic of the spiral of violence definitely remain instructive, and are arguably unsurpassed, to this day.

Camara's analysis begins with a point reminiscent of those made emphatically and persuasively by Fanon, whose justly celebrated book "begins with the fact that colonialism is institutionalised violence – institutionalized and internalized" (Wolfenstein 1993, p.103). Likewise, Camara starts by arguing, albeit in somewhat more general terms, that if you "look closely at the injustices" inside poor countries, much less the relations between poor countries and rich ones, "you will find that everywhere the injustices are a form of violence". This violence he calls "violence No. 1".

Camara continues by stating two premises, which he derives from his liberationist interpretation of Christian theology, but which can be derived from many other theological, metaphysical, and even perhaps post-metaphysical traditions as well. These premises are: (1) that "no-one is born to be a slave," and, somewhat more controversially, (2) that no one sets out "to suffer injustices, humiliations, restrictions". From these premises, Camara goes on to insist that wherever human beings are subjected to such "subhuman" conditions, wherever they "suffer restrictions, humiliations, injustices; without prospects, without hope," wherever they are effectively enslaved, "this established violence No. 1 attracts violence No. 2, revolt, either of the oppressed themselves or of youth, firmly resolved to battle for a more just and human world" (1971, p.30). In short, violence No. 1 begets violence No. 2.

Simple as it may seem, those in positions of power tend to adamantly deny the connection. "They pretend to believe that without the presence of 'agitators', the oppressed masses would remain with their eyes closed, passive and immobile" (1971, p.32).

But such finger-pointing and attempts at denial notwithstanding, it is ultimately undeniable for anyone with a modicum of intellectual honesty to recognize that, *at the root*, it is violence No.1 which begets violence No.2.

And then comes violence No. 3: repression. As Camara explains: "When conflict comes out in the streets, when violence No. 2 tries to resist violence No. 1, the authorities consider themselves obliged to re-establish public order, even if this means using force. This is violence No. 3". What's more, he warns: "Sometimes they go even further, and this is becoming increasingly common: in order to obtain information which may indeed be important to public security, the logic of violence leads them to use moral and physical torture," and he makes sure to add, "as though any information extracted through torture deserved the slightest attention!"

Camara ends his illumination of the logic of the spiral by striking a prophetic chord. He notes that "the reaction of the oppressed also shows clear signs of becoming sharper," and thus predicts that "the world is headed for [more] trouble, protest, violence, coming from the youth". He then poses the question, "Who has any illusions about the stepping up of governmental re-actions?" For those who might feel tempted to succumb to such illusions, he simply reminds them: "We need only consider how many countries have sub-mitted to extra-constitutional governments or dictatorships. Look at the map and count the number of countries in the hands of the military". This is be-fore coming to the "inescapable conclusion … that there is a real threat" of a further "escalation of violence," indeed, a "threat of seeing the world fall into a spiral of violence" (1971, pp.39-40).

To illustrate and add to the force of this prophetic, apocalyptic chord, Ca-mara next turns his attention to the War in Vietnam, which was still raging when he wrote. He highlights what he perceptively considers "the saddest and gravest lesson of the Vietnamese war" – namely, the fact that the National Liberation Front, in "accepting and desiring tacit alliances at the moment of battle against the common enemy," ends up with "a political philosophy im-posed on it by the Empire which finances it," a philosophy which includes not only militant atheism, but also "blind obedience to the Party and all its methods of insecurity". These methods included actions such as "encourage-ment of informers and [the] periodic purges inherent in the dictatorships of left or right" (1971, pp.43-44).

Thus, he comes to a crucial challenge, indeed a conundrum, if not a stale-mate, in terms of the prospects for an emancipatory outcome to the spiral of violence between oppressors and oppressed. On the one hand, "even a first-rate power cannot defeat guerrillas if it cannot count on the support of the population". But on the other hand, the guerrillas can only "tackle the warlike power with great force" when they have "another great power" behind them. In short, "the liberation of Vietnam (and of the countries that will suffer the same fate) is very relative: either the people continue to be a satellite in the capitalist orbit, or they are condemned to revolve as a satellite in the socialist orbit" (pp.44-45). A good dose of intellectual pessimism, to say the least.

Situating and Complicating the Model

Camara's nightmare vision, first published in 1971, was certainly prophetic when it came to events in the Republic of Turkey, where the violence and counter-violence between far-right and left would provide the justification for two military coups in less than a decade, first in the spring of 1971, and then again in 1980. And both coups would effectively bring with them successive crackdowns on the legal space for political opposition, not to mention the plight of Turkish workers, much less the Kurds.

But prophetic as it was, and useful as it remains, the model of the negative dialectic sketched by Camara remains oversimplified. As happens so often with models, its parsimony is both its virtue and its vice. Here again it makes sense to return to Fanon, and to Camara's fellow Catholic, compatriot, and comrade, the critical pedagogue Paolo Freire. These two thinkers help supplement, and subtly complicate, the model of the spiral of violence, albeit rendering its predictive capacity somewhat weaker. Alas, such are the contingencies of human freedom.

They certainly also help to correct the tendency to interpret the "lessons of history" as the basis for a dogmatic commitment to pacifism. Not surprisingly, coming as he does from the hierarchy within the Catholic Church, Camara's arguments are directed mostly at people who are at least complicit in oppression. And so, perhaps it is effective for him to end his analysis with an ode to the virtues of Gandhi. But even if Gandhi were a saint, which he wasn't, as a tactical matter, *in matters of this world*, it remains far from clear in which concrete conditions Gandhi's method is likely to lead to emancipation, and in which conditions his method is likely to reify and reproduce the "false peace," the "deceptive beauty" of "stagnant marshes in moonlight" that Camara himself so eloquently and passionately denounces (1971, p.59).

Frantz Fanon, of course, was positioned very differently. He was an Afro-Caribbean intellectual who came to be organically linked to the Algerian Freedom Movement. He was thus very far from any temptation to end up, in affairs of this world, to pledge his allegiance to the Vatican. To the contrary, he was a militant atheist, a "dialectical materialist". But he was, of course, also a trained psychiatrist. His understanding of the consciousness of the oppressed was thus based on tons of direct lived experience and professional training, not to mention professional treatment. In this respect, it is not surprising that his account of the psychoanalytic dynamics at work among the oppressed, including especially his passionate presentation of the psychic costs of the workings of violence No. 1 on their consciousness, his account of their trauma, is understandably more subtle, and therefore less teleological, than the oversimplified model so parsimoniously if skilfully sketched by the Archbishop.

Crucially, Fanon observes that the first manifestations, and indeed, the vast majority of violence committed by the oppressed is directed "horizontally," not "vertically;" that is, it tends to be aimed not at oppressors, but rather, pits oppressed against oppressed. As Wolfenstein has ably summarized Fanon's argument: "institutionalized violence engenders a self-destructive counter-violence in the colonized individual". In *Black Skin, White Masks* he had analysed the phenomenon of self-hatred; in *The Wretched of the Earth*, Fanon extends his line of argument towards an explanation of "intraracial violence" (Wolfenstein 1993, p.103).

For Fanon, the first step towards transcending self-destructive self-hatred and horizontal violence, the first step towards decolonization, is to "negate the negation," to recover one's own sense of dignity and humanity through a "violent rejection of the master-slave relationship". Fanon thus explicitly invokes Hegel, with whose work he was intimately familiar, having even self-consciously set out in *Black Skin, White Masks* to adapt and correct Hegel's analysis of the master-slave dialectic, via a materialist inversion of the motives of the master (if not those of the slave) – "For Hegel there is reciprocity; here the master laughs at the consciousness of the slave. What he wants from the slave is not recognition but work" (Graves 1997).

However, this moment of "negating the negation," the act of violent insurrection, of bloody rebellion is thus a necessary condition for emancipation; but it is clearly not sufficient. This is because, as Fanon also insists, "violent action is pathologizing even if, in the colonial context, it is also humanizing". Indeed, according to Fanon, only if "spontaneous rebellion evolves into organized mass movement," only if "spontaneous anger is transformed into critical consciousness, will the energies released in the violent action not be dissipated". Political commitment, political organization, even revolutionary discipline and active participation in the collective struggle, are thus depicted by Fanon as imperative for the mental health of the oppressed (Wolfenstein 1993, p.103).

Mental health should not be expected to be the norm, perhaps especially in the traumatizing context of colonial wars, as the Archbishop's more simplistic model would seem to suggest. To the contrary, in a pathological situation, pathologies should be expected as the order of the day. The impulse towards emancipation, the will towards life, need not win out over the impulse to self-destruction, the will towards death. Necrophilia can reign supreme. Horizontal violence need not ever give way to collective insurgency. And collective insurgency always runs the risk of devolving back into internecine violence amongst the oppressed.

This is a spectre that looms in the background of Fanon's thinking, hauntingly, one he tries to exorcise by shifting the focus from "self-hatred" to "intraracial violence". This shift, however, requires further justification and explanation. Unfortunately, Fanon didn't live long enough to clarify how "intra-psychic" dynamics are translated into "inter-personal" acts.

Paolo Freire's short but suggestive analysis of horizontal violence is helpful in filling in the gaps left by Fanon's silence in this regard. Freire emphasizes the ways in which the hatred and prejudices of the oppressors can get internalized in the self-images and worldviews of the oppressed. Indeed, their consciousness and consciences can come to be corrupted by disregard and even hatred for their fellow oppressed, which manifests itself in the phenomenon of horizontal violence. As Freire explains it, apologetically, "Because the oppressor exists within their oppressed comrades, when they attack those comrades they are indirectly attacking the oppressor as well" (1972, p.44). But he could have put it the other way around just as well, if less apologetically: that because the oppressor exists within the oppressed, when the oppressed attack their comrades, it is the oppressors within them who are lashing out. In a word, the enemy is also within us. And so the ability, the willingness, to redirect the rage away from the fellow oppressed, to channel it instead towards the oppressor, requires confronting this "enemy within".

Such successful confrontation requires constant dialogue. Even more, it requires cultivating a culture open to critical self-reflection, a willingness to question hollow dogmas, tolerance of ruthless critique, in order to vanquish the oppressor within, as well as to make sure that he is not resurrected. This is why Freire goes on to "emphasize that there is no dichotomy between dialogue and revolutionary action," though he perhaps overstates the case when he goes even further and asserts that "dialogue is the essence of revolutionary action" (1972, p.116).

The Necrophilia of Oppression

For Freire, revolution is about love for life. This is a point implicit in Fanon's account as well, but Freire's work spells it out explicitly. Not only do oppressive social relations literally kill, both through acts of omission and acts of commission, so too do such oppressive relations condemn all too many to "an almost unnatural *living* death: life which is fully denied". Oppressive social relations constrict people's creativity; they restrict and confine their lives. In this respect, the emergence of a revolutionary will to struggle to overthrow such oppression is best understood as a labour of love – love for life, love for creation. Indeed, Freire insists, the revolution seeks to create life, even if, in order to do so "it may be obliged to prevent some men from circumscribing life" (1972, p.152).

Oppression, by contrast, is "necrophilic". It, too, may be "nourished by love," but of a very different kind – not love of life, but "love of death" (1972, p.58). The dilemma, though, is this: anyone who engages in violence, anyone who takes the life of another, even if it is a necessary act, one done in the name of life and creation, anyone who commits such an act of violence will always run a heightened risk of falling victim to a resurgent bout of "necrophilia". There is a risk of resurrecting the vanquished oppressor within, of rekindling the romance with death and destruction.

This necrophilia of oppression, this love of death and destruction, is ubiquitous in the contemporary world. This is a point powerfully made by Walter Benjamin, who provides a final complement and refinement to the model of the spiral of violence sketched by Archbishop Da Camara. In his prophetic essay "The Work of Art in the Age of Mechanical Reproduction," originally published in 1936, Benjamin offered a prescient and piercing early diagnosis of "mass society," and even "the society of the spectacle" — a condition (a) underpinned and propelled forward by transformations in art and in the "mass media" in the age of mechanical reproduction; and (b) intimately intertwined with the rise of fascism. Benjamin honed in on the significance of the Futurist movement's glamorization and glorification of the alleged beauty of war, adducing it as evidence of the extent of human "self-alienation" experienced in "mass society". In his words: "Mankind's ... self-alienation has reached such a degree that it can experience its own destruction as an aesthetic pleasure of the first order" (1999, pp.234-235).

Benjamin, following Freud, held the modern experience to be centred principally on "shock". As Buck-Morss has explained: "In industrial production no less than modern warfare, in street crowds and erotic encounters, in amusement parks and gambling casinos, shock is the very essence of modern experience". Under such conditions, "response to stimuli *without* thinking has become necessary for survival". Consciousness comes to serve largely as a "shield" and a "buffer," protecting the organism by preventing the retention of external stimuli from being "impressed as memory," even "isolating present consciousness from past memory". The depth of memory thus flattened, "experience is impoverished". This "crisis in cognitive experience" is in turn linked to the cultivation of narcissism, a narcissism which "functions as an anaesthetizing tactic against the shock of modern experience," and which is "appealed to daily by the image-phantasmagoria of mass culture". It also renders fertile "the ground from which fascism" can spring forth (1999, pp.16, 41).

The romance with death and destruction thus runs deep. It is a romance inherent in oppressive social relations of any sort; but it is greatly exacerbated by the alienation, the shock and the traumas experienced in, and the reactive narcissism generated by, everyday life in modern, industrial society.

Apocalyptic Undertones in the Model

All of these important addendums – Fanon's emphasis on the significance of horizontal violence; Freire's emphasis on the internalization of the oppressor within the psyches of the oppressed, as well as his emphasis on the intimate links between oppression and necrophilia; and Benjamin's emphasis on how the shock and traumas of life in industrial society tend to undermine the very capacity for reflective "consciousness" – all of these additions ultimately serve to reinforce the apocalyptic undertones already evident in the Archbishop's parsimonious sketch of the spiral of violence, even if they also render the model's predictive power somewhat less robust. But the most basic point of Archbishop Da Camara's parsimonious model remains intact: institutional violence begets violence, either of the self-destructive or the insurrectionary sort, or both.

Bob Marley, quoting Haile Selassie, puts the basic point about oppression begetting violence in a similar apocalyptic vein:

"Until the philosophy that holds one race superior and another inferior
Is finally and permanently discredited and abandoned
Everywhere is war
Me say war.
That until there is no longer
First class and second class citizens of any nation
Until the colour of a man's skin is no more significant than the colour
    of his eyes
Me say war.
That until the basic human rights are equally guaranteed to all
Without regard to race
Dis a war.
That until that day the dream of lasting peace
World Citizenship
The Rule of international morality
Will remain but a fleeting illusion to be pursued
But never attained
Now everywhere is war.
War". (Marley 1976)

Of course, one need not be fully persuaded by such grandiose, apocalyptic motifs. But at the very least, if one takes into account the insights of this adapted model of the spiral of violence, it can help overcome the temptation to fetishize violence, and so help when it comes to tactical considerations about the likely consequences and costs in terms of human suffering of engaging in insurrectionary violence.

In a word, it can help avoid falling into the same trap of over-confidence, if not blind faith, in the redemptive powers and emancipatory potential of violent insurrection that gradually came to dominate many left wing circles, both in the West and in the Republic of Turkey, over the course of the 1960s and into the 1970s.

But at the same time, crucially, it can also help undermine any temptation to believe the tactical arguments made by those who promise peace without being willing to deliver even a modicum of justice, without any amelioration of institutional violence.

Abdullah Öcalan and the Legitimacy of Self-Defence

Enter Abdullah Öcalan. One of the aspects of the democratic confederal project that Öcalan emphasizes is the imperative of self-defence. This is a point of clear discrepancy between Öcalan's radical, anti-statist understanding of democracy and contemporary mainstream liberal, statist appropriations of the term. Not surprisingly, it has also proven a major obstacle for Turkish authorities the times in which they have opted to engage with Öcalan in always aborted negotiations for peace. For Öcalan is adamant that "only self-defence will make peace possible," indeed, that "[a] peace with no self-defence can only be an expression of submission and slavery". He objects to the imposition by contemporary liberalism of "peace with no self-defence on societies and peoples," dismissing such a "unilateral game of democratic stability and reconciliation" as "nothing but a fig leaf on the bourgeois class domination achieved by armed forces," or even "a covert state of war". To this end, he insists that "[t]he major plank in capitalist ideological hegemony is the idea that a true peace is a peace that requires no self-defence" (2020, p.129).

He further specifies that "[t]here are different parties to any peace," only to add that "the complete dominance of one party over another does not and cannot denote peace" (2020, p.129). Though he admits that it may in fact be "possible to achieve stability and quiescence under the rule of the gun," he nevertheless contends that "this cannot be called peace" (2020, p.130). For this reason, he stakes out an unmovable position, as a point of principle, that "a complete disarmament of the different parties is not on the table" (p.130). "In the final analysis," he concludes, "peace is the conditional reconciliation of democracy and the state" (2020, p.131). Accordingly, "[a] cease-fire that does not include a moral and political solution cannot be called peace" (2020, p.130).

Öcalan's position is in an important respect reminiscent of the classic argument advanced by Helder Cámara in *The Spiral of Violence*, where the archbishop distinguishes between genuine peace and a state of stagnant quiescence; nevertheless, Öcalan draws a very different conclusion than does the more pacifistic Cámara about the consequences of a violent response to systemic oppression. Whereas for Cámara such recourse to counter-violence is likely to trigger a spiral of repression, Öcalan seems to suggest that it could also serve to re-equilibrate power relations, and in so doing lead to an opening for genuine peace. While, conversely, Öcalan also contends that "[c]apital and power monopolies are like wolves pursuing their prey; they seize what they want from those who lack self-defence – like grabbing a stray sheep from a disbanded flock" (2020, p.191).

Öcalan has elsewhere justified armed insurgency in the Kurdish context as an historic necessity which achieved the consolidation of Kurdish identity. In *The Sociology of Freedom*, he renders this reasoning in more generalizable terms, by contending that "self-defence for societies is not simply military defence," for "[i]t is intertwined with the protection of identities ..." (2020, p.261). This line of argument draws him close to the militant anti-colonial tradition of the likes of Frantz Fanon. However, Öcalan embraces a substantive vision for self-determination that differs dramatically from the statist strategy espoused by Fanon – since, in his words, "[d]emocratic confederalism leaves no room for hegemony of any sort" (2020, p.220).

Self-defence as a prerequisite for democratic peace, otherwise the wolves will prey upon the stray sheep: here we can glimpse that Öcalan's will to resist remains unbroken. Even so, his consequentialist calculation is questionable. The spiral of violence is at least as likely as the opening for democratic reconciliation. Yet Öcalan's intuition, his reasoning, is perhaps not reducible to an account of costs and benefits, even if his logic cannot be plausibly portrayed as deontological either. Rather, it has to do with the concept of democracy, the core democratic ideal of self-determination. For Öcalan is adamant: "[a] society that insists on determining its own course, that rejects colonization or any form of imposed dependency, must be capable of self-defence" (2020, p.190).

Self-defence and strong institutions can be seen as preconditions, or constituent components, of self-determination. "Societies without self-defence," Öcalan insists, "are societies that have surrendered and been colonized by the capital and power monopolies" (2020, p.191). This formulation reveals that Öcalan is attune to a dual danger for freedom: on one hand, capital, on the other, the state, or "power monopolies". Both of these forces constitute a credible threat to democratic society, and render it imperative for self-defence to "be established" and "always ready to defend," to "inhibit the attacks and exploitation" emanating from the two.

If these are two dangers against which self-defence is imperative, there are also two mistakes which must be scrupulously avoided. The first of these is "to entrust self-defence to the monopolistic order". But conversely, the second is "to try to become a power apparatus under the rubric of forming a state to counter the existing state" (2020, p.191). Here we glimpse the anti-statist dimension of Öcalan's logic at work. For if the problem is framed as one of monopoly, then forming a state of one's own can only mean cancelling out the democratic credentials of the struggle. Rather, a reconciliation of sorts, at minimum, if not a smashing of the bureaucratic apparatus, more maximally, must be sought.

But Öcalan is not sanguine about the prospect for abolishing the state altogether, or for that matter, for abolishing capitalism, at least in the short term. To the contrary, he foresees "we will be living with capital and with power apparatuses for a while" (2020, p.191).

Öcalan is particularly attuned to the militaristic dimension of the nation-state system, which he juxtaposes with the framework of democratic confederalism, within which "social self-defence is best realized" (2020, p.260). According to Öcalan, the nation-state is only conceivable as "a product of war," and "[t]he institutions of power and the state, referred to as the civil administration, are essentially a veil over this military armour". Indeed, he contends, even "[t]he apparatuses known as bourgeois democracies" are best interpreted as but "efforts to apply a coat of democratic polish to this militarist structure and mentality" (2020, p.261).

The "nation-state," Öcalan surmises, is intimately and inextricably linked to the phenomenon of fascism, the various power practices of which can best be interpreted as "the formal expression" of the nation-state's "purest form" (2020, p.261). As such, he insists, the militarization of the nation-state can only be stopped by democratic confederalism's resort to self-defence. The tight connection between the nation-state form and militarism and fascism, then, are what justify for Öcalan the imperative of the capacity for societal self-defence. In his judgment, "[s]ocieties deprived of self-defence face the danger of losing their identities, political qualities, and democratization" (2020, p.261). In contrast, even dialectical contradiction, to the militaristic and fascistic tendencies of the nation-state, "[s]elf-defence can, in fact, be defined as the concentrated expression of democratic politics" (2020, p.260).

But are not the units of self-defence themselves vulnerable to emulating the very militaristic tendencies against which they are meant to serve as bulwarks? Öcalan has elsewhere contemplated this very real possibility, in the form of a thorough-going self-criticism of the state-like behaviour of the PKK, over which he long presided and remains, at least formally, the head. In *The Sociology of Freedom*, Öcalan suggests that the kind of self-defence militias he has in mind have a considerably different command structure than the classic paramilitary guerrilla. In this vein, he argues that such units "are not a military monopoly but are under the tight control of democratic organs in accordance with society's internal and external security needs" (2020, p.220). In short, the suggestion here is that the self-defence units are conceived as subordinate to the citizens' direct-democratic assemblies. Such an interpretation is certainly consistent with their objective, which Öcalan characterizes as "to validate the will of democratic politics," and further, "to render harmless any internal or external force that attempts to frustrate, prevent, or otherwise undermine this will" (2020, p.220). Indeed, Öcalan would doubly subordinate the command structures of these self-defence units to democratic accountability – both to the participatory assemblies and to the members of the units themselves, though he remains silent about just how such double-subordination would be effectively coordinated and secured. He simply writes: "The command structure of the units is under the dual control of both the organs of democratic politics and unit members and can easily be changed, if necessary, by motions and their democratic approval" (2020, p.220). Despite its ambiguities, this formulation remains most instructive, for it points well beyond the actual balance and relation of forces within the Kurdish freedom movement as it is currently structured.

NOTE

1 This chapter was originally published as an essay by *Peace in Kurdistan*. Accessible at: https://www.peaceinkurdistancampaign.com/wp-content/uploads/2021/09/ PIK-Issue-7-Reflections_Spiral_Legitimacy-Miley-6pp-A4.pdf

REFERENCES

Benjamin, W. 1999. "The Work of Art in the Age of Mechanical Reproduction," in *Illuminations*. London: Pimlico. pp.211-244.

Buck-Morss, S. 1992. "Aesthetics and Anaesthetics: Walter Benjamin's Artwork Essay Reconsidered," *October*, Vol. 62, pp.3-41.

Da Camara, H. 1971. *The Spiral of Violence*. London: Sheed and Ward Ltd.

Debray, R. 1967. *Revolution in the Revolution?* New York: Monthly Review Press.

Fanon, F. 2001. *The Wretched of the Earth*. London: Penguin Classics.

Freire, P. 1972. *The Pedagogy of the Oppressed*. Middlesex: Penguin Books.

Graves, B. 1997. "Hegel and Fanon," http://www.postcolonialweb.org/sa/gordimer/ july6.html

Marley, B. 1976. "War," on the album *Rastaman Vibration*. https://www.youtube.com/ watch?v=4XHEPoMNPoI.

Öcalan, A. 2020. *The Sociology of Freedom*. Oakland, CA: PM Press.

Wolfenstein, E.V. 1993. *Psychoanalytic Marxism: Groundwork*. New York, NY: The Guilford Press.

CHAPTER 9

Revolutionary Consciousness beyond Militant Secularism

Militant Secularism and the Bias against Belief in the Spirit-World Reconsidered

The left has long been dominated by "dialectical materialism," and thus remains too quick to dismiss as mystified, "backward," ultimately "uncivilized," any appeal to the divine or the mystical realm.

Frantz Fanon is emblematic in this regard, doubly biased against the "religious," doubly indebted to the tradition of European secularism, to the militant atheism of both Marx and of Freud. In *The Wretched of the Earth*, for example, he is explicit in his contempt for religious worldviews, such as when he dogmatically conflates belief in God as but a manifestation of fatalism: "A belief in fatality removes all blame from the oppressor; the cause of misfortunes is attributed to God; He is Fate. In this way the individual accepts the disintegration ordained by God, bows down before the settler and his lot, and by a kind of interior restabilization acquires a stony calm" (2001, p.42). As if secularism were somehow immune to similar manifestations of fatalism; and as if religious convictions, or mystical experiences, were incapable of galvanizing the will to resist oppressive relations in this world.

Fanon is equally dismissive of folk religious practices, of "myths and magic" structured around popular beliefs in the "supernatural," such as "maleficent spirits, leopardmen, serpent-men, six-legged dogs, zombies": "By entangling myself in this inextricable network where actions are repeated with crystalline inevitability, I find the everlasting world which belongs to me, and the perenniality which is thereby affirmed of the world belonging to us. Believe me, the zombies are more terrifying than the settlers; and in consequence the problem is no longer that of keeping oneself right with the colonial world and its barbed-wire entanglements, but of considering three times before urinating, spitting, or going out into the night" (2001, p.43).

Part of the problem has to do with the modernist and Eurocentric limits to the revolutionary imagination of the left, a left that remains much more familiar with the master/slave dialectic as described by Hegel than as lived and narrated by Frederick Douglass, a former slave. Which is not to deny any points of convergence between the insights of the two great thinkers. As captured by Hegel's pithy formulation in his *Phenomenology of Mind*, that "[i]t is solely by risking life that freedom is obtained" (Buck-Morss 2009, p.55).

There is a crucial scene in *The Narrative of the Life of Frederick Douglass*, where Douglass recounts in detail the precise moment in which the flame of the will to struggle was lit in him. The details of the scene are most revealing, and certainly contradict the secular dogmatists' insistence that belief in the spirit world is necessarily an obstacle for forging the will to struggle against oppression. Douglass begins the scene, which takes place towards the middle of his *Narrative*, by serving notice, with dramatic flair: "You have seen how a man was made a slave; you shall see how a slave was made a man".

It is a scene set in the summer of 1833, when Douglass was fifteen. On a hot summer day, he was fanning wheat. By early afternoon, Douglass falls faint, his strength breaks down, he has to stop. Over comes Mr. Covey, a relatively poor man himself, a farm-renter, but also a slaveholder, and a man with "a high reputation for breaking young slaves," to whom Douglass's owner had leased him out. Mr. Covey proceeds to beat Douglass viciously. Douglass manages to flee Mr. Covey's premises, disregarding Covey's calls and threats beckoning him to return or else. Douglass returns to his master, and implores him to let him get a new home, but the master refuses, even threatening to whip him if he did not return to Mr. Covey's farm the next morning. Douglass at first obeys, but upon approaching Mr. Covey's place, he catches a glimpse of the proud "nigger-breaker" grabbing his whip, looking very angry. Douglass figures he is probably coming to finish him off. So he takes off running, back into the woods. Mr. Covey chases him, but can't catch him, and eventually gives up.

Douglass spends most of the day in the woods, contemplating his seemingly bleak alternatives – "to go home and be whipped to death, or stay in the woods to starve to death". But then a stroke of fortune strikes. Douglass runs into Sandy Jenkins, a fellow slave with whom he is vaguely acquainted. He asks Jenkins for advice. Jenkins tells him, "with great solemnity," that he must return to Mr. Covey. But before that, Douglass must accompany him to another part of the woods, where a certain root can be found; and that as long as Douglass carries that root on him, on his right side, he can rest assured that Mr. Covey, nor any other white, will ever be able to lay a whip on him. Douglass is at first sceptical, but decides to do it anyway, figuring it can do no harm.

Douglass makes his way back to Mr. Covey's one more time. Mr. Covey at first receives him kindly, no trace of the previous rage. Douglass now begins to believe in the root, though because it is Sunday, and Mr. Covey fashions himself a pious man, Douglass still isn't sure. Monday morning rolls around, and Mr. Covey comes after him again. He catches Douglass, and begins to tie him up, when all of a sudden, "*from whence came the spirit I don't know*," Douglass resolves to fight. He seizes Mr. Covey by the throat, and thus the battle begins. For two hours they duke it out, Douglass more than holds his own. After that day, Mr. Covey never dares lay a hand on him again.

Douglass recalls the day in terms of which Fanon would certainly broadly approve. Douglass calls it a "turning-point in his career as a slave". He insists that the violent episode, his insurrection, had "rekindled the few expiring embers of freedom," revived his sense of "manhood," brought back his self-confidence, and inspired him with the determination to be free no matter what comes his way, even if he has to die. He is filled with a sense of "deep satisfaction," about which he eloquently describes:

"He only can understand the deep satisfaction which I experienced, who has himself repelled by force the bloody arm of slavery. I felt as I never felt before. It was a glorious resurrection, from the tomb of slavery, to the heaven of freedom. My long-crushed spirit rose, cowardice departed, bold defiance took its place; and I now resolved that, however long I might remain a slave in form, the day had passed forever when I could be a slave in fact. I did not hesitate to let it be known of me, that the white man who expected to succeed in whipping, must also succeed in killing me" (1995, p.43).

It is noteworthy that Douglass describes his "glorious resurrection" in terms of vanquishing his fear of death, or at least successfully subordinating such fear to his thirst for freedom. He also emphasizes that he let it be known that he was willing to fight and was not afraid to die. But he utters not a word about any willingness to kill. Perhaps such a willingness can be inferred, but he even reports feeling no anger, just a deep satisfaction and an even deeper resolve, the resolve to be free, even if it means a fight to the death.

All of this sounds right in line with Fanon's analysis, though Fanon would probably not approve of Douglass's use of the term "resurrection," given its deep religious associations. And for that matter, what would Fanon make of the *root*? At the very least it seems to have served what the pharmacy folks like to call a *placebo effect*, capable of producing courage. And it certainly didn't have the effect of an opiate, inducing quiescence. Mystified consciousness? Hard to say. Who's to say it wasn't magic? But either way, it seems to have galvanized his will to struggle, not to have thwarted it. *"From whence came the spirit I don't know".*

One of the more influential books in terms of making a dent in the Eurocentrism of the revolutionary imaginary on the left – at least in the Anglosphere, which is not just any sphere – is the brilliant account of the Haitian Revolution (1791-1803) penned by C.L.R. James, an Afro-Caribbean Marxist like Fanon. James, too, was an atheist, but one who has been aptly described as a man exuding a "Marxist spirituality" (O'Donnell 2013).

There is a curious detail included in James' account of the revolution, one often brushed over without comment, perhaps even downplayed by James himself. It is about the role played by Voodoo in the outbreak of the revolution. As James puts the point evocatively, "Voodoo was the medium of conspiracy". A conspiracy hatched in early 1791, among slaves across the island, who "in spite of all prohibitions … travelled miles to sing and dance and practice the rites and talk". News about the Revolution in France was among the subjects about which they spoke. In these discussions, the plans for an insurrection were hatched. The leader was a slave named Boukman, a Paploi, or Voodoo High Priest.

James recounts with particular aplomb the events on the eve of the insurrection, a summer night in which "a tropical storm raged, with lightning and gusts of wind and heavy showers of rain". The leaders of the revolt met in an open space, again in the forest:

> "There Boukman gave the last instructions and, after Voodoo incantations and the sucking of the blood of a stuck pig, he stimulated his fol-

lowers by a prayer spoken in creole which, like so much spoken on such
occasions, has remained. 'The God who created the sun which gives us
light, who rouses the waves and rules the storm, though hidden in the
clouds, he watches us. He sees all that the white man does. The god of
the white man inspires him with crime, but our god calls upon us to do
good works. Our god who is good to us orders us to revenge our wrongs.
He will direct our arms and aid us. Throw away the symbol of the god
of the whites who has so often caused us to weep, and listen to the voice
of liberty, which speaks in the hearts of us all'.

"The symbol of the god of the whites was the cross which, as Catho-
lics, they wore around their necks" (1989, p.87).

Again we find powerful empirical evidence directly contradicting the dogmatic and condescending prejudice that would equate belief in the spirit-
world with fatalism and quiescence. To the contrary, as James's account ably
documents, in Haiti, "Voodoo" was the medium from which revolutionary
insurrection was born among the slaves who worked the land.

Revolutionary Consciousness: Beyond Homogenous Empty Time

Like the early Christians, the early "dialectical materialists" were prone to the
mistaken belief that the Kingdom of Heaven was imminent, not imminent.
But as decades passed, their confidence became shaken, in both traditions.
Among the "dialectical materialists," as once surging internationalist solidarity
increasingly succumbed to the politics of divide and conquer, some of the
best and the brightest began to catch a glimpse of the possible unfolding of
a nightmare scenario strikingly similar to the one sketched by Da Camara
decades later.

In her classic account of *The Crisis in German Social Democracy*, better
known as *The Junius Pamphlet*, a most instructive pamphlet penned in the
wake of the outbreak of the First World War, which consummated the tragic
defeat of internationalism and the collapse of the Second International, Rosa
Luxemburg comes close to despair, even glimpses briefly into the abyss. She

quotes a phrase that she attributes to Engels, that "bourgeois society stands at the crossroads, either transition to socialism or regression into barbarism," and goes on to insist that the victory of imperialism, "[i]ts bloody sword of genocide, has brutally tilted the scale toward the abyss of misery". Either the victory of socialism, or "one great cemetery" are the only options left for humanity. She stares into the "one great cemetery" for a second before stepping back, and doubles down with resolve: "The only compensation for all the misery and all the shame would be if we learn from the war how the proletariat can seize mastery of its own destiny and escape the role of the lackey to the ruling classes" (1915).

But alas, the lessons would not be learned. Instead, her prophetic alternative of thoroughgoing internationalist militancy, the ruthless and consistent critique of all nationalist mystifications died with her, brutally murdered and dumped into the Landwehr Canal, pushed into the abyss. And yet, Red Rosa speaks to us still, her final words of defiance ringing out, as if an echo, from beyond the grave. Those who can hear, must listen: "Your 'order' is built on sand. Tomorrow the revolution will 'rise up again, clashing its weapons', and to your horror it will proclaim with trumpets blazing: I was, I am, I shall be!" (1919).

It is as if, in the frenzy of activity that characterized the last days of her life, Rosa's consciousness somehow transcended the confines of homogeneous, empty time. She was transported into the realm of the *messianic*, the realm of the eternal "now".

It was a state of revolutionary consciousness not reducible to Gramsci's often-cited, secular formulation of "pessimism of the intellect, optimism of the will". She had become a pure conduit, thoroughly possessed by immortal spirits, on the way to deliver the verdict of divine justice. She transcended into the now-time, but she was cut off at the pass, gunned down at the crossroads. Gunned down by thugs, attack dogs, the vicious lap-dogs of an Evil Empire, with the complicity of her former comrades, the Social Democrats. Martyred on 19 January, 1919. Dead, but not forgotten.

The word "revolution" originally meant a return to the origins or a turning of the wheel. It used to point backwards, as in "rolling back," when it did not refer to "recurrent cyclical motions, as in Copernicus's *On the Revolutions of Heavenly Spheres*". At least until the French Revolution came along. Indeed, even on the eve of that decisive rupture, a future-oriented understanding of the term "revolution" was still nowhere to be found, as the main entry for the term in the *Encyclopédie* reveals, referring as it does to "clocks and clock-making. Only after 1789 did 'revolution' become a door to the future, as did, a little later, another 're-' term: 'reform'" (Therborn 2008, pp.121-122).

But in Haiti, as we have seen, the ideological underpinnings of revolution-ary struggle, even when they were explicitly influenced by the news about Revolution in the metropole, were not reflective of such modernist under-standings and experiences of homogenous empty temporality. Indeed, as Walter Benjamin points out, such understandings are ultimately contradicted by the understandings and experiences of the French revolutionaries them-selves, who may have declared themselves to be living in year zero, but also viewed themselves as "Rome reincarnate" (1999, Thesis XIV).

Walter Benjamin was the person within the Marxist tradition who reflected perhaps most profoundly on the confines and contours of homogeneous empty time. He was a mystic and, like Luxemburg, also a martyr, in his own way, on his own terms. But still, he was snuffed out by the same fascist tide that silenced Luxemburg two decades before him. In his *Theses on the Philos-ophy of History*, penned in exile in Paris in January of 1940, less than six months before the conquering *Wehrmacht* came marching in, Benjamin takes up the task of re-founding the Marxist "dialectic," on foundations free from any naïve and discredited commitment to the high modernist cult of progress. In the process, he attempts a re-orientation of revolutionary faith, away from the future, back towards the past, to those moments of heroic rup-ture, where the "now-time" blasted through the continuum of history, pre-figuring the world to come. In this regard, he pushes much further than Luxemburg, who incarnated this *"jeitzeit"* but could not, or at least did not live to theorize it.

Benjamin attempts to disentangle the Marxist conception of history from problematic binaries such as the one in which Luxemburg's articulation of the glimpse into the abyss remains embroiled, as exemplified by her choice of the loaded term "barbarism" as the only remaining alternative to "social-ism". Since, after all, as Benjamin rightly emphasizes in a famous turn of phrase, "There is no document of culture which is not at the same time a document of barbarism" (1999, Thesis VII). Progress? Unlikely. More likely, "a storm blowing in from Paradise" (1999, Thesis IX).

Benjamin chose an overdose of morphine, after he and the group of Jewish refugees with whom he had fled were detained at a border crossing, in the grip of the fascist police who patrolled the border in Spain, and who had been ordered to return them to meet their fate in occupied France. His arrest by the Spanish authorities was itself an act of "international" solidarity of sorts, solidarity among fascists. Benjamin opted for a dignified death on Spanish (more precisely, Catalan) soil, refusing to consent to the fate of being herded back and brutalized by the Nazis.

Death in Portbou, the very same border crossing, the very same crossroad, through which so many Spanish Republican refugees had passed just a couple of years earlier, into exile, fleeing Franco's conquering troops. It was not far from Barcelona, the site of the great anarchist revolution of 1936, a revolution rolled back by the henchmen of Stalin, who may or may not have known what they were doing when they extinguished the sacred flame.

One of the central figures in that tremendous upheaval, Buenaventura Durruti, was interviewed just a few months before he fell in battle while defending Madrid. He was asked a tough question, one most likely motivated by a well-intentioned pessimism-of-the-intellect on the part of the journalist who posed it, Pierre Van Passen. It was a question reminiscent of Benjamin's reference to the "catastrophe, which keeps piling wreckage upon wreckage". Van Passen would remark in passing: "You will be sitting upon a pile of ruins if you are victorious". To which, the soon-to-be revolutionary martyr Durruti would reply: "We are not in the least afraid of ruins. We are going to inherit the earth. There is not the slightest doubt about that. The bourgeoisie might blast and ruin its own world before it leaves the stage of history. We carry a new world, here in our hearts. That world is growing this minute" (Van Passen, 1936). His state of consciousness, in the pitch of the battle, near the eve of his martyrdom, like that of Rosa Luxemburg's, showed signs of transcendence into the realm of the eternal "now".

REFERENCES

Benjamin, W. (1999). "Theses on the Philosophy of History," in *Illuminations*. London: Pimlico.

Buck-Morss, S. (2009). *Hegel, Haiti, and Universal History*. Pittsburgh, PA: University of Pittsburgh Press.

Douglass, F. (1995). *The Narrative of the Life of Frederick Douglass*. New York, NY: Dover Publications Inc.

Fanon, F. (2001). *The Wretched of the Earth*. London: Penguin Classics.

James, C.L.R. (1989). *The Black Jacobins*. New York: Vintage Books.

Luxemburg, R. (1915). *The Junius Pamphlet. The Crisis of German Social Democracy*. Accessible at: https://www.marxists.org/archive/luxemburg/1915/junius/

Luxemburg, R. (1919). "Order Prevails in Berlin". Accessible at: https://www.marxists.org/archive/luxemburg/1919/01/14.htm

O'Donnell, P. (2013). "The Marxist Spirituality of C.L.R. James". Accessible at: http://www.religiousleftlaw.com/2013/05/the-marxist-spirituality-of-clr-james.html

Therborn, G. (2008). *From Marxism to Post-Marxism?* London: Verso Books.

Van Passen, P. (1936). "Interview with Buenaventura Durruti". Accessible at: https://libcom.org/history/buenaventura-durruti-interview-pierre-van-paasen

CHAPTER 10

Murray Bookchin and Democratic Theory

Introduction

Murray Bookchin is undoubtedly one of the most important Anglo-American political thinkers of the twentieth century, and yet, somewhat "astonishingly," as Frank Fischer has recently observed, he "remains more or less unknown in the academic world". Indeed, Fischer quotes Gundersen to the effect that Bookchin is "almost wholly ignored by political scientists, including political theorists" (2017, p.237; Morris 2019, p.12).

This is a great shame, for few twentieth-century Anglo-American theorists can rival the scope and systematicity of Bookchin's body of work. Bookchin manages to elaborate and combine in an original and creative way a compelling ecological philosophy with an overarching social history, an account of the emergence of hierarchy, alongside a rather detailed sketch of the contours of a complex political program, libertarian municipalism, intended to combat and ultimately dissolve hierarchy in all its forms. In the process, he provides a coherent, and to a large extent plausible, meta-narrative which grounds a unique synthesis of ecological and anarchist, or perhaps more precisely, libertarian socialist, politics. Bookchin is best known as a founder of social ecology, which represents, in his words, a "*philosophy* of evolution," one that posits a "dialectical *unfolding* of life-forms from simple to complex, or more precisely, from the simple to the diverse". As Bookchin would characterize it in the year before his death, "[s]ocial ecology … is a concept of an ever-developing universe, indeed a vast process of achieving *wholeness* (to the extent that it can ever be fully achieved), by means of unity in diversity, with creative potentialities that thematically intertwine two *legacies* or traditions:

a legacy of freedom and a legacy of domination. These legacies interact to expand independently and interdependently the landscape of freedom and domination" (2005, pp.10-11).

Bookchin's articulation of social ecology thus includes several interrelated dimensions, incorporating the presentation of "a philosophy, a conception of natural and social development, an in-depth analysis of our social and environmental problems, and a radical utopian alternative" (2005, p.21).

Bookchin was a master of the much-maligned genre of the meta-narrative. He not only intervened in classic debates to sketch a unique and synthetic account of the emergence of hierarchy. He also grounded this account in a particular, Kropotkin-inspired, cooperative interpretation of evolutionary science. In turn, he related both of these to an elaborate account of the dialectical intertwining, or "double helix," of the legacies of domination and freedom as they interacted in the course of over two millennia of European history. He sought to draw a series of libertarian-socialist lessons from the European revolutionary tradition and to use all of these to provide robust philosophical and historical foundations for the advocacy of his creative synthesis of Marxism and anarchism with ecological politics and face-to-face, direct democracy.

The Meta-Narrative of the Emergence of Hierarchy

Against pernicious and pervasive social-Darwinist interpretations of evolutionary science, Bookchin recuperates "the tradition of Peter Kropotkin's *Mutual Aid*". He emphasizes, in contradistinction to the competitive and conflictual imaginary reflected in the oft-repeated mantra of "the survival of the fittest," that "the survival of living beings greatly depends on their ability to be supportive of one another" (2005, p.30). Indeed, Bookchin cites William Trager's notion of "symbiosis" in support of an extension of Kropotkin's "mutualistic naturalism" to apply not only "to relationships within and among species," but "among complex cellular forms" as well (2005, p.459). To this end, he reproduces Trager's words to the effect that "few people realize that mutual cooperation between different kinds of organisms – symbiosis – is just as important [as the 'survival of the fittest'], and that the 'fittest' may be the one that most helps another to survive" (2005, p.459). He references, too, the work of Lynn Margulis, and goes on to conclude: "*Mutualism*, not predation, seems to have been the guiding principle for the evolution of the highly complex aerobic forms that are common today" (2005, p.460).

Again and again, Bookchin stresses the theme of mutualism in what he refers to as "first nature". In such a vein, he maintains that "[t]he thrust of biotic evolution over greater eras of organic evolution has been towards the increasing diversification of species and their interlocking into highly complex, basically mutualistic relationships" (1999, p.41). From this, he infers that a principle of "unity in diversity" is operative in "first nature," and he proceeds to argue that "this ecological principle … grades into a richly mediated social principle," which is why he uses the term "social ecology". He posits: "[S]ociety, in turn, attains its 'truth', its self-actualization, in the form of richly articulated, mutualistic networks of people based on community, roundedness of personality, diversity of stimuli and activities, an increasing wealth of experience, and a variety of tasks" (1999, pp.41-42).

Bookchin is likewise careful to stress the intrinsic connection between ecological issues and social issues. He insists that, "like it or not, nearly every ecological issue is also a social issue," and that, in fact, "our present-day ecological dislocations have their basic sources in social dislocations" (2005, p.32). One of his core arguments is that "the very notion of the domination of nature by man stems from the very real domination of human by human" (2005, p.65). This leads him to sense an urgent "need to explain the emergence of social hierarchy and domination and to elucidate the means, sensibility, and practice that could yield a truly harmonious ecological society" (2005, p.65). As he contends in the 1991 introduction to *The Ecology of Freedom*, "we have to know *how* hierarchy arose if we are to undo it". He continues: "Without a clear insight into the nature of hierarchy and domination, we will not only fail to understand how the social and biotic interact with each other; we will fail to realize that the very *idea* of dominating first nature has its origins in the domination of human by human …" (2005, p.34).

Bookchin takes from Cicero the distinction between "first nature" and "second nature," the latter of which, unique among animals, incorporates cultural tradition, complex language, elaborate conceptual powers, and "an impressive capacity to restructure the environment purposefully according to human needs" (1999, pp.46, 48). "Second nature" is embedded within but emerges out of "first nature," and is associated with the phenomena and notion of "societies". These have differed immensely from one another over the course of history, Bookchin stresses, and in *The Ecology of Freedom* he provides a composite sketch of just "how simple differences in status were elaborated into firmly established hierarchies, [and] hierarchies into economic classes" (1999, p.49).

He is at pains to emphasize throughout that, when it comes to such hierarchies, we are not "dealing with inherent, unalterable features," but rather, "fabricated structures that can be modified, improved, worsened – or simply abandoned" (1999, p.49). Indeed, he insists, "[t]he trick of every ruling elite from the beginning of history to modern times has been to identify its own socially created hierarchical systems of domination with community life *as such*, with the result that human-made institutions acquire divine or biological sanction" (1999, p.49). By tracing the origins of hierarchies Bookchin hopes to help foster a critical consciousness capable of unravelling them. The urgent task, as he characterizes it, is for us "to go beyond existing second nature to fulfil the potentiality of combining first and second nature in a new synthesis that I have elsewhere called 'free nature'" (2005, p.50).

In the chapter on "The Emergence of Hierarchy," Bookchin draws on anthropological evidence to produce an, albeit admittedly rather speculative, account of the "development toward a complex hierarchical society, from gerontocracy, through patricentricity, shamanistic guilds, warrior groups, chiefdoms, and finally to state-like formations, even before classes begin to emerge" (2005, p.26). Biehl has cogently and concisely summarized Bookchin's hierarchy narrative in her compelling biography, *Ecology or Catastrophe*, as follows: "The earliest human societies ... had been small-scale, nonhierarchical, and egalitarian in nature ... [They] were not only egalitarian, they were mutualistic and matricentric. Tribespeople gathered in groups and shared. Everyone had a right to what Radin called the 'irreducible minimum' of subsistence goods – the means of life. People took what they needed and nothing more, operating on an unspoken principle of usufruct ... Early societies lived in harmony, indeed in symbiosis, with the natural world ... Out of this 'organic society', hierarchy had gradually emerged, immanently" (2015, pp.142-143).

This is a central point of contention surrounding Bookchin's hierarchy narrative, as Andy Price has explained. *When* and *how* did hierarchy emerge? The answer to when, according to Bookchin, is "before society started to bifurcate into economic classes around the emergence of surplus from the early Neolithic onwards" (Price 2012, p.132). But this, in turn, begs the question of *how*. Specifically, if mutualistic, symbiotic relations, rather than competition, conflict, and the struggle for existence (à la the 'survival of the fittest'), characterize "organic society," then why should hierarchy have emerged at all? Bookchin's claim "to have reversed the traditional formula of the emergence of hierarchy stemming from an attempt to dominate nature by humanity" turns out to be somewhat suspect (Price 2012, p.139).

The story he tells is that "[e]lderly people, feeling vulnerable as their powers failed, claimed privileges over the young for self-protection, giving rise to gerontocracy" (Price 2012, p.143). But this story seems to contradict the thrust of Bookchin's claims about mutuality and symbiosis in "organic society". For, as Price has aptly summarized an objection raised by Rudy:

> "[I]f, as Bookchin contends, nature is 'a participatory realm of interactive life-forms whose most outstanding attributes are fecundity, creativity, and directiveness', and that as such, organic societies are the social expression of this, operating along these same participatory processes— as denoted by 'their intense solidarity internally and with the natural world'—then what are we to make of the fact that Bookchin sees the genesis of hierarchy stemming from an instance—the precariousness of the old—which seems not to represent the fecundity and creativity of the natural evolution but in fact its 'stinginess' or cruelty?" (2012, p.139).

Be that as it may, for Bookchin, the blame for the emergence of hierarchy rests not only on the elderly *per se*, but more specifically, on "the sensibility and experience of the elderly *cum* shaman" (2005, p.153). As Biehl puts the point: "Shamans also experienced insecurity (magic being an unreliable means of healing), so for protection, they sought alliances with warriors". Conversely, "[i]n return for protection, shamans validated warriors' authority by endowing it with a magico-political aura" (2015, p.143).

After this step, further differentiations ensued. "Priests then emerged, as privileged religious formulators. Male warriors became patriarchs who dominated women and young men; tribal chiefs became commanding rulers". It was with such developments that hierarchy "became part of the unconscious apparatus of humanity," while "concepts of ownership developed, and words connoting inferiority and superiority entered vocabularies" (Biehl 2015, p.143).

All of this took place before the emergence of the state and of social classes. Institutionalized hierarchical mentalities preceded and paved the way for such subsequent developments. Biehl continues: "The advent of agriculture and the domestication of animals produced surpluses, which created social classes – privileged minorities who could live off the labor of others, using them for production;" and consequently, "[c]ollective societies became states, with armies, monarchs, and kings" (2015, p.143).

Next, with the rise of capitalism and the market economy, "mutualistic social ties" were dissolved, as "[t]he quest for the maximum profitable deal replaced usufruct, and once-cooperative groups became mutually competing buyers and sellers," while "[c]ities became marketplaces" (Biehl 2015, p.143). And overall, "[o]nce social hierarchies were in place, people projected a hierarchical mentality outward onto nature" (Biehl 2015, p.143).

For Bookchin, then, the rise of hierarchy comes well before the emergence of property ownership, and operates crucially at the level of consciousness – "incipient hierarchies gave rise to a hierarchical sensibility that ranked people as superior or inferior by a given standard and then used that ranking to justify the domination of the latter by the former" (1999, pp.75-76). Moreover, Bookchin himself is concerned to affect a revolution in consciousness. Revolution understood in the original sense of a return to origins. To this end, he traces the origins of hierarchy in order to historicize, and therefore denaturalize it. Whereas ruling elites have always sought to naturalize such hierarchies, Bookchin's project does the opposite.iIt takes the "emancipatory step to try to expand the realm of what convention holds to be social at the expense of what it defines as biological, precisely to open up possibilities for the transformation of existing social relationships" (1999, pp.76-77).

The story that Bookchin tells about the ascendancy of hierarchy he characterizes as a "legacy of domination;" but he is at pains to juxtapose and counter this legacy with one of freedom. These two legacies, he contends, are dialectically intertwined. They run throughout history like a "double helix". Where there is domination, so too is there resistance. As Biehl has succinctly summarized: "Through history and across cultures, people have dreamed of achieving freedom, 'the land of Cokaygne', a utopia of peace and harmony, where the lion and lamb lie down alongside each other". The examples of this legacy of freedom to which Bookchin recurs include "[t]he slave revolts of the ancient Mediterranean, the peasant upsurges of the European Middle Ages, the heretical Christians, the Levellers and Diggers of the English Civil War, the Enragés of the French Revolution, the Paris Communards of 1871, the Russian Socialist Revolutionaries of 1917, and the anarchists of the 1936 Spanish revolution". All of these examples, Biehl surmises, "to one degree or another, had sought a redistribution of wealth and an end to social hierarchies". Indeed, she continues, "[t]hese recurrent goals were, in essence, unconscious yearnings for the principles of organic society – usufruct, complementarity, and the irreducible minimum" (2015, p.145).

In both *The Ecology of Freedom* and *Urbanization without Cities*, Bookchin would spend significant time sketching the contours and content of this counter-legacy of freedom. In *The Third Revolution* he would take up the complementary task of providing a comprehensive account of popular movements that underpinned and propelled revolutionary episodes in Europe and the United States. This is a means of grounding his forward-oriented, utopian vision of an eco-anarchist, democratic-confederal, or libertarian municipal project. Bookchin intended to fortify that vision by recovering its deep historical precedents, by exploring "past possibilities that remain unfulfilled" (1999, p.152). He tried to keep alive a memory of the distinctly libertarian currents that can be found within the revolutionary tradition, in the hopes that such currents might be learned from, their vices transcended, their virtues resuscitated.

The Re-Articulation of the Democratic Ideal

This brings us to Bookchin's utopian vision of an eco-anarchist social order, sometimes called communalism, other times either democratic confederalism or libertarian-municipalism. Bookchin was determined to "move beyond critique to offer a reconstructive vision of a fundamentally different society – directly democratic, anticapitalist, ecological, and opposed to all forms of domination – that actualizes freedom in popular assemblies bound together in confederation" (2015, pp. xiv-xv). To this end, he was particularly concerned to revive the revolutionary imagination by exorcising it from the authoritarian, statist legacy bequeathed by the tradition of Marxism-Leninism. He was at the same time eager to re-articulate the democratic ideal in a radical way that allowed for a clear distinction between democracy and representative modes of rule.

Indeed, Bookchin is at perhaps his most eloquent and persuasive in his elaboration of the contrast between politics and statecraft, and his related advocacy of direct democracy over representative modes of rule. He is, in this regard, emphatic that citizens should not be conflated with "constituents" or "voters". According to Bookchin, political parties are best conceived as "miniature states," they are normally organised as "highly structured hierarchies," and are "fleshed out by a membership that functions in a top-down manner" (1992, p.243). In a word, "parties are replications of the state when they are out of power and often synonymous with the state when they are in power. They are formed to mobilize, to command, to acquire power, and to rule" (1992, p.243).

Janet Biehl has deftly summarized Bookchin's critique of political parties in the following terms: "They are essentially hierarchically structured, top-down bureaucracies that are seeking to gain State power for themselves through their candidates". She continues: "Their main concerns are the practical exigencies of faction, power, and mobilization, not the social well-being of the officeholders' 'constituents', except insofar as professions of concern for the well-being of ordinary men and women attracts votes". Nevertheless, she goes on to contend: "But in no sense are these kinds of political parties either derivative of the body politic or constituted by it". Indeed, she concludes: "Far from expressing the will of citizens, parties function precisely to contain the body politic, to control it and to manipulate it – indeed, to prevent it from developing an independent will" (1998, p.4).

Bookchin contrasts "inorganic" parties to "organic" and "authentic" political movements, the latter of which "emerge out of the body politic itself," and which "articulate the deepest social and political aspirations" of the populace. Examples that Bookchin provides of these include "the populist movements that swept out of agrarian America and tsarist Russia" and "the anarchosyndicalist and peasant movements of Spain and Mexico" (1992, p.244).

Bookchin further emphasizes "the public's power to create its own political institutions and forms of organization". To this end, he points to "twentieth century popular uprisings such as the Russian, German, Spanish, and most recently, Hungarian revolutions," all of which "witnessed the widespread self-organization of the people into councils …, popular assemblies …, and autonomous municipalities". And, he underscores, this occurred "often without party leadership" (1992, p.244).

He goes on to reference approvingly the work of Robert Michels, who "despite his jaundiced view of the 'competence' of the 'masses' in *Political Parties* and his proclivity for charismatic leaders, provides a compelling argument for the inertial effect of conventional political parties in periods of rapid social change". In effect, Bookchin concludes, parties "tend to take over institutions that the people create rather than innovate them, indeed, ultimately reworking them along statist lines" (1992, p.245). The "textbook case" illustrating this tendency, he notes, is the Bolshevik revolution.

Indeed, Bookchin insists that "[t]he words 'representative democracy', taken literally, are a contradiction in terms" (1992, p.245). Along these lines, he furthermore articulates a strident critique of the act of voting, which, he argues, "like registering one's 'preferences' for soap and detergents in opinion polls, is the total quantification of citizenship, politics, individuality, and the very formation of ideas as a mutually informative process". In his words, "[t]he mere vote reflects a preformulated 'percentage' of our perceptions and values, not their full expression. It is the technical debasing of views into mere preferences, of ideals into mere tastes, of overall comprehension into quantification such that human aspirations and beliefs can be reduced to numerical digits" (1992, p.250).

Or, as Janet Biehl has summarized Bookchin's position: "Mass voting in the privacy of a booth is but a pale substitute for an active political life. Here personal preferences for candidates are registered, tabulated, and quantified, like consumers' preferences in a market research survey, then processed in order to devise more effective marketing strategies for the next set of candidates" (1998, p.84).

Nor, for that matter, can voting in referenda be meaningfully distinguished from voting for representatives. Bookchin is not one who would conflate the institutional mechanism of the referendum with the ideals of direct democracy. To the contrary, he insists: "The autonomous individual *qua* 'voter' who forms the social unit of the referendum process in liberal theory is a fiction – whether in seemingly democratic notions at one extreme or a totalitarian politics of mass mobilization at the other". Furthermore, he continues: "The individual, left to his or her own destiny in the name of autonomy and independence, becomes a seemingly asocial being whose very freedom is denuded of vital traits that provide the necessary flesh and blood for genuine individuality" (1992, p.248).

Or, as Biehl has again clarified this line of critique: "[R]eferenda merely offer preformulated options; they do not allow for the collective formulation of policies or the expression of a broad range of possibilities. As with mass voting for candidates, mass voting for referenda continues the degradation of political participation into the mere registration of preferences. It debases citizens into consumers, broad ideals into personal tastes, and political ideas into percentages" (1992, pp.84-85).

Bookchin's critique of voting resembles that of Sartre, who in a polemical article from 1973 titled, "Elections: A Trap for Fools," argued: "When I vote, I abdicate my power — that is, the possibility everyone has of joining others to form a sovereign group, which would have no need of representatives. By voting I confirm the fact that we, the voters, are always other than ourselves and that none of us can ever desert the seriality in favour of the group, except through intermediaries. For the serialized citizen, to vote is undoubtedly to give his support to a party. But it is even more to vote for voting, as Kravetz says; that is, to vote for the political institution that keeps us in a state of powerless serialization".

Bookchin's line of reasoning, like that of Sartre, comes from a venerable tradition of critique of representative modes of rule, espoused perhaps most emblematically by Rousseau in *The Social Contract*, from which Bookchin cites approvingly one of the most famous passages in his chapter on "The Legacy of Domination" in *The Ecology of Freedom* (2005, p.202). The passage in question by Rousseau reads:

"Sovereignty, for the same reason as it makes it inalienable, cannot be represented. It lies essentially in the general will and does not admit of representation: it is either the same, or other; there is no intermediate possibility. The deputies of the people, therefore, are not and cannot be its representatives: they are merely its stewards, and can carry through no definitive acts. Every law the people have not ratified in person is null and void – is, in fact, not a law. The people of England regards itself as free, but it is grossly mistaken: it is free only during the election of members of parliament. As soon as they are elected, slavery overtakes it, and it is nothing".

Bookchin contends in relation to this Rousseauian argument that "the decisive shift from society to the State occurs with the most supreme political act of all: the delegation of power" (2005, p.201). He explicitly lauds Rousseau for his "clear distinction between deputation and delegation, direct democracy and representation," and adds: "[t]o delegate power is to divest personality of its most integral traits; it denies the very notion that the individual is competent to deal not only with the management of his personal life but with its most important context: the social context" (2005, p.202).

And yet, Bookchin does not follow Sartre, or for that matter "orthodox" currents of anarchism, in renouncing elections altogether. To the contrary, he advocates the contesting of elections at the local level, as a key component of his libertarian municipalist agenda. Specifically, Bookchin espouses the view that libertarian municipalists should run for local office with the goal of creating "fully empowered citizens' assemblies" (1998, p.73).

Bookchin conceives of the citizens' assemblies as the institutional space in which the democratic ideal of self-determination can be realized. In this vein, when asked by Janet Biehl what the relationship between libertarian municipalism and direct action is, Bookchin would respond: "Libertarian municipalism is the highest form of direct action. It is the direct – indeed, face-to-face – self-administration of a community. People act directly on society and directly shape their own destinies. There's no higher form of direct action than self-determination" (1998, p.163).

Whereas the "representative-democratic" model depends on a largely passive citizenry, and tends to assume the incompetence of the average person when it comes to managing civic affairs, Bookchin's libertarian municipal alternative requires and "assumes quite the opposite" (Biehl 1998, p.88). This is why Bookchin is careful to emphasize the educational dimension of his political project. In such a vein, he underscores the importance of "moral education and character building – what the Greeks called *paideia*," which he refers to as "indispensable," if we are to transform and transcend the role "of the passive constituents and consumers that we have today" (1992, p.299). But where is such education supposed to take place? To a large extent, it is through active engagement in citizens' assemblies themselves.

For Bookchin, political activity is formative and transformative; it promises to trigger the realization of human potentiality, and "challenges the citizenry to take control of its own community" (1992, p.276). By thus conceiving of his political project as fundamentally an educational project, Bookchin builds into his account the possibility of a self-reinforcing, expansionary dynamic in relation to the prospect of self-determination. As he pithily, and optimistically, puts the point: "self-governance begets self-governance" (1992, p.277). The ultimate vision of the political world which he sketches is one "in which the state as such will finally be replaced by a confederal network of municipal assemblies," and in which "the corporate economy reduced to a truly political economy" (1992, p.286).

Bookchin would locate the locus of self-governance, of sovereignty, in local citizens' assemblies. This distinguishes his vision of direct democracy from that of *workerist* alternatives which emphasize the democratization of the workplace as critical for the realization of self-determination. Not that Bookchin is opposed to the democratization of the workplace. He is indeed generally supportive of the establishment of workers' councils and of cooperatives, but he is quick to stress that the diffusion of such democratic workplace relations – that is, of democratic relations at the point of production – would not be sufficient for achieving the urgent task of democratizing social life. To the contrary, he contends, absent of a more all-encompassing, territorial basis for the exercise of direct democracy, so-called *workerist* alternatives can be all too easily incorporated into a competitive, corporate-capitalist *modus operandi*. To this end, he advocates the municipalization of the economy. In his words: "In a libertarian municipalist society, the assembly would decide the policies of the entire economy. Workers would shed their unique vocational identity and interests, at least as far as the public realm is concerned, and see themselves as citizens in their community. The municipality, through the assembly of its citizens, would control and make the broad decisions for its shops, lay down the policies that they should follow, always working with a civic outlook rather than an occupational one" (in Biehl 1998, pp.161-162).

Bookchin's vision of direct democracy, centred on local citizens' assemblies, requires radical decentralization, for face-to face participation, as well as a "localist emphasis on community values" (1992, p.293). However, Bookchin also emphasizes that "decentralized communities are inevitably dependent on one another". He warns against the spectres of "parochialism and chauvinism," and even underscores "the need for confederation … to counteract" such tendencies (1992, pp.293, 296). Indeed, this confederal level, he foresees, would have to constitute "a scrupulously supervised system of coordination," and goes on to refer to "the dialectical development of independence and dependence into a more richly articulated form of interdependence" (1992, p.299).

Nevertheless, as Fischer has perceptively argued, "Bookchin's concept of an associational confederation … suffers from a potentially serious weakness". Bookchin insists on the distinction between policymaking, on the one hand, and coordination and execution on the other, claiming that the confederal level would be engaged in the latter forms of activity alone. Even so, this "conceptualization of a central committee that would only be an administrative body concerned with implementation seems both worrisome and unlikely". This because, first, "it fails to recognize that central administration is already a form of political activity, one that often hides behind the pretense of neutrality;" and furthermore, "it is unclear that this body, as an administrative unit, would be capable of guiding action to protect the members of the confederation from incursions from the outside (or perhaps dissension or revolt from within)" (2017, pp.256-257).

Nor are the difficulties conceivably involved in the coordination of confederation the only problematic aspect of Bookchin's political project. There is also the crucial question of how we are supposed to get from here to there. Bookchin was in many respects quite optimistic about the prospect of building a movement that could effectively establish a confederated libertarian municipalist order. But he was by no means naïve. At one point towards the end of *Urbanization without Cities*, he hints at the spectre of a violent conflict with the state, specifically, when he suggests that "whether or not the people have power depends upon whether or not it is armed and creates its own grass-roots militia, not only to guard itself from criminals or invaders but also from the ever-encroaching power of the state itself" (1992, p.285). Even so, he tends to emphasize that the path towards the realization of libertarian municipalism is best conceived as a process, indeed, "an admittedly long development in which existing institutions and traditions of freedom are slowly enlarged and expanded" (1992, p.287). And to this end, he would stress the need "to democratize the republic, and radicalize our democracy," a task he framed as perhaps a long process, but nevertheless nothing less than "a precondition for our survival as a species" (1992, p.288).

Ultimately, Bookchin conceived of the construction of libertarian municipalism in relation to the notion of "dual power," and anticipated a growing tension between the direct-democratic institutions of people power and the nation-state. Indeed, according to Bookchin, "[l]ibertarian municipalists seek to exacerbate the tension between municipalities and the State, to become an oppositional dual power that will, under propitious conditions, abolish the state for a confederal system of social administration" (in Biehl 1998, p.175). Just four years before his death, he would reflect upon the difficulties of such a task. In his words: "Libertarian municipalists do not delude themselves that the state will view with equanimity their attempts to replace professionalized power with popular power. They harbor no illusions that the ruling classes will indefinitely allow a Communalist movement to demand rights that infringe on the state's sovereignty over towns and cities". Furthermore, he would continue: "Communalists' attempt to restore the power of towns and cities and to knit them together into confederations can be expected to evoke increasing resistance from national institutions". Here he invokes the term dual power explicitly. He asserts: "That the new popular-assemblyist municipal confederations will embody a dual power against the state that becomes the source of growing political tension is obvious". This is when the movement will face a critical challenge. He contends: "Either a Communalist movement will be radicalized by this tension and will resolutely face all its consequences or it will surely sink into a morass of compromises that absorb it back into the social order that it once sought to change". Indeed, he concludes: "How the movement meets this challenge is a clear measure of its seriousness in seeking to change the existing political system and the social consciousness it develops as a source of public education and leadership" (2017, pp.18-19). A very tall task, to say the least.

The Problems of Eurocentrism and Secularist Sectarianism

Where Bookchin's meta-narrative and framework proves least convincing has to do with his unapologetic Eurocentrism, which in turn is related to an albeit perhaps less pronounced, but nevertheless still detectable, streak of secular dogmatism. Despite his compelling and often strident critique of the nation-state, his efforts to recover and promote a legacy of freedom in the United States lead him to articulate a rather whitewashed version of US history at the same time that he systematically underestimates the pernicious and insidious nature of US nationalism.

The original sins of settler colonial genocide and chattel slavery, not to mention their continuing impact upon hegemonic mentalities in the United States, are not altogether ignored; but they certainly occupy a less central place in Bookchin's narrative than they should. Likewise with the brutality associated with ongoing and pervasive US imperialism. At a certain point in *Urbanization without Cities*, Bookchin goes so far as to dismiss those who would dwell on such ugly realities as "self-indulgent," and "liv[ing] on a diet of hating America" (1992, pp.280-281). Indeed, he even chastises these critics on the US left for "snarling perpetually at [their] most natural allies at home – the ordinary citizen desiccated by his or her own spiritual poverty" (1992, p.282).

This seems to miss the mark, and indeed even cuts against Bookchin's own emphasis on the importance of the project of political education, of consciousness-raising, or *paideia*, for the purpose of movement building. The deconstruction of hegemonic myths associated with the legacy of domination, the effort to extirpate the authoritarian detritus that has accumulated in the common sense, is at least as important as the recuperation of freedom traditions. And indeed, the freedom traditions themselves have to be subjected to a critical hermeneutic capable of revealing the complex and dialectical intertwining of emancipatory aspirations with projects and practices of domination and exclusion.

In a word, we might say that where Bookchin is sharpest is related to his critique of the state. But he could be sharper when it comes to the critique of the nation. And here he is guilty of a certain double standard – since he is highly critical of anti-colonial nationalisms, but in fact complicit with European and US chauvinism.

How could the freedom tradition be exclusively European? C.L.R. James's *Black Jacobins* was originally published in 1938, and yet, it is as if Bookchin never heard of him, or for that matter, the Haitian revolution. As for Frantz Fanon, he is nowhere cited in either *The Ecology of Freedom* or *Urbanization without Cities*. This despite his influence on the radical left in the 1960s. In Biehl's biography of Bookchin, Fanon is only mentioned as a pernicious influence on the US left, associated with his writings on violence. She writes, in relation to Fanon's influence: "Bookchin, aghast, recognized that the whole plan was foolhardy. Ordinary Americans were repulsed by posters of Mao and Ho and Che and Fidel, and they didn't like cops being provoked. Revolutionary rhetoric and quotations from the Little Red Book would do nothing but drive them away" (2015, p.118).

And yet, there is a clear affinity between important aspects of Fanon's political program and the thrust of Bookchin's libertarian municipalist agenda, as for example, when in *The Wretched of the Earth*, Fanon emphasizes that "in order really to incarnate the people … there must be decentralization in the extreme" (1963, pp.197-198).

In *Urbanization without Cities*, Bookchin goes so far as to wax eloquent about "the American Dream". He lectures the left to this effect, insisting that "[a] municipal agenda that does not piece together the emancipatory features of the 'American Dream' such that this agenda can speak in a clear and unqualified voice to the American people will not be worth the paper on which it was written". He continues: "For decades, social innovators have talked to the American people in German (Marx), Russian (Lenin), Chinese (Mao), Vietnamese (Ho Chi Minh), indeed in virtually every language but English – which is to say, in the language of the traditions and 'isms' that are largely incomprehensible to Americans" (1992, p.281). If only Americans were fluent in such languages! The call to "speak English" to Americans, albeit intended metaphorically, strikes this reader as too much of a concession to the xenophobia and jingoism so ubiquitous on the American political right. To foster an internationalist consciousness, embedded in a thoroughgoing critique of US nationalism, should not be equated with "debark[ing] to a 'Third World' ideological ghetto" (1992, p.281).

Besides, there is a clear disjuncture between the call for a municipally-centered politics, and the national (as well as Eurocentric) framing of his narrative appeal about the traditions to which "Americans" belong. Why not make the effort to deconstruct rather than reify the national(ist) framing altogether, by recovering municipal and regional local traditions, below the nation-state, alongside a deliberate effort to foster internationalist consciousness beyond it? Not that Bookchin is opposed to internationalism – far from it. In this vein, in an interview with Janet Biehl from 1996, he would insist that "[i]f capital is going to function in an international way, a libertarian municipalist movement will have to be international too" (1998, p.147).

Bookchin's attempt to appeal to "ordinary citizens," indeed, to "ordinary Americans," is certainly understandable, but at the same time it reflects a clear dilemma shared by all who aspire to radical political transformation – the need to appeal to common sense in a world in which such common sense has been thoroughly distorted by hegemonic machinations and manipulations. How to successfully appeal to common sense without pandering to pervasive and insidious prejudices? If you do not appeal to such prejudices, how can you avoid the fate of being rendered a marginal, even irrelevant, sectarian force? But if you do, what will remain of your transformative aims?

When national chauvinism is not confronted head on, it can end up festering. Likewise with civilizational conceits, such as the idea that the legacy of freedom somehow uniquely belongs to Europe and the United States.

In the preface to *The Third Revolution*, Bookchin acknowledges his failure to address "in any great detail certain shortcomings of the great democratic revolutions, such as the limited role that women were permitted to play in them and the oppression that African-Americans suffered even as the American Revolution honoured their 'natural rights' in the breach", though he pleads innocent to the charge of being "oblivious to the rights and interests of women, homosexuals, and ethnic minorities". Rather, he excuses these omissions on the grounds that "any introductory account of the revolutionary era must necessarily be highly selective in its choice of events and facts," before adding that "[f]ortunately, there are now many books available that deal in considerable detail with issues of gender and ethnicity in these revolutions and that adequately fill out my own gaps" (1996, p.x). This is not good enough.

Like with his beloved Athens, the exclusionary/oppressive dimensions of the social orders and processes upon which Bookchin focuses cannot be so easily bracketed or marginalized from the narrative of the emancipatory traditions that he is seeking to recover. After all, the freedom of the Athenian citizen was in a very literal sense founded upon patriarchal domination and slavery – this was not just an unfortunate accident; nor can it be merely chalked up "to the era of which it was a part" (1998, p.20), that is, to the dominant prejudices of the age. Rather, it was a constitutive feature of the social-property relations upon which the practices of citizen freedom depended.

Not only are the exclusionary/oppressive dimensions of the emancipatory traditions upon which Bookchin focuses given short shrift. There is a broader problem as well, having to do with the fact that the vast majority of humanity is effectively excluded from the metanarrative Bookchin elaborates about the legacy of freedom.

Virtually every single example which Bookchin provides comes from Europe or the United States – though he does mention agrarian populism in Mexico, and at one point in *Urbanization without Cities* even claims that "John Ball and Thomas Munzer were the ancestors of a host of later agrarian leaders such as Emilian Pugachev in Russia and Emiliano Zapata in Mexico," all of whom "shared the central goal of preserving the village community" (1992, p.185).

Elsewhere, in his discussion of German confederacy, in relation to Engels' negative assessment, he writes: "The problem is not merely an academic one. It raises the crucial question of whether or not seemingly 'undeveloped' peoples today are to achieve what we so flippantly call 'modernization' – by confederalism or nationalism, decentralism or centralism, libertarian institutions or authoritarian ones" (1992, p.163).

And yet, for the most part, he remains aloof to the fate of what he at one point refers to disparagingly as the "Third World ghetto". This attitude surfaces most problematically in his last major work, the four volumes on *The Third Revolution*, in which his account of the revolutionary tradition explicitly excludes any examples from beyond Europe and the US In the introduction to the first volume, he goes so far as to contend that the charge of Eurocentrism "leaves [him] singularly untroubled". Indeed, according to Bookchin, "[t]he fact is that the authentic center of the revolutionary era was the European continent, including Russia, and the United States (whose revolution belongs very much in the European tradition)". He proceeds to offer a thoroughly diffusionist framing of revolutionary traditions elsewhere, claiming that "[t]o the extent that revolutions in the 'Third World' had certain universal features and sought or professed to establish a radically new social dispensation for humanity as a whole, they emulated the great European rev-olutions discussed in this book". Even worse, not only does he dismiss 'Third World' revolutions as unoriginal; he also argues that they cannot compare in terms of "universal appeal" to the revolutions of their European counterparts. In his words: "Their nationalistic and anti-imperialistic aspects may be un-derstandable in the context in which they occurred; but these revolutions should not be mystified, nor should their justifiable claims to freedom from imperialism be viewed as comparable to the universal appeals to humanity that marked the great revolutions that occurred in Europe" (1996, p.18).

He would have done well to read (more closely?) his Fanon, who ever so wisely advises: "Leave this Europe where they are never done talking of Man, yet murder men everywhere they find them, at the corner of every one of their own streets, in all the corners of the globe" (1963, p.311).

If Bookchin's unabashed Eurocentrism, his insensitivity to the "colonial matrix of power," and relatedly, the ease with which he dissociates the legacies of domination from the legacies of freedom, thus constitutes one of the main weaknesses of his social-ecological paradigm, the streak of secular dogmatism that can be detected at least at points in his work constitutes another. Bookchin is perhaps right when he insists that "[f]alsehoods and dogmatic beliefs, how-ever benign they may seem at first glance, inevitably imprison the mind and diminish its critical thrust" (2005, p.53). But he is wrong to suggest that sec-ularism, too, cannot breed such a dogmatic mentality. Indeed, his critiques of scientism and of rationalism point in precisely this direction. Nevertheless, when he asserts that "[n]either religion nor a spiritualistic vision of experience has any place in an ecological lexicon" (2005, p.23), he would seem to err on the side of dogmatism himself, of a distinctly sectarian, secular variety. That this "secular fundamentalist" formulation comes from the 1991 introduction of *The Ecology of Freedom* is of course no coincidence. Evidently, the polemical falling out with the deep ecologists had exacerbated his secularist sensibilities, to the point of provoking (or possibly revealing) a prejudice against mysticism, and against faith. This despite the fact that his own utopian proclivities cer-tainly require faith, in their own right – faith that another world beyond cap-italism is in fact possible, faith that the struggle to realize such a world would not make things even worse. As such, the "proclivity for faith" cannot be so easily dismissed as Bookchin would have it, for example, in his unfortunate and caricatured articulation that the "arbitrary nature" of such a proclivity "renders their acolytes manipulable by assorted New Age gurus, priests, priestesses, witches, and orchestrators of mass culture" (2005, p.53).

Conclusion

If Bookchin's very rich body of work remains unfortunately largely ignored in the hallowed halls of academia, a decade and a half after his death, his legacy has in other important respects begun to blossom. This is no small part due to the influence his work has had on the imprisoned leader of the Kurdish freedom movement, Abdullah Öcalan, and through this influence, the spread of "democratic confederal" ideals and practices embodied in the Kurdish-led revolutionary project in northeastern Syria, in Rojava. The confluence of social ecology, and of libertarian municipalism, with the re-articulation of self-determination by Öcalan and his followers, the emergence of this joint project as an historical force in a revolutionary context, albeit a very different context from the one Bookchin had in mind, is a subject worthy of serious, in-depth investigation in its own right. This author, for one, first came into contact with Bookchin's ideas through engagement with the Kurdish movement. The affinity between Bookchin's utopian vision and the radical, direct-democratic alternative to the nation-state under construction in Rojava is in significant ways uncanny – for Rojava represents an alternative characterized by citizens' assemblies and self-defence militias, by an emphasis on gender emancipation and multi-cultural accommodation, and by a sensitivity to the urgency of ecological sustainability in a region where the soil bleeds oil. Indeed, in Rojava, Bookchin's social-ecological, communalist project has, through dialectical synthesis with the creative and dynamic Kurdish movement, managed definitively to transcend its Eurocentric origins and to become part of humanity's legacy of freedom.

REFERENCES

Biehl, Janet. 1998. *The Politics of Social Ecology. Libertarian Municipalism* (Montreal: Black Rose Books).

Biehl, Janet. Editor. 1999. *The Murray Bookchin Reader* (Montreal: Black Rose Books).

Biehl, Janet. 2015. *Ecology or Catastrophe. The Life of Murray Bookchin* (Oxford: Oxford University Press).

Bookchin, Murray. 1992. *Urbanization without Cities. The Rise and Decline of Citizenship* (Montreal: Black Rose Books).

Bookchin, Murray. 1996. *The Third Revolution. Popular Movements in the Revolutionary Era* (London: Cassell).

Bookchin, Murray. 2005. *The Ecology of Freedom. The Emergence and Dissolution of Hierarchy* (Oakland, CA: AK Press).

Bookchin, Murray. 2015. *The Next Revolution. Popular Assemblies and the Promise of Direct Democracy* (London: Verso).

Fanon, Frantz. 1963. *The Wretched of the Earth* (New York, NY: Grove Press). Accessible at: https://libcom.org/files/[Frantz_Fanon]_Wretched_of_the_earth_(tran(BookZZ.org).pdf

Fischer, Frank. 2017. *Climate Crisis and the Democratic Prospect. Participatory Governance in Sustainable Communities* (Oxford: Oxford University Press).

Morris, Brian. 2019. "The Legacy of Murray Bookchin," in Federico Venturini, Emet Degirmenci, and Inés Morales, editors, *Social Ecology and the Right to the City. Towards Ecological and Democratic Cities* (Montreal: Black Rose Books), pp.12-31.

Price, Andy. 2012. *Recovering Bookchin. Social Ecology and the Crises of Our Time* (Porsgrunn, Norway: New Compass Press).

Rousseau, Jean Jaques. 1762. *The Social Contract.* Accessible at: https://socialpolicy.ucc.ie/Rousseau_contrat-social.pdf

Sartre, Jean Paul. 1973. "Elections: A Trap for Fools". Accessible at: https://goodmorningrev.wordpress.com/2008/08/14/elections-a-trap-for-fools/

CHAPTER 11

Marx, Marxism, and the Problem of Eurocentrism
Reflections Inspired by Esteban Torres, La gran transformación de la sociología

In an essay titled, "Marx, Eurocentrism and Structural Change in Latin America,"[1] originally presented as an intervention in a dialogue with Álvaro García Linera, Atilio Borón, and Elvira Concheiro Borquez on the occasion of the presentation of the book, *Marx at 200: Present, Past and Future,* and now included as a stand-alone chapter in the section on "Marx and the Lefts Facing the Regional Future" in *The Great Transformation of Sociology* (2021), Esteban Torres addresses the crucial question and charge of Eurocentrism in the work of Marx and in the tradition of Marxism.

On the surface, at least, Torres would seem to acquit Marx of the charge. He contends, instead, that "Marx offers a European vision of the world, not a Eurocentric vision". And he goes on to argue that "Marx, or any other great author, no matter how internationalist their emancipatory interest may be, cannot be asked to think for us, nor to take charge of the situation, from the particularity of our own historical location, to recognize for us which are the most fundamental and urgent problems" (2021, pp. 363-364).

It is worth considering the substance and significance of Torres's claim in some greater detail. Torres is clearly familiar with the too-often neglected Latin American contributions to the Marxist tradition – as is apparent from his reference to such emblematic, albeit "heterodox," figures as José María Aricó, Mariátegui, Scalabrini Ortiz, Jorge Abelardo Ramos, and Zabaleta Mercado. Even so, he insists, such thinkers were well aware of the fact that "Marx's theoretical framework was not created from Latin America, nor in the first instance for the region" (2021, p.364). To comprehend Marx, Torres contends, requires situating him within the European context from which his work emerged. In Torres's words, "Marx cannot be delocalized" (2021, p.364). But this does not lead Torres to reject the prospect of a fruitful dialogue with Marx and with Marxism, from perspectives rooted in other world regions. To the contrary, he claims, such a dialogue is most urgent and necessary. This is because, he argues, "[j]ust as the world is not the product of only one locality, a theory of world society cannot be either" (2021, pp.364-365).

Torres is insistent that "it cannot be demanded of Marx or of anybody that they supplant our work of substantive theoretical creation" (2021, p.366). Furthermore, he goes on to sketch what he takes to be one of the fundamental challenges for critical social sciences (in which he includes Marxism), as being the propagation and development "of new theories of world society, from and for Latin America, from which categories can be generated that allow us to explain, among other things, how in objective terms national and popular governments in the region and in the peripheral world more generally are functioning" (2021, p.366).

In sum, Torres thus champions the proliferation of theories of global society both from and for the global peripheries. To this end, he calls for a "paradigmatic renovation" of the social sciences, a renovation which consists in "the recreation of a 'spirit' that is at the same time *mundialista* and *autonomista*" (2021, p.368). He admits the possibility that these theories and this 'spirit' can take inspiration in the work of Marx and can indeed be situated within the Marxist tradition. And yet, he argues, "throughout history, in the few moments and countries of Latin America in which Marxist ideas prospered on a grand scale, these ideas were subjected to a process of autonomist theoretical creation, of 'creative destruction' in relation to Marx" (2021, p.367). Likewise, in the political terrain, Torres cites the examples of Castro's Cuba, Allende's Chile, and Evo Morales' Bolivia as instances of national victories associated with the Marxist movement in the region, but at the same time he is careful to stress "the creative and irreverent theoretical force of its leaders and reference groups". In all these cases, he contends, "the implementation of an autonomist theoretical and political practice implied discarding a good part of the Marxian postulates" (2021, p.367).

Nor is the link between the theoretical and the political levels that Torres makes tangential or incidental. To the contrary, it reflects his deeply held conviction of the necessity – indeed, the "existential imperative" – for left-wing social sciences to generate "institutional conditions to effectively influence the process of social change" (2021, p.369).

All this is fine and good, but where does this leave us with respect to the problematic of Eurocentrism? One might be tempted to say that, according to Torres, Marx generated a theory of global society from and for Europe.

Indeed, Torres would seem to substantially concur with the judgment of Salah Hassan, that "in spite of his visionary work and enduring legacy, Marx was a product of his time and of Europe as a rising colonial empire with ambitions of conquest and domination, and the larger framework of his analysis was bound by the evolutionary thinking of that time" (and place) (2012, p.3).

Moreover, like Hassan, Torres's reflex response to help transcend this limitation is to centre the contributions to the Marxist tradition made by organic intellectuals writing from and for the global south. In such a vein, both Hassan and Torres effectively follow Benita Parry's strategy of attempting to correct the Eurocentric tendency within so-called Western Marxist thought that would ignore and exclude non-Metropolitan contributions to the tradition, by emphasizing the creativity and innovation of contributions to that tradition made by figures from the global south (Parry 2011). They likewise evoke the same pertinent question posed by Sarah Salem, namely, "what are we assuming to be the Marxist 'canon'?" For, as Salem has argued, "[i]f we take seriously the work of Samir Amin, C.L.R. James, Frantz Fanon and Claudia Jones, then the Marxist canon itself is not as stable as often imagined" (Salem 2019).

Even so, as we shall see, such a move, which Robinson (2019) has perhaps a bit unfairly caricatured as a strategy of "parading out images of … revolutionaries of colour," cannot ultimately put to rest the critique of Eurocentrism.

Nevertheless, Torres actually rejects the charge against not only Marxism in general but also against Marx himself of Eurocentrism, perhaps only because he sees such "centrism" to be inevitable, insofar as all universalizing theories inevitably bear the mark of the particular circumstances and local problematics to which the theorist is responding, not to mention the particular interlocutors with whom the theorist is corresponding. In a word, all theories, regardless of their universalizing aspirations, are theories elaborated from and for somewhere. As such, Torres would seem to suggest, the only way to approximate universality is through the proliferation of dialogue among theorists thinking both from and for a variety of different global regions, with an emphasis on the "*conjunto*" of the world peripheries, or global south.

But is the aspiration to approximate universality itself a reflection of a Eurocentric bias, as post-colonial critics have so often claimed? Or to put the point another way, is such an aspiration "inherently epistemically colonial" (Robinson 2019), as some latter-day decolonial champions of the "pluriverse" have argued? Torres is basically right to resist such a sweeping dismissal of universalizing aspirations per se, even if he is too quick to acquit Marx of the charge of Eurocentrism. Nevertheless, in order to more deftly navigate the terrain of such claims, it might prove worthwhile to take a closer look at the debate about Marx and Eurocentrism.

There have been rivers of ink spilled over this question of Marx's – and Marxism's – alleged Eurocentrism. What is the nature of this accusation against Marx of which Torres seems all too quick to acquit him? For starters, what precisely does Eurocentrism entail? In one of the more persuasive recent interventions in the debate, in an article titled "Marx's Eurocentrism: Post-colonial Studies and Marx Scholarship," Kolja Lindner has provided an analytically incisive four-dimensional definition of the concept of Eurocentrism. According to Lindner, in its first dimension, Eurocentrism can be considered "a form of ethnocentrism distinguished not only by the presumption that Western societies are superior, but also by the attempt to justify this presumption in rational, scientific terms". In its second dimension, Eurocentrism has to do with "[a]n 'Orientalist' way of looking at the non-Western world which has less to do with the real conditions prevailing there than with what [Edward] Said calls the "'European Western Experience'. The world as whole is imagined from a regional standpoint". Moreover, in its third dimension, Eurocentrism is reflected in "a conception of development which, by means of a 'false universalism… uncritically makes the cultural and historical patterns of capitalist Western Europe the established standards for all human history and culture'". And finally, in its fourth dimension, Eurocentrism is characterised by the "[e]ffacement of non-European history, or, more precisely, of its influence on European development" (2010, pp.2-3).

Rahul Rao has recently argued that blanket dismissals of Marxism as Eurocentric "fail to attend to the nuances embedded within Marx's position on imperialism" (as summarized by Salem 2019). There is, nevertheless, no doubt that Marx's own views on imperialism and/or colonialism were decidedly more ambivalent and ambiguous than those of Lenin, much less those of Mao or Fanon. And in striking contrast to such later Marxists, nowhere does Marx himself offer any "emancipatory programme specifically for colonial revolution" (Young 2016, p.102).

It is, nevertheless, also the case that, for Marx (and for Engels), colonial expansion constituted a necessary precondition for the subsequent rise of industrial capitalism. In Robert C. Young's words: "it was colonial expansion which enabled the bourgeoisie to accumulate enough capital to revolutionize the whole economic and social system on a global scale – an observation which would later be developed into world-system theory" (2016, p.102).

As Marx put the point most eloquently in Volume 1 of *Capital*, first published in 1867, towards the very end, in Chapter XXXI on the "Genesis of the Industrial Capitalist": "The discovery of gold and silver in America, the extirpation, enslavement and entombment in mines of the aboriginal population, the beginning of the conquest and looting of the East Indies, the turning of Africa into a warren for the commercial hunting of black-skins, signalised the rosy dawn of the era of capitalist production. These idyllic proceedings are the chief moments of primitive accumulation" (1867/2015, p.533).

As such, Marx saw capitalism and imperialism to be intimately intertwined. At the root of his ambivalence was his whole-hearted commitment to socialist revolution, coupled with his conviction that the path to socialism had necessarily to pass through the transition to industrial capitalism first. To the extent that colonial conquest could be viewed as clearing the way for the subsequent development of capitalism, in other words, to the extent that colonialism could be seen as "a necessary instrument for the introduction of modernity" (Young 2016, p.105), for Marx, colonialism could be considered as part of a dialectical unfolding. This despite the despicable brutality involved, which Marx was always careful to document in meticulous detail.

As Marx would infamously argue in an 1853 article written for the *New York Daily Tribune*, on "The British Rule in India": "England, it is true, in causing a social revolution in Hindostan, was actuated only by the vilest interests, and was stupid in her manner of enforcing them. But that is not the question. The question is, can mankind fulfil its destiny without a fundamental revolution in the social state of Asia? If not, whatever may have been the crimes of England she was the unconscious tool of history in bringing about that revolution" (1853/2005).

As Young puts the point: "Colonialism therefore, for Marx, was fiercely dialectical: both a ruthless system of economic exploitation and a significant positive move towards a Utopian future" (2016, p.109).

If Marx's writings from the 1850's on India display a clear ambivalence towards European imperialism, his and Engels' treatment of Ireland would be more categorical in their condemnation of the phenomenon. This is because, as Kevin Anderson has emphasised, Marx saw Ireland "as an important source of opposition to Britain and to global capital" (2010, p.115), indeed, progressively so, and by 1870 he even came to consider Ireland potentially as "the lever" of the revolution (2010, p.144). By all means, as Lindner has highlighted, Marx's observations of colonized Ireland stand in rather stark contrast with those he made of colonized India: "In the case of India, Marx observes that destruction and progress go hand-in-hand; this explains his ambivalent appreciation of England's 'double mission'. The example of Ireland, in contrast, shows him that colonialism ultimately brings the colonies asymmetrical integration into the world market, while actually throwing up barriers before the establishment of a capitalist mode of production, rather than promoting it" (2010, p.12).

There is an evolution in Marx's thought, which bears rather directly on his attitude towards imperialism/colonialism. As Anderson has perceptively elucidated in his earlier writings, Marx "exhibited more of a sense of capitalism's progressiveness vis à vis earlier social forms, whether this concerned Western feudalism or non-Western societies. By the late 1850s and early 1860s, however, Marx's perspectives on non-Western societies began to evolve. This was true of India, where he attacked British colonialism far more sharply during the 1857 Sepoy Uprising than in his 1853 writings on that country … It was also true of Russia, where by 1858 he began to consider the possibility of peasant-based upheaval in a society he had previously viewed as utterly conservative from top to bottom" (2010, pp.162-163).

The substantial differences between the first edition of Volume I of *Capital*, published in 1867, and the French edition, published serially between 1872 and 1875, which have been highlighted both by Anderson (2010, pp.171-180) and by the Latin American liberation philosopher Enrique Dussel (2000, p.9), are also worth noting in this regard. For in the latter version, Marx explicitly distances himself from a unilinear evolutionary narrative about the succession of social formations and the emergence of industrial capitalism, and embraces instead a more multilinear approach.

Intimately related to this, there is considerable evidence that towards the end of his life, Marx had begun to contemplate the possibility that there could be multiple paths towards socialism, indeed, that in some circumstances, it might be possible to arrive at socialism without having to make the painful transition to industrial capitalism first. To this end, Anderson and Dussel have both emphasized that, "[i]n his correspondence with the Russian exile Vera Zasulich and elsewhere, Marx began to suggest that agrarian Russia's communal villages could be a starting point for a socialist transformation, one that might avoid the brutal process of the primitive accumulation of capital" (Anderson 2010, p.196; see also Dussel 2000, p.9). The consequences for his earlier ambivalence towards colonialism would seem clear – the notion of "dialectical necessity" need no longer be countenanced, much less maintained.

And yet, the considerable shifts in Marx's thought, his increasing scepticism towards the progressive features of capitalist modernity, and, correspondingly, his increasing appreciation of the virtues of a more multilinear evolutionary narrative. This culminated in Marx's correspondence late in life with Vera Zasulich, which would remain much less well known, much less influential, than the more mechanistic, developmentalist, and teleological line of argument that he and Engels had sketched in their early work, most emblematically, in the 1848 *Communist Manifesto*. And so, the ambivalent chord that they struck towards colonialism would become an important part of the inheritance of the Marxist tradition, destined to be "fought out in the extended discussions of the Second International and left unresolved" (Young 2016, p.110).

It would be left unto Lenin to "inaugurate a major shift of emphasis" (Young 2016, p.110), to unequivocally condemn the course of imperialist aggression, and to decisively embrace the revolutionary repercussions of anti-colonial revolt.

In his critically acclaimed and highly influential 1979 post-colonial classic, *Orientalism*, Edward Said levels perhaps the most famous critique of Marx for his Eurocentrism. Said accuses Marx of being guilty of the sin of orientalism, in particular in Marx's 1853 analyses of British rule in India, where Marx advances "the idea that even in destroying Asia, Britain was making possible there a real social revolution," that, indeed, the brutality of the violent transformations wrought by the British were, albeit repugnant, at the same time the expression of "historical necessity" (1979, p.153).

Said hones in on Marx's quotation of a famous passage from Goethe's *West-Eastern Divan*, in which the renowned German poet writes: "Should this torture then torment us / Since it brings us greater pleasure? / Were not through the rule of Timur / Souls devoured without measure?" (1979, p.154). According to Said, Marx's recourse to Goethe is most revealing. It allegedly allows us to identify the "sources of Marx's conceptions about the Orient," to locate them in a "Romantic redemptive project," more specifically, in "the idea of regenerating a fundamentally lifeless Asia" (1979, p.154). Said here goes on to equate Marx with so many other Orientalists and "early-nineteenth century thinkers," who tended to "conceive of humanity in abstract generalities," who were "neither interested nor capable of discussing individuals," and for whom, "between Orient and Occident, as if in a self-fulfilling proclamation, only the vast anonymous collectivity mattered, or existed" (1979, pp.154-155).

The fact that Marx seemed able to express some sympathy for those who suffered so much at the hands of the British, the fact that he could "identify even a little with poor Asia," Said contends, "suggests that something happened before the labels took over, before he was dispatched to Goethe as his source of wisdom on the Orient" (1979, p.155). Even so, Said concludes, "the very vocabulary [Marx] found himself forced to employ" worked "to stop and chase away the sympathy," and his "sentiment therefore disappeared as it encountered the unshakeable definitions built up by Orientalist science, supported by 'Oriental' lore (e.g. the *Diwan*) supposed to be appropriate for it" (1979, p.155). Accordingly, "what finally occurs is that something forces [Marx] to scurry back to Goethe, there to stand in his protective Orientalized Orient" (1979, p.155).

Kevin Anderson has addressed Said's charge at some length in a section titled "Marx, Goethe, and Edward Said's Critique of Eurocentrism," in his authoritative book, *Marx at the Margins. On Nationalism, Ethnicity, and Non-Western Societies*, in which he offers at least a partial defence of Marx against Said's accusation. Anderson begins by conceding that Said is certainly "correct in pointing to elements of Eurocentrism in Marx's 'The British Rule in India'". Nevertheless, he objects, Said "is surely mistaken … when he has Marx relying on a poet, even one as brilliant as Goethe, as his 'source of wisdom on the Orient'" (2010, p.17).

Anderson expresses surprise at Said's failure to mention "the nineteenth-century context of the stanza from Goethe" in question – specifically, the link to Napoleon and the French Revolution. And he goes on to excavate a variety of different occasions on which Marx would make reference to the same stanza, but with respect to a context very different to that of India – namely, "the dehumanization of the industrial worker". That in relation to this latter context, Marx cannot plausibly be seen to agree with the sentiments expressed in the lines of Goethe's stanza, leads Anderson to wonder whether, in the former, Marx might not have also used it "to characterize the British colonialist perspective rather than his own" (2010, p.18)?

To this end, Anderson mentions the German critical theorist Irving Fletscher, who makes a similar point in relation to a passage from Marx's 1861-1863 economic manuscripts where Marx again makes reference to Goethe's stanza, again with respect to the brutal plight of English workers. Anderson goes on to insist, with Fletscher, that, "[o]bviously, there is nothing specifically Orientalist at work … in Marx's discussion of English workers, in which he does not mention any society outside capitalist England" (2010, p.19).

From all this, Anderson concludes, against Said, that Marx's use of Goethe's stanza on Timur in his 1853 article "On the British Rule in India" in no way implies a lack of sympathy for humans suffering from the brutal destruction of British colonialism. Anderson nevertheless admits that none of this "invalidate[s] Said's more generalized attack on Marx's uncritically modernist perspective of 1853, with its evocation of the ultimate progressiveness of British imperialism in India," though he is quick to add that Marx later came to revise such an uncritical modernist perspective.

Anderson further cites the "spirited response" to Said's attack on Marx penned by Aijaz Ahmad in his polemical 1992 book, *In Theory: Classes, Nations, Literature* – a book in which Ahmad excoriates Said's brand of "postmodern postcolonialism" for ignoring "issues like caste oppression and the needed 'transformation … within Asian societies' that Marx and progressive Indians have long supported" (2010, p.20).

Ahmad's rejoinder to Said is certainly a "spirited" one, to say the least. Nevertheless, like Kevin Anderson after him, Ahmad concedes "that the writings of Marx and Engels are indeed contaminated in several places with the usual banalities of nineteenth-century Eurocentrism, and the general prognosis they offered about the social stagnation of our societies was often based on unexamined staples of conventional European histories" (p.229). Indeed, more specifically, Ahmad enumerates a host of inaccuracies to be found in Marx's judgment and account. Among these, the fact that "it is obviously true that colonialism did not bring us a revolution," as Marx seemed to suggest it would. "Likewise," Ahmad continues, "it is doubtless true that the image of Asia as an unchanging, 'vegetative' place was part of the inherited world-view in nineteenth-century Europe, and had been hallowed by such figures of the Enlightenment as Hobbes and Montesquieu". So too, Ahmad adds, "though Said does not say so," it is the case "that the image of the so-called self-sufficient Indian village community that we find in Marx was lifted, almost verbatim, out of Hegel. All of this," Ahmad reminds the reader, "had been reiterated for the left, yet again, by Perry Anderson, in his *Lineages of the Absolutist State*, which had circulated widely while *Orientalism* was being drafted". As such, Ahmad concludes, what was original about Said's critique "was not that he pointed towards these facts … but that he fashioned a rhetoric of dismissal" (1992, p.224).

A rhetoric of dismissal, grounded in a convenient use of a couple of quotations of "journalistic flourishes" from two of Marx's dispatches on India for the *New York Daily Tribune* from 1853 – predictable enough, Ahmad contends, though "there is no evidence in *Orientalism* that [Said] has come to regard [these] as representative passage[s] after some considerable engagement with Marx's many and highly complex writings on colonialism as such and on the encounter between non-capitalist and capitalist societies" (1992, p.222). This "combined in very curious ways with indifference to – possibly ignorance of – how the complex issues raised by Marx's cryptic writings on India have actually been seen in the research of key Indian historians" (1992, p.222).

Be that as it may, Said's critique, though perhaps the most famous, is far from the only influential critique of Marx for his alleged Eurocentrism that has emerged from post-colonial quarters. In the widely-touted book, *Provincializing Europe*, Dipesh Chakrabarty seeks to explore "the tension between the European roots of Marx's thoughts and their global significance" (2007, p.xi). In so doing, he advances the accusation that Marx's conception of time is Eurocentric, or at the very least that "Marxist" historical narratives tend to display a "historicist" bias. Such narratives, he argues, "turn around the theme of historical transition" (2007, p.31), and would appear to consign the third world to an "idea of history as a waiting room, a period which is needed for the transition to capitalism at any particular time and place" (2007, p.65). Chakrabarty attempts an alternative reading of Marx's category of abstract labour – an interpretation blended with Heideggerian motifs, that is intended to be less hostile to difference, and less inflected with "developmental and stadial" (2007, p.xv) "historicist" presuppositions.

In the preface to the 2007 re-edition of his book, Chakrabarty recounts how the question that he addresses in the book first began to gestate. He re-calls how, the more he "tried to imagine relations in Indian factories through categories made available by Marx and his followers," the more he "became aware of a tension that arose from the profoundly—and one might say, parochially—European origins of Marx's thoughts and their undoubted international significance". He goes on to contend: "To call historical characters whose analogues I knew in everyday life as familiar types by names or categories derived from revolutions in Europe in 1789 or 1848 or 1871 or 1917 felt increasingly like a doubly distancing activity" (2007, p.x). At the same time, Chakrabarty expresses a sense of dissatisfaction he came increasingly to feel with the 1970s Marxist milieu in Calcutta with which he was familiar, since there seemed to be, among them, "no room for thinking about Marx as someone belonging to certain European traditions of thought that he may have even shared with intellectuals who were not Marxists or who thought in a manner opposed to his" (2007, xi).

The main such European tradition of thought to which Marx is alleged to belong and upon which Chakrabarty seizes as the principal target of his critique is what he refers to as "historicism". According to Chakrabarty, "[h]istoricism enabled European domination of the world in the nineteenth century". He characterizes this "-ism" as "one important form that the ideology of progress or 'development' took from the nineteenth century on". He further contends, it "is what made modernity or capitalism look not simply global but rather as something that became global over time, by originating in one place (Europe) and then spreading outside it". It was, in other words, a "structure of global historical time," conceived as "first in Europe, then elsewhere". Such a conception, he insists, was what allowed Marx, in the preface to the first edition to Volume 1 of *Capital*, to declare that the "country that is more developed industrially only shows, to the less developed, the image of its own future". It correspondingly "posited historical time as a measure of the cultural distance (at least in institutional development) that was assumed to exist between the West and the non-West" and "legitimated the idea of civilization," while rendering "possible completely internalist histories of Europe in which Europe was described as the site of the first occurrence of capitalism, modernity, or Enlightenment". Historical movement thereby took place inside of Europe, while "inhabitants of the colonies ... were assigned a place 'elsewhere' in the 'first in Europe and then elsewhere' structure of time". It led, in sum, "to what Johannes Fabian has called 'the denial of coevalness'" (2007, pp.7-8).

Chakrabarty is careful to address and judge as ultimately inadequate for overcoming the basic problems associated with "historicism" an array of "sophisticated strategies" employed by Marxist intellectuals "that allow them to acknowledge the evidence of "incompleteness" of capitalist transformation in Europe and other places while retaining the idea of a general historical movement from a premodern stage to that of modernity". These strategies go beyond "the old and now discredited evolutionist paradigms of the nineteenth century — the language of 'survivals' and 'remnants' — sometimes found in Marx's own prose," but are all basically "variations on the theme of 'uneven development'," picked up from Marx's use of the concept in his 1859 *Critique of Political Economy*, and from subsequent elaborations by Lenin and Trotsky. Chakrabarty singles out both Ernst Bloch's notion of the "synchronicity of the non-synchronous" and Althusser's reference to "structural causality" as two such instantiations of these strategies, accusing them of "retain[ing] elements of historicism in the direction of their thought (in spite of Althusser's explicit opposition to historicism)," enabling them "to identify certain elements in the present as 'anachronistic'" (2007, pp.11-12).

For Chakrabarty, at the core of "historicism" lies a fetishization of "the universal" at the expense of "the local". Accordingly, Chakrabarty argues that the excessive valorization of the universalizing aspects of capitalism by Marxists leads them to be hostile to local differences. More specifically, he contends that "[c]ommon to their thinking is the idea that any sense of the 'local' is a surface phenomenon of social life; it is, in the ultimate analysis, some kind of an effect of capital," and he therefore stresses how Marxists "emphasize the need to understand how one's sense of the local is actually produced". Yet, he continues, "these critics usually do not ask of themselves any questions about the place from where their own thinking comes. They presumably produce their criticisms from 'nowhere' or — what is the same thing — the 'everywhere' of a capitalism that always seems to be global in scope". In so doing, they tend to "evacuate all lived sense of place by assigning it to what is assumed to be a deeper and a more determining level, the level at which the capitalist mode of production creates abstract space", and thereby fail to do justice to "the heterotemporal horizons of innumerable … singular and unique histories" (2007, pp.xvi-xvii).

In his extended polemic against postcolonial theory and in defence of what he fashions to be a rather orthodox version of Marxism, in *Postcolonial Theory and the Specter of Capital*, Vivek Chibber responds to Chakrabarty, addressing his charge of "historicism" at some length. He begins by complaining that "Chakrabarty not only fails to provide the reader with a clear understanding of historicism, but … seems quite committed to preserving the concept's opacity" (2013, p.18). Chibber goes on to dedicate an entire chapter to what he refers to as "the (non)problem of historicism". In the chapter, he is at pains to demonstrate, *pace* Chakrabarty, that "[t]heories committed to the reality of capital's universalization do not … have to be blind to historical diversity" (2013, p.243). In the discussion, he emphasizes two main points – the first, "that capitalism is not only compatible with social difference, but systematically produces it"; the second, "that, insofar as a great deal of what we take to be social difference is in fact causally related to capitalist reproduction, it follows that the analysis of that diversity must, of necessity, draw on the universalizing categories of post-Enlightenment theories" (2013, p.243).

Slavoj Zizek, too, has taken aim at Chakrabarty's critique of the alleged parochiality of the universal. In one of his more incisive recent contributions, *Living in the End Times*, the perhaps too ubiquitous Slovenian psycho-analytic Marxist would pose a version of Chakrabarty's question – "Does the universal dimension to which we refer really exist?," only to turn this question around, and ask instead, "But what if it is our particular identity which does not exist, that is, which is always already traversed by universalities, caught up in them?" Along the same lines, he would continue: "What if, in today's global civilization, we are more universal than we think, and it is our particular identity which is a fragile ideological fantasy?" This before insisting that, "by taking particular lifeworld identities as his starting point, Chakrabarty ignores how universality manifests itself through the gaps, failures, and antagonisms at the heart of those very identities …" (2010, pp.285-286).

Furthermore, in a line of argument similar to the one advanced by Ahmad in response to Said, Zizek presses ahead by countering "[t]he standard complaint about how global capitalism corrodes and destroys particular lifeworlds". He instead insists, against the particular and in defence of the universal, "that such lifeworlds are invariably based on some form of domination and oppression, that to a greater or lesser extent they conceal hidden antagonisms, and that any emerging emancipatory universality therein is the universality of those who have no 'proper place' within their particular world, a universality that forms the lateral link between the excluded in each lifeworld" (2010, p.286).

The sometimes, perhaps too often, vituperative debate between postcolonial theorists and Marxists over the question of Marx's alleged Eurocentrism thus continues relatively unabated nearly four decades on, despite pleas by the likes of Rahul Rao to seek "reparative possibilities immanent within the theoretical formations being criticized" (2017, p.555). In the meantime, a new self-fashioned paradigm or tradition, that of "decoloniality," has emerged, which has re-articulated many similar critiques of Marx and Marxism. Paradoxically enough, like its postcolonial predecessor, this new decolonial paradigm is again centred in the US academy, albeit with more of a Latin American rather than South Asian, diasporic frame of reference.

According to Walter Mignolo, for example, Marxism is best conceived as but "an outgrowth of Western civilization". For East and Southeast Asian Marxists, this means they must "deal with a system of ideas that came from afar". They are forced to balance this foreign system with "local histories, languages, and systems of sacred and moral belief that conform to their subjectivities". Though, he contends, "[i]t is always possible to suppress or repress feelings and to replace them with conceptual structures," such suppression/

repression is not necessary. To the contrary, he suggests, "it may be painful to be forced to inhabit memories that are not the ones inscribed in your body (the so-called colonial wound) since birth" (2011, p.51).

As an outgrowth and internal critique of the West, Mignolo insists, Marxism shares many of the same presuppositions and prejudices of its erstwhile adversaries. Invoking Alonso Quijano, he argues that Marxism remains within the so-called "colonial matrix of power" (Mignolo and Walsh 2018, p.222). Consequently, "in the disputes between (neo)liberalism and (neo) Marxism, both sides of the coin belong to the same bank: the disputes are entrenched within the same rules of the game, where the contenders defend different positions but do not question the terms of the conversation" (2011, p.92). Mignolo goes on to urge "a shift in the geo- and body-politics of knowledge that focuses on changing the rules of the game rather than its content". He intends this shift to entail a definitive displacement of Descartes' famous "I think, therefore I am," with the alternative, "I am where I do and think" (2011, p.92).

This emphasis on place, on the particular provenance from which thought emerges, is certainly reminiscent of Chakrabarty's concerns. As Ramón Grosfoguel has articulated the decolonial complaint against Marxism, "Marxists … still tend to produce knowledge from the zero-point, that is, without questioning the place from which they speak and produce this knowledge" (2012, p.89). Likewise, linked to this preoccupation with the particular place from which a system of thought is originally enunciated, is the suggestion that the problems and methods central to Marxism are perhaps appropriate for the "First World," but not the "Third". As such, to transpose these problems and methods from the "First World" to the "Third" is to commit an act of epistemic violence. Mignolo provocatively puts the point thus: "in the Third World the problems are not the same as in the First, and therefore to transplant both the problems and methods from the First to the Third World is no less a colonial operation than transplanting armies or factories to satisfy the needs of the First World" (2011, p.129).

Grosfoguel has condensed and articulated a rather robust decolonial critique along such lines. He begins by arguing that "[w]hat Marx maintains in common with the Western Bourgeois philosophical tradition is that his universalism, despite having emerged from a particular location—in this case, the proletariat—does not problematize the fact that this subject is European, masculine, heterosexual, white, Judeo-Christian, etc". Built into this articulation is thus an emphasis on what feminist theory has labelled "intersectionality". Marx's lack of intersectional reflexivity is, in Grosfoguel's judgment, intimately linked to his Eurocentrism. He contends: "Marx's proletariat is a conflictive subject internal to Europe, which does not allow him to think outside the Eurocentric limits of Western thought". Grosfoguel goes further still, openly accusing Marx's "epistemic universalism" of "epistemic racism," too. "Just like the Western thinkers that preceded him," Grosfoguel insists, "Marx participates in the epistemic racism in which there only exists a single epistemology with access to universality: the Western tradition". In Marx, he concludes, "the subject of enunciation remains concealed, camouflaged, hidden beneath a new abstract universal that is no longer 'man', 'the transcendental subject', 'the ego', but instead 'the proletariat' and its universal political project, 'communism'".

Grosfoguel further elaborates on the charge of "epistemic racism" by advancing an argument again reminiscent of Chakrabarty's critique of Marx's "historicism". He thus writes: "Marx reproduces an epistemic racism much like that of Hegel, which does not allow him to grant to non-European peoples and societies either temporal coevalness or the capacity to produce thought worthy of being considered part of the philosophical legacy of humanity or world history. For Marx," he continues, "non-European peoples and societies were primitive, backwards, that is, Europe's past". Indeed, he contends, "Marx participated in the linearity of time characteristic of Western evolutionist thought," and "this economistic evolutionism would lead 20th-century Marxists down a blind alley". As such, he concludes, "Marxist thought, despite being from the left, ended up trapped in the same problems of Eurocentrism and colonialism that had imprisoned Eurocentered thinkers of the right" (2012, pp.93-94).

In the process, Grosfoguel adds to the list of Marx's colonialist credentials not only his supposed support for the British conquest of India, making no mention even of Marx's oft-noted ambivalence in this regard; but he also accuses Marx of having supported the invasion by the United States of Mexico. There is of course some substance to this latter accusation, since Engels did write in 1848 that he "rejoiced" at the US conquest of Mexico, believing it to be "an advance when a country which has hitherto been exclusively wrapped up in its own affairs, perpetually rent with civil wars, and completely hindered in its development, a country whose best prospect had been to become in-dustrially subject to Britain – when such a country is forcibly drawn into the historical process" (*Workers' Vanguard* 2013). Even so, Grosfoguel leaves the reader with little sense of the ambiguities, much less the subsequent shifts, in Marx's and Engels' position(s).

There is, however, some tension in the decolonial account and prescription. On the one hand, decolonial thinkers argue for a strategy of "delinking" from Eurocentric theoretical inspirations such as those found in the Marxist tra-dition; but on the other, they revindicate figures such as Fanon and Césaire, who situated themselves within that tradition. Fanon famously argued, in *The Wretched of the Earth*, that "Marxist analysis should always be slightly stretched every time we have to do with the colonial problem," adding that "[e]verything up to and including the very nature of pre-capitalist society, so well explained by Marx, must here be thought out again" (1963, p.40). But to stretch Marxism is a different prescription from "delinking," or breaking away from it.

Likewise, when it comes to the revindication of the universal versus the "pluriversal" or particular, Césaire's formulation is most instructive. Césaire argues for a third way of sorts, against both "narrow particularism" and "dis-embodied universalism," in favour of embracing a truer, more concretely-sit-uated, less abstract and less Eurocentric universalism. In his words: "I'm not going to confine myself to some narrow particularism. But I don't intend ei-ther to become lost in a disembodied universalism ... I have a different idea of a universal. It is a universal rich with all that is particular, rich with all the particulars there are, the deepening of each particular, the coexistence of them all" (in Kelley 2000, pp.25-26). Tellingly, in an exchange with René Depestre that would take place a decade after his resignation from the French Com-munist party, significantly, at the 1967 Cultural Congress in Havana, Césaire would emphasize: "Marx is all right, but we need to complete Marx ..." (De-pestre 2000, pp.85-86).

Which brings us back to the thought of Esteban Torres, with which we began this chapter. Whereas the decolonial thinkers argue, perhaps somewhat disingenuously, for a thorough "delinking" from the Marxist tradition, Torres calls for an approach more consistent with the articulations of the likes of Fanon and Césaire, and other heterodox figures thinking *from* and *for* the global south, but from within the Marxist tradition. Torres calls not for "delinking" altogether, but for combining *autonomismo* with *mundialismo*.

Decolonial thinkers are concerned to reject logics of diffusion, imitation, and mimicry. But what is at work in such figures as Fanon and Césaire, and other heterodox Marxists thinking *from* and *for* particular locations within the global south, is perhaps more accurately portrayed as translation, reinvention, and reappropriation. Adom Getachew's book on *Worldmaking after Empire: The Rise and Fall of Self-Determination* is quite illuminating in this regard. In it, she takes up David Scott's notion of a "problem space" as a useful "conceptual tool for conceiving of the way in which political thought and practice are responses to specific, historically situated questions" (2019, p.77). The "tool" of the "problem space" allows us to "rethink the politics of appropriation as a creative intervention, responding to specific political questions and conditions" (2019, p.77), in a manner more subtle and receptive to agency than such notions as diffusion, imitation, or mimicry would suggest.

Torres's call for a combination of *autonomismo* with *mundialismo* likewise resonates with Gary Wilder's critique of Chakrabarty and his followers, in his book *Freedom Time: Negritude, Decolonization, and the Future of the World*. Though Wilder acknowledges that "[u]nderstandable fears of totalizing explanation and Eurocentric evaluation have led a generation of scholars to insist on the singularity of black, African, and non-Western forms of thought," he nevertheless goes on to contend that "we now need to be less concerned with unmasking universalisms as covert European particularisms than with challenging the assumption that the universal is European property" (pp.9-10).

The debate over Marx, Marxism and Eurocentrism is unlikely to abate anytime soon. Among the virtues of Torres' articulation of the problem is his ability to sketch a position which points in a decidedly "reparative" (Rao 2017) direction. Moreover, to all sides engaged in this often rancorous debate, that nevertheless tends towards a version of radical scholasticism, Torres reminds us of the still urgent imperative entailed in Marx's eleventh thesis on Feuerbach, that the point is not merely to understand the world, but to change it. Let us hope that the dialogue initiated by his book can help generate momentum in such a direction, at both the theoretical and the praxiological levels.

NOTES

1 Translations from the original Spanish are the author's.

REFERENCES

Ahmad, A. (1992). *In Theory. Classes, Nations, Literatures* (London: Verso).

Anderson, K. (2010). *Marx at the Margins. On Nationalism, Ethnicity, and Non-Western Societies* (The University of Chicago Press).

Chakrabarty, D. (2007). *Provincializing Europe. Postcolonial Thought and Historical Difference* (Princeton, NJ: Princeton University Press).

Chibber, V. (2013). *Postcolonial Theory and the Specter of Capital* (London: Verso).

Depestre, R. (2000). "An Interview with Aimé Césaire," in A. Césaire, *Discourse on Colonialism* (New York, NY: Monthly Review Press), pp.79-94.

Dussel, E. (2000). "The Four Drafts of *Capital*. Towards a New Interpretation of the Dialectical Thought of Marx," https://www.mtholyoke.edu/~fmoseley/Dussel.pdf

Fanon, F. (1963). *The Wretched of the Earth* (New York, NY: Grove Press).

Getachew, A. (2019). *Worldmaking after Empire. The Rise and Fall of Self-Determination* (Princeton, NJ: Princeton University Press, 2019).

Grosfoguel, R. (2012). "Decolonizing Western Uni-versalisms. Decolonial Pluriversalism from Aimé Césaire to the Zapatistas," *Transmodernity*, pp.88-102.

Hassan, S. (2012). "How to Liberate Marx from his Eurocentrism: Notes on African/ Black Marxism," *100 Notes – 100 Thoughts*, No. 91, pp.3-8.

Kelley, R. (2000). "A Poetics of Anticolonialism". Introduction to A. Césaire, *Discourse on Colonialism* (New York, NY: Monthly Review Press), pp.7-28.

Lindner, K. (2010). "Marx's Eurocentrism. Postcolonial Studies and Marx Scholarship," *Radical Philosophy*, Vol. 161, pp.27-41.

Marx, K. (1853/2005). "The British Rule in India," https://www.marxists.org/archive/marx/works/1853/06/25.htm

Marx, K. (1867/2015). *Capital. Volume One.* https://www.marxists.org/archive/marx/works/download/pdf/Capital-Volume-I.pdf

Mignolo, W. (2011). *The Darker Side of Modernity. Global Futures, Decolonial Options* (Durham, NC: Duke University Press).

Mignolo, W. and Walsh, C. eds. (2018). *On Decoloniality: Concepts, Analytics, Praxis* (Durham, NC: Duke University Press).

Parry, B. (2011). "Liberation Theory: Variations on Themes of Marxism and Modernity," in C. Bartolovitch and N. Lazarus, *Marxism, Modernity and Postcolonial Studies* (Cambridge University Press), pp.125-149.

Rao, R. (2017). "Recovering Reparative Readings of Postcolonialism and Marxism," *Critical Sociology*, Vol. 43, No. 4-5, pp.587-598.

Robinson, R. (2019). "Decolonization, Decoloniality, Marxism," Marxism, Coloniality, "Man", & Euromodern Science – Maehk n Ahp htesewen (wordpress.com)

Said, E. (1979). *Orientalism* (New York: Vintage Books).

Salem, S. (2019). "'Stretching' Marxism in the Postcolonial World. Egyptian Decolonization and the Contradictions of National Sovereignty," *Historical Materialism*, Vol. 27, No. 4, pp.3-28.

Torres, E. (2021). *La gran transformación de la sociología* (1a ed. Córdoba: Universidad Nacional de Córdoba, Facultad de Ciencias Sociales; Buenos Aires: CLACSO).

Wilder, G. (2015). *Freedom Time. Negritude, Decolonization, and the Future of the World* (Duke University Press).

Workers' Vanguard. (2013). "Reply to Letter on Marx, Maximilian, and Mexico," *WV*, No. 1015, 11 January. https://www.icl-fi.org/english/wv/1015/let-mexico.html

Young, R. (2016). *Postcolonialism. An Historical Introduction* (Wiley Blackwell).

Zizek, S. (2010). *Living in the End Times* (London: Verso).

CHAPTER 12

"Double Consciousness" among Moroccan Migrants in the Metropolitan Region of Barcelona

Co-authored with Dr. Djaouida Moualhi

Abstract: *This chapter foregrounds the perspectives of Moroccan migrants in the Metropolitan Region of Barcelona. It is based on a set of focus group discussions conducted with Moroccan migrants in the municipalities of Badalona and Hospitalet de Llobregat, in the Spring of 2013. The focus group discussions related to the subject of "integration," and brought to light lived experiences with and reactions to systemic discrimination, offset in part by material opportunities. The chapter documents these experiences and reactions, interpreting them through the lens of W.E.B. Dubois' concept of "double consciousness". It emphasises the ambivalence produced by the simultaneous recognition of the existence of concrete material advantages associated with life in Catalan society, contrasted with grievances generated by so many racist, xenophobic, and Islamophobic everyday encounters. It highlights the salience and affective responses triggered among Moroccan migrant women by mention of controversies surrounding the practice of veiling. It concludes with reflections about the appeal of the ideal of the Umma, the community of believers, among postcolonial subjects in the former European metropoles, as a response to the experience of systemic discrimination on racialized and religious grounds, especially in contexts in which "integrationist" narratives about "the land of opportunity" begin to ring hollow.*

Introduction

Across Europe, resurgent right-wing populist forces have managed to successfully frame migration as a problem, and have targeted migrant communities, especially Muslim migrants (Brubaker 2017; Mudde 2016; Katsambekis 2017). To understand the ideological efficacy of such framing and targeting, the legacy of colonial histories, and of neo-colonial realities, needs to be taken into account (Gilroy 2005a; Bhambra 2007). These festering histories, these unacknowledged realities, condition the content and contours of dominant social imaginaries; they contaminate the collective consciousness; they corrupt the terms and constrict the horizons of public debate.

An important task for critical social science, perhaps particularly at this most troublesome conjuncture, is to counter and contest the omissions, the distortions, the lies and propaganda, that proliferate in mainstream discourse and debate (Burawoy 2005). It is indeed urgent to cultivate the ability to empathize with the plight of the oppressed, of the excluded, of those at the margins; and more than this, to learn to look at the social world from their perspectives, through their eyes (Strega and Brown 2015).

This chapter is intended as a modest contribution along such lines. It foregrounds the experiences and perspectives of Moroccan migrants in the Metropolitan Region of Barcelona, in Catalonia, Spain. It is based on a set of focus group discussions that were conducted with Moroccan migrants in the spring of 2013 in the municipalities of Badalona and Hospitalet de Llobregat, contexts which have witnessed varying degrees of anti-immigrant mobilization (Astor 2017; Hernández-Carr 2011; Moreras 2008). The focus group discussions were centred around a series of themes related to the subject of "integration," and they brought to light a whole host of lived experiences with and reactions to systemic discrimination, offset in part by material opportunities. The article seeks to document these experiences and reactions, and to interpret them through the lens of W.E.B. Dubois' concept of "double consciousness" ([1903]2008). It emphasizes the ambivalence produced by the simultaneous recognition of the existence of concrete material advantages associated with life in Catalan society, on the one hand, contrasted with serious grievances generated by so many racist, xenophobic, and Islamophobic everyday encounters, on the other. It highlights in particular the special salience and affective responses triggered among Moroccan migrant women by mention of controversies surrounding the practice of veiling. And it concludes with some theoretical reflections about the appeal of the ideal of the *Umma*, the community of believers, among postcolonial subjects in the former European metropoles, as a response to the experience of systemic discrimination on racialized and religious grounds, especially in contexts in which "integrationist" narratives about "the land of opportunity" begin to ring ever more hollow.

The Coast is Clear

In Castilian Spanish, the translation for the phrase, "the coast is clear," is "*no hay moros en la costa*," which means, literally, that "there are no moors on the coast". According to Wikipedia, the term "moors" refers "primarily to the Muslim inhabitants of the Maghreb, the Iberian Peninsula, Sicily, and Malta during the Middle Ages". The on-line, open-sourced encyclopaedia adds that "[t]he moors initially were the indigenous Maghrebine Berbers," but that "[t]he name was later applied to Arabs" as well. It goes on, further, to note that "[t]he term has also been used in Europe in a broader, somewhat derogatory sense to refer to Muslims in general," but also mentions, in passing, that the term does not refer to "a distinct or self-defined people" (Wikipedia 2019a).

Those interested in etymology can find, via Wiktionary, that the phrase, "*no hay moros en la costa*," "comes from a time when the Moors, inhabitants of North Africa, used to invade from the sea and sack coastal villages in Spain" (2019). While those familiar with Shakespeare may recall that the subtitle for *The Tragedy of Othello*, is none other than *The Moor of Venice*.

Needless to say, the term is a loaded one, and one that Moroccan migrants in Spain, as well as people born in Spain who are of Moroccan descent, will almost certainly have come across, experienced as verbal violence, in the form of a hurled insult. As one Moroccan man complained, during one of the several focus groups dedicated to the subject of "integration" that were organized across the Metropolitan Region of Barcelona back in the spring of 2013: "[N]o matter how you are, even if you are married to one of them, go to their churches, eat pork, you remain, and you will always be, a '*moro*', even a '*moro de mierda'* ('shitty *moro*')." From which, he would conclude: "It is for that reason that I will never be integrated 100% in this society, nor will I ever feel like I am one of them".

Disparaging attitudes towards Moroccans are deeply ingrained in the Spanish, as well as Catalan, national imaginations (Dietz 2010; Greenough 2016; Dotson-Renta 2012; García Sánchez 2009; Zapata-Barrero 2005; Zapata-Barrero and DeWitte 2010). Indeed, the myth of the *Reconquista* has long been framed as foundational in the forging of Spanish identity, its unity initially constructed around commitment to a religious cause, that of Catholicism, "in the course of a centuries' long struggle against an enemy, an 'other', a foil. The virtues of the Spanish *reconquistadores* were long portrayed and imagined to stand out in relief against the projected vices of an Islamic foe" (Miley 2015, p.414; Rogozen-Soltar 2012, 2017). A foe frequently referred to simply as the "*moro*".

Layered over top of this deep historical legacy, in the nineteenth century, belief in Spain's "historic destiny in North Africa" came to occupy a significant space in the Spanish imagination, with nationalist repertoire replete with calls for a "new crusade against the infidel Moors" (Carr 1982, pp.517, 261). In this vein, the capture of Tetouan in 1860 "evoked a nation-wide apotheosis," in Carr's judgment, "a reflex action of a nation that felt itself growing in prosperity and ripe for colonial responsibility," the Moroccan war's popularity in Catalonia "proof that national patriotism could still subsume regional loyalties" (1982, p.261).

Though subsequent colonial incursions would prove significantly more complicated and controversial, the ideological efficacy of appeals to anti-"*moro*" sentiment would, and still does, remain. So much so that hostility to the "*moro*" can be considered a constitutive feature of the Spanish imagination, symbolic violence perpetrated against those labelled as such is structural, ubiquitous, nearly impossible to avoid (Flesler 2008; Gillespie 1996; Pérez Yruela and Desrues 2007, p.21; Savelkoul et. al. 2012). As is Islamophobia more generally (Cebolla Boada and González Ferrer 2008, p.263; Goytisolo and Naïr 2000). A feature further exacerbated in the context of the ongoing Orwellian "war on terror" (Fekete 2004; Karlsen and Nazroo 2013; Pérez Yruela and Desrues 2008; White 2007). Thus the dialectic of distancing described by the Moroccan informant from the focus group, a dialectic recognizable to anyone familiar with group relations in contexts of structured oppression. The hostility of the Spaniard, or Catalan, can, and often does, breed a sense of alienation among those targeted – "I will never be integrated 100% in this society, nor will I ever feel like I am one of them." Boundaries between "us" and "them" are reified, reproduced and constantly guarded by acts of verbal violence such as *"moro de mierda".*

Some studies have documented a relatively low level of more objective indicators of "socio-cultural integration" among Moroccan migrants and their offspring in Spain, as well as in other countries in Europe (e.g. Cebolla and Requena 2010), though others have contested such claims (Aparicio 2007; Fokkema and de Haas 2011). Our focus here, however, is on the sense of subjective experiences, on perceptions of grievance and alienation, which are relatively autonomous, though not independent from, other more objective indicators of "acculturation" and/or "integration".

One of the more interesting facts about that proud Moroccan informant, which emerged in the course of the focus group, was that he was married to a Spanish woman. This fact, however, did not lead him to temper his judgment about the prejudices harboured by Spaniards against Moroccans. To the contrary, he maintained, it only served to provide him with an epistemic privilege of sorts – in his words, "I know how they think". He would argue, emphatically: "Spaniards don't want to be friends with us. They might work with us, but to be our friends they would first have to get rid of the ideas they have in their heads about us – 'moros de mierda'." To this, he would add: "They even call our king that. No matter what you have, money, education, you will always be the same to them. They always look down on us." Even worse, he would insist: "If, in the middle of the day, in the Plaza Catalunya, you stop to ask someone something, if they have something valuable in their hands, they will grab it real tight, because they think you are going to rob them." And to conclude, he would go on to claim: "They say we governed them for 800 years, they are afraid we will return. They hate us!"

Push and Pull

Such a defiant response to the experience of systemic discrimination is, of course, neither uniform nor even necessarily the most common. Personal experiences, networks, perceptions, psychological proclivities, and social context all vary (Kadianaki 2010; Lubbers et. al. 2007; Van Oudenhoven et. al. 2006; Zlobina and Paez 2018). Some would opt to deflect, downplay, even deny, the cultural-cum-racial dimension at work, attributing the experience of hostility to class position instead. This was the case with another of the male Moroccan informants, who interjected in response: "I have to say I don't fully agree with this man, because I believe we live in a materialist society that judges people based on money. If they need you they will be your friend, but if not, you will be marginalized." To which, he would add: "Let me give a real-life example. When people from Abu Dhabi, Qatar, or Saudi Arabia come here, those with money, Spaniards always suck up to them; but when someone comes from Morocco to work, the matter is very different." This before going on to insist: "Especially now with the economic crisis, rejection of the other is on the rise, because the people who live here think that you are taking their money, their food."

However unsatisfactory this kind of "class, not race" response might ultimately be, from an intersectional perspective, it does at least have the virtue of directing attention to dynamics of divide and conquer at work among workers, exacerbated under conditions of neoliberal austerity (Rinken and Escobar Villegas 2011; Moreno-Colom and De Alós 2015), an explanation which emphasises the situationally irrational character of such horizontally-directed aggression coming from one, racially-privileged faction of the working class, directed at another faction of the same class (Roemer 1979; Wolfenstein 1993). A dynamic very much encouraged by right-wing demagogues operating in the political sphere, whose views are propagated by important segments of the mass media (Desrues 2008; Martínez Zurita 2008), the ideological efficacy of which is nevertheless conditioned by a much longer tradition of recourse to racist tropes by the ruling class, for the purpose of legitimating policies of Imperial plunder, of manufacturing consent, of fending off the threat of working class unity, and thereby securing the reproduction of hierarchical and oppressive social-property relations (Balibar 2007; Gilroy 2005b).

Spain is a country with a relatively long history of very high levels of structural unemployment, and it witnessed as well a very high level of immigration throughout the 1990s and well into the 2000s, during which period the demography of the country was significantly transformed, from less than 1% to over 10% immigrant population (Arango and Finotelli 2009; Bardají Ruiz 2006; Cebolla Boado and González Ferrer 2008; Domínguez-Mujica et. al. 2014; Sperling 2013). Moroccans constitute the biggest "foreign" population resident in Spain – in 2017, they made up over 16% of the 4.5 million "foreigners" in the country, according to official Spanish statistics, which means close to three quarters of a million who are "seen by the state". Of these, just over 218,000 Moroccans with residency permits live in Catalonia (IDESCAT 2019). This despite the fact that, as recently as 1990, official statistics registered barely over 16,000 Moroccans residing in all of Spain. Between 1990 and 2010, there was thus a rapid influx of Moroccans into Spain (Arango and González Quiñones 2009; López García and Berriane 2004; Ostergaard-Nielsen 2009). Over the past decade, against the backdrop of the financial crisis, with resurgent unemployment, the influx has stopped, but the number of Moroccans residing in Spain has nevertheless remained more or less constant (González Enriquez 2019).

A so-called "pull factor" (Castles 2004; Portes and Böröcz 1989; Zimmerman 1996) has certainly been operative, since GDP per capita in Spain is approximately eleven times that of Morocco. Moroccans have come to Spain, and to Catalonia, first and foremost in search of employment opportunities, to work in agriculture, construction, hospitality, and in the service sector (Garreta Bochaca 2000; López García and Berriane 2004; White 2001; Wikipedia 2019b). Prominent among the arenas in which they experience racial, xenophobic and Islamophobic discrimination is in the labour market itself, as has been fairly well-documented (Solé and Parella 2003; Kalter and Kogan 2006; López García and García Ortiz 2006).

Inter-ethnic competition for relatively scarce employment opportunities in tight labour markets was a factor mentioned by some of the Moroccan participants themselves in our focus groups, in order to help explain the hostility that they had come up against in their time in Catalonia. Such perceptions accord with "ethnic competition theory" (Olzak 1992), and, more specifically, with findings in the literature on "ethnic exclusionism" towards migrants in Europe (Scheepers et. al. 2002). For example, in discussing their experiences with discrimination, one man stopped to make explicit reference to what he saw as a distinction between "Catalans" and those with Andalusian origins, insisting that the "Catalans are more inclusive". To which point, the moderator interjected, making the assumption that he was referring to the significant internal migrant population of Andalusians (and perhaps their descendants) who reside in Catalonia, to opine: "Because they are immigrants, too, like you." Which in turn prompted the man to conjecture: "Because we bother them in cleaning work, in construction work, because the majority of them have a low level of education like us."

Nor would the material comforts and opportunities associated with living in the context of a more advanced capitalist economy go unnoticed or unmentioned among the participants in our focus groups. As one Moroccan woman would put the point: "I can't deny that they've done me well in Catalonia. I have seen many good things, I have managed to eat, to drink, to live." Among the material comforts mentioned by our participants, the social rights and benefits linked to the welfare state – "they help with food, they help with children," the same woman went on to remark.

In a similar vein, another woman would comment: "I wish my country had even 10% of what Spain has. When you live here, you get used to a different standard of living than in Morocco, which makes it difficult to return." To which point, she would add the comparative facility of dealing with the state in Spain: "For example, just to get an administrative document in Morocco is a huge ordeal, unlike here."

Sticks and Stones May Break My Bones

Recognition of these material comforts, these benefits, available in Spain works to temper some of the indignation caused by the experience of systemic discrimination, resulting in a certain ambivalence, even double consciousness, of sorts. Such feelings of ambivalence, resulting from direct personal experience with racism and Islamophobia, among Moroccan migrants in Spain, and elsewhere in Europe, have been detected in other studies (e.g. Anneas et. al. 2011; Ennaji 2010; Fresno and Chahin 2011; Karlsen and Nazroo 2013; Narbona Reina 1992; Ouassini 2008; Veredas Muñoz 2011). The focus groups clearly confirm such findings. For example, one man, after listening to others complain about the everyday racism they had to put up with, intervened to say: "I was going to say that I feel moderately identified with this place, I was going to put a five out of ten, because the social assistance has helped me out a lot, and continues to. But when we talk about racism, that's the truth, it exists, and we all know it."

This man's intervention, in turn, led another participant to reply: "Listen, it's true, when I broke my hand, they helped me out quite a bit, they gave me

200 euros a month, they treated me well." And yet, he would go on to insist: "But I am not talking about that; I am talking about having to face insults like, '*moro, vete a tu tierra*' ('Moor, go back to your country')."

Yet another participant shrugged his shoulders and said, "I hear what you all are saying, but at the end of the day, so long as I have a good job and my boss treats me well, I will remain content here." This response seemed to anger the most defiant man among the participants, who suddenly interjected: "Excuse me for interrupting, but no! You say so long as your boss treats you well; well, I was the boss. I was working in a very big supermarket. I was the store manager. I was in charge of dealing with any problems, and yet, people would insult me constantly. They would say, 'I'm having a problem here, and on top of it all, they bring a *moro* to come and help!'" The man would add, nevertheless, that not all Spaniards acted in the same way, that, indeed, "others would try to console me, saying 'God help you, because people here are very rude'." Even so, he would conclude: "In the end, I quit the job, I couldn't take it anymore. Even my Spanish wife had to agree with me."

He would then go on to make a distinction between the material and the sentimental, so to speak, by insisting: "I'm not speaking about money, about the economy, but about my feelings. I have no economic complaints; I've always had a good job here." Leave that to one side – "I'm not talking about that." What is he talking about, then? "I am talking about everyday life, about how they treat you when they see you in the subway, on the street, about the envy they have." To which, he would add, emphatically: "I don't want to live with a person who doesn't respect me, when they see me with a woman on the street and they insult me with swear words."

The verbal aggressions elicited by the innocent act of walking down the street with a Spanish woman, with his Spanish wife, have left an intangible but still undeniable scar on this man. Nor was he alone in communicating considerable psychological pain inflicted by having to endure so many petty racist acts intended to denigrate, to humiliate. Another man chimed in, to share his experience of being repeatedly disrespected: "I was working, and I still work, with Spaniards, but they don't respect you," he began. He stopped, cleared his throat, and then continued: "You say, for example, 'Give me some water to drink', but they won't give it to you in a glass or a bottle, I swear. No, they give it to you in a tin can instead, and they warn you, 'Don't dare touch my cups.'" For emphasis, he would add: "And I can't count the times I've heard, 'Go back to your land! What are you doing here?'"

"Double Consciousness" in Action

And yet, gratitude for the opportunities and amenities available in Spanish society, and even a sense of shame about the behaviour and reputation of fellow Moroccans, were attitudes that were not uncommon among the focus group participants. Double consciousness did abound, indeed, even if traces of liberationist transcendence, of "acculturative integration" (García-Ramirez et. al. 2010), alongside incipient signs of an emergent "tactical ethnicity" (Colombo 2014, pp.32-34), could be detected as well.

The phenomenon of double consciousness was famously described by W.E.B. Dubois as the propensity to "look at oneself through the eyes" of a racist society, to "measure one's soul by the tape of a world that looks on in amused contempt and pity". It proves difficult to avoid internalising the racist gaze, to transcend the horizons of consciousness imposed upon us by the powers that be.

A conversation that occurred among three women in another focus group is most indicative in this regard. The exchange began with one woman remarking how much she appreciated the order and the cleanliness in Barcelona, which she compared favourably to Morocco. In her words: "I like the order here. It is very different from my country. I don't like speaking bad about my country, but the system is different. Here I have learned not to throw trash in the street, here I have learned to recycle paper in its place. I like this." Having made this point, she then continued by honing in on the issue of safety, beginning with the flow of traffic: "When it comes to crossing the street, I feel safe, not like in some countries where the rules of circulation are not respected." From here, she would move to make a more general point about her greater sense of security in Spain: "There is peace and tranquillity here in Spain. In Morocco, from the moment I arrive, from when I pass the police control at the border, I feel unsafe." This before concluding, with a full-fledged embrace of the paradigm of development and underdevelopment: "Morocco still has a long way to come, a long way to advance."

Nodding her head in agreement, a second woman intervened to add: "Here there are security cameras, there are police." To which point, the first woman would reply with little short of an homage to the police in Spain: "Exactly! Here you have nothing to be afraid of. If someone comes after you, you call the police and they arrive quickly. By contrast, there you have nobody to call. The police in Morocco won't come, even if you call them."

It is perhaps worth noting that Spain has the highest rate of imprisonment in the European Union, even higher than the United Kingdom, and that Moroccans are significantly over-represented among Spain's prison population (Morocco World News 2015). But such considerations were far from the minds of this woman, who instead continued: "Even though they don't like us and they would prefer for us to leave, they are better than us, their country is well-organized."

The claim that Spaniards want Moroccans to leave disturbed the second woman, who again interjected, this time to insist: "They don't want us to leave, no!" Which in turn caused the first woman to shake her head affirmatively and reply: "Yes, it's true, really, they want us to leave."

At this point, a third woman intervened, to agree that Spaniards do indeed want Moroccans to leave, and she would offer an explanation for why this is the case. In her words: "They want us to leave because we dirty everything, we are problematic." To which the first woman would again reply: "It's true, it's true." The second woman now assented, adding her own explanation: "Some of us have stained the atmosphere, with lies, fights, robbing, begging." And the first woman then concluded: "It's not their fault. We are the ones who have created the problems."

Such self-denigrating attitudes, however, were but part of a much more ambivalent repertoire, and certainly cannot be said to be a sign of "integration," at least not in any straightforward sense. Indeed, the very same first woman went on to admit that though she likes how Spaniards live, "I don't have any Spanish friends, I just watch them from afar." This before mentioning, as if in passing: "What I don't like is that they reject us. The majority of them laugh and they act nice to you, but deep down, they detest us."

The Veil as a Bone of Contention

Most tellingly, this note of ambivalence would give way to an openly confrontational attitude as soon as the subject of the veil was raised. There has been much written about the controversies over the practice of veiling, which have occurred across Europe, with scholars originally paying particular attention to the highly charged atmosphere in France, but more recently working to elaborate a broader comparative European perspective on the phenomenon (e.g. Bedmar and Cobano-Delgado Palma 2010; Joppke 2009; Mancini 2012; McCauley 2018; McGoldrick 2006; Scott 2007; Woodhead 2009). The salience of these controversies certainly serves to illustrate the aptness of Seyla Benhabib's claim that "women and their bodies are the symbolic and cultural place where human societies write their moral system" (2002, p.84, quoted in Mancini 2012, p.411).

Joan Scott has famously depicted the public debate in France as "a sustained polemic, a political discourse" which has "attempted to enact a particular version of reality, one which [has] insisted on assimilation as the only way for Muslims to become French" (2007, pp.7-8). For her part, Linda Woodhead has attributed the fierceness of European reactions to the practice of veiling to what she identifies as "the sacred value attributed to secularism and a narrative of secular progress" (2009, p.2). While Susana Mancini has deciphered in these controversies "a pattern of false projection," by which "majority cultures have projected on minorities some features of their own which they seek to hide from themselves" (2012, p.411).

But the impact of these controversies on the everyday lives of Muslim women in Europe has arguably received less consideration (Birge 2010; Pham 2014). When the focus group moderator asked what the women thought about controversies surrounding girls wearing hijabs or other Islamic veils in schools, this opened up a very robust discussion, in which the other side of the double consciousness came to the fore. The first arguments advanced had to do with freedom of expression, but these would soon be followed by more strident, religious claims, provided in response to one of the women in the group who disagreed with the rest.

The discussion began with one of the women asserting her right to dress how she pleases. In her words: "I dress how I like, whether it be with a veil or a mini-skirt, I dress how I please. If one day I want to wear a veil, I will not permit anybody to tell me how to dress. I don't think it is right for people to tell people how they should dress." Another joined in to emphasize that individual beliefs had to be respected as well. She began by insisting that "[e]veryone is free to dress how they please, it is an individual right," but then continued: "The veil has to do with individual beliefs, and nobody has a right to mess with people's beliefs."

At this point, however, a woman intervened to express a dissenting opinion. She would argue: "Spaniards who worry about the veil, you know what? They are right. You know why? Because we came to their country. We have to respect their rules."

This triggered a torrent of objections, with the woman who just a few minutes earlier had been the most vocal in expressing self-denigrating attitudes now turning to shout, "No! No!" And another, who had also been adamant in denouncing the behaviour of her fellow Moroccans in Spain, now raising her voice to exclaim, "Excuse me! Excuse me!"

The moderator stepped in to try to calm things down, by saying: "Let her express herself. Afterwards you can speak." The dissenter accepted the offer, and chose to continue: "Listen, you come to their land, and on top of that, you want to send your children to school with the hijab? Some even wear burkas! You have to respect the Spaniards. You can dress how you please, but you have to respect their rules. We owe them respect."

By now, the woman who had been so vocal before was visibly eager to be vocal again: "Let me respond," she requested, impatiently. "Let her finish," the moderator insisted. "She already has finished," she replied. But the dissenting woman had more to say. She now added: "When the Spaniards come to Morocco, they respect us, they don't go into our mosques."

This prompted another woman to interject: "But we don't tell them how to dress, we don't tell them they have to wear a tunic." While yet another would add: "Everyone has their religion. For example, if I go to your house, even as a guest, would you oblige me to eat something I don't like?"

"No," replied the dissenting woman. "Well, it's the same," said the other.

"No, it's not the same," declared the dissenter. "If you go to a country where everyone dresses a certain way, where they wear a certain uniform to school, what would you do? Would you wear a veil?"

"I would wear the uniform and a veil as well," answered the other.

At this point, the woman who had been so vocal before again got the chance to speak her mind. She began by saying, "Everyone has their own opinion," before turning to point out: "We also have Spaniards who live in Morocco, but we never tell them, 'you have to dress this way or that way.'" She then continued: "Above all else, we are talking about a modern veil. Not the burka. You can't wear the burka here." This before concluding: "But the hijab, yes, we will wear it, and our children will wear it, and we will not let them impede us from doing so, because our reference point is God, and we are Muslims."

Such stridence caused one of the women in the group to waiver: "But we have to live with them." To which the dissenting woman would reply: "No, not just live with them, we have to respect their way of dressing." This in turn seemed to resolve the waverer's lingering doubts, for she now insisted, rather resolutely: "No, it is not just a way of dressing. It has to do with religion. For them it is a simple dress, for us it is a religious obligation. My religion is worth more than their way of seeing things."

The woman who had been so vocal again intervened, to assert: "They are only human beings; by contrast, the veil is something revealed by God, in the Koran, which we should obey."

To which, the dissenter replied: "If we think like that, then we should go back to our own country, that way we will avoid conflict."

Again, voices were raised: "Yes, go to my country! God is great," replied the vocal woman, sardonically.

"Indeed, God is powerful," quipped in response to the dissenter.

It was, indeed, rather remarkable to witness the shift in this focus group, from a near consensus in favour of self-denigrating attitudes towards a near consensus in favour of more confrontational, more openly defiant, more proud postures, when the subject of the Islamic veil was raised. Which goes to show the salience and sensitivity of matters associated with religious conviction, in a European context characterised by rising Islamophobia, just how polarizing the debate about the veil can be.

The example of the woman who had been so vocal in denouncing her fellow Moroccans, but who in a matter of minutes found herself defending quite stridently those who wear the veil, is particularly poignant in this regard. Perhaps even more so, when we take into consideration the fact that she herself did not wear a veil, a point about which she openly reflected: "I don't wear the veil, but if I were to put it on again, it would be to not go to hell; and if they try to oblige me not to wear it, I would prefer to go to my country rather than obey." The counterpoint to her admiration for how the Spaniards live, for her enjoyment of all the material comforts available in Spain, a sense of being spiritually adrift. In her own words: "I am weak when it comes to practicing my religion. I am not even praying these days. In my country, I was better, I wore the veil correctly, I never missed my daily prayers. But since I arrived here I am lost. Even so, despite everything, I will enthusiastically defend my religion. I am not afraid of human beings, I am only afraid of God."

In the context of post-colonial Europe, we can conclude, the phenomenon of double consciousness cannot be dissociated from the question of Islam. Moreover, the subject of the hijab and other Islamic veils, in particular, proves capable of triggering the most intense of emotions. Fanon had noted already, in his *Discourse on a Dying Colonialism*, how in the context of colonial Algeria, the veil "had become the bone of contention in a grandiose battle, on account of which the occupation forces were to mobilize their most powerful and most varied resources" (1965, pp.36-37). A battle in which, according to Fanon, "converting the woman, winning her over to the foreign values, wrenching her free from her status, was at the same time achieving a real power over the man and attaining a practical, effective means of destructuring Algerian culture" (p.39). In contemporary Spain, much like contemporary France, stereotypes about the oppression of Muslim women continue to prevail (Moualhi 2000) while the residues and resentments of past colonial confrontations prove most easily resuscitated among post-colonial subjects by the "bone of contention" that remains the veil (Githens-Mazer 2009).

Indeed, across the focus groups, informants proved especially emphatic in registering their concerns about the treatment to which women wearing the hijab are being subjected. In another group, one woman remarked: "I think this problem of the veil is very grave, because, for example, when you do a preparatory course for some kind of job, when it comes time for the practice sessions, they oblige you to take off the veil. I was on such a course, training to become a waitress, and the company accepted me, but only on the condition that I take off my veil." In this woman's opinion, the veil was but an excuse to discriminate, for she would add: "They always find an excuse to push you away."

Another woman at this point intervened to insist: "The majority of Spaniards are good people. There are some who understand you, and others who don't, just like in any other place." She would then go on to make a point about job market competition underlying discriminatory attitudes, by claiming: "Those who look badly at you, it is because you are the person who has come to their country to take away their job and their money." Even so, she would also emphasize: "What I don't like about Spaniards is that they are racist towards people who wear the veil, because they think a woman who wears a veil is uncultured, illiterate, comes from the village."

This in turn provoked another woman to remark: "I personally have faced a lot of problems because I wear the veil. When you look for a job, they can reject you just because you wear the veil. They will even accept someone with lower qualifications than you just for that reason." From which she would conclude: "I have lost many job opportunities because of the problem of the veil."

"And you won't take it off?" asked another woman in the group.

"No, I won't," she replied.

"Very well, then," responded a third. "I was forced to take it off by my employers as a condition for taking me. When you are obliged like me, you'll take it off."

"I don't think so," she again replied.

As this exchange demonstrates, the controversies surrounding the wearing of the hijab and other Islamic veils have a direct material impact on the lives and livelihoods of women in Spain who choose to persist in the practice of veiling, despite the clear pressures they receive from the dominant society to desist.

"Double Consciousness," Take Two

The quickness with which attitudes of self-denigration gave way to postures of defiance as soon as the practice of veiling was raised as a subject for discussion certainly speaks to the special salience of this practice, as a clear "bone of contention" in the public debate about "integration;" at the same time, it helps to illuminate the contours of double consciousness among Moroccan migrants in the Metropolitan Region of Barcelona.

Dubois originally coined the term "double consciousness" in the early twentieth century, to refer to a condition that he diagnosed to be then prevalent among the community to whom he referred as "American Negroes." In his classic, *The Souls of Black Folk*, Dubois famously described double-consciousness as "a peculiar sensation … this sense of always looking at oneself through the eyes of others, of measuring one's soul through the tape of a world that looks on in amused contempt and pity". He continued: "One ever feels his two-ness, an American, a Negro; two souls, two thoughts, two unreconciled strivings; two warring ideals in one dark body, whose dogged strength alone keeps it from being torn asunder". According to Dubois, "[t]he history of the American Negro" could be summed up as "the history of this strife," as a constant struggle to "merge his double self into a better and truer self," and thereby "to attain self-conscious manhood;" indeed, "to make it possible for a man to be both a Negro and an American without being cursed and spit upon by his fellows, without having the doors of opportunity closed roughly in his face".

Though the term was thus originally employed to refer to the plight of the descendants of slaves in the United States, it has since been employed more generally in debates about multiculturalism and transnationalism, especially in relation to diaspora experiences (Dayal 1996). Indeed, there is an emergent literature that employs Dubois' concept of "double consciousness" to make sense of a diverse array of migrant, diasporic experiences (Abdul-Jabbar 2015; Kinefuchi 2010; Upegui-Hernández 2009; Vertovec 1997; Wang 1997; Werbner 2013), upon which this chapter builds.

Dayal has explicitly argued that double consciousness "need not be conceived in the restricted sense in which W.E.B. Dubois casts it," in fact, that the term is "more productively conceived" in reference to "fracturings of the subject that resist falsely comforting identifications and reifications" (Dayal 1996, p.48), and that, "by posing the challenge of an *internal* hybridity," the term effectively "interrupts the narratives of national purity or autonomy" (p.49).

For postcolonial subjects who find themselves living in former metropoles, who are traversed by racialized and religious boundaries, who are symbolically excluded from belonging to the imagined communities of the "nations" in which they reside, no more than what Frantz Fanon "bitterly termed 'honorary citizenship'" would seem to be on offer, at best (Dayal 1996, p.50). Diasporic double-consciousness thus prevails (Tsolidis 2014). A consciousness in part complicit with the dominant terms of metropolitan discourse; but simultaneously, in part defiantly opposed to such terms, attempting to negate them, while assuming a posture of internal critique.

As we have seen in the focus group discussions, recognition of the material advantages and social benefits associated with living in a rich country often at least partially offsets the sense of grievance caused by the everyday experience of racism, xenophobia, and Islamophobia. Indeed, such recognition helps account for the complicity with the dominant terms of metropolitan discourse, for the tendency "to look at oneself through the eyes of others." Such recognition is in turn born out of the horizons of comparison between the concrete life opportunities that are available in Morocco and those available in Catalonia.

The "integrationist" narrative of the rich country as "a land of opportunity" is difficult for an economic migrant from a poorer country to disassociate oneself from entirely – for it is a myth that corresponds, at least in part, with the lived experience of the migrant, a myth that helps to justify the migrant's many sacrifices, a myth that helps to make sense of the migrant's difficult life choices. Even if the encounter with racism, xenophobia, and Islamophobia works to disabuse the migrant of the urge to embrace this "integrationist" myth, without hesitation, in its entirety.

The migrant's children, however, frequently find themselves in a somewhat more difficult psychological bind, paradoxical though it may seem. They remain traversed by racialized and religious boundaries, symbolically excluded from fully belonging to the imagined communities of the "nations" in which they have grown up. Their fluency in the local languages and dominant cultures, if anything, can serve to exacerbate the sense of grievance and alienation provoked by everyday encounters with systemic discrimination and symbolic exclusion. Nor do they have any horizons of comparison to offset such real grievances; for they have no "home country" with which their current situation can favourably compare. And so, the "integrationist" narrative of the "land of opportunity" rings ever more hollow to them.

If "diasporic double-consciousness" makes more sense than the language of "integration" to describe the condition of postcolonial migrants in the former metropoles, for their children the very notion of a "home country" becomes increasingly problematic. Thus in part the seductive appeal of the *Umma*, the community of believers, a transnational ideal, a community to which one can belong no matter where one has grown up, no matter where one resides (Dalgaard-Nielsen 2010, p.800; Just et. al. 2014; Ouassini 2013; Roy 2003). The *Umma* promises to provide a sense of belonging for those symbolically excluded from the "nation," a "home land" for the homeless, an imagined community for those postcolonial subjects who find themselves adrift, scattered across the globe. For those postcolonial subjects, always already traversed by racialized and religious boundaries, to embrace the *Umma* is an act of positive self-affirmation, of trans-valuation, of negating a negation. Indeed, it is a response to the experience of systemic discrimination along racialized and religious lines; or as Marx once put it, "it is the sigh of the oppressed creature, the heart of a heartless world, and the soul of soulless conditions".

Which is why, as we have seen in our focus group discussions, the phenomenon of double consciousness cannot be dissociated from the question of Islam in the former European metropoles. It is also why the subject of the hijab and other Islamic veils, in particular, proves capable of triggering the most intense of emotions. Nor should we expect such associations to die, or such intense emotions to be assuaged, among the children of these postcolonial migrants (Just et. al. 2014; Voas and Fleischman 2012). To the contrary, if anything, we should expect such associations to be strengthened, such emotional reactions to be further intensified, as the "integrationist" narrative of the "land of opportunity" loses its appeal and its power to offset the sense of alienation provoked by the experience of systemic discrimination on racialized and religious grounds.

Conclusion

This chapter foregrounds the perspectives of Moroccan migrants in the Metropolitan Region of Barcelona on a variety of themes associated with the ongoing public debate about "integration". In so doing, it attempts to contest and counter the terms of dominant discourse, which have been corrupted across Europe by resurgent reactionary populist forces, who have successfully managed to frame migration as a problem, and who have targeted migrant communities through recurrent recourse to racist, xenophobic, and Islamophobic tropes.

The empirical basis for the chapter is a set of focus group discussions conducted with migrant Moroccan men and women in the municipalities of Badalona and Hospitalet de Llobregat in the Spring of 2013, right in the midst of the so-called Eurozone crisis, in local contexts which had experienced different degrees of anti-immigrant mobilization (Astor 2017). The focus group moderators probed participants for their views about local, regional, and "national" political and social dynamics, and about personal experiences with and perceptions of systemic discrimination, in addition to explicitly eliciting their perspectives on the prospects and challenges of "integration". Such priming was intended as a means of not only prompting but also amplifying the voices and multiple perspectives of a migrant community too often *spoken over* or *spoken about* rather than *spoken with*. In other words, it was intended as a means of taking them seriously as *political subjects*, with both agency and often eloquent convictions, and thereby contradicting their frequent portrayal in dominant discourse and public debate as either villains, or at best, passive victims.

The chapter documents the prevalence of a sense of alienation and grievance provoked by everyday encounters with racism, xenophobia, and Islamophobia. It goes on to show, however, how such feelings are at least partially offset by the widespread recognition of the material opportunities and benefits associated with living in a rich country. It employs W.E.B. Dubois' concept of "double consciousness" to interpret and describe the resulting set of ambivalent attitudes expressed by our focus group participants. It adapts the concept from its original application to the condition of African-Americans, to relate it as well to the plight of diasporic postcolonial subjects who find themselves living in the former metropoles of Europe. It brings to light the appeal of "integrationist" narratives about a "land of opportunity" and even about a "land of security" among Moroccan migrants, a clear note of complicity with the terms of dominant discourse, at the same time evidence of a tendency "to look at oneself through the eyes of others".

However, the chapter also demonstrates just how quickly attitudes of self-denigration give way to postures of open resistance and defiance as soon as the controversial subject of the practice of veiling is broached. This response allows us to conclude that, in the context of post-colonial Europe, the phenomenon of double consciousness cannot be dissociated from the question of Islam. The practice of veiling turns out to be a "bone of contention," capable of triggering the most intense of emotions, of resuscitating among postcolonial subjects the residues and resentments of past colonial confrontations.

For postcolonial subjects traversed by racialized and religious boundaries, symbolically excluded from belonging to the "nations" in which they reside, diasporic double-consciousness prevails. Nor should this condition of ambivalence so evident among Moroccan migrants be expected to give way to full-fledged "integration" among their children. To the contrary, as the horizons of comparison with the life opportunities available in the "home country" fade – indeed, as the very notion of a "home country" vanishes – the sting of the everyday experience of systemic discrimination and symbolic exclusion along racialized and religious lines can come to be felt all the more acutely (Franz 2007; Lyons-Padilla et. al. 2015; Pumares Fernández 1993, pp.143-144). Thus the ever more seductive appeal of the *Umma*, the ideal of the community of believers, of a community that transcends "national" belonging, even transcends place, the embrace of which is best interpreted as an act of self-affirmation, as the negation of a negation, as the response to so many everyday encounters with racism, xenophobia, and Islamophobia.

REFERENCES

Abdul-Jabbar, W. "Internalized Arab Diasporic Identity: Revisiting the Duboisian Double Consciousness," *Contemporary Arab Affairs*, Vol. 8, No. 1, 2015, pp. 54-64.

Anneas, A., J. Garreta and F. Molina Luque, "Ethnocultural Conflict in Spain: Moroccans in Spain – So Near, Yet So Far. A Long History of Meeting While Not Meeting," in D. Landis and R. Albert, eds., *Handbook of Ethnic Conflict. International and Cultural Psychology* (Boston, MA: Springer, 2012), pp.493-482.

Aparicio, R. "The Integration of the Second and 1.5 Generations of Moroccan, Dominican and Peruvian Origin in Madrid and Barcelona," *Journal of Ethnic and Migration Studies*, Vol. 33, No. 7, 2007, pp.1169-1193.

Arango, J. and C. Finotelli, "Past and Future Challenges of a Southern European Migration Regime: The Spanish Case," *IDEA Working Papers*, No. 8, May 2009. Accessible at: http://www.idea6fp.uw.edu.pl/pliki/WP8_Spain.pdf

Arango, J. and F. González Quiñones, "The Impacts of the Current Financial and Economic Crisis on Migration in the Spain-Morocco Corridor," CARIM 2009/39. Accessible at: *https://cadmus.eui.eu/bitstream/handle/1814/12994/CARIM_ASN_2009_39. pdf?sequence=1&isAllowed=y*

Astor, A. *Rebuilding Islam in Contemporary Spain. The Politics of Mosque Establishment, 1976-2013* (Sussex Academic, 2017), especially chapter 3, "Migration, Urbanization, and Social Stratification in Catalonia."

Balibar, E. *The Philosophy of Marx* (London: Verso, 2007).

Bardají Ruíz, F. *Literatura sobre inmigrantes en España.* Madrid: Observatorio Permanente de la Inmigración (OPI), 2006. Accessible at: http://extranjeros.mitramiss.gob.es/es/ObservatorioPermanenteInmigracion/Publicaciones/fichas/archivos/LITERATURA_SOBRE.pdf

Bhambra, G. *Rethinking Modernity: Postcolonialism and the Sociological Imagination* (New York, NY: Palgrave MacMillan, 2007).

Birge, S. "Beyond Resistance versus Subordination: An Intersectional Approach to the Agency of Veiled Muslim Women," *Journal of Intercultural Studies*, Vol. 31, No. 1, 2010, pp.9-28.

Brubaker, R. "Between Nationalism and Civilizationalism: The European Populist Moment in Comparative Perspective," *Ethnic and Racial Studies*, Vol. 40, No. 8, 2017, pp.1191-1226.

Burawoy, M. "For Public Sociology," *American Sociological Review*, Vol. 70, No. 1, 2005, pp.4-28.

Carr, R. 1982. *Spain 1808-1975* (Oxford: Clarendon Press, 1982).

Castles, S. "Why Migration Policies Fail," *Ethnic and Racial Studies*, Vol. 27, No. 2, 2004, pp.205-227.

Cebolla Boada and A. González Ferrer, *La inmigración en España (2000-2007). De la gestión de flujos a la integración de los inmigrantes* (Madrid: Centro de Estudios Políticos y Constitucionales, 2008).

Cebolla, H. and M. Requena, "Marroquíes en España, Holanda y Francia: ¿Importa el modelo de gestión de la diversidad para explicar la integración?," *Historia y Política*, No. 23, 2010, pp.55-83.

Colombo, E. "Living on the Move: Belonging and Identification among Adolescent Children of Immigrants in Italy," in G. Tsolidis, ed., *Migration, Diaspora and Identity. Cross-National Experiences* (London: Springer, 2014), pp.19-36.

Dalgaard-Nielsen, A. "Violent Radicalization in Europe: What We Know and What We Do Not Know," *Studies in Conflict & Terrorism*, Vol. 33, No. 9, 2010, pp.797-814.

Dayal, S. "Diaspora and Double Consciousness," *The Journal of Midwest Modern Language Association*, Vol. 29, No. 1, 1996, pp.46-62.

Desrues, T. "Percepciones del Islam y de los musulmanes en los medios de comunicación en España," *El diálogo intercultural: un reto para las creencias y las convicciones.
Seminario a la Comisión Europea.* Brussels, Nov. 11, 2008. Accessible at: https://core.
ac.uk/download/pdf/36041109.pdf

Dietz, J. "Frontier Hybridization or Culture Clash?" *Journal of Ethnic and Migration
Studies,* Vol. 30, No. 6, 2004, pp.1087-1112.

Domínguez-Mujica, R. Guerra-Talavera, and J.M. Parreño-Castellano, "Migration at
a Time of Global Economic Crisis: The Situation in Spain," *International Migration,*
Vol. 52, No. 6, 2014, pp.113-127.

Dotson-Renta, L.N. *Immigration, Popular Culture, and Re-routing of European Muslim
Identity* (Palgrave Macmillan, 2011).

Dubois, W.E.B. *The Souls of Black Folks.* Oxford: Oxford University Press, [1903]2008.

Ennaji, M. "Moroccan Migrants in Europe and Islamophobia," *Comparative Studies
of South Asia, Africa and the Middle East,* Vol. 30, No. 1, 2010, pp.14-20.

Fanon, F. *A Dying Colonialism* (New York, NY: Grove Press, 1965). Accessible at: http://
abahlali.org/wp-content/uploads/2011/04/Frantz-Fanon-A-Dying-Colonialism.pdf

Fekete, L. "Anti-Muslim Racism and the European Security State," *Race and Class,* Vol.
46, No. 1, 2004, pp.3-29.

Flesler, D. "Contemporary Moroccan Immigration and its Ghosts," in S.R. Doubleday
and D. Coleman, eds., *In the Light of Medieval Spain. The New Middle Ages* (New
York: Palgrave MacMillan, 2008), pp.115-132.

Fokkema, T. and H. de Haas, "Pre- and Post-Migration Determinants of Socio-Cultural
Integration of African Immigrants in Italy and Spain," *International Migration,*
Vol. 53, No. 6, pp.3-26.

Franz, B. "Europe's Muslim Youth: An Inquiry into the Politics of Discrimination,
Relative Deprivation, and Identity Formation," *Mediterranean Quarterly,* Vol. 18,
No. 1, 2007, pp.89-112.

Fresno, J.M. and A. Chahin, "La discriminación racial o étnica percibida por la
población inmigrante," *Documentación Social. Revista de Estudios Sociales y de Sociología Aplicada,* No. 162, 2011, pp.31-56. Accessible at: https://caritas-web.s3.amazon
aws.com/main-files/uploads/2012/02/DS100162-LA-DISCRIMINACI%C3%93N-
%C3%89TNICA-HACIA-LA-POBLACI%C3%93N-INMIGRANTE.pdf

García-Ramírez, M., et. al., "A Liberation Psychology Approach to Acculturative Integration of Migrant Populations," *American Journal of Community Psychology,* Vol. 47,
No.1-2, 2011, pp.86-97.

García Sanchez, I. *Moroccan Immigrant Children in a Time of Surveillance: Navigating Sameness and Difference in Contemporary Spain* (UCLA Ph.D. Dissertation, 2009).

Garreta Bochaca, J. "Inmigrantes musulmanes en Cataluña," *Revista Internacional de Sociología*, Vol. 25, 2000, pp.151-176.

Gillespie, R. "Spain and the Mediterranean: Southern Sensitivity, European Aspirations," *Mediterranean Politics*, Vol. 1, No. 2, 1996, pp.193-211.

Gilroy, P. *Postcolonial Melancholia* (New York, NY: Columbia University Press, 2005a).

Gilroy, P. "Multiculture, Double Consciousness and the 'War on Terror'," *Patterns of Prejudice*, Vol. 35, No. 4, 2005b, pp.431-443.

Githens-Mazer, J. "The Blowback of Repression and the Dynamics of North African Radicalization," Vol. 85, No. 5, 2009, pp.1015-1029.

González Enriquez, C. "Inmigración en España: una nueva fase de llegadas," *Real Instituto Elcano*< March 2019. Accessible at: http://www.realinstitutoelcano.org/wps/por tal/rielcano_es/contenido?WCM_GLOBAL_CONTEXT=/elcano/elcano_es/zonas_es/ demografia+y+poblacion/ari28-2019-gonzalezenriquez-inmigracion-espana-nueva-fase-llegadas

Goytisolo, J. and S. Naïr, *El peaje de la vida. Integración o rechazo de la emigración en España* (Madrid: Aguilar, 2000).

Greenough, E. "Spain's Historical Paradox: Racism and Reliance on African Migrants," *CERS Working Papers*, 2016. Accessible at: http://cers.leeds.ac.uk/wp-content/up loads/sites/97/2013/05/Spain%E2%80%99s-Historical-Paradox-Racism-and-Reliance-on-African-Migrants-Emma_Greenough.pdf

Hernández-Carr, A. "¿La hora del populismo? Elementos para comprender el 'éxito' electoral de Plataforma per Catalunya," *Revista de Estudios Políticos*, No. 153, 2011, pp.47-74.

Institut de Estadística de Catalunya (IDESCAT). "Estrangers amb tarjeta de residencia," 2019. Accessible at: https://www.idescat.cat/pub/?id=aec&n=272&lang=es

Joppke, C. 2009, *Veil: Measure of Identity* (Cambridge: Polity Press, 2009).

Just, A., M.E. Sandovici, and O. Listhaug, "Islam, Religiosity, and Immigrant Political Action in Western Europe," *Social Science Research*, Vol. 43, 2014, pp.127-144.

Kadianaki, I. "Making Sense of Immigrant Identity Dialogues," *Culture & Psychology*, Vol. 16, No. 3, 2010, pp.437-448.

Kalter, F. and I. Kogan, "Ethnic Inequalities at the Transition from School to Work in Belgium and Spain: Discrimination or Self-Exclusion?," *Research in Social Mobility and Stratification*, Vol. 24, No. 3, 2006, pp.259-274.

Karlsen, S. and J.Y. Nazroo, "Influence on Forms of National Identity and Feeling 'At Home' among Muslim Groups in Britain, Germany, and Spain," *Ethnicities*, Vol. 13, No. 6, 2013, pp.689-708.

Katsambekis, G. "The Populist Surge in Post-Democratic Times: Theoretical and Political Challenges," *The Political Quarterly*, Vo. 88, No. 2, 2017, pp.202-210.

Kinefuchi, E. "Finding Home in Migration: Montagnard Refugees and Post-Migration Identity," *Journal of International and Intercultural Communication*, Vol. 3, No. 3, pp.228-248.

Llorent Bedmar, V.L., and V. Cobano-Delgado Palma, "The Muslim Veil Controversy in French and Spanish Schools," *Islam and Christian-Muslim Relations*, Vol. 21, No. 1, 2010, pp.61-73.

López García, B. and M. Berriane, eds., *Atlas de la inmigración marroquí en España* (Madrid: Universidad Autónoma de Madrid, 2004). Accessible at: http://extran jeros.mitramiss.gob.es/es/ObservatorioPermanenteInmigracion/Publicaciones/Otros Documentos/archivos/19.2_Atlas_de_la_inmigracixn_marroqux_en_Espaxa.pdf

López García, B. and P. García Ortiz, "Jóvenes y menores en la inmigración magrebí actual en España," *Anales de Historia Contemporánea*, Vol. 22, 2006, pp.57-78.

Lubbers, M., J.L. Molina, and C. McCarty, "Personal Networks and Ethnic Identifications" *International Sociology*, Vol. 22, No. 6, 2007, pp.721-741.

Lyons-Padilla, S. et. al. "Belonging Nowhere: Marginalization & Radicalization Risk among Muslim Immigrants," *Behavioral Science & Policy*, Vol. 1, No. 2, 2015, pp.1-12.

Mancini, S. "Patriarchy as the Exclusive Domain of the Other: The Veil Controversy, False Projection and Cultural Racism," *International Journal of Constitutional Law*, Vol. 10, No. 2, 2012, pp. 411–428.

McCauley, A. "In Islam, Wearing a Hijab Is a Choice. But in Spain, This Choice Comes at a Price," *Euroviews*, April 15, 2018. Accessible at: http://www.euroviews.eu/2018/ 2018/04/15/wearing-comes-at-a-price-in-spain/

McGoldrick, D. *Human Rights and Religion – The Islamic Headscarf Debate in Europe* (Oxford: Hart Publishing, 2006).

Martínez Zurita, D. "The Enemy Within: Media Discourses and Moroccans in Spain" (The Hague, Netherlands: Institute of Social Studies Masters' Dissertation, 2008). Accessible at: http://citeseerx.ist.psu.edu/viewdoc/download?doi=10.1.1.976.9451 &rep=rep1&type=pdf

Miley, T. "Constitutional Politics and Religious Accommodation: Lessons from Spain," *Politics, Religion & Ideology*. Vol. 16, No. 4, 2015, pp. 411–433.

Moreno-Colom, S. and R. De Alós, "La inmigración en España: ¿Una integración con pies de barro?," *Política y Sociedad*, Vol. 53, No. 2, 2016, pp.509-528.

Moreras, J. "¿Conflictos por el reconocimiento? Las polémicas en torno a los oratorios musulmanes en Cataluña," in A.I. Planet Contreras and J. Moreras, eds., *Islam e inmigración* (Madrid: Centro de Estudios Políticos y Constitucionales, 2008), pp.53-79.

Morocco World News, "Moroccans, Largest Foreign Prison Population in Spain," August 11, 2015. Accessible at: https://www.moroccoworldnews.com/2015/08/165313/moroccans-largest-foreign-prison-population-in-spain/

Moualhi, D. "Mujeres musulmanes: estereotipos occidentales versus realidad social," *Papers* 60, 2000, pp.291-304.

Mudde, C. "Europe's Populist Surge: A Long Time in the Making," *Foreign Affairs*, Vol. 95, 2016, pp.25-30.

Narbona Reina, L.M. *Marroquíes en Viladecans* (Ajuntament de Viladecans, 1992).

Ostergaard-Nielsen, E. "Mobilising the Moroccans: Policies and Perceptions of Transnational Co-Development Engagement Among Moroccan Migrants in Catalonia," *Journal of Ethnic and Migration Studies* Vol. 35, No. 10, 2009, pp.1623-1641.

Olzak, S. *The Dynamics of Ethnic Competition and Conflict* (Stanford, CA: Stanford University Press, 1992).

Ouassini, A. "Between Islamophobia and the Ummah: How Spanish Moroccans Are Negotiating Their Identities in Post-3/11 Madrid," (University of New Mexico Dissertation, 2013).

Pérez Yruela, M. and T. Desrues, *Opinión de los españoles en materia de racismo y xenofobia*. Madrid: Ministerio de Trabajo y Asuntos Sociales. Observatorio Español del Racismo y la Xenofobia, 2007. Accessible at: http://www.carm.es/ctra/cendoc/haddock/14708.pdf

Pérez Yruela, M. and T. Desrues, *Percepcioes y actitudes hacia el Islam y los musulmanes en España>* Madrid: Ministerio de Trabajo y Asuntos Sociales, 2008. Accessible at: http://www.ikuspegi.eus/documentos/investigacion/es/percep_acti_islam_avance marzo2008.pdf

Pham, T. *Moroccan Immigrant Women in Spain* (Lanham, MD: Lexington Books, 2014).

Portes, A. and J. Böröcz, "Contemporary immigration: Theoretical Perspectives on its Determinants and Modes of Incorporation," *International Migration Review*, Vol. 23, No.3, 1989, pp.606-630.

Pumares Fernández, P. "Problemática de la inmigración marroquí en España," *Política y Sociedad*, No. 12, 1993, pp.139-147. Accessible on-line at: https://core.ac.uk/download/pdf/38819549.pdf

Rinken, S. and M.S. Escobar Villegas, "Opiniones y actitudes ante la inmigración en un contexto de crisis económica: datos y reflexiones," *Documentación Social. Revista de Estudios Sociales y de Sociología Aplicada*, No. 162, 2011, pp.99-116. Accessible at: https://caritas-web.s3.amazonaws.com/main-files/uploads/2012/02/DS100162-LA-DISCRIMINACI%C3%93N-%C3%89TNICA-HACIA-LA-POBLACI%C3%93N-INMIGRANTE.pdf

Roemer, J. "Divide and Conquer: Microfoundations of a Marxian Theory of Wage Discrimination," *The Bell Journal of Economics*, Vol. 10, No. 2, 1979, pp.695-705.

Rogozen-Soltar, M. "Managing Muslim Visibility: Conversion, Immigration, and Spanish Imaginaries of Islam," *American Anthropologist* 114(4), 2012, pp.611-623.

Rogozen-Soltar, M. *Spain Unmoored: Migration, Conversion, and the Politics of Islam* (Bloomington, IN: Indiana University Press, 2017).

Roy, O. "EuroIslam: The Jihad Within?," *The National Interest*, No. 71, 2003, pp.63-73.

Roy, O. *Secularism Confronts Islam* (New York, NY: Columbia University Press, 2007).

Savelkoul, M., et. al., "Comparing Levels of Anti-Muslim Attitudes across Western Countries," *Quality & Quantity*, Vol. 46, No. 5, 2012, pp.1617-1624.

Scheepers, P., M. Gijsberts, and M. Coenders, "Ethnic Exclusionism in European Countries. Public Opposition to Legal Rights for Migrants as a Response to Perceived Ethnic Threat," *European Sociological Review*, Vol. 18, No. 1, 2002, pp.17-34.

Scott, J. *The Politics of the Veil* (Princeton, NJ: Princeton University Press, 2007).

Solé, C. and S. Parella, "The Labour Market and Racial Discrimination in Spain," *Journal of Ethnic and Migration Studies*, Vol. 29, No. 1, 2003, pp.121-140.

Sperling, J. "Spain: Migration 1960s to Present," *The Encyclopedia of Global Human Migration* (Hoboken, NJ: Blackwell Publishing, 2013).

Strega, S. and L. Brown, eds., *Research as Resistance. Revisiting Critical, Indigenous, and Anti-Oppressive Approaches* (Toronto, Ontario: Canadian Scholars' Press Inc., 2015).

Tsolidis, G. "Introduction: Does Diaspora Matter When Living Cultural Difference," in G. Tsolidis, ed., *Migration, Diaspora and Identity. Cross-National Experiences* (London: Springer, 2014), pp.1-18.

Upegui-Hernández, D. "Double Consciousness: A Journey through the Multiplicity of Personal and Social Selves in the Context of Migration," in J.L. Chin, ed., *Diversity in Mind and in Action. Volume 1. Multiple Faces of Identity* (Oxford: Praeger Perspectives, 2009), pp.129-148.

Van Oudenhoven, J.P., C. Ward, and A.M. Masgoret, "Patterns of Relations between Immigrants and Host Societies," *International Journal of Intercultural Relations*, Vol. 30, No. 6, 2006, pp.637-651.

Veredas Muñoz, S. "Identidad étnica y de género entre adolescentes de origen marroquí," *Papers* 96/1, 2011, pp.117-144. Accessible at: https://core.ac.uk/download/pdf/13300115.pdf

Vertovec, S. "Three Meanings of 'Diaspora', Exemplified among South Asian Religions," *Diaspora*, Vol. 6, No. 3, pp.277-299.

Voas, D. and F. Fleischman, "Islam Moves West: Religious Change in the First and Second Generations," *Annual Review of Sociology*, Vol. 38, 2012, pp.525-545.

Wang, Q. "'Double consciousness', Sociological Imagination, and the Asian American Experience," *Race, Gender & Class*, Vol. 4, No. 3, 1997, pp.88-94.

Werbner, P. "Mothers and Daughters in Historical perspective: Home, Identity and Double Consciousness in British Pakistanis' Migration and Return," *Journal of Historical Sociology*, Vol. 26, No. 1, pp.41-61.

White, G. "Risking the Strait: Moroccan labour Migration to Spain, *Middle East Report*, No. 218, Spring 2001, pp.26-29, 48.

White, G. "Sovereignty and International Labour Migration: The 'Security Mentality' in Spanish-Moroccan Relations as an Assertion of Sovereignty," *Review of International Political Economy*, Vol. 14, No. 4, 2007, pp.690-718.

Wikipedia, "Moors," 2019a. Accessible at: https://en.wikipedia.org/wiki/Moors

Wikipedia, "Moroccans in Spain," 2019b. Accessible at: https://en.wikipedia.org/wiki/Moroccans_in_Spain

Wiktionary, "No hay moros en la costa," 2019. Accessible at: https://en.wiktionary.org/wiki/no_hay_moros_en_la_costa

Wolfenstein, E.V. *Psychoanalytic Marxism. Groundwork* (London: Free Association Books, 1993).

Woodhead, L. "The Muslim Veil Controversy and European Values," *Swedish Missiological Themes*, Vol. 97, No. 1, 2009, pp.89-105.

Zapata-Barrero, R. "The Muslim Community and the Spanish Tradition: Maurophobia as a Fact and Impartiality as a Desideratum," in T. Modood, A. Traindafyllidou, and R. Zapata-Barrero, eds., *Multiculturalism, Muslims and Citizenship: A European Approach* (London: Routledge, 2005).

Zapata-Barrero, R. and N. De Witte, "Muslims in Spain: Blurring Past and Present Moors," in A. Triandafyllidou, ed., *Muslims in 21st Century Europe* (London: Routledge, 2010).

Zimmermann, K.F. "European Migration: Push and Pull," *International Regional Science Review*, Vol. 19, No. 2, 1996, pp.95-128.

Zlobina, A. and D. Páez, "Aculturación y comunicación intercultural: el caso de inmigración en España," *Revista del Centro de Estudos de Comunicação e Sociedade*, 2018. Accessible at: http://revistacomsoc.pt/index.php/cecs_ebooks/article/view/2836